# Street Entrepreneurs

T0313308

Whether they are at relatively sedate farmers' markets in the United States and Europe or the more chaotic street bazaars of Latin America, Africa and Asia, street traders are making a comeback after a century in which they were supposed to disappear, replaced by the more "sanitary" and "efficient" Supermarket. But both consumers and government planners are finding that street vendors and markets energize social landscapes, whether in urban or rural locations, as well as providing an important source of employment and the efficient supply of vital goods, especially for the neglected urban poor. However, while they are no longer universally seen as pariahs, street traders still face considerable harassment from officials in many locations as well as the general perception that they are merely relevant at the local level as "curiosities" and survival mechanisms.

This volume collects essays from authors around the world about the markets and vendors they know best. The essays speak to the struggles that vendors have faced to legitimize their activity, the role that they play in helping societies adapt or to survive catastrophes, as well as the practical role that they play in both the local and global social and economic system within which we live. They speak to the ways in which street traders challenge the dominant system of control of space, as well as the conception of property rights in other ways.

While focusing attention on the importance of street markets as a phenomenon of interest in itself to a growing body of scholarship, the essays also show how the study of street vending can provide insights not only into economic anthropology, but also urban studies, post modernism, spatial geography, political sociology and globalization theory.

**John Cross** is Visiting Assistant Professor of Sociology at Kent State University. **Alfonso Morales** is Visiting Professor of Sociology at the University of Wisconsin.

# Routledge Studies in the Modern World Economy

# Street Entrepreneurs

People, place and politics in local and global perspective

**Edited by**
**John Cross and Alfonso Morales**

Routledge
Taylor & Francis Group

LONDON AND NEW YORK

First published 2007
by Routledge
2 Park Square, Milton Park, Abingdon, Oxon OX14 4RN

Simultaneously published in the USA and Canada
by Routledge
711 Third Ave, New York, NY 10017

*Routledge is an imprint of the Taylor & Francis Group, an informa business*

Typeset in Times by
Book Now Ltd, London

First issued in paperback in 2013

*British Library Cataloguing in Publication Data*
A catalogue record for this book is available from the British Library

*Library of Congress Cataloging in Publication Data*
Street entrepreneurs: people, place, and politics in local and global
perspective/edited by John Cross and Alfonso Morales.
    p. cm. – (Routledge studies in the modern world economy; 66)
Includes bibliographical references and index.
1. Street vendors–Political activity. 2. Informal sector (Economics)–Political
aspects. 3. Vending stands–Political aspects. I. Cross, John C. (John
Christopher), 1964– II. Morales, Alfonso, 1961–

HF5458.S77 2007
381'.18–dc22                                                2006032205


ISBN13: 978–0–415–77028–6 (hbk)
ISBN13: 978–0–415–74847–6 (pbk)
ISBN13: 978–0–203–08674–2 (ebk)

To
**Crisostomo and Aurelia Romero**
**Gustavo and Frances Morales**
and
**Catalina Peña Noriega**

**They worked the streets**

**And to their fellow vendors**
**Around the world.**

*A.M. and J.C.*

# Contents

# Illustrations

## Tables

## Figures

# Contributors

**Danielle Berman** is a PhD candidate in Sociology and Rural Sociology at the University of Wisconsin–Madison. Her dissertation research explores the role of foreign governments and corporations in transforming Russia's agriculture and food system.

**Sharit K. Bhowmik** is Professor of Labour Studies, School of Management and Labour, Tata Institute of Social Sciences, Mumbai 400098, India. His research focuses on the urban informal sector in developing countries. He works closely with the National Alliance of Street Vendors of India and WIEGO.

**Michèle Companion** is Assistant Professor of Sociology at the University of Colorado – Colorado Springs and a food/livelihood security consultant. She does research in the areas of international development, indigenous rights, Native American health, law and society, and social movements.

**John C. Cross** is Visiting Assistant Professor at Kent State University. He does research on the political economy of poverty, focusing on informal and illegal activities as responses to systems of inequality. He serves as advisor to a number of international organizations.

**Anne de Bruin** is Professor of Economics, Massey University, Auckland, New Zealand. Her research interests include entrepreneurship, labor market dynamics, regional employment strategies, and career theory.

**Ann Dupuis** is Associate Professor of Sociology at Massey University, Auckland, New Zealand. Her research and publishing interests include sustainable employment and younger workers, entrepreneurship, labor market change, and non-standard work.

**María Fernanda García-Rincón** is a PhD candidate at the Department of Land Economy, University of Cambridge. Her research interests include: urban development, relationship between state and society, informal economy, and Latin America.

**Marina Karides** is Assistant Professor of Sociology at Florida Atlantic University. Her research includes micro-enterprise development and

Lefebvrian analysis of space and gender, race, and vendors in the Caribbean and Mediterranean.

**Gregg W. Kettles** is Professor of Law at Mississippi College School of Law in Jackson, Mississippi. He writes about environmental law and the formal and informal rules governing the use of public space.

**Fergus Lyon** is a reader and principal consultant at the Centre for Enterprise and Economic Development Research, Middlesex University. His research interests cover the role of entrepreneurship in local economic development in the UK and Africa.

**Alfonso Morales** is Visiting Assistant Professor of Sociology at the University of Wisconsin at Madison. He is writing a book about Chicago's Maxwell Street Market. He consults on markets and does research on law and society and economic sociology.

**Oleg Pachenkov** is Senior Research Fellow and Deputy Director of the Centre for Independent Social Research (CISR) in St Petersburg, Russia. He studies ethnic, migrant, and informal economy issues and is currently conducting a comparative study of flea markets and street vending.

**Colin Sage** is Senior Lecturer in Geography at University College Cork, Ireland. He has a particular interest in geographies of food and is currently engaged in interrogating constructions of quality and the role of science in discourses of safe food.

**Kathleen Staudt** is Professor of Political Science and Director of the Center for Civic Engagement at the University of Texas at El Paso. She has published a dozen books; her forthcoming book is entitled *Violence and Activism at the Border*.

**Joel Stillerman** is Associate Professor of Sociology and Coordinator of Latin American Studies at Grand Valley State University. His publications focus on workers, consumer culture, and cities in Santiago, Chile and he is completing a book on Chilean metalworkers.

**Catherine Sundt** is a graduate of Grand Valley State University, and a doctoral student in Spanish at The Ohio State University. She is interested in gender issues in twentieth-century Hispanic literature.

**Recep Varcin** is Associate Professor of Sociology at the Faculty of Political Sciences and Director of the Center for the Study of Human Resources Management and Career Counseling, Ankara University. His current research focuses on national innovation systems.

# Foreword

Street vending is one of the world's oldest and most widespread occupations, yet it has never received the scholarly attention it deserves. I am writing as one of the few who wrote several articles on street vending in the late 1970s and early 1980s, but who never considered compiling a global collection of essays like this one and publishing through a major international publisher. The time was not right a quarter-century ago, as most twentieth-century scholars put their heads in the sand and sought to minimize the significance of street vending. Some thought it worthy of a few articles, but few considered it appropriate for book-length treatment. Most scholars viewed street vending as unimportant and destined to disappear!

Why was street vending so pervasively ignored and disdained? It was simultaneously a victim of Marxism, modernity, and capitalism. Those who chose to study it were variously cast as anarchists, neo-Marxists, or simply as lovers of the quaint and exotic.

In orthodox Marxist–Leninist analysis, street vending was petty trading, varying from marginal and lumpen proletarian to micro-entrepreneurial and petty bourgeois. Street vendors were "urban kulaks" – inconvenient non-peasant, non-proletarian, non-revolutionary remnants. Their views and occupations were considered irrelevant to the inevitable revolution. After the revolution, it was assumed that they would be replaced by rational planned distribution systems and that they would have to be re-educated to perform new roles in the new economy. Street vendors were viewed as archetypal "parasitic middlemen" in economies where all real value derived from the extraction and processing of raw materials, and from industries manufacturing commodities. Services were mere adjuncts to the fundamental commodity-producing activities that underpinned the economy. Street vendors were not worthy of study because they were parasitic and dysfunctional, had no political significance, and were destined to disappear.

To advocates of "modernity," both socialist and capitalist, street vending was a disorderly and superfluous activity that cluttered the urban environment, interrupted efficient traffic flows, and competed unfairly with new, large, hygienic commercial establishments. Street vending was the antithesis of everything modern – the supermarket, the department store, and the shopping mall. Most modernists believed that these gleaming commercial establishments enabled shoppers to obtain all they needed under a single roof with maximum speed, economy, comfort, and hygiene. In sharp contrast, they thought that street vending could only survive by dodging taxes, hood-winking customers, and pandering to antiquated traditions. Street vending was seen as a disappearing occupation, unworthy of serious study because it had no future.

In much twentieth-century capitalist thinking, most small businesses had no future. The world was increasingly dominated by giant corporations, and pushcarts, stalls, shops, workshops, handicrafts, and peasant farms all seemed uncompetitive. It was assumed that slowly but surely, the "surplus labor" of these pre-capitalist activities would be absorbed into the expanding, dynamic capitalist economy. In the face of corporate competition, only a few high-technology, business services and fashion-trend start-ups had a chance, and the few that survived would soon grow large or be bought up by giant corporations. Corporate success was attributed to modern management, scale economies, horizontal and vertical integration, sophisticated R&D, and aggressive marketing campaigns through the mass media. Giant corporations became increasingly global, and many assumed that small businesses would disappear or be concentrated in narrow, specific niches of the economy.

This book shows how crude and absurd many of these ideas were. Never-theless, they were prevailing conventional wisdoms just a quarter-century ago, in a Cold War era shaped by the titanic struggle between the capitalist west and the Soviet Bloc. Just as few envisioned the fall of communism, few imagined the persistence and variety of street vending. By mistakenly seeing street vending as disappearing, irrelevant, or parasitic, most scholars and policy-makers ignored its economic, social, and political significance. Regu-lation has never received the serious attention it deserves, and in most countries and localities street vendors have had to deal with petty officials, often arbitrary and corrupt, administering outdated and impractical rules.

I came to street vendor studies after doing spatial and socio-economic analyses of marketplace trade, a much more popular field of study in the 1960s and 1970s. Marketplace trade usually takes place in public plazas and market buildings, but often extends into neighboring streets as "street markets." Street vendors fan out further to "forestall" customers walking in towards the markets, and some work the streets as "peddlers" or "hawkers," offering their wares door-to-door and to passers-by. For most 1960s scholars, however, the focus was not the street vendor, but the marketplace, an economic anthropological laboratory of social interaction and commercial behavior. It was assumed that both street vendors and marketplace trade were destined to disappear as modern retailing and mass communications grew in significance, but marketplace trade was viewed as being much more authentic, traditional, and worthy of study.

Though I had recognized the significance of street vendors and street markets through my work on marketplace trade, the golden opportunity to do more studies came because of an advance in "development theory" – the early-1970s emergence of the concepts of formal and informal sectors, as a modification of the modern–traditional dichotomy established in the 1950s. Preferences varied as to whether to call the new category small enterprises, informal enterprises, the informal sector, or petty commodity production, but most scholars now saw it as normal, embracing a wide range of occupations including street vending. A labor-intensive sector was now recognized, paralleling, complementing, and/or serving corporate and governmental production and employment. Intense debates ensued about the structure and long-term future of the overall economy, and about the articulation of the two sectors that most scholars identified.

Like many other researchers, I participated in these "informal sector debates," using case studies of individual occupations in specific places as ways to illustrate much broader arguments. Street vendors were not studied in their own right, but because of their capacity to illustrate features of the overall economic system. Most researchers, however, preferred to focus on other small-scale participants in that system – peasant farmers, artisans, and small industries – activities which seemed more "productive," following the prevailing commodity obsessions of the era.

The transitions of the last quarter-century have included the fall of communism, the decline of developmentalism, the rise of China, continued growth of other Far Eastern economies, accelerating globalization, massive international financial flows, the rising power of transnational corporations, and the diminishing power of most nation-states to make independent policies. Manufacturing industries have declined in many parts of the world, and new technologies have emphasized electronics, software, and the elegance of miniaturization. "The service sector" is now the principal employer in most countries, both rich and poor. In the midst of all this global change, street vendors have continued to innovate and grow in numbers. They should no longer be forgotten, condemned, ignored, or bundled into some much larger "sector." The occupation is economically, socially, and politically important, and it serves substantial and enduring consumer demands. The population of vendors, customers, and their dependents is too large to ignore.

John Cross and Alfonso Morales have assembled a fascinating variety of researchers and case studies from across the world. At last, street entrepreneurs are beginning to get the attention they deserve!

Ray Bromley
University at Albany, SUNY
Albany, NY 12222, USA

# Preface and acknowledgments

Paradoxically, this book about street merchants has its roots in the internet. The editors are co-sponsors with Steve Balkin of *openair.org*, the world's primary portal for research on street markets, vendors, and associated activities. Balkin founded the webpage in 1995 and since then it has provided a forum for researchers, policy makers, markets, and merchants. In 2005 Robert Langham, an editor at Routledge, approached Balkin about editing a book on vendors and vending and, given his many commitments at the time, he asked us if we would co-edit this volume.

Our interest at *openair.org*, as well as in editing this book, is to both highlight the overlooked importance of street markets in today's globalized world, as well as to advocate for a more humane treatment of vendors, who are often struggling to survive in the face of government neglect or outright antagonism. Long seen as parasites, petty criminals, or at the least an "inconvenience" to the elites who dominate our cities, we wanted to provide a forum for challenging these stereotypes. Since then the Web page has spurred much research into the economic and social benefits that street markets bring to their communities. We have been called upon as consultants to conduct applied research for private and government organizations about making street markets more effective. At the same time, we have also pursued intellectual goals. As political and economic sociologists, we wanted to show that street markets provide a fascinating and vital perspective on the political, economic, and social processes in today's society where everything is both local and global at the same time.

Our scholarship is tempered by scientific norms and our peers. Our advocacy is founded on building capabilities for people to cope with uncertainties and inequalities of the postmodern world. But our approach is balanced: we recognize that street markets can sometimes have negative as well as positive effects. Yet our applied research has successfully enabled cities and organizations to incorporate markets appropriately into their locally complex political-economic environments. Despite some success there have been times when the dominant perspective is all one-sided, making our more neutral perspective seem very partisan. John Cross can remember being shouted down at a conference in Mexico City by members of a neighborhood association who were angry about a street market that had invaded their wealthy neighborhood. They assumed, since he didn't simply denounce street vending, that he was getting a cut of the fees that street vendors were paying to their leaders for protection. Alas, he has no such luck. Likewise Alfonso Morales confronted a skeptical and even boisterous audience when he was invited to speak at an Internal Revenue Service Tax Conference. Among otherwise quiet presentations among pocket-protected tax practitioners and scholars his work was derided by audience members claiming he supported thieves and vagrants. Even so, the work was acknowledged by others in the audience who appreciated the conceptual and policy innovations advocated.

It bodes well for debate when government and civil society take scholars seriously and more scholars are taking these debates even more seriously. We are happy to see that others have subsequently taken up these issues, including the urban geographer Jerome Monnet of France, who has helped organize a number of international conferences in Mexico City and Brazil. But we are especially pleased that organizations have joined scholars interested in markets and vendors, The Project for Public Spaces, which has been supported by the Ford Foundation and the Rockefeller Foundation and has helped urban planners see street markets as a valuable addition to public spaces in the United States, and especially WIEGO (Women in the Informal Economy – Globalizing and Organizing), founded by Ela Bhatt of India, and StreetNet, founded by Pat Horn of South Africa, which has brought together a number of street vendor organizations in Asia and Africa and is reaching out to Latin America. Among many others, these new voices are going beyond the old perception that street markets were local nuisances, to the realization that they are a part of an increasingly globalized economy.

One goal in putting together this book was to encourage contributions from new scholars as well as established ones, and to reach out to an international perspective, not just in terms of case studies but in terms of authorship. We had a lot of work to do to select among a total of 43 excellent contributors while making sure that the studies represented a variety of world regions and cultural standards. Knowing the complexity of the phenomena and unhappy with simple or reductionist accounts we selected chapters that treated vendors and vending from several dimensions at the same time. We also wanted to make sure that each chapter could "stand by itself" in terms of making an important contribution to the literature while still creating a coherent whole.

Because we wanted to include work by new and international scholars, we committed ourselves to working extensively with authors who perhaps did not speak English as a first language, or come from English-speaking regions with very different writing styles. As a result, the final product includes the contribution of authors from seven different countries. We also wanted to spur cross-fertilization and collaboration. Thus, while we followed standard academic procedure in using outside peer reviewers, we also asked the authors to read and comment on each other's work. In some cases, the process of rewriting, and even reconceptualization, took place over several years. We believe that the essays that emerged from this process reflect scholarly excellence, theoretical innovation, and geographical reach. We hope the reader agrees.

A work like this is, as we found out to our chagrin, a lot of work, and we would have been unable to accomplish it without the help of many others, beginning, of course, with the authors and the many others who sent in contributions that we were unable to include. All of them were interesting, and we hope to see their work published soon elsewhere. Outside readers who volunteered their time and considerable expertise to help select and perfect the chapters in this book included (in random order): Peter Walker of Tufts University, Dan Maxwell of CARE International, Sally Roever of the University of California, Berkeley, Jon Shefner of the University of Tennessee, Patricia Fernandez-Kelly of Princeton University, Fatima Gomes of the Federal University of Rio de Janeiro, Sergio Pena of the University of Texas–El Paso, Caroline Skinner of the University of Kwazulu-Natal, Loretta Bass of Oklahoma University, Allison Brown of the University of London, Meine Pieter van Dijk, of Erasmus University, Jerome Monnet of the University of Paris, and Amy Todd of Brandeis University. The help of Megan Rosengren, Ana Leos, Rebekah Harrison, and Criselda Brooks was essential in providing editorial assistance, and equally essential was the help of Arifa (Sideeka) Boyer in preparing the initial index, and Kevin Konieczko in finishing it. At Routledge, we would like to thank our initial editor, Robert Langham, for his vision and good taste in encouraging us to initiate this process, as well as his successor Terry Clague and editorial assistants Taiba Batool and Tom Sutton for helping to nurse us through it and answering all our questions. Kate McMillian at the Department of Sociology at the University of Wisconsin helped to make sure everything got to Routledge in one piece. Finally, we would like to thank the Departments of Sociology at the Wisconsin, the University of Texas–Pan American, and Kent State University for their support of the project. Of course our spouses Becky and Manuela, and our children Alex and Cruz, were supportive, directly and as welcome distractions over the last few years.

Finally, we would like to thank the many people – vendors, officials, and others – whose participation in these studies helped to make them possible, and you, our reader, for your interest in this subject matter. We realize that this is a topic that is of interest to a wide variety of people, both within and outside academia. As a result, we tried to ensure that the chapters would be accessible and meaningful not just to scholars and graduate students but to anyone with an interest in street markets. We say "tried" because, of course, we are both academics and it is almost inevitable that we will slip into jargonese from time to time, as well as the fact that we must follow academic standards in bibliographic citations which often seems like Greek to the non-academic reader. Nevertheless, we hope that the reader will persevere.

In our next project, we would also like to include more voices of activists, vendors, and leaders themselves, as well as the voices of those who find street vending problematic, through the *openair.org* website, which will hopefully lead to subsequent publications. All the royalties from this book will be used to support that process, and anyone – scholar, activist, official, or interested bystander – who wishes to contribute to that discussion are invited to join us.

John Cross and Alfonso Morales

# 1 Introduction

## Locating street markets in the modern/postmodern world

*John C. Cross and Alfonso Morales*[1]

We typically think of street vending as a part of the premodern economic order surviving only on the fringes of modern society. How could something thought of as premodern be associated with, even revived by, modernity and completely at home with postmodernity? Our reasons for presenting the reader with this conundrum are rooted in our research on street vending in various countries – research initially rooted in the assumption that street vending should, by all logical criteria, eventually disappear. What we found, however, is that street vending, despite some problems and frequent attacks, is a thriving and growing phenomenon ironically driven, we believe, by government policy, and rooted to modernity's economic successes and subsequent inequalities, and most fully appreciated in terms of contemporary global economic changes authors associate with postmodernity.

If someone were asked 100 years ago about the future of commercial activity they would have gushed over the diverse products available in the variety of street markets around the United States. They might have been thankful for government regulation of food safety and have celebrated the employment opportunities government created by constituting markets. But how could they foresee the Walgreens opening in Chicago in 1912, the same year Chicago formalized street markets in the City, which would become the norm for retail business? On the other hand, asking that person's grandchild 50 years ago about the future of commercial activity they would have waxed enthusiastically about shopping centers, supermarkets, and department stores: places where consumers could enjoy a variety of choices within a convenient, comfortable environment. That person enjoyed the specifics of that context and could not have anticipated the chains, lengthening and multiplying, linking raw materials, producers, and themselves, nor would they have foreseen the displacement of productive processes to industrializing nations, but they would have understood the consequences of plant closings for employment. Today mass media, particularly internet shopping, dominate business pages. Almost every retail business has a web presence, but Craig's list, Freecycle, and other trade or barter webpages are changing our expectations for how we acquire many goods and services.

In the United States, street commerce shrank in relative importance in the middle of the twentieth century; experts believed that it belonged to the past, catered only to tourists, and would only survive in less industrialized countries until replaced by modern practices. But, in the latter half of the twentieth century, in the United States and elsewhere, open air markets and merchants became more popular rather than less.

The reasons for this revival are many. Some factors are local and idiosyncratic, such as, in the First World, the popularity of flea markets in the hippie culture of the 1960s and 70s, and the popularity of farmers' markets in the yuppie culture of the 1990s. Others are economic, such as the inability of large, capital-intensive (and tax-paying) retailers to make a profit in low-income neighborhoods (Tokman 1978), and the overall growth of inequality and exploitation that force some into informality in order to survive (Fernández-Kelly and García 1989). Others are political, such as the ability of street vendors to defend themselves against attempts by formal stores and government officials to legislate them out of existence (Cross 1998). Monnet notes that street vending has become more acceptable partly because it fits ideologically with "postfordist flexible capitalism, where the dominant ideal is that each person is a businessperson, solely responsible for themselves." (2005 – author's translation.)

But most important is that markets and merchants have adapted to government action and economic problems and opportunities. This chapter introduces the book by exploring a far broader theme that has been generally overlooked in the literature on street vending and the informal sector: the global transformation from a "modern" economic/political system, which saw street vendors and the informal sector as parasitic or at best inefficient, to a "postmodern" economic/political system in which street commerce is often seen as a source of growth and flexibility.

Research on street vending usually categorizes it as part of the "informal" economy, a concept popularized by Keith Hart (1973) and probably best defined by Portes and Castells (1989) as activity that produces or distributes legal goods while avoiding regulatory controls. While the term is used in a number of different ways by the authors in this volume, we emphasize that it is of limited usefulness for the same reasons "formalism" was useless to economic anthropologists in the 1950s and 60s, particularly if it is seen as a reified and rigid category. Some street markets may be fully regulated, but still informal in terms of the relationships between vendors and clients (and the ability to hide cash income), such as farmers' markets in the United States. In other cases, street markets may include clearly illegal activities, such as the sale of contraband goods (Cross, this volume). Markets and merchants represent a complex intersection of social, political, and economic processes. Markets are more than price-setting mechanisms: exchange represents and reinforces social ties. Vendors earn income, but that simple act takes place within complex social and household dynamics. Whatever the other analytic schemes that might apply, fundamentally vendors and vending provision consumers, produce income for merchants and relate to government policy. Rather than simply labeling markets or merchants as "informal" and descending into an interminable language game, we recommend policy makers and scientists take government, family, and market in their empirical reality, taking great care while employing abstract categories, and embracing the various aspects of what they want to understand and explain.

## Modernity and postmodernity: a rough sketch

While there is some debate about whether or not it is appropriate to use the term postmodernity to describe today's world, "At the least it is obvious that the world which for a long time has been thought of as 'modern' is experiencing a crisis of grave and global proportions" (Lemert 1997:32). Lemert associates this crisis with three factors: the collapse of the Euro-American colonial system; the disappearance of a coherent imperial world center; and the rise of a global opposition to a single, unified world culture associated with Euro-American value systems. These broader changes are also associated with changes in the global economic system, which have seriously undermined the central logic of modernism itself – the Fordist/Keynesian economic order. This system emphasized, on the one hand, the centralization of production and distribution in the hands of mega-corporations built around the theory of economies of scale. On the other hand, it emphasized the regulatory role of the state in managing relations between workers, managers, owners, and consumers. This regulatory role is the basis of the massive increase in the size of the state bureaucracy at every level even as it has intervened into every aspect of social life, a process shown clearly in Foucault's archeology of ideas.

Obviously, this modern project began long before the advent of Ford and Keynes. Many tie its origins to the enlightenment (Harvey 1990), but the Fordist/Keynesian approach to economic management, the former at the corporate level and the latter at the state level, exemplified the process and theory behind economic centralization and regulation that became a hallmark of the "modern" world, whether it was capitalist or socialist. While the grand rationale behind modernism was the creation of more and more "efficient" and "productive" individuals by controlling and ordering the relations between them, in fact modern efficiency and productivity could only fully thrive under optimal conditions that had to be molded gradually over time. These conditions not only required massive changes in state structure, roles and revenues, business organization, factory structure, and market systems, but also in the very culture and social life of individuals, families, and communities. As a total system, it required that every aspect of society should be molded according to its requirements. Fordism represents above all the formal recognition that mass production *requires* a mass market, and that mass markets do not simply spring into being – they must be manufactured!

Yet even in the growth of this modernist system, analysts complained of "irrational" remnants of premodern life. Bairoch (1973) was among modernists who lamented the vestiges and even redevelopment of an "over-distended tertiary" – encompassing services and commerce that, in his view, threatened to undermine national development plans by placing a drag on the economy. Like many analysts of the day his work tended to dualistic, either/or analysis masquerading as explanation (Morales 2001). Such work substituted assumptions of cultural and educational backwardness for questions about and comparative descriptions of behavior. The persistence and growth of merchants and markets as reasoned adaptation to circumstances beyond one's immediate control was rarely considered, or theorists discarded these remnants as ill-fitted to modernistic theoretical edifices of empty categories by which they sorted behavior.

Nor did modernist architecture or urban planning fit street markets well. The best representative of modernist design was Le Corbusier, a French architect who influenced the field greatly in the mid-war period with his emphasis on grand-scale design and planning. In his 1923 keynote text, *Towards a New Architecture*, Le Corbusier (1996) expressed the modern focus on creating the "ideal" society through a planned structure that would assign each individual to his or her place in life, regulating and caring for each need and demand:

> ... without plan there can be neither grandeur of aim and expression, nor rhythm, nor mass, nor coherence. Without plan we have the sensation, so insupportable to man, of shapelessness, of poverty, of disorder, of willfulness.
>
> (1996:207)

Thus Corbusier exhibits the modernist dream of a model society run from above, similar in scope and design to the model of the "pan-opticon" prison discussed by Foucault (1979) and in another sense to the non-political administration of socialism envisioned by Marxists such as Lenin. The relative disorder of markets and merchants has little refuge in such a world. In modernism everything is ordered, efficient, and structured: nothing is left to chance. It is little wonder, indeed, that Corbusier, like many others in Europe during this period of chaos, was attracted to more and more authoritarian regimes that could effect such an order. The result could perhaps be more appropriately termed the modernist nightmare, as Fascism and Stalinist socialism arose to crash against each other and against the more liberal (but no less modern) democracies in the second world war (Harvey 1990: 128–29).[2]

Planning and architecture dovetailed neatly into like-minded economic modernism which penetrated deeply into society such that it profoundly influenced other social institutions, even if it did not produce a uniformly nightmarish social life. Economic modernism's heyday was reached in the 1950s and 60s, with rapid economic growth in the United States and, later,

Europe and Japan, but even as Bairoch was writing in the 1970s cracks showed in modernist economic structure. Not only did increased competition from Europe and Japan slow economic growth in the United States, but unemployment and inflation became problematic. Even as international economic planning organizations, like the IMF, took hold, their legitimacy decreased and their modernist promises faded as Third World growth strategies, built around protectionist import substitution policies, produced socio-economic crises (Harvey 1990:141).

Economic modernism was built on government policy and international agreements, it created economic growth, temporarily reducing economic inequality in the United States and Europe, as it fostered growing inequalities around the world. Clearly not everyone benefited equally. Racial and gender dynamics in the United States produced wealth discrepancies and persisting discrimination (Oliver and Shapiro 1997; Brown *et al.* 2004). In Third World nations, growth benefited an even smaller class of elite workers and managers while the "marginalized" masses struggled to survive outside modernist enclaves. First/Third World urban redevelopment schemes created new forms of ghettos devoid of even the ability to control local space earlier enjoyed by the neglected poor. In the United States, "Modernism failed as mass-housing and city building partly because it failed to communicate with its inhabitants and users who might not have liked the style, understood what it meant or even known how to use it." (Jencks 1996:475.) Thus, those excluded from modernist dreams became victims blamed for adapting to precarious circumstances.

If anything, the decline of economic modernism enlarged the number of people who could be blamed for not adapting to "new" economic opportunities. The shift from Fordism to flexible accumulation "spelled danger for traditionally organized businesses, sparking a wave of bankruptcies, plant closures, deindustrialization, and restructuring ... " (Harvey 1990:155). The economies of scale sought by Fordist mass production were supplanted, at least to some degree, by economies of flexibility. In effect, the growth of regulatory and labor power in the First World economies grew to the point that they produced a competitive disadvantage, leading "either to the rise of entirely new industrial forms or to the integration of Fordism with a network of subcontracting and 'outsourcing' to give greater flexibility in the face of heightened competition and greater risks." (Harvey 1990:155–56; see also Lozano 1989.) In effect, the modernist compromise whereby workers gave up control over their labor in exchange for a modicum of wealth and security unraveled in the face of competitive pressures. Not only were workers paid less in the aggregate, but they also took greater risks as jobs moved overseas to find the lowest wages.

The "great sucking sound to the south" that Ross Perot alluded to in the 1992 debate over the passage of the North American Free Trade Agreement with Mexico and Canada had really begun decades before as plants and production relocated to Mexico, Taiwan, South Korea, and other nations (or even poorer regions of the same nation) where labor costs were lower and regulatory enforcement was less complete. Despite this new investment, wage levels in the receiving nations remained low for the vast majority of the population. For the First World, moreover, new forms of employment lacked the security and wage guarantees of modernist industry. Average wages decreased and economic inequality increased around the world. Outside a few privileged sectors, people are paid less for doing more, violating the laws of supply and demand, questioning the logic of classical and neoclassical economics, and reinvigorating segments of the population in labor and economic justice movements bridging modernist boundaries of race, nation, and gender.

Postmodernity, then, reflects a moment in economic history in which capital is free to go wherever profits are higher without the need to worry about the welfare of workers or consumers. Mass production remains important, but "just-in-time" and other responsive production practices respond to consumer-/advertising-driven market segmentation. International investment escaped from the Fordist need to pay wages and benefits high enough so that the workers could themselves consume the products they produce. Consumers could be found elsewhere, and if not products began to flow through a retail system that included discount and retail outlets of "last" resort. Simultaneously the growing numbers of poor consumers were embracing deep discount retail, while the more affluent consumers were rejecting mass production in favor of local, organic, or other initiatives and workers, squeezed from the middle class wages provided by Fordism, began to reorganize themselves and their households to "reserve" some labor to replace wage income earning activities with other means of support (Uzzell 1980).

## Street vending, modernity, and postmodernity

Following Le Corbusier's modernist vision of urban space, the informal economy, and street vending in particular, would very much provoke in the modernist that "sensation, so insupportable to man, of shapelessness, of poverty, of disorder, of willfulness." To the extent that the modernist ideal was shared by elites in the First and Third Worlds alike (particularly in as much as Third World elites considered "modernization" to imply the approximation of the western modernist ideal in external form), the presence of large street markets was the clearest sign of the "disorder" and "willfulness" of the informal economy that needed to be stamped out.

In his classic study *Peddlers and Princes* (1963) the anthropologist Clifford Geertz reflected the belief shared by most scholars at the time – that street markets and bazaars were part of a romantic past that had little place in the "modern" world. According to the modernist developmental vision that permeated the scholarship of the 1950s and 60s, these forms of commerce were seen as backward, inefficient, and detrimental to national development schemes, taking up and wasting resources that could be better spent in more productive fashion. From a cultural perspective Geertz argued that the "bazaar economy" hampered the development of a western-style "firm-centered" economy. Even though it employs huge numbers of individuals, Geertz maintained that this market system "has the disadvantage that it turns even the established businessman away from an interest in reducing costs and developing markets and toward petty speculation and short-run opportunism" (28–29).

The irrationalities implied in price setting and relationships were one rationale for attacks on markets and merchants throughout the modernist era. But while the criticism decried their purported inefficiency the real problem was that they successfully competed against modern retail outlets, unless they were located in optimal "modern" areas. Since supermarkets could not put street vendors out of business through market mechanisms, business in league with politicians used the police system to do it.

The solution, therefore, was to ban or over-regulate street vendors while also redesigning urban spaces so that street vending could no longer exist. Suburban subdivisions, urban decay, and urban renewal projects were all a vigorous part of this process in the First World. In the Third World, the same processes were attempted, but with varying success stymied by modernism's uneven penetration of society and the merchants' ability to evade or resist the modernist encroachment on their livelihoods. In Mexico City, for example, an extraordinarily expensive program of repression and market construction managed to banish street vending for just under a decade in the 1960s, but merchants reemerged stronger than ever (Cross 1998). In Los Angeles, California, on the other hand, while street vending was effectively banished in the late 1950s it became a significant factor again in the 1980s (Kettles, this volume).

This reemergence occurred as the modernist dream crumbled into post-modern reality. However, street merchants have not simply returned to a romanticized past but created reasoned reactions to local manifestations of today's economic, cultural, and social world. Postmodernism as a movement, if we can think of it as such, is concerned first and foremost with the individual's attempt to regain control over their lives – control that is lost in modern society's mass-production factories and corporate offices. This is reflected in the renewed growth of small businesses since the 1980s, as the middle class seeks to avoid the control of salaried labor. But many are finding that the burden of regulations means that they have simply exchanged one form of control for another (Kuratko *et al.* 1999).

The relationship between street merchants and modernity was obviously problematic from the start. As the state's regulatory system expanded to encompass every aspect of economic activity in order to regulate and order the relations between owners, employees, and consumers, it became more and more difficult for the poor, in particular, to establish businesses that met the varied and complex regulatory environment. Requirements are costly, both financially and in terms of transactions that require the assistance of lawyers, accountants, or other specialists – services typically out of the reach of the poor. De Soto (1989) argues that this over-regulation is directly responsible for creating entrepreneurial incentives to skirt the regulatory system, thus allowing competition with multinational corporations.

The persistence and reinvigoration of the street is a strategy for survival and upward mobility conducted by entrepreneurs across the globe while at the same time policy makers are, as they did 100 years ago, perceiving markets and merchants as policy tools. For instance supermarket chains, the quintessence of modernist retailing, cannot compete, apparently, with the boutiques of wealthy areas nor the street markets in poor areas (Tokman 1978). Where regulations are strictly applied, food and other essential goods are *more* expensive in poor neighborhoods than they are in middle class areas, while the wealthy demand personalized services that are difficult for formal organizations to provide. However, street markets can flexibly fill this niche passing the savings on to the poor (or rich) of these areas.[3] Likewise, popular products often filter into impoverished areas by way of street markets. Alonso (1980) argued that small vendors are a form of disguised employees of large corporations. Bromley (1978) makes a similar argument with respect to some street vendors (particularly ice cream and newspaper vendors) in Colombia. Finally, buy local and organic initiatives fostering farmers' markets are of a kind with luxury markets for tourists that fit into "identity based" economic development strategies for tourism.

## Turning to street markets and merchants as policy prescription

About 100 years ago street markets were an important policy tool in the United States to alleviate problems with unemployment, food safety, and distribution (Morales 2000; Tangiers 2003). Once again, policy makers today see such markets playing a role in economic policy. Street vending minimizes overhead costs of rent and utilities, is ideally suited for low-skilled employment, and fits with a new ideology of independence and entrepreneurship, but can it withstand attempts to over-regulate it while provisioning consumers safely? While markets may be attractive to some and vilified by others, it should be kept in mind that part of the problem lies not in the phenomenon occurring in their streets, but in preconceived notions of the "appropriate" (read western or modernist) use of public space or appropriate retail trade discussed in chapters throughout the book and focused on by the next chapter.

Markets and merchants are now often called upon by today's development experts to take over where the formal sector has failed (Peattie 1987; Cornwall 1998). Throughout the Third World and increasingly in the First, government and non-government (NGO) development agencies have turned to the "micro-business" sector to absorb excess unemployment and pick up the slack on economic growth. The most popular mechanism of "supporting" this sector is the use of micro-loans: small amounts of money lent out for relatively short periods of time for use in establishing or expanding a small business. While this may seem like an equitable solution, we have significant doubts that such programs can be sufficient without a broader change in attitude.[4]

While earlier attacks on markets were rooted in an erroneous belief that they were parasitic or irrational because they did not fit with the "modernist" economic vision, this new belief repeats the error of thinking about markets simply in negative terms: that is, in terms of how vendors are *not* formal. We call this "formalomorphism" – the tendency to reify a formal category, retail trade, and diagnose problems with street markets or other residual activities as if it were a bad copy of the privileged category instead of appreciating them for what they are and what they do contribute. For example, as Rakowski (1994) points out, the vast bulk of economic literature emphasizes what "informals" lack with respect to the formal sector (Sethuraman 1981; PREALC/OIT 1988). It is smaller (less efficiencies of scale); it is undercapitalized (lack of machinery and/or inventory); it is underskilled (lack of managerial skill, credentials); and it is not growth oriented (Yusuf and Schindehutte 2000).

Policy designed to develop the informal sector tends to ignore or minimize the potential or the benefits of street merchants and underestimate the difficulties of making micro-businesses bear the development burden of formal enterprises. "Entrepreneurs" are taught accounting, project goals focus on loan repayment, businesses are encouraged or required to conform to existing regulations, all goals that look great from a formal point of view. But this is exactly the danger: they potentially undermine the very factors that make many informal enterprises successful while imposing formal rules that they are unable to deal with. From engaging in a flexible and evolving economic activity focused on family subsistence needs (and often involving the avoidance of control by authorities), they are sucked into a rigid set of rules that they can barely understand and even less likely to be able to challenge or manipulate. While their businesses may be more "accountable" they may in fact be less successful.

Informality should be seen, for example, not only as a violation of rules, but as a particular way in which people interact. The micro-business perspective overlooks the features that make markets and merchants successful – the ability to interact informally with clients and suppliers, thus promoting the spirit of survival and flexibility that attracted scholars to this activity in the first place (Wirth 1928; Hart 1970, 1973; Birbeck 1978). It seems to us that those who would champion the street as policy tool should eschew reified categories and embrace local and historical context as they understand the organization of markets, the role played, and thence the ways to link merchants as part of more encompassing development strategies.[5]

We have argued elements of this approach elsewhere. Morales *et al.* (1995) enumerated the economic and non-economic benefits by attending to social, legal, and economic concerns intersecting in a century-old market. Cross (1998:33; 1999) comprehended implications associated with combinations of costs and benefits for different types of retail trade. Instead of a sterile typology, his examination focused on organizational and policy implications of the trade-offs merchants make between operating in a store or on the street. Morales (1992; 2001) critiqued tax compliance theory, arguing that policy should foster the entrepreneurial spirit of new immigrant street merchants and critiqued theory privileging categories over description and understanding, which the contributors to this volume illuminate splendidly.

Our efforts indicate no single "solution" to the tension between markets and modernity. Instead, postmodernity suggests to us many working hypotheses where every successful solution attends to context, experimentation, history, and close understanding of local organization relating wider-spread networks and practices. Government policy makers and other organizations should use and promote street markets while preserving their advantages. We believe this approach is not at all new or radical: in fact it is rooted metaphorically in one of the oldest of activities, the gardener. Organizational decision-makers should simply define markets as legitimate places for business, then like a prudent gardener, better still a Franciscan gardener, they should let everything bloom and flourish, acknowledging the most accepted norms, but experimenting with the delimited space, redirecting and encouraging, pruning and transplanting, educating themselves and their choices in dialog with merchants. In other words, we suggest recognizing and experimenting with systems of production and distribution provided by micro-enterprises but intersecting with large firms and fostering growth and development of each. An example of this is Morales' (2002) investigation of interdependencies between households and radio stations in producing economic opportunities for each.

While modernity presented a complete *unilateral* system of ideas and behaviors, postmodernity implies multiple distinct but *interwoven* systems of ideas and behaviors, demanding analysts to adapt their practices to the more complex reality.

Street markets have resurfaced reinvigorated by successfully exploiting consumer segmentation, rich or poor, and, typically in the latter case although depending on local circumstances, avoiding state control focused on the needs and concerns of large business enterprises. But as the modernist dream fades into postmodern reality, policy makers who use street markets to supplant unsuccessful economics endanger the very factors that clients, vendors, and suppliers find attractive in such markets. The solution, therefore, is to take advantage of the pragmatist postmodern emphasis on experimentation in multiple layers of reality. Rather than "lowering" the formal system to the level of the informal sector, as some have advocated (De Soto 1989), or "raising" the informal sector to the level of the formal sector, as many development projects focusing on the micro-business sector seem to attempt, our suggestion is that policy makers create ways in which distinct systems can intersect while existing side-to-side. Continue to maintain and support the "modern" formal system, but also allow spaces, or massive micro-business incubators, in which those overlooked by the formal sector can develop their own solutions to the circumstances of their lives, their aspirations, and the larger political-economic context they face.

## The essays that follow

For this to happen successfully, of course, far more research is necessary about the political, economic, business, and social reality of street markets. This book, by pulling together research conducted around the world, is a small first step in that direction.

These authors make great strides in our appreciation of street vendors and vending by describing the complexity of empirical settings around the world. The main tool they bring is the notion of embeddedness first used by Polanyi and later by Granovetter (1985). Thus these chapters each take economic activity, but understand it as embedded *with* other aspects of social life. Vendors around the world do recognizably similar things, but not always in the same way or for the same reasons as their institutional contexts vary. Likewise, laws and regulations vary due to socio-historical trajectory (without any straight-line determinism) and contestation over the role of markets and merchants in each time and place. The results are delightfully complex, but rendered understandable with reference to embeddedness.

The book that follows is organized into two parts that roughly correspond to "context" versus "practice," although generally each essay makes some comment on each aspect. The essays on context in Part I focus mostly on regulatory issues rather than economic ones. This is not because economic factors are unimportant, but because we feel that historically far less attention has been made to the regulatory system in the academic literature. Nevertheless, economic considerations are raised by almost all the authors as part of their broader arguments. The essays on practice in Part II tend to focus more on the embeddedness of street markets in broader social relations, whether between vendors or between these and their suppliers and clients.

Markets are most famous for their assault on our senses, but underlying the compounded perceptions are equally numerous and complex social processes, information, and ideas acted upon bringing commerce to the streets of our increasingly interconnected and globalized world.

## Notes

1 This chapter is based in part on an article written by the first author (Cross 2000).
2 The same modernist nightmare influenced such novels as Huxley's *Brave New World* and Orwell's *1984*, differing versions of the same theme of modernist utopias gone wild.

3  This is why street markets exist on both sides of the spectrum: think Santa Fe or
   Milano for the wealthy, and Chicago's Maxwell Street market or Mexico's Tepito
   for the poor.
4  See also Sreenivasan (2000), Woller *et al.* (1999), and Yunus (1999) for discussion
   of the benefits and drawbacks of this approach.
5  Excellent statements of the general approach are found in Leaf (1979; 1998) and
   Cernea (1985).

# Bibliography

Alonso, J. (1980) *Lucha Urbana y Acumulación de Capital*, Mexico City: La Casa
   Chata.
Bairoch, P. (1973) *Urban Unemployment in Developing Countries*, Geneva:
   International Labor Office.
Birbeck, C. (1978) "Self-Employed Proletarians in an Informal Factory: The Case of
   Cali's Garbage Dump," *World Development*, 6: 1173–86.
Bromley, R. (1978) "Organization, Regulation and Exploitation in the So-Called
   'Urban Informal Sector': The Street Traders of Cali, Colombia," *World
   Development*, 6: 1161–72.
Brown, M. K., Carnoy, M., Currie, E., Duster, T., Oppenheimer, D. B., Shultz, M. M.,
   and Wellman, D. (2003) *Whitewashing Race: The Myth of a Color-Blind Society*,
   CA: University of California Press.
Cernea, M. M. (1985) *Putting People First: Sociological Variables in Rural
   Development*, London: Oxford University Press.
Cornwall, J. R. (1998) "The Entrepreneur as a Building Block for Community,"
   *Journal of Developmental Entrepreneurship*, 3: 141–48.
Cross, J. (1998) *Informal Politics: Street Vendors and the State in Mexico City*,
   Stanford, CA: Stanford University Press.
——(1999) "Informal Sector," in P. O'Hara (ed.) *Encyclopedia of Political Economy*,
   London: Routledge.
——(2000) "Street Vendors, Modernity and Postmodernity: Conflict and Compro-
   mise in the Global Economy," *International Journal of Sociology and Social
   Planning*, 21(1): 29–51.
De Soto, H. (1989) *The Other Path: The Invisible Revolution in the Third World*, New
   York: Harper & Row.
Fernández-Kelly, M. P. and García, A. M. (1989) "Informalization at the Core:
   Hispanic Women, Homework, and the Advanced Capitalist State," in A. Portes,
   M. Castells, and L. A. Benton (eds) *The Informal Economy: Studies in Advanced
   and Less Developed Countries*, Baltimore, MA: Johns Hopkins University Press.
Foucault, M. (1979) *Discipline and Punish: The Birth of the Prison*, New York:
   Vintage.
Geertz, C. (1963) *Peddlers and Princes: Social Change and Economic Modernization
   in Two Indonesian Towns*, Chicago, IL: University of Chicago Press.
Granovetter, M. (1985) "Economic Structure and Social Action: The Problem of
   Embeddedness," *American Journal of Sociology*, 91(3): 481–510.
Hart, J. K. (1970) "Small Scale Entrepreneurs in Ghana and Development Planning,"
   *The Journal of Development Studies*, 6: 104–20.
——(1973) "Informal Income Opportunities and Urban Employment in Ghana,"
   *Journal of Modern African Studies*, 11: 61–89.

Harvey, D. (1990) *The Condition of Postmodernity*, Oxford: Blackwell.

Jencks, C. (1996) "What is Postmodernism?," in L. Cahoone (ed.) *From Modernism to Postmodernism: An Anthology*, Oxford: Blackwell.

Kuratko, D. F., Hornsby, J. S., and Naffziger, D. W. (1999) "The Adverse Effect of Public Policy on Microenterprises: An Exploratory Study of Owner's Perceptions," *Journal of Developmental Entrepreneurship*, 4: 81–93.

Leaf, M. J. (1979) *Man, Mind, and Science: A History of Anthropology*, New York: Columbia University Press.

——(1998) *Pragmatism and Development; The Prospect for Pluralist Transformation in the Third World*, Westport, CT: Bergin & Garvey.

Le Corbusier (1996) "Towards a New Architecture," in L. Cahoone (ed.) *From Modernism to Postmodernism: An Anthology*, Oxford: Blackwell.

Lemert, C. (1997) *Postmodernism Is Not What You Think*, Oxford: Blackwell.

Lozano, B. (1989) *The Invisible Work Force: Transforming American Business With Outside and Home-Based Workers*, New York: The Free Press.

Monnet, J. (2005) "Conceptualización del ambulantaje; de los vendedores a los clientes: un acercamiento a la metropolis posfordista," in J. Monnet and J. Bonnafé (eds) *Memoria del Seminario El Ambulantaje en la Ciudad de México: Investigaciones Recientes*, Mexico, D.F.: UNAM/PUEC/CEMCA.

Morales, A. (1992) "Tax Problems of New Immigrants," *IRS Research Conference Publications*.

——(1998) "Income Tax Compliance and Alternative Views of Ethics and Human Nature," *Journal of Accounting, Ethics and Public Policy*, 1(3): 380–400.

——(2000) "Peddling Policy: Street Vending in Historical and Contemporary Context," *International Journal of Sociology and Social Policy*, 20(3/4): 76–99.

——(2001) "Policy from Theory: A Critical Reconstruction of Theory on the 'Informal' Economy," *Sociological Imagination*, 38(3): 190–203.

——(2002) "Radio Mercado: Radio Stations and Subsistence Marketing," *Journal of Borderlands Studies*, 17: 79–102.

——, Balkin, S., and Persky, J. (1995) "The Value of Benefits of a Public Street Market: The Case of Maxwell Street," *Economic Development Quarterly*, 9: 304–20.

Oliver, M. and Shapiro, T. (1997) *Black Wealth, White Wealth: A New Perspective on Racial Inequality*, London and New York: Routledge.

Peattie, L. (1987) "An Idea in Good Currency and How It Grew: The Informal Sector," *World Development*, 15(7): 851–60.

Polanyi, K. (1957) "The Economy as Instituted Process," in K. Polanyi, C. M. Arensberg, and H. W. Pearson (eds) *The Trade and Market in the Early Empires*, Glencoe: Free Press.

Portes, A. and Castells, M. (1989) "Introduction," in A. Portes, M. Castells, and L. A. Benton (eds), *The Informal Economy: Studies in Advanced and Less Developed Countries*, Baltimore, MA: Johns Hopkins University Press.

PREALC/OIT (1988) *Sobrevivir en la Calle: El Comercio Ambulante en Santiago*, Santiago: PREALC/OIT.

Rakowski, C. A. (1994) "Convergence and Divergence in the Informal Sector Debate: A Focus on Latin America," *World Development*, 22: 501–16.

Romero, M. (1991) *Maid in the U.S.A.*, New York: Routledge.

Sethuraman, S. V. (1981) "Technology Adoption and Small Enterprise Development," in P. A. Neck and R. E. Nelson (eds) *Small Enterprise Development:*

*Policies and Programme*, Geneva: ILO-ARTEP, International Labour Organization, pp. 187–202.

Sreenivasan, J. (2000) *Ela Bhatt: Uniting Women in India*, New York: The Feminist Press at CUNY.

Tangiers, H. (2003) *Public Markets and Civic Culture in Nineteenth-Century America*, Baltimore, MD: The Johns Hopkins University Press.

Tokman, V. E. (1978) "Competition between the Informal and Formal Sectors in Retailing: The Case of Santiago," *World Development*, 6: 1187–98.

Uzzell, J. D. (1980) "Mixed Strategies and the Informal Sector: Three Faces of Reverse Labor," *Human Organization*, 39: 40–49.

Wirth, L. (1928) *The Ghetto*, Chicago, IL: University of Chicago Press.

Woller, G. M., Wheeler, G., and Checketts, N. (1999) "Evaluation Practices in Microcredit Institutions," *Journal of Developmental Entrepreneurship*, 4: 59–80.

Yunus, M. (1999) *Banker to the Poor: Micro-lending and the Battle Against World Poverty*, Washington, DC: Public Affairs.

Yusuf, A. and Schindehutte, M. (2000) "Exploring Entrepreneurship in a Declining Economy," *Journal of Developmental Entrepreneurship*, 5: 41–56.

# Part I

# Appropriating space

## Political and social regulation of street markets

The literature on street markets has usually been subsumed within the context of the "informal economy," a concept that embodies both economic and regulatory, and thus political, dimensions. In the following chapters we showcase research focusing primarily on regulatory systems within which street vendors and street markets operate, and the implications they have on urban space, political systems, and even legal systems. For example, where street markets are discouraged or repressed, vendors must often invade (illegally or informally) the space in which to gain access to their clients. This process often puts them in conflict with other local stakeholders who are usually more powerful – local businesses and local franchises of multi-nationals, but also middle-class and upper-class elites who see street stalls as an infringement of "their" right to use public space.

To open this part, Cross and Karides present a discussion of the notion of urban space, and why street markets are often seen as violating the "appropriate" use of that space. Making use of Lefebvre's Marxist analysis of urban theory, the chapter demonstrates that the study of street markets, as a part of street life more broadly speaking, provides a unique perspective on urban theory itself, as street vendors can be seen challenging the dominant use of space, and thus the dominant spatial value system. Rather than pointing to a revolutionary outcome, however, the authors suggest that urban planners must reassess the ways that they think about space to incorporate the needs of the urban poor.

García-Rincón analyzes the effect of the populist Chavez government in Venezuela on the delicate balance of power between street vendors and municipal authorities in Caracas. Vendors and authorities contest the appropriate use of public space in two ways, by physical presence and in terms of contested definitions of appropriate use. The original repressive anti-vendor policy was enacted by the local authorities on advice from Rudolph Giuliani, the "law and order" ex-Mayor of New York. But the public support given by the president for the rights of vendors, a part of his broader populist strategy, created regulatory confusion at the municipal level, where vendors used the moral support of the presidency to undermine and sabotage the

Giuliani-inspired policy. The chapter amply demonstrates that local level physical and ideological conflicts must be analyzed in terms of the broader political as well as economic context.

The chapters by Kettles and Staudt provide an important contrast between First and Third Worlds. By examining Los Angeles and El Paso we see how street vending, often assumed to be a thing of the past, is in fact reemerging but often stymied by over-regulation. In Los Angeles, Kettles focuses on a new regulatory policy implemented in the early 1990s that was supposed to help underprivileged vendors by allowing street vending for the first time in three decades. However, the emphasis on controlling vendors created a confusing, over-constraining regulatory system that implied high costs for vendors, few benefits, and a series of bureaucratic obstacles. As a result, the policy never achieved its aim: vendors were forced to continue to sell illegally because the permits were too expensive and too difficult to obtain. Kettles also enumerates the broader political-policy-related arguments in favor of vending in a way that is analogous to Morales *et al.*'s (1995) estimates of monetary and nonmonetary benefits of vending. Staudt, while revisiting her 15-year-old case study of El Paso, Texas, also incorporates a comparison with Ciudad Juarez, the Mexican city across the border from El Paso. One unique contribution she makes is to specify the patron–client relationships organizing merchants in dissimilar marketing contexts. Whether the merchant is found on the street, in a market, or even in a mall, their entrepreneurial efforts are limited by patron–client relationships. However, like Kettles, she points out that regulatory controls are constantly threatening to strangle the potential for the poor to participate in street vending in El Paso, while in Ciudad Juarez vendors are able to negotiate far more effectively to maintain their access to public space. One of the factors in both cases is that US regulatory systems tend to emphasize individual rights, which in effect pits the individual vendor against the bureaucratic might of the state. On the other hand, in Mexico vendors work collectively, giving them far more leverage against a state that is often far less cohesive bureaucratically.

Bhowmik and Varcin each provide vital case studies of regulatory systems in two societies – India and Turkey – that are in some ways similar and in others totally different. In both societies street markets form a vital source of employment and provision, particularly for the poor. However, in India the remnants of British colonial policy and a perverse focus on "modernization at any cost" led scholars to completely ignore the reality of street merchants, with official policy alternating between benign neglect, bribery, and repression, while in Turkey the tradition of oriental despotism blended with the modernization of the Ataturk state to create a system of hyper-regulation that incorporated vendors as an important part of the fiscal system but often forced them to find ways around the regulatory system in order to survive. Bhowmik's chapter, which focuses on how street vendor organizations helped to write a federal law in India on behalf of street merchants, is also a case in point of how an idea becomes law on the books, but whose crusade is only symbolic without practical application. Bhowmik begs for resources and a real place at the policy table for street merchants, but, as in many other societies, they cannot match the lobbying that western-style and western-brand retailers bring to negotiations with government. Varcin's chapter on Turkey contrasts with India in that merchants are expected to support the state, but the burden falls unevenly on vendors unable to pay both official and unofficial taxes. Yet despite their struggle with capricious regulators they have had some success in mobilizing against unfavorable policies in part because they are considered an essential part of the political, fiscal, and regulatory system.

In the final chapter of the first part, Cross focuses on the sale of contraband items in a popular street market in Mexico. Questioning the boundary between the "informal" and "illegal" markets, Cross shows how vendors justify their production and sale of pirated music and movie CDs and DVDs within the context of their experience in struggling for legitimacy against the state and large businesses. The broad spectrum of individuals involved in this activity, the ease with which it is done, and the available counter-hegemonic justifications that legitimate, at least in their eyes, their illegal activity as a form of survival, illustrates the role of street markets as a site of resistance to the dominant normative system in societies where it cannot be repressed. While this could obviously be seen by some as a reason for destroying such sites in the modernist tradition of control, it could also be seen by others as a potential site of "utopian possibilities" (Harvey 2000).

## Bibliography

Harvey, David (2000) *Spaces of Hope,* Berkeley, CA: University of California Press.
Morales, Alfonso, Steve Balkin, and Joe Persky (1995) "The Value of Benefits of a Public Street Market: The Case of Maxwell Street," *Economic Development Quarterly,* 9: 304–20.

# 2 Capitalism, modernity, and the "appropriate" use of space

*John C. Cross and Marina Karides*

Street vendors are accused of many things: of being dirty and "ugly," of not paying their share of taxes, of selling illegal or contraband goods, of being unhygienic, of blocking public transit, and of making too much noise. But while many of these issues could be subsumed within the concept of the "Informal Sector," the underlying complaint by many city administrators, local businesses, or residents is that they are *there*. As the president of Mexico City's Chamber of Commerce argued when the city government planned to tax and regulate vendors: "the solution is not to tax the vendors, but to take them off the streets" (Soto 2005). In a similar fashion, even though the Indian government has passed laws requiring states to approve street vending, only two of the states have done so due to the opposition of local interests (Bhowmik, this volume). Certainly, it is not our intent to argue that the use of space is the only conflictive issue between vendors and the state (see Cross, this volume, for a discussion of contraband and piracy), but the spatial crisis of global capitalism is one of the primordial cross-cutting issues that street vendors all over the world have to face.

Vendors' struggles for space are particularly acute in downtown areas, especially in cities where the local government and business want to "renovate" urban areas for tourism or to increase local real-estate values. Businesses claim that street vendors usurp space that is intended to allow their customers to drive and walk to their stores. These complaints are compounded by the argument that vendors compete "unfairly" because they are not paying rents (or taxes) equivalent to those paid by established businesses. City officials, anxious to collect their share of rents and taxes, have a direct interest in siding with those businesses. But the argument is not entirely one-sided. Street vendors, for their part, often argue that they have historical rights to their market zones and that they deserve the right to make an "honest living" in the context of economic insecurity, an argument that sometimes provokes the state and the public to side with their interests (Morales 2000).

There are even some contexts in which local businesses look favorably on the presence of street vendors. For instance, in Port of Spain, Trinidad, government and local developers used street vendors to revitalize downtown streets that were destroyed when the nation experienced a political coup (Karides 2001). In other cities, even in the United States, street markets may also be seen as a way to add color to downtown areas. Some shop owners also see street vendors as providing informal security, reducing shop lifting and other petty crimes that may occur in vacant streets. However, the interests of vendors are almost always seen as subsidiary to those of "established" businesses. In the case of Trinidad, when the nation experienced economic strain and the size of the vending population began to increase, business owners began to complain of congestion and competition. Overall, despite the fact that a sizeable portion of workers in the post-colonial world is involved in some form of street trade, they are not fully realized for the contributions that they make to these national economies (de Soto 1989; Morales *et al.* 1995a, 1995b). Ultimately, the problem with vendors is that they contest assumptions about how "public space" should be used, and in whose interests. In effect, the conflict between businesses, governments, residents, development interests, and vendors is over the very definition of "appropriate use" of space.

It is not just the "formal" definition of appropriate use that is at stake here, but the "practical" definition that takes place between regulation and enforcement. Police officers or other officials who are primarily responsible for enforcing what is legally defined as the appropriate use of space often have a complicated relationship with street vendors. While some officers attempt to regulate vendors according to government law, others engage in a system of bribes, or have friendly relationships with some vendors and not others. Many officers who are in a similar class position as vendors are sympathetic to their wish to make an honest living and are hesitant to harass or arrest vendors that are elderly or differently-abled. This "street level enforcement" is often complicated by the fact that local agencies have contradictory mandates, while local regulations are antiquated or simply fail to reflect social reality on the ground, creating a condition of "low state integration" (Cross 1998) or a "frustrated state" (Centeno and Portes 2006). Such a condition is reflected in every essay in the first part of this book.

These struggles over space are indicative of Lefebvre's argument of the centrality of space in the current era of global capitalism (Karides and Balaguer 2005). In effect, from the perspective of city planners eager to increase their tax rolls and businesses eager to supplement their bottom line, the desire to increase urban land values is challenged by the presence of "uncontrolled" vendors that violate the strictly limited (and highly regulated) role of "quaint" tourist attractions. To the extent that they violate these norms, vendors are reconfiguring space to suit their own needs, contrary to the desires of the state and capital.

Although written in 1974, Lefebvre's *The Production of Space* (1991) has enormous relevance to this conflict (Karides and Balaguer 2005). Lefebvre's work put Marxian thought squarely within the framework of urban spatial theory. While Marxists generally thought of space as a part of the superstructure of society, and therefore of secondary importance to issues of class, Lefebvre argued that how space is "produced" is a central part of the mode of production (Smith 2003). The organization of space not only reflects power, but produces power. These concepts were used in different ways by new urbanists such as Manuel Castells and David Harvey, giving rise to the field of human geography (Gottendier 1993: 129). Foucault, with a different theoretical base, still arrives at a similar conclusion that each epoch must create "*functional sites* ... [that] correspond not only to the need to supervise, to break dangerous communications, but also to create a useful space" (1979: 143–44, emphasis in original).

Historically, neither Marxist nor liberal visions of development paid much heed to the role of street markets, even though they had been the predominant form of commerce in the developing world.[1] Despite his advocacy of the downtrodden worker, Marx placed street peddlers into the "reactionary" lumpen-proletariate, a belief shared by liberal Victorian social reformers such as Booth who lumped street vendors into the lowest class of urban dwellers who could "render no useful service ... and ... degrade everything they touch" (quoted in Parker 2004). Despite a more "scientific" approach, basic views did not change during most of the twentieth century. Early academic investigation into street vending typically identified these economic pursuits as part of the pre-modern traditional economic order (Murphy 1990; Smith 1988). Some even argued that these small and informal economic activities were antithetical to development (Lewis 1954). Liberal anthropologists such as Geertz (1963) lambasted the cultural backwardness of the "Bazaar Economy," while academic Marxists pinpointed the "informal sector" as an arena of super-exploitation that subsidized and maintained a low-wage formal sector (Portes and Walton 1978; Evans and Timberlake 1980). Furthermore, because they infringed on public space, street vendors who congregated in capital cities throughout the Global South presented a visible challenge to nations trying to shape themselves into Western images of modernized society.

Both Marxist and liberal visionaries argued for the development of large industrial urban production and commercial units to trigger economic growth and to replace smaller enterprises that they assumed were less efficient (Mattera 1985; Portes and Castells 1989; Rakowski 1994; Varcin, this volume). The political role of the modern state was to facilitate the "development" process of large firms and to hinder informal, small, or micro businesses. Thus, governments typically removed unauthorized street traders who they identified as interfering with public order, "legitimate" trade, and state control.

As detailed in the previous chapter, even as later scholars and policy analysts identified the informal sector as an area of possible economic growth (Hart 1973; Sethuraman 1981; de Soto 1989), street vendors were considered problematic due to their occupation of public space. When governments tried to support small merchants, their primary method was the building of market buildings that took vendors off the streets, and often had a devastating effect for the fortunes of the vendors so "benefited." Even when vendors were tolerated by development practitioners and academics who deemed it "an activity of subsistence that served as a pole of attraction for the least able, the most vulnerable, the invalids ... an occupation that employed the *unemployable*" (López Santillán 2005) it was regarded as an occupation that was doomed to disappear. However, toleration soon disappeared when it seemed that the vendors would not. As the cases in this volume show, street vending has, if anything, increased.

Street vendors make up a large percentage of global workers – in Latin America up to 50 percent of the retail workforce along with a great many children engage in street trade (NACLA 1994). The majority of the African trade sector is conducted by street vendors, and in Asia the informal sector makes up between 45 and 85 percent of non-agricultural work (Charmes 1998).

The failures of "relocation" programs such as that of Mexico City in the early 1990s (Cross 1997; Stamm 2005), illustrate that street vendors are far from passive actors in this process. In Mexico City, faced with rising payments for their stalls and declining sales, relocated vendors argued that they had to return to the streets just to pay for their "formal" stalls. Whether this process was organized or individual (with vendors slowly creeping back into street areas they had been relocated from), and whether it assumed a political or simply economic face, the problem for authorities and "appropriate" users of space was the same: their *de jure* "rights" were being usurped by the *de facto* rights of vendors.

Similarly, in Port of Spain, Trinidad, venues were built for street vendors who had assisted the city's redevelopment after the conflagration of Port of Spain. While the Prime Minister boasted that the venue was turning vendors into micro-businesses, the vendors themselves consistently ran behind on rent that was priced not too far below the rents paid in private malls on more actively used downtown avenues. Many of these vendors began to use their vending booths as a storage space. In addition, a nighttime vending practice began when vendors would head to the streets to sell their wares "after hours" when the formal shops were closed and they were less likely to be subject to police harassment and arrest.[2]

## Space and the urban setting: the definition of "appropriate" use

Why is it all right to sell oranges in an established store but not on the street or out of one's own home? Far from evoking moral outrage, the average pedestrian might praise the vendor for her entrepreneurship. However, depending on political and economic circumstances praise can turn to complaints: vendors are blocking traffic, disrupting pedestrian flow, and competing unfairly with "proper" retail outlets. But why not invert these claims? Why should "traffic" trump the need to earn a living? Why does that "living" have to take place in an "approved" place? Our objective is not to claim that traffic is unproblematic, or that business should not be regulated, but to problematize the way in which we think of appropriate uses of space as a part of a specific "mode of production" in the Marxist sense.

Applying Lefebvre's logic, space is not only where class conflict is expressed, but also where class relations are constituted (Gregory 1994). Each mode of production produces and is sustained by a particular dominant way of organizing space. Changes in the way this power is expressed, Lefebvre argued, can be explained by the Marxist notion of Dialecticism – produced spaces also produce subordinate forms of the use of space. The public plazas so necessary for organizing the mercantile and political/ritual life of feudal society, for example, also produced, over time, the very mercantile and political bourgeois forces that overthrew the system to implant capitalism. However, even though, or more specifically, precisely because, it was born out of the chaos of feudal street life, capitalism also needs to control that public space and specialize it so that it increases exchange value.

Just as factories must be "organized" spatially to maximize production, so urban space must be organized to maximize social production. Under capitalism, urban development is carefully managed to ensure that "residential," "commercial," "leisure," and "industrial" districts are laid out with intervening corridors designed to connect them together in a way that maximizes the dependence of worker/consumers in the residential areas on their employer/providers in the industrial/business/commercial areas. The fact that street vendors are absent in both the planning of modern space and in the modernization paradigm illuminates Lefebvre's spatial social link. The attempts to plan urban centers that did not provide a venue for petty market exchange is a clear example of how space was used to create a certain set of capitalist relations: modern capitalist development assumed that all workers would be incorporated into formal units of mass production.

The alienation of space represents not just the idea that space can be bought and sold – a concept that emerged with and was essential to the development of early capitalism – it is completed in late capitalism by the designation of appropriate uses of given spaces in the "urban plan" or zoning map. Not only the tools of production, but even a *space* for production is stripped from the common citizen and thus reserved for corporate entities that control the large concentrations of capital necessary to control "productive" space.

The paradox is that the "right" to privacy, limited for most citizens to interior residential spaces, actually creates a lack of rights to use that space for productive uses and a lack of almost all rights to privacy in the "private" domains of the employer or formal merchant. Privacy is limited to a domestic sphere where one "lives," but not to the productive and distributive spheres where "life" is made possible.

The notion of "public space" also becomes inverted in capitalism. The sanctification of private property implies that each citizen has their "private space," reserving public space for the "public good" as determined by the representative for the "community" – the state. A private citizen may have certain rights to public space, but those rights are severely circumscribed. They have the right to transit – to use public space temporarily as they move from one private space (their own) to another (their employer's or their supplier's) – but always under the surveillance of the state's agents. In effect, the street "belongs" to the state, and therefore to those who dominate the political process. As Slater (2004) states, "The scenery, the public space, is a class hegemony, a dictatorship over the community, the culture, and the private viewer."

Of course, no mode of production is absolute, but is best seen as a form of contested domination. Control is never uniform: within the dialectical process there are not only the remnants of "old" modes of production but also new reactions created by the new modes of production: contradictions created by the system itself. A "crisis of space" is created particularly in late capitalism as the commodification of space – the shift of property sales and speculation to a leading economic role – contributes to a scarcity of space, representing the triumph of the exchange value of space over the use value of space.

This contradiction is best explained by using an example relevant to the middle-class reader: the cost of housing. When the use value of space is emphasized, such as when a family is renting a home to live in, the tendency is to expend the fewest possible resources to obtain it in order to reserve resources for other useful purposes. Why rent a mansion when a two-bedroom flat will suffice? However, realtors happily tell the future homeowner that a house is an "investment." As an investment the house changes from a "use value" into an "exchange value." Now, the family wants to buy the biggest house possible: after all, if the price goes up 10 percent, the larger the initial investment the larger the reward.

The effect is two-fold and dramatic. First, as everyone attempts to spend as much as they can on housing, demand and size both increase. In the United States, for example, the average new home now has over 2,300 square feet compared to 1,100 in the 1950s, despite the fact that household size has declined (Wilson and Boehland 2005). Prices skyrocket as land and materials become relatively scarce. The resulting urban sprawl, which is now occurring in cities all over the globe, has an even more dramatic effect on central shopping and commercial districts, where land values reach thousands of dollars per square inch.

The second part of the effect derives from the speculative nature of exchange value: value is determined by the "market," which ultimately reflects what people think *other* people think about the value (rather than the value the space has for themselves). To paraphrase Benjamin Franklin, the slightest apparent discord can have a huge impact on perceptions, and thus value. Just as the neighbor's uncut lawn may have an impact on one's own housing price, so something as seemingly insignificant as a street market can have a huge impact on "upscale" areas because the appearance of chaos and disruption may deter potential investors. Thus, it becomes crucial to control not only one's own "use" space, but also the "exchange value" of the surrounding area. Again, while these effects are dramatic enough in the suburbs, in central areas they can affect billions of dollars of real-estate values. In essence, the capitalist crisis of space reflects the fact that, as an exchange commodity, space no longer becomes *available* for use.

Lefebvre expands dialecticism in order to conceptualize this fluid notion of space. Space is seen as envisioning three characteristics: as a spatial practice (that is, as it is perceived by and directs the behavior of its occupants as a product); as an ideal representation (that is, as conceived by dominant elites – in this case the state and capitalists); and as "representational space," which refers to the process by which space is invested with meaning and in some sense reappropriated by those living within it. While the first characteristic represents the "objective" nature of space as it is seen in day-to-day usage, the second and third characteristics represent the class struggle between the dominant and subordinate classes in society.

To give an example from Mexico City, in the 1970s the administration built a series of major thoroughfares that bisected the city to facilitate automobile traffic. One of these runs through an inner-city neighborhood famous for its second-hand street market – Tepito. To prevent the market from interfering with traffic flows, the city forced vendor organizations in the area to move off the thoroughfare – based on the logic of the need for rapid transportation between residential and commercial areas. However, the new avenue also made a perfect entry to the market area for the city's growing middle class. The result was a shift in the market towards electronic goods, smuggled around the high import tariff system, that appealed to the new clientele, resulting in a dramatic burst of informal/illegal economic activity. Within a decade, vendors had forced their way back on the thoroughfare and today (after another market shift to pirated movies and music) they routinely block up to half the road in order to provide safe areas around their stalls. In order to make the post-modern irony of the situation perfect, the street in question is the most direct route from the richest area of the city to the airport.

It is this ability to reconfigure space that is "the means by which people can take back power in their everyday lives" (Stewart 1995: 610). Indeed, it is interesting that street vendors in Mexico have developed their commercial occupation of space into a political art form – combining protests with trade by setting up their markets outside government offices in order to pressure officials to recognize their rights in other areas of the city, a practice possible because of their high level of organization in that city (Cross 1998: 140). In essence, the very concentration of spatial value itself creates a potential point of disruption by subordinate powers, creating "utopian possibilities" (Harvey 2000) for resisting the process of capitalist/statist rationalization. By corollary, it also creates greater needs for surveillance and repression by those powers which may be untenable for "frustrated states" in the developing world that lack the financial and legitimization resources necessary for such surveillance and repression.

Thus, even though street vendors are generally focused on simply making a living and are usually politically apathetic (Cross 1998: 123), their practical occupation of the street places them in the forefront of the political struggle over space (Karides and Balaguer 2005).

To say that this conflict is only a result of the economic crisis of late capitalism (and more specifically, the recurrent global restructurings of the 1980s and 1990s) would be an oversimplification that hides a larger truth behind a smaller one. Cross (1998) has argued the necessity of studying the political factors behind the growth of street trade rather than simply the economic ones, a call taken up more recently by Fernández-Kelly (2006). While these are important, a Lefebvrian spatial analysis improves the formulation of the street vending problematic (Karides and Balaguer 2005). As Lefebvre argues, the real focus of study should not be of "things in space ... but the political economy of space." (1991: 299.) In other words, instead of focusing on the fact that the numbers of vendors have grown, our focus is on how the political economy of urban space – especially in the Global South but also in the "developed" North – has changed to create expanding pockets of "gray zone" where the informal street economy can thrive.[3]

Today, street vendors are clearly competitors in the post-modern scarcity of space (Brenner 1997). Given the precarious development of capitalism itself, particularly but not only in the Third World, the urban poor are forced to find some space within which they could survive, pushing them into constant conflict with the state's spatial regulations. While marginality theory has been critiqued for implying that these activities are irrelevant to the modern economy (Perlman 1980), the central point that needs to be made is that they were marginalized by the very spatial practices of the state/capitalist nexus itself.

The result of this process was the opening of "gray zones," especially in Third World cities, where regulatory enforcement was lax given the frustrated nature of the state – its simple inability to police all areas of the city. Enforcement centered around areas occupied by elites, which typically moved out of old city centers into suburban areas. Many cities such as Mexico City saw the rise of new elite centers on the "edge" of the city (Polanco, Lomas de Chapultepec, Satélite, San Angel, etc.), as it was cheaper to build out than to rebuild the old city center.[4] The old city centers became occupied by the poor, for whom the deteriorating palaces of the colonial elites were subdivided into tenement housing. In many cases the tenements also doubled as productive space for workshops while the streets doubled as market areas.

However, as the capitalist system matured, focus shifted back to the old centers. Spatial intensification for increasing exchange value is certainly apparent in the struggle of city governments to "liberate" decayed areas of their city centers from vendors or poor and low-income communities in order to make room for urban renovation. As new international investment plans attempt to take back these neglected areas, they are faced with the contradiction that the very neo-liberal policies that have concentrated the wealth and power to do so have also contributed to a solidification and politicization of the impoverished classes that currently occupy them.

The inner city presents a special arena of conflict for another reason. Since suburban areas in developed countries were typically designed around the automobile, they effectively undercut the kind of active pedestrian street life that could potentially provide clients for street vendors (Duany *et al.* 2001). The very same "street life" qualities, a lively mix of residential and commercial activity, narrow streets with building fronts pushed up to the sidewalk, and ample access to public transportation that make areas like Greenwich Village and Times Square in New York a prime target of gentrification, also make them prime street market areas, leading to the need for constant repression against these activities (or in some cases enlightened, but highly regulated, "tourist" markets). In the Global South these qualities are multiplied a hundred-fold. Since development often took place outside of the "old" city center, these areas retained the qualities that Jacobs (1967) long ago described as desirable for community life. Mexico City's Historical Center, for example, provides over two square miles of such streets, which is one of the reasons it has proven so resistant to the expulsion of over 20,000 vendors in the area.

Finally, Monnet (2005) points out another reason why street vending has become so difficult to eradicate in the modern and postmodern city: not only are street markets able to capitalize on the geographic elements of proximity (with neighborhood markets) and centrality (with downtown markets), he argues that it also responds to the very mobility required of the modern urbanite as he rushes from home to work to "entertainment." Using Mexico City as an example, he states:

> Street vending responds ... to those changes in urban life, offering the consumer, during his multiple trips, mobile services: information (newspapers sold in the street); communication (cell phone cards distributed at stoplights by uniformed salespersons); car services (windshield cleaners, body cleaners, caretakers, and valet parking); shoe services (shoe shiners); refreshment (sodas in the congested freeways; morning orange juice in the entrances to offices, candies and gum at the exits); entertainment while waiting (pirate disk vendors in the metro trains, jugglers, clowns, and fire eaters at the stoplights); protection (street sales of umbrellas and rain coats during the rainy season), etcetera.
>
> (Monnet 2005, translated by author)

## From modernist space to post-modernist space

To the extent that they use the concept of "post-modernism" (or post-industrialism), many scholars argue that the shift from modernism to post-modernism implies a shift within capitalism, rather than a change to a new form (Jencks 1996; Harvey 1990). As detailed in the previous chapter, it signifies a shift from Fordist principles of mass production and mass consumption to principles of flexibility and to what some might call the McDonaldization of society (Ritzer 2004) – mass-produced forms of individuality. However, this shift has meaning principally for the privileged middle classes of the "developed" world. As industrialization has shifted from the First World to the Third, many blue-collar workers have lost their jobs and the wages of white-collar workers have decreased relative to their earnings in the past. It has also led to the explosion in the numbers of cheap goods subsidized by the low wage rates of industrial plants located in the Third World. The result has meant both greater impoverishment for the poor (Goldsmith 2002) but also greater purchasing power for the well-to-do in both "north" and "south" areas. At the same time, control over wealth has become even more concentrated in "globalized" cities such as New York, Tokyo, and London. Cities and regions develop plans to become "global" cities and they must compete with each other to attract resources, for instance the dwindling numbers of major corporate headquarters (Abu-Lughod 2000; Fainstein 2002; Sassen 2001).

The result of this process is that many city centers have seen a new revitalization, but not one that bodes well for the poor who were left to languish there while the middle class moved to suburbia. Instead, businesses are offered direct control over the streets in order to create "street malls" such as New York's Times Square where a "Business Investment District" (BID) is able to hire its own rent-a-cops to push peddlers not only away from the entrances of the Disney Store and other upscale retail establishments, but out of the neighborhood altogether.

Although post-modernism emphasizes flexibility, the objective of flexibility is to increase profit margins, not allow independent operators to make a living. Street markets are allowed only when they are seen as beneficial to established businesses, a rare enough occasion in itself, but one that even so rarely incorporates truly independent vendors.[5]

Thus, "post-modernism" alone does not provide any clear-cut solution to the issue of street vending, even though it might celebrate it as a form of de-centered "other." The subject of the next section is what to do with the pockets of vendors who refuse to give up their subsistence. While development agencies and some governments around the world have grudgingly accepted the logic of street markets – still more as a necessary evil than as an ideal – it is still almost impossible to put this grudging acceptance into practical form due to the resistance of officials, local businesses, and politicians pandering to "law and order" constituencies. Besides the examples of

India and Mexico City discussed above, another example of the latter phenomenon was given by the nationwide crackdown on street vendors in Zimbabwe by the dictatorial Mugabe government in order to distract the public from the government's economic incompetence (Cross *et al*. 2005).

## Turning to the informal sector as solution?

Since it takes advantage of public space and minimizes overhead costs of rent and utilities, street vending is ideally suited for informal growth. To the extent that street vending withstands hostile attempts to over-regulate or eliminate it, either through evasion, negotiation, or conflict, vendors can maintain an economic existence that ranges from basic survival to middle-class existence. While street vending is most widely associated with over-urbanization in cities of the Global South, it has been sustained throughout colonial occupation, modernization in developed or advanced capitalists, and socialist and post-socialist contexts. Yet urban planning still does not take account of the numerous vendors that fill city streets. In part this is due to planners and officials alike who have preconceived notions of the "appropriate" use of public space: street stalls get in the way of traffic precisely because city planners have left them with no other viable place to go.

Thus, the solution to the problems that vendors face, and which cities face with street vending, cannot be focused on the individual vendor but must be spatial and ecological in design. Micro-business programs may provide some assistance to specific vendors, but they ignore the broader context around them that is rarely supportive and often downright hostile. As we have also seen, attempts to simply legislate street vending into oblivion have rarely worked. This is why we believe that the solution must be spatial – it must look at ways in which space can be redefined and localized, not to eliminate the notion of "appropriate" behavior but to recognize that each area requires its own notion of appropriateness.

A first set of strategies is to expand or create spatial zones of informality or semi-formality, rather than expand specific informal enterprises. Specific geographic areas and/or economic sectors could be created in which small, low-capital, individual, or family-run firms are allowed to operate under a self-regulating system with government tax and regulatory enforcement reduced to the bare necessities. By recognizing a system of semi-formality on the level of entire low-income neighborhoods formal organizations could formalize the informal by permitting the flow of goods and services that can be provided by micro-enterprises.

Street markets are an excellent example of the benefits of this approach. Where street markets have become vibrant sources of economic growth, it is due to the fact that they have been able to avoid rigid regulatory control and regulate themselves. Mexico City provides one example of this (Cross 1998), but another is given by the growth of flea markets and farmers' markets in the United States and Europe (see Sage, this volume). These became popular precisely because they exist in a form of suspended space with regard to regulatory control and as a result allowed informal relations between vendors and their clients to flourish. The rules still exist, but it is understood that enforcement would be tuned to the limited means available to the individual vendors. Often, flea markets regulate themselves to avoid the perception that they are conduits for illegally obtained goods.

The advantage of making such a policy official is that it is already occurring unofficially and therefore there would be minimal actual effect. By allowing micro-firms to remain largely informal within certain broad guidelines, the only negative effect is to recognize a *fait accompli*. On the positive side, however, more people would be encouraged to open up micro-businesses within these sectors while enforcement resources could be focused on key issues such as public health concerns (Adeoti 2000; Blackman and Bannister 1998). Such an environment would allow at least some informal firms to naturally grow until the point at which it makes more sense to become formal in order to protect their capital and resources.

Second, related to the first issue is that city planners need to incorporate street market zones into their urban planning. Many streets in downtown areas can benefit tremendously by being essentially transformed into open-air malls with stores on the sides and stalls down the middle. Traffic can be shifted onto other streets (or out of the area altogether, which would encourage more use of public transportation and less pollution) while parking garages would encourage people to park the car and walk to their destination through the mall area. Open plazas should be designed with areas for street markets, while street corner vendors, which are often prohibited but in fact are highly lucrative, could be encouraged by making sidewalks at junctions wider. In addition, while some streets could be more strictly regulated to be tourist-attractive, it should be kept in mind that more "chaotic" market areas should be provided to allow for vendors who cannot meet rigid regulations: these would be the equivalent of flea markets where access to vending would be far easier.

Third, city officials should resist the tendency to keep the number of such markets as low as possible. In fact markets should be counted and incorporated into census mechanisms, and vendors should be counted as an occupational category, as they were until 1940 in the United States. Markets substitute for storefront retail in many poor inner-city areas bereft of retail establishments, where less-efficient existing retailers charge high prices. Street markets can provide a vital retail function at low costs due to their lack of overhead and high levels of competition. Over-managing such markets by reducing competition, requiring elaborate carts or facades, or "direct from producer" distribution chains such as in a farmers' market, may be appropriate in an exclusive area, but not in such poor areas. They can also provide a source of additional income and perhaps a way out of welfare dependency for local residents (Morales *et al.* 1995b).

Fourth, street vendors need to be organized spatially to present their interests before city officials and balance the interests of established businesses and automobile drivers. This could be in the form of "civil associations" as takes place in Mexico, "Block Coordinators" as in Venezuela (García-Rincón, this volume), or in the form of a "Chamber of Street Commerce." Such organizations, because of their closeness to the vending base, would be able to regulate certain aspects of each market zone, such as cleanliness, hours of operation, and conflicts that emerge between vendors or between these and clients, neighbors, and the city. In Mexico City such organizations often provide access to social programs and informal insurance systems. They could also be used in a broader capacity to funnel vendors into social security systems, group insurance programs, and even tax systems. Above all, they would reduce the cost of regulatory enforcement on the municipality.

Finally, street markets can function as economical outlets for locally produced goods and services, encouraging growth in the local formal sector. In Mexico City, a chain of Popsicle franchises called "Bon Ice" has already capitalized on this by hiring vendors as distinctively dressed independent contractors who can often earn many times the minimum wage while being eligible for formal status. While such relations can sometimes be exploitative, as long as they are one option among many they will have to compete with the earnings of other vendors in the market. The establishment of wholesale centers for locally produced goods, similar to wholesale produce markets, can also allow independent vendors to buy goods for resale in their market zones. To date, this function is being carried out far more effectively by importers, resulting in a shift in sales to cheap imports from Asia rather than local goods that could be provided just as economically.

But it should be kept in mind that the problems of spatial access are part of a broader system of social inequality. "Neo-liberalism" has led to drastic reductions in government responsibility for the work lives of the urban poor. Even if street vendors engage in commendable business practices, are given low interest loans, and are granted a low-cost business location, the survival and success of a business enterprise is not guaranteed. Assisting micro-entrepreneurs in order to create more alternatives for the poor is a laudable goal, but it cannot successfully replace government social and unemployment programs (Karides 2005). Rather, government social programs must be expanded so that all workers have the security of knowing that their basic needs will be met even when they cannot attend to their businesses for reasons such as health problems or childcare. The paradox is that the neo-liberal argument that such benefits are burdensome subsidies for the poor is often contradicted by increased subsidies for large-scale businesses. Reinstating such programs is a good start in reversing the trend towards increased social inequality.

## Conclusion

Despite initial assumptions that information technology would lead to dispersion of workers, spatial concentration is a feature of the post-modern world (Sassen 2001). The post-modern or global city is characterized both by an increase in high-income residents (gentrification) and the growth of the informal sector. Street vendors pose a significant challenge to dealing with the limits of urban space, and its constant reformation and reconfiguration to increase value. Yet street vendors also serve the local economy, for instance by providing products that are regularly consumed or unique and particular products that cater to the consumption demands of young urban professionals, becoming embedded in the new geography of centrality and marginality that globalization creates. The small or micro-businesses operated by street vendors are struggling, to be sure, but they are hardly at the fringe of contemporary society. Rather, street vendors not only participate in commercial exchange and urban politics, but also shape the spatial organization of cities. Instead of fighting that process, urban planning should learn to take advantage of it.

## Notes

1 See Sage (this volume) for a brief discussion of the history of street markets in Europe.
2 In both cases, vendors argued that they faced a Hobbesian choice, since the areas they abandoned might be taken over by other vendors, leading to a self-fulfilling prophesy as they themselves led the re-invasion process.
3 The paradox is that modern urban planning was supposed to eliminate such "gray zones," a point implied by Le Corbusier (1996) and noted tangentially by Duneier (2000).
4 Some cities took the opposite path such as Rio de Janeiro, where the poor were forced to move out of the center (Meade 1997).
5 For example, when the Atlanta Olympic Games organizing committee wanted to include street vendors in their marketing plans, their first step was to evict the already existing vendors in order to resell the spaces to the highest bidder (Miller 1995).

## Bibliography

Abu-Lughod, J.L. (2000) 'Can Chicago Make it as a Global City?' Great Cities Publication no. GCP-00-2, Institute working paper series, University of Illinois at Chicago.
Adeoti, J.O. (2000) 'Small Enterprise Promotion and Sustainable Development: An Attempt at Integration,' *Journal of Developmental Entrepreneurship*, 5: 57–71.
Birbeck, C. (1978) 'Self-Employed Proletarians in an Informal Factory: The Case of Cali's Garbage Dump,' *World Development*, 6: 1173–86.
Blackman, A. and Bannister, G. (1998) *Pollution Control in the Informal Sector: The Ciudad Juárez Brickmaker's Project*, Washington, DC: Resource for the Future.

Brenner, N. (1997) 'State Territorial Restructuring and the Production of Spatial Scale,' *Political Geography*, 16(4): 273–306.

Centeno, M.A. and Portes, A. (2006) 'The Informal Economy in the Shadow of the State,' in P. Fernández-Kelly and J. Shefner (eds) *Out of the Shadows: Political Action and the Informal Economy in Latin America*, University Park, PA: Pennsylvania State University Press.

Charmes, J. (1998) *Informal Sector, Poverty and Gender: A Review of Empirical Evidence*, Washington DC: The World Bank.

Cross, J. (1997) 'Debilitando el clientelismo: la formalización del ambulantaje en la Ciudad de Mexico,' *Revista Mexicana de Sociología*, 59(4): 93–116.

—— (1998) *Informal Politics: Street Vendors and the State in Mexico City*, Stanford, CA: Stanford University Press.

—— (1999) 'Informal Sector,' *Encyclopedia of Political Economy*, London: Routledge: 580–82.

—— (2000) 'Passing the Buck: Risk Avoidance and Risk Management in the Illegal/ Informal Drug Trade,' *International Journal of Sociology and Social Policy*, 20(9–10): 68–94.

Cross, J. and Johnson, B. (2000) 'Expanding Dual Labor Market Theory: Crack Dealers and the Informal Economy,' *International Journal of Sociology and Social Policy*, 20(1–2): 96–134.

Cross, J., Balkin, S., and Morales, A. (2005) 'Street Vending Good for the Economy,' *The Zimbabwean*, 29 July.

De Soto, H. (1989) *The Other Path: The Invisible Revolution in the Third World*, New York: Harper & Row.

Duany, A., Plater-Zyberk, E., and Speck, J. (2001) *Suburban Nation: The Rise of Sprawl and the Decline of the American Dream*, New York: North Point Press.

Duneier, M. (2000) *Sidewalk*, New York: Farrar, Strause and Giroux.

Eastwood, C. (2002) *Near West Side Stories: Struggles for Community in Chicago's Maxwell Street Neighborhood*, Chicago, IL: Lake Claremont Press.

Evans, P. and Timberlake, M. (1980) 'Dependence, Inequality, and the Growth of the Tertiary: A Comparative Analysis of Less Developed Countries,' *American Sociological Review*, 45: 532–52.

Fainstein, S. (2002) 'The Changing World Economy and Urban Restructuring,' in S. Fainstein and S. Campbell (eds) *Readings in Urban Theory*, 2nd edn, New York: Blackwell.

Fernández-Kelly, M.P. (2006) 'Introduction,' in M.P. Fernández-Kelly and J. Shefner (eds) *Out of the Shadows: Political Action and the Informal Sector in Latin America*, University Park, PA: Pennsylvania State University Press.

—— and Garcia, A.M. (1989) 'Informalization at the Core: Hispanic Women, Homework, and the Advanced Capitalist State,' in A. Portes, M. Castells, and L.A. Benton (eds) *The Informal Economy: Studies in Advanced and Less Developed Countries*, Baltimore, MA: Johns Hopkins University Press.

Foucault, M. (1979) *Discipline and Punish: The Birth of the Prison*, New York: Vintage.

Geertz, C. (1963) *Peddlers & Princes: Social Change and Economic Modernization in Two Indonesian Towns*, Chicago, IL: University of Chicago Press.

Goldsmith, W. (2002) 'From the Metropolis to Globalization: the Dialectics of Race and Urban Form,' in S. Fainstein and S. Campbell (eds) *Readings in Urban Theory*, 2nd edn, New York: Blackwell.

Gottendier, M. (1993) 'A Marx for Our Time: Henri Lefebvre and the Production of Space,' *Sociological Theory*, 11(1): 129–34.

Gregory, D. (1994) *Geographical Imaginations*, Cambridge, MA: Blackwell.

Hart, J.K. (1973) 'Informal Income Opportunities and Urban Employment in Ghana,' *Journal of Modern African Studies*, 11: 61–89.

Harvey, D. (1990) *The Condition of Postmodernity*, Cambridge, MA: Blackwell.

—— (2000) *Spaces of Hope*, Berkeley, CA: University of California Press.

Jacobs, J. (1967) *The Economy of Cities*, New York: Random House.

Jencks, C. (1996) 'What is Postmodernism?' in L. Cahoone (ed.) *From Modernism to Postmodernism: An Anthology*, Oxford: Blackwell.

Karides, M. (2001) 'Self-Employment for All: Race, Gender, and Micro-Enterprise Development in Port of Spain, Trinidad,' Ph.D. Dissertation, University of Georgia.

—— (2005) 'Whose Solution Is It? Development Ideology and the Work of Micro-entrepreneurs in Caribbean Context,' *International Sociology and Social Policy*, 25(1/2): 30–62.

Karides, M. and Balaguer, G. (2005) 'Claiming Space and Globalizing Streets: Street Vendors and Transnational Resistance to Capitalist Expansion.' Paper presented at the Global Labor Mini-Conference cosponsored by the PEWS, Labor, and Political Sociology sections of the American Sociological Association in August, Philadelphia, PA.

Le Corbusier (1996) 'Towards a New Architecture,' in L. Cahoone (ed.) *From Modernism to Postmodernism: An Anthology*, Oxford: Blackwell.

Lefebvre, H. (1991) *The Production of Space*, Oxford: Blackwell.

Lemert, C. (1997) *Postmodernism Is Not What You Think*, Oxford: Blackwell.

Lewis, A.W. (1954) 'Economic Development with Unlimited Supplies of Labor,' *Manchester School of Economics and Social Studies*, 22: 139–91.

López Santillán, R. (2005) 'Algunos actores sociales y sus representaciones de la venta callejera en la Ciudad de México,' in J. Monnet and J. Bonnafé (eds) *El Ambulantaje en la Ciudad de México: Investigaciones Recientes*, Mexico, D.F.: UNAM/PUEC/CEMCA.

Mattera, P. (1985) *Off the Books*, New York: St. Martin's Press.

Meade, T. (1997) *'Civilizing' Rio: Reform and Resistance in a Brazilian City 1889–1930*, University Park, PA: Pennsylvania State University Press.

Miller, L. (1995) 'Vendor News from Atlanta.' Online. Available: www.openair.org/alerts/atlan.html (accessed 3 January 2004).

Monnet, J. (2005) 'Conceptualización del ambulantaje; de los vendedores a los clients: un acercamiento a la metropolis posfordista,' in J. Monnet and J. Bonnafé (eds) *Memoria del Seminario El Ambulantaje en la Ciudad de México: Investigaciones Recientes*, Mexico, D.F.: UNAM/PUEC/CEMCA.

Morales, A. (1998) 'Income Tax Compliance and Alternative Views of Ethics and Human Nature,' in R.W. McGee (ed.) *The Ethics of Tax Evasion*, NJ: The Dumont Institute for Public Policy Research.

—— (2000) 'Peddling Policy: Street Vending in Historical and Contemporary Context,' *International Journal of Sociology and Social Policy*, 20(3/4): 76–99.

—— (2001) 'Policy from Theory: A Critical Reconstruction of Theory on the "Informal" Economy,' *Sociological Imagination*, 38(3): 190–203.

Morales, A., Balkin, S., and Persky, J. (1995a) 'The Value of Benefits of a Public Street Market: The Case of Maxwell Street,' *Economic Development Quarterly*, 9(4): 304–20.

—— (1995b) 'Contradictions and Irony in Policy Research on the Informal Economy: A Reply,' *Economic Development Quarterly*, 9(4): 327–30.

Murphy, M.F. (1990) 'The Need for a Re-evaluation of the Concept "Informal Sector": A Reinterpretation,' *Population and Development Review*, 10: 586–611.

NACLA (1994) *Disposable Children: The Hazards of Growing up Poor in Latin America.*

Parker, S. (2004) *Urban Theory and the Urban Experience*, London: Routledge.

Peattie, L. (1987) 'An Idea in Good Currency and How it Grew: The Informal Sector,' *World Development*, 15(7): 851–60.

Perlman, J.E. (1980) *Myth of Marginality: Urban Poverty and Politics in Rio De Janeiro*, Berkeley, CA: University of California Press.

Portes, A. and Castells, M. (1989) 'Introduction,' in A. Portes, M. Castells, and L.A. Benton (eds), *The Informal Economy: Studies in Advanced and Less Developed Countries*, Baltimore, MA: Johns Hopkins University Press.

Portes, A. and Walton, J. (1978) *Urban Latin America*, Austin, TX: University of Texas Press.

PREALC/OIT (1988) *Sobrevivir en la Calle: El Comercio Ambulante en Santiago*, Santiago: PREALC/OIT.

Raheim, S., Alter, C.A., and Yarbrough, D. (1996) 'Evaluating Microenterprise Programs: Issues and Lessons Learned,' *Journal of Developmental Entrepreneurship*, 1: 87–103.

Rakowski, C.A. (1994) 'Convergence and Divergence in the Informal Sector Debate: A Focus on Latin America,' *World Development*, 22: 501–16.

Ritzer, G. (2004) *The McDonaldization of Society*, Thousand Oaks, CA: Pine View Press.

Sassen, S. (2001) *The Global City: New York, London, Tokyo*, Princeton, NJ: Princeton University Press.

Sethuraman, S.V. (1981) *The Urban Informal Sector in Developing Countries: Employment, Poverty and Environment*, Geneva: ILO Publications.

Slater, J. (2004) 'The Erosion of Public Space,' in D.M. Callejo Pâerez, J.J. Slater, and S.M. Fain (eds) *Pedagogy of Place: Seeing Space as Cultural Education*, New York: Counterpoints.

Smith, D. (1988) 'Overurbanization Reconceptualized: A Political Economy of the World-System Approach,' *Urban Affairs Quarterly*, 23: 270–94.

Smith, N. (2003) *'Forward' to The Urban Revolution by Henri Lefebvre*, Minneapolis, MN: University of Minnesota Press.

Soto, O. (2005) 'Facilitará el SAT la regularización de ambulantes,' *El Universal Online* (accessed 28 January 2005). Finanzas: 3.

Stamm, C. (2005) 'Balance de las plazas de comercio popular del Centro Histórico de la Ciudad de México,' in J. Monnet and J. Bonnafé (eds) *El Ambulantaje en la Ciudad de México: Investigaciones Recientes*, Mexico, D.F.: UNAM/PUEC/CEMCA.

Stewart, L. (1995) 'Bodies, Visions, and Spatial Politics: A Review Essay of Henri Lefebvre's *The Production of Space*,' *Environment and Planning D: Society and Space*, 13: 609–18.

Wilson, A. and Boehland, J. (2005) 'Small Is Beautiful: US House Size, Resource Use and the Environment,' *Journal of Industrial Ecology*, 9: 277–87.

# 3 Redefining rules

## A market for public space in Caracas, Venezuela

*María Fernanda García-Rincón*[1]

Following President Chávez's 1999 speech demanding that street vendors in Caracas "not be touched," earlier efforts to evict informal merchants from public spaces were immediately curtailed. In areas of high demand for space, the state no longer enforces regulations regarding public space, a role informally assumed by individuals, who privately gain from the market transaction of buying, selling, and renting the constitutionally given "right to work."

## Introduction

Throughout history, traders and vendors who pursue their work in public space have formed contested sites of interaction (Picavet 1989; Cross 1998; Hansen 2004). The specific relationship that takes place between states and informal economic activity depends on the cultural, political, and economic dynamics of their time and place. The narrative that follows in this chapter will focus on Caracas' street vending scene, to discuss issues of policy, regulation, and appropriation of public space.

Forty-eight thousand people – better known as *buhoneros* – take the streets of Metropolitan Caracas to make a daily living (INE 2001).[2] Most of these individuals are located in the Libertador's Municipality, one of the five municipalities that constitute Metropolitan Caracas, and where vending is most prominent. They work selling fruits, vegetables, pirated CDs and DVDs, the latest fashions in shirts and jeans, toys, cosmetics, and other "*Made in China*" products.

"Urban space is a key element of physical capital in livelihood strategies for the urban poor ... as a place for trade and communal activities, or as a channel of movement" (Brown and Lloyd-Jones 2002: 191). Yet how street vendors access or use public space has not been studied in depth (Pratt 2002). Access to public space is important because income generation depends on location. Locations near subway stops, financial institutions, and areas of higher-income clients are considered a competitive advantage for vendors.[3] The ability to work on the street depends on the resistance by municipal regulations, the police, leaders of street vending organizations, and other stakeholders, which vary by area. How that resistance is evaded or negotiated is important. During policy change or where there is weak state integration, vendors take advantage by strategically legitimizing activity and rights over that space. Such policy changes can also lead to some vendors materially benefiting from the "privatization" of space.

In this chapter I will first describe street vending in Caracas and narrate the eviction that cleared vendors off the streets of Caracas in 1999. Second, I evaluate the policy change that occurred 1998–99, when President Hugo Chávez was elected. Third, I discuss theoretical considerations with regard to usage and appropriation of public space. Fourth, I discuss the different ways in which people obtain the space to work in. Last, I propose a possible explanation for how the management of public space is undertaken by non-state organizations and individuals with substantial symbolic capital.[4]

The information presented here is based on the field research conducted over nine months (August 2004–May 2005) on informal trading in Caracas. In a collaborative effort with the Centre for the Dissemination of Economic Knowledge (CEDICE), 366 garment traders in Caracas' most critical areas for street vending – Sabana Grande, El Cementerio, El Centro, and Catia – were interviewed.[5] The information collected in the survey is complemented with field observations, a follow-up of newspaper coverage since 1985, documentation of planning, open-ended questions, narratives, and in-depth interviews with vendors, residents, formal stores, and state officials.

## Street vending in Caracas

Although street vending stretches back to at least the nineteenth century, when immigrants from the Middle East (and Europe) would sell imported merchandise by going house to house, it doesn't become "problematic" until the mid-1980s (El Universal 1985). It is occasionally noted that the "*boom buhoneril*" came hand in hand with the "oil boom" of the mid-1970s, and is the result of excessive petrodollars and political clientelism (Buitrago 1985). In the media, street vending has largely been associated with illegal immigration, inefficiency of state policies, relocation, bribes, corruption, and the buying and selling of space. The first ordinance to regulate the activity in Caracas was published on June 12, 1985 (Gaceta Municipal del Distrito Federal Extra 634) by the Governor of Caracas (GC), and it wasn't until 1990 that the Libertador's Municipal Office (LMO) began to regulate the activity.

Most of the 1980s and early 1990s were characterized by uncoordinated policies by different state agencies: clearing, harassment, and relocation all formed parts of the complete recipe. Plans to relocate vendors into municipal markets started in 1989 with the building of the market of La Hoyada, along with the relocation of 1,400 street vendors in the first phase of the project. This market was built on the most expensive bit of land in Caracas (T.N. 1989). The action excluded 3,600 vendors, who were removed but soon after returned to the streets. Vendors in the market could not adequately compete with vendors on the street, as the latter have a competitive advantage of holding a valuable asset: public space. As a result, La Hoyada was empty at the beginning, and only began to be filled when vendors were sanctioned with five days of jail for selling on public space (El Universal 1990).

For example, in 1993, while the GC prohibited the activity with decree 96, the Municipal Office would give permits to vendors in selected areas. In other cases, the municipal councilors, although not authorized to give vending permits to its constituents, would do so. The Mayor's office would then revoke the permits and give the order to clear vendors, and withhold merchandise. Political opposition and competition between state officials created conflict, producing a policy vacuum within which the vendors could gain leeway. Venezuela is very similar to the case discussed by Cross (1998), where state power should be analyzed in terms of "state integration." Lack of coordination or political rivalry allows vendors to effectively adapt and manipulate the nature of the state itself. The state in its relationship with vendors, on the one hand, uses legal ordinances and regulation and repressive police action while on the other tolerates vendors' actions, specially for those with political affiliation (Febres *et al.* 1995). Repression and clearing of vendors was legally carried out, since vendors had violated the regulation. Yet police would 'do a favor' for the vendors by letting them work, turning a blind eye, and not confiscating merchandise in exchange for a *tarifa* or rate (Lara 1997). For example, in 1995, the distribution of *matraca*, or informal payment to authorities for 70 stands of economic activity in the Christmas season in the Municipality Libertador, Caracas, was Bs. 4,200,000 (US$ 24,706) (Marquez undated).

Within the dynamic of state–vendor interaction, policies and actions are cyclical. When December comes around, street vendors put pressure on the Mayor's office to be allowed to work, as that is the month when sales are at their highest. The municipality formally or informally would agree with the commitment that in January the streets would be cleared and new discussions, censuses, and proposals on how to solve the street vending problem would begin. As the year progresses, street vendors would gradually re-claim space. When the high season begins in October, so do rumors of "clearing" of streets. Round about December, a small "clearing" takes place on behalf of authorities, and there is usually a violent protest on behalf of the vendors. Authorities then grant special permits for December (as everyone needs a holiday bonus). New resolutions are put into place to validate this "special December circumstance." When the year ends, the story begins all over again (Lara 1997). Public space is regulated through a series of ordinances, decrees, and regulations by the local municipality, which is contradictory, confusing, and inapplicable (Marquez undated).

## The crackdown on street vendors

Antonio Ledezma was elected in 1995 as Mayor of Caracas (1996–2000) and began a crackdown on vendors in an effort to restore public space. He sought advice from Rudolph Guiliani's government in New York as he demolished La Hoyada market, Nuevo Circo, and stalls at the bus station La Bandera and other rundown areas in need of restoration. Although during his campaign he told vendors "Here we are talking about the right to work, which like all Venezuelans you have. I will defend that right because even in the plaza of the Vatican in Rome there are street vendors," he denies having carried out an ambiguous electoral campaign, but rather that he had a clear mandate to clean and clear the streets (Herrera 1996).[6] In 1996, this new municipal government, in cooperation with the Governor of Caracas, local neighborhood associations, parish council, and formal commercial sector, decided to keep public areas free from vendors during the year. In some areas his policies were successful, such as in Sabana Grande and El Centro, but not without protest. In others like Catia they were not. In Catia, although the police and neighbors worked together to clear the boulevard, vendors appropriated the streets adjacent to the boulevard, where "presumably" the neighborhood association had given them permits (Lara 1997). Part of the mayor's relocation scheme included finding abandoned and empty lots in shopping centers and the commercial floors of many buildings. Some *buhoneros* took advantage of this and are now considered formal entrepreneurs.[7]

La Hoyada market, built as part of a relocation policy in the late 1980s, had by 1998 become associated with drugs, violence, and prostitution – a public order problem. The state also saw alternative uses for this prime location. In addition to the action to demolish the market La Hoyada, there came a series of evictions of vendors in Sabana Grande and El Centro. As a result of several years of restrictive policies, 1999 was a year with highly visible riots and protests on behalf of the vendors. While the Municipal Office evicted vendors the GO was giving permits to vendors for the December season. Street vending organizations collected Bs. 1,000 (approximately US$ 1) from each vendor in El Centro for police security. Plans to relocate vendors and to build new markets (such as San Martin and El Calvario) began. Yet in 2005 the San Martin market, a three-story building with 800 stands, sits abandoned as a reminder of the inconsistencies in state policies, and El Calvario market has not been built.

Government policy makers and the media discussed the crackdown of vendors as an issue of law, order, sanitation, and health. Yet it all came to a halt when President Chávez intervened by publicly supporting the vendors. In a system of "personalistic politics," informal statements and political discourse are taken to be equal to or higher than the law. Many political, social, and institutional issues and changes converged at this particular time.

## The President and street vendors

Venezuela as a petro-state is characterized by a highly wealthy, petrolized economy, with a weak institutional framework, power concentrated in the executive office, low accountability, and oil-related development plans. Once the oil boom disappeared, it was hard for political parties to reform the system, thus creating a political crisis in a populist and democratic regimen. As the oil rents decreased, economic measures needed to be taken, but this did not fit with what Venezuelans expected from the "magical state" (Coronil 1997). IMF reforms and a structural adjustment program implemented in the late 1980s caused riots, and subsequently a group of young military officials, which included Chávez, seized the opportunity to attempt a coup d'etat in 1992. He was put in jail, where he gained popularity and later released by presidential decree. Chávez ran for the presidency and was elected in December 1998. He came into power at a time when Venezuela's political system and institutions were perceived as corrupt, illegitimate, and in need of reform. The first reform was to change the 1961 Constitution, which required a lengthy consultation process. A deteriorating economic situation had impoverished many Venezuelans. Poverty had risen from 26.1 percent in 1975 to 49 percent in 1998, and later rose even more to 67.9 percent in 2003 (España 2001; INE 2004). Chávez's supporters include many of the poor informal workers (McCaughan 2004).

By the time President Chávez had been sworn into office in February 1999, street vending in Caracas, Venezuela's capital, with a population of 2,762,759 (INE 2001), was in the process of completely being cleared from the main streets. It was the first time such an action had been taken to such a magnitude. Previous attempts by the Municipal Office to remove vendors from the capital's main streets had been temporary, and vendors usually returned within a few days, following intense negotiations. It came as a surprise to the Mayor and many of the city's residents that the attempt to clear the vendors had been brought to a halt after the president had stated that the "*buhoneros* were not to be touched." This statement was directed towards the Municipal Office, which had just completed the demolishment of the market La Hoyada I, II, and III, and was aggressively clearing the vendors from the streets of Caracas. This statement was also taken by vendors as direct support of their activity: "the president ... gave us permission." The presidential statement added a new dimension to the legal discussion of whether the vendors have a right to work on public space.

It was also a year of institutional change, as the Constituent Assembly gathered to draft a new constitution. As the festive season approached, the President said that "no regional authority could use public force to mistreat the people" (Sotillo Silva 1999).[8] The mayor was having a difficult time carrying out his policies because, as he stated, "As I am taking [vendors] out from one side, they are going in through the other side." Although the Governor of Caracas' decree of 1993 legally backed his action, he said that the vendors "didn't pay any attention to it because they are supported," implying in this instance the support from the President (Canizales 1999). In an address to the Interior Minster he said, "I have been fighting [to restore public space] in the last couple of years but the national authorities sabotage the work" (Sotillo Silva 1999).

The statement was clearly a sign that Ledezma was left without any institutional support (except an ordinance and decree that prohibited in theory the activity). The Organic Labor Law had previously, in 1997, defined non-dependent workers in Article 40: "It is understood that non-dependent workers are the persons who habitually make a living by his/her work without being in a situation of dependence with respect to one or various patrons."[9] So, although the labor law recognized non-dependent workers as legitimate actors, public space was regulated by municipal regulations and generally given different treatment. Over the year, vendors had made appeals to the courts over the alleged unconstitutional nature of the ordinances and decrees, yet they were never successful due to technical issues.

These interventions by the executive can complicate governance. Another example occurred in 2001, when the president powerfully articulated a discourse of resistance by the poor. In a speech on 4 February commemorating the anniversary of his coup attempt, Chávez directly addressed a visible conflict between *buhoneros* and the Municipal Office in Sabana Grande, promising never to use public force to "assault" the vendors. He praised the actions of the mayor of Caracas, Freddy Bernal (elected in 2000), while asking vendors to be patient while negotiations over relocation took place and markets were built. He reminded the *buhoneros* that their problems were "rooted in the failures of *puntofijism*" and could not be rectified overnight. It is interesting to note that although the approach and discourse has changed from one of confrontation during Ledezma to one of direct intervention by the executive with a more understanding and empathetic speech, the policy of relocation is still being used (Hellinger 2001).

Seeking to appropriate visibly their right to work in June, a group of street vendors invaded an empty lot near the Sabana Grande Boulevard. They were claiming an empty lot (state land) so that the municipal authorities would build them a shopping center. Inspired by the speech President Chávez had given in February, the leader of the invasion, José Chauran, told the invaders: "There's the lot that belongs to you in the name of God." He then added: "Claim your rights." As they took the lot, they shouted: "*Viva Chávez!*" When the police came to evict them from this state-owned lot, a woman was heard telling the police: "Chavez said not to touch the *buhoneros*" (El Universal 2001).

The statements made by the president have resulted in the police and municipal authorities withdrawing their enforcement capacity in the areas where street vendors work. Enforcement is now lower as a consequence. With the municipal ordinance alienated, the monopoly that the state has over public space is now managed, in many cases, by local street-vending organizations. Consumption and exchange of space, as a commodity, is "inspired and regulated by those in power ... if not it would likely appear to threaten them" (Appadurai 1986: 28). The political discourse has affected the demand for space. On the one hand we can say that in this case demand is determined by social and economic factors, while on the other, it can, within limits, manipulate the conditions under which such a demand is articulated (ibid.: 31). A change in the use of material and virtual space affects the social process of the city, where rights are contested through everyday practices.

## The law and institutional reform

The institutional reform that began with the drafting of a new constitution has added to the complexity in attempting to address the issues of the excluded and impoverished sectors, while maintaining order and the rule of law. One of the achievements of the Federation of Non-Dependent Workers of Venezuela (FUTRAND) was to have the new constitution recognize non-dependent workers. This federation, encompassing five labor unions, four guild associations, and 10,000 informal workers, was created in 1992 as a result of the approval of the Organic Labor Law (Article 40) that explicitly recognized informal workers and their right to organize (Llerena 2005). Since then they have battled to secure the rights of informal workers as non-dependent workers. As a result of their lobby they proposed and negotiated Article 87 (of the Constitution) in the National Constituent Assembly in 1999, which recognizes non-dependent workers as legitimate actors.[10] FUTRAND argues that this was an important recognition and achievement, yet these workers have limited gains from a formal recognition. They are still victims of harassment, bribes, and manipulation; not only by the state but also by the representatives of these organizations. Yet ever since the new constitution no area has been cleared, securing public space for vendors despite the lack of a specific right of usage.

Organized groups have taken this as the platform from which to demand state recognition for their activity. In conversations with Yolanda Wunde-heiler, labor union leader, for example, I was reminded several times that as workers of the informal economy, the constitution gave them the right to work, and that in so doing they are merely exercising that right.

Only 33 percent of the street vendors interviewed agree with Ms Wunde-heiler's argument and think that the constitution gives them a right to work on the street. Sixty-five percent do not agree.[11] Those that do agree give arguments of citizenship and labor exclusion, although they disagree over the constitutional right and municipal regulation.

> "I have a right to work according to the constitution but it is not of use by the Municipal organism."[12]

> "[President] Chavez said that the streets belong to the people."

> "Because of the right to work and if there is no supply of employment, I have a right to work and above all I have right to life and if I don't work I can't live."

> "We are Venezuelan."

The Municipal Office still regulates the usage of public space through ordinance 1789–2, published 9 September 1998, the same ordinance which Antonio Ledezma used to clear the vendors. It establishes the norms through which natural persons may trade articles on public space. The ordinance, the highest municipal legal instrument, prohibits trading in areas such as boulevards, street corners, metro exits, and near public offices and historical buildings. Yet those are precisely the areas with the higher concentration of street vendors: Sabana Grande, El Cementerio, El Centro, and Catia.

In practice, the ordinance is ignored and a decree published in January 2004 by the Municipal Office is used to set a series of norms that the vendors should follow.[13] It is an instrument that attempts to hold in balance the right to work and the right to the use of public space; yet the police, the governmental authorities, and the street vendors are all accused of disrespecting the agreement. Everyday resistance includes the pleading of ignorance with regard to this instrument, since it was reached in consensus with street vending leaders but not through general participation of the sector.

When discussing the law, only 9 percent of street vendors thought they were well defined, 34 percent agreed they were badly defined, and 39 percent said they were not applicable. The ordinances and decrees that regulate public space, according to 47 percent, went against the right to work.[14] Their strategies are to ignore and evade such legislation, law, or rule, and continue to fight to work on the street. Over the last 15 years, the acts of everyday resistance have changed and/or narrowed the policy options available to the state (Scott 1998: 36).

## Public space: negotiating inclusion

Public space, as a public good, is a space that anyone has a right to use without being excluded in terms of social or economic requirements. However, the working reality is that much of the public space in Caracas has been privately appropriated. The entrance of new actors is also limited as space is appropriated by actors; it cannot be simultaneously consumed, thus producing exclusion. Vendors apply their exclusion of the formal economic and labor system to the visible and public sphere. Spaces, like time and history, shape social processes and determine outcomes. The informal no longer is an issue of the periphery, since the traders have taken the informal – if it can really be described as such – to the center, and have reshaped the way we see and understand public space by gaining support of the bureaucracy and general public.

Within the informal economy literature (Mingione 1994: 25; Chichlow 1998: 62; Morales 2001), scholars argue that the informal/formal dichotomy has distorted sociological tradition, overlooking complex social relations and strategies. In particular, while there are differences of interest between those working on the street and those working off the street, the distinction of informal/formal may not be the most appropriate (Pratt 2002). The formal and informal should be reconceptualized, as it is an interconnected and fluid relational structure of strategies existing between the people and the state. The law, however, defines territories inside and outside the law, which means that there are spaces of full citizenship and limited citizenship (Morales 2001).

Street vendors struggle for the legitimization of their activities – defined by the dominant as informal – in practice; however, the activities are very much everyday ones, and recognizable by the general public.[15] For the day-to-day practices lie underneath the conceptual dualism; the formal and informal are inseparable and continuous responses and links to structures.

Democratic collective action in the public sphere has opened a space for popular participation in the economy and in claiming certain rights (Habermas 1989). But additionally they have transformed public space into social space, which "contains specific representation of ... interaction between the social relations of production and reproduction" (Lefebvre *et al.* 1996). It is a symbolic representation of a social space where inclusion and rights are being negotiated, simultaneously excluding others. It is a space that actively contests the state's legitimacy, showing its inability to comply with what it legislates.

In this context the informal economy is the result of excessive legality and bureaucracy (de Soto 1989). This has resulted in many entrepreneurs being excluded from the formal sphere. In the face of legislation that is complex, bureaucratic, contradictory, and often ambiguous, Venezuelan street vendors strategically decide to resist the state's regulations through everyday acts of resistance and negotiation. When the state openly decides to clear an area, thereby affecting their livelihood, they take the silent protest to a public protest, which may bring the city to a halt. Both parts acknowledge the contradiction of the law and thus agree to ignore it by establishing informal norms of cooperation. In the case of street vendors, the state gives them the "green light" to sell on the street.[16] It does not change the norm, yet extra-officially regulates the sector, avoiding its legitimacy from being questioned.

There is usually the assumption that there is a technocratic worldview of the rule of law and that they share in the state a "monopoly of legitimate symbolic violence, have grounds socially, and are encouraged to regard themselves as the functionaries and missionaries of the universal" (Bourdieu 2005). This is not always the case, particularly in the context of Caracas: public officials can also "bend the rules" to please the local constituency or to do someone a favor. Public officials enforce regulations only to the extent that enforcing them serves their interest in "turning a blind eye" or "making an exception."

Bourdieu further contends:

> the option of opening up the possibility of an exception of the rule represents the most common and effective way of acquiring that particular

form of bureaucratic charisma that is acquired by distancing oneself from the bureaucratic definition of the civil service role.

(ibid.: 132)

The public official can seek acquaintance to the group by building social capital "of useful relations and a symbolic capital of gratitude that pertain to that very particular form of exchange in which the 'currency' is nothing other than exceptions to rules or accommodations to regulations granted or offered as a 'favor.'" The application of the rule depends on the dispositions and interests of agents that derive their power from their monopoly control of interpreting and imposing the regulation. The "exception to the rule" and "bureaucratic charisma" has been ingrained in the institutional framework, thus reproducing certain logic of day-to-day practices (ibid.).

The demand of the street as a physical space

> entails in its turn logic and a strategy of property in space: "places and things belonging to you do not belong to me." The fact remains, however, that communal or shared spaces, the possession or consumption of which cannot be entirely privatized, continue to exist.
>
> (Lefebvre *et al.* 1996)

Street vendors, therefore, maintain a right to use that shared space.[17] The street, as a commodity, is traded; some bits are bought and sold, for the right to use and consume that space, but it cannot be privatized completely nor will full rights to own it be transferred from the state. The practice of informal negotiation allows space to be distributed, with the law remaining formal in its prohibition. Thus we begin to see two parallel systems operating simultaneously: one of inclusion, the other of exclusion.

The street as a social space is determined by a specific configuration of a physical and real space, where actions and practices are determined by past actions and rules of the game (Bourdieu 1990; Lefebvre 1991). For the street vendor, the street includes not only physical objects, such as the merchandise, tables, and metal structure, but also a practical expression of the day-to-day, of informality as a manifestation or continuity of the rigidity in the economic structures which do not give them space to carry out their work. It also includes space of the public sphere, where discourses of inclusion and citizenship are contested. As "the people" or "the sovereign body" (*el pueblo* or *el soberano*), they seek to participate not only in the economic but also in the political.

Those of the informal segment struggle against the dominant discourse of the formal segment. They compete for space, rights, and livelihood by appropriating public space for private use of production and reproduction. The informal strategies used to compete with the formal institutional context simultaneously reproduce an informal sphere that takes the form of the dominant structure "in practice," but is neither legitimized nor accepted as a working reality. The struggle exists because, as José Chauran[18] has observed on street vending: "There is a culture that considers the street vendor as a third class citizen." The kinds of capital used by subordinate groups tend to be ignored or devalued in the functioning of dominant institutions. In a sense, informality becomes the counter-culture of the formal or ideal, while simply seeking inclusion in the structure and not attempting to change the structure itself.

In areas of high demand, other private actors have taken the supply of space monopolized by the state. The organizational structure of the sector will determine the barriers to entry. In areas of poor organization, individuals that sell from their own stand supply the market, but that does not make a business out of managing space. In areas where organizations are stronger, in some cases individuals with substantial social and political capital manage the space. Management and allocation of space may require payment in money or support. The state still maintains a right to revoke those permits allocated by leaders or coordinators, who might have privately gained from the transaction. The contacts with the government determine those that are most successful at making a business of the street.

The state has the monopoly to determine the legal and illegal, in the name of social well being, although "individual behavior and social practice are often regulated by other, unofficial criteria" (Fernandes and Varley 1998: 4). However, these transactions could not take place without the indirect support of the state through its institutions and personal representatives. This form of "illegal" appropriation of space tends to be accepted and/or tolerated by both the state and public opinion (ibid.). The retreat of the state has allowed the street vendors with the highest level of cultural, economic, and symbolic capital (usually the leaders, block coordinators) to make use of that capital for income generation schemes that include, but are not limited to, the exchange of space for monetary and/or symbolic value.

As we will see in the next section, there are many ways of appropriating space. Contacts, or simply knowing people in the sector, will facilitate entry.

## Ways of appropriating public space

As Weber argues, "one obeys the rule when the interest in obeying it predominates over the interest in disobeying it" (Bourdieu 2005). Or as one street vendor, Norma Jaramillo, put it:

> I will comply with the norm only when everyone follows it ... The truth is that I have very little hope that the norms will work. That is why I came back to work and I don't lose time in [listening to promises from] the municipal office.
>
> (El Nacional 2004)

*Guapear*, false compliance, feigned ignorance, sabotage: all of these are everyday forms of resistance.[19] They require little planning and depend on informal networks and the use of implicit understanding of the rules in operation. This resistance, however, never seeks openly to contest formal definitions of hierarchy and power, but rather seeks participation in the public sphere (Scott 1985). For this reason, street vendors use the bits of law that are beneficial to them. Some regard the right to work over the right of others to use public space. Others state that they are merely borrowing the space, which either belongs to the general public or the government, to make a living, as they have a right and necessity to make a livelihood. The state holds a monopoly of the supply of public space, and although social and legal conditions prohibit the activity, it is supported and regulated informally, allowing the demand for space to be satisfied.

### Obtaining space: exchange and value

The value of the street is exemplified by its capacity to be exchanged as a commodity (as a monetary or symbolic good). The link between the exchange and the value of the exchange is in the politics (Appadurai 1986). Need, demand, and power interact to create economic value from this specific social situation, where use of space by vendors is prohibited, yet authority can turn a blind eye, creating a market for such transactions. For this reason, people obtain a stand in the streets in many different ways (see Table 3.1). In some cases, it is handed over by family or friends, invaded violently, occupied non-violently (by fighting against police and authority for the space for years) or through the acquisition of a permit from the municipality, local street-vending organization, or local leader. Following what the legislature says, one would assume that those that work on the street have been given a permit or license. In practice this is not true.

Fifty-six percent have used non-violent occupation, that is, by going out every day, talking to people, looking at the area, and selling things like souvenirs and other paraphernalia easily produced and readily purchased. Non-violent occupation was very common in the phase after the Ledezma crackdown period. Thirty-four-year-old Gustavo explains how he obtained

*Table 3.1* Ways in which vendors in Caracas obtain a stand/spot

| Mechanism | % |
| --- | --- |
| Non-violent occupation | 56 |
| Bought/let | 18 |
| Informal permit | 11 |
| Transfer from family/friend | 10 |
| Violent occupation | 3 |
| Other | 3 |

Source: CEDICE, December 2004.

his current location: "*Guapeando* and coming everyday; placing my black rag [on the floor] and selling the merchandise." Others that have been selling on the street longer have had to:

> "*Guapear* with merchandise in the hand and run [from the] police when they came."

> "Talk to two neighbors to see if I could occupy [the space] and they said yes."

> "Become familiar with all the rest of the street vendors; it was a transfer, I was an employee here."

Still others (11 percent) have spoken to the local street vendor leader or the local organization of street vendors and have been given a permit to work there. This permission or "okay" is given by the president of the street vending organization, the block coordinator, or the natural leader of the area. Sometimes it requires payment to those coordinators of a yearly fee of up to Bs. 1,150,000 (US$ 534), while at other times the person only needs an "okay" from the leader.[20] Obtaining permission depends on your friend and/or family ties in the area, who introduces you to the leader, and whether the leader charges for giving a piece of the sidewalk. Other times, payment is given for security from police, and cleaning services, among other sources. As some interviewed put how they obtained their current stand:

> "Talk[ing] to the coordinator and pay[ing] her."

> "Becom[ing] familiar [with area] and talk with neighbors that a friend introduced me to and with the block coordinator."

> "Talk to the leaders which are the ones that negotiated the permit with the Mayor's office."

Other ways of obtaining a stand include: transfer from family/friend, or violent occupation. But what about the "privatization of space" that is consistently referred to in interviews, surveys, and newspapers? The trading of street-vending stands seems to constitute an institutionalized way of obtaining a right to work on the street, although the legislature makes no reference to what is actually occurring on the ground as a day-to-day practice.

Although not particularly significant, it is increasingly common for people to buy or rent the stands where they work. In our survey 18 percent had done so. In other words, a private market allows for the exchange of space as a commodity. This is most common among people that have recently undertaken the activity. For example, 26-year-old Pedro "talk[ed] with the owner, [and] negotiate[d] the payment with him." This sale, however, does not give any security, as he could still be evicted from the spot. When the stand is sold, the owner lets others around him know that this new person has bought the stand and will be the new occupier of the spot. This allows for others to recognize him as the legitimate holder of that space. This is in itself an act of resistance, since it defies the ordinance that clearly denies the transferring of stands, even more so for a monetary exchange.

For others, no negotiation is needed, as this is a market transaction, following demand and supply principles. For example, during Christmas, the research team saw a sign in Sabana Grande that said: "Letting stand Bs 1,500,000 (US$ 698) during season" (García-Rincón 2005).[21] Or, as Pedro, a 42-year-old man, best indicated when stating, "I put the transaction together for you, but I get something out of it."[22] But not all street transactions follow the demand and supply principle, whereby a seller and a buyer exchange goods. For example, Octavio, a 42-year-old street vendor of Catia, claims he was forced to abandon his stall and space, between the Second and Third Avenues of Catia, three years ago because a leader, Carmen, was harassing him. "She sells space as if it were private property. And nothing can be done because she says she is *Chavista*. She wants to run for office in the local elections and is looking for support." He then had to find a new place to set up business. Currently Carmen has let and privately profits from his old stand.[23]

### Politics of exchange

Even when there is no security in the transactions for obtaining a stand, they must have someone's backing to feel secure for claiming a right of usage over public space. Of the 366 street vendors interviewed, 66 percent think that they have a right of use over public space to carry out commercial activities. Public institutions and/or their representatives have given such a prerogative to work on the street.

For the right of use of a particular stand to be respected, the most important factors are not formal ones such as having a permit or following the decree, but rather aspects such as the amount of time with the stand (53 percent). The longer the person has been working a particular space with a stand, the more his or her right will be respected. Municipal laws were also mentioned (19 percent): the more the person has complied with the regulations set out, the more his or her right will be respected. Fifteen percent mentioned labor law, 6 percent having bought the stand, and 7 percent other factors. Going every day, time spent with the stand, having friends and family working in the area, knowing street-vending leaders, having contacts with the government, and having bought the stand were also considered important for having the right of usage respected.[24]

Table 3.2 shows which institution was seen as giving them the right of usage, which does not necessarily reflect a permit but an institutional backing of some sort. Thirty-four percent mentioned the Municipal Office, 22 percent a street-vendor's organization, 16 percent no-one, 12 percent the Presidential Palace *Miraflores*, 9 percent Metropolitan Municipal Office, and the other 7 percent mentioned options such as ministries, did not know or other.

At times, this right to use public space is attributed to a permit given by a person (see Table 3.3). When asked which individuals had given them that right, 25 percent mentioned the President, 20 percent "myself," 17 percent the Libertador Mayor, 14 percent the block coordinator, and 12 percent the Metropolitan Mayor; the rest answered "other" (8 percent), no one (3 percent), or they did not know (1 percent).

I have mentioned informal payments throughout this section. Discussing bribes and/or monetary transactions is not an easy thing, since people, due to fear, are not willing to discuss it openly, but rather in passing. What seems to be consistent is that prior to President Chávez's statement on "leaving the street vendors alone," the police periodically harassed street vendors, but that after that statement the police and state in general have withdrawn from enforcing the ordinance. Therefore, bribes have also (apparently) decreased, as public officials are no longer obligated to enforce the law but rather provide security to the sector. In a 1992 survey of 634 vendors, 32 percent identified police harassment as their main problem in the development of

*Table 3.2* Organizations that grant right over the street to vendors in Caracas

| Organization | % |
| --- | --- |
| LMO | 34 |
| Street vendors' organization | 22 |
| No institution | 16 |
| Presidential office | 12 |
| MMO | 10 |
| Other | 4 |
| Does not know | 2 |
| Other state agency | 1 |

Source: CEDICE, December 2004.

*Table 3.3* Individuals that grant right over the street to vendors in Caracas

| Individual | % |
| --- | --- |
| President | 25 |
| Me, myself, and I | 20 |
| Libertador Mayor | 17 |
| Block coordinator | 14 |
| Metropolitan Mayor | 12 |
| Other/ Does not know | 9 |
| No one | 3 |

Source: CEDICE, December 2004.

their commercial activity (Contreras *et al.* 1992; Lara 1997).[25] Yet in our survey it was not identified as a problem: only 8 percent of those interviewed had paid a bribe to the police in the previous year. When we asked about bribes in the survey we started to notice that people were referring to payments made to block coordinators and street-vending associations, rather than the police. Naturally, this complicated our understanding of bribes. I will now look briefly at the role of coordinators.

### *Privatization of space? The role of coordinators*

"Block coordinators," or street vendor leaders, were seen as the most important factor in obtaining a stall (Contreras *et al.* 1992). Thirty-six percent of street vendors interviewed claimed to be a member of one of these organizations, although participation varies by area: Sabana Grande (58 percent), Cementerio (16 percent), Centre (36 percent), and Catia (58 percent). Not all street vendors want to pay fees to the organizations and their leaders, while others have had problems with block coordinators and leaders and thus prefer to be independent. Yet, the organizations play an important role in negotiating public policies with the Municipal Office, looking for solutions to the problem of street vending and calling the media's attention to the sector. Street vendors suggest that belonging to these organizations is very important and useful. On top of this, dynamics in each area are different.

Catia is historically the oldest street-vending area (established in the mid-1970s) and the first to consist of many small organizations, resulting in dynamics differing from one block to the next. So while between Second and Third Avenue the management exploits workers, in the next block the opposite occurs. Dynamics in El Centro were similar to those in Catia. Sabana Grande, newer to vending (established in the mid-1980s and cleared during several periods), is divided into two organizations. Being more to the east of the city, and its boulevard being a landmark in the 1960s, it is always the first area to be considered for restoration by authorities (such as Ledezma). Yet payment in this area is hardly heard of. The leaders are more political in their representation of workers on the local planning council. El Cementerio is an area with little or no organization, although as a cluster for selling garment products it is the most profitable area. Stands here are readily available for letting and individuals sell and buy stands with limited intervention by authorities or organizations. We tried renting a stand for December at a cost of Bs. 3,000,000, yet in January we could buy it for the same cost.[26]

The coordinator is a recently developed role. Ten years ago it did not exist. The role emerged with respect to the increase in the number of vendors; the need to coordinate information, actions, and the control of space in areas of high demand and limited supply; and because the state used direct action of confrontation, clearing, and not allowing street vending to proliferate. Although it is still unclear what the relationship between block coordinators and the state is, on 7 January 2004 the Mayor of Libertador stated that they "will designate an individual responsible per block, who will be responsible for ensuring that everyone takes down their stands ..., " so the position was given official recognition. In some areas, they are elected, while in others they are self-named. They are, however, a link between the street-vending community at large, street-vending leaders, and the Municipal Office, and they are in a position to create informal institutional arrangements for public space management.

Today, the question of who manages the rules of the street is unclear. Cornelio Torres is of the opinion that: "Now there aren't any leaders, but bandits, who have the luxury of selling space and negotiating space."[27] While José Chauran stated: "What mafia? The mafia is within the same municipal office!"[28] What appears to be occurring, in the end, is that the leaders and block coordinators collaborate with the state, contesting the field in which they operate, and seeing the opportunity of participating in the political sphere. In short, leaders and block coordinators are reproducing informality that operates within the field and that has shaped the *habitus*[29] of its actors. The relationship and actions between actors is determined by "rules" learned from everyday practices in the context of ongoing relationships. Morales (2001: 196) states, "each means of acquiring space reflects the variable presence of expectations learned from social institutions." Here I am not referring to informality as an economic activity, or the activity outside the formal realm, but rather I am talking about the way in which things are done, and the way rules are negotiated and implemented. I am talking about the social capital that excludes certain groups of people, while others benefit from state contracts, and negotiate the law to operate and generate private profit from a public good.

## Conclusion

Historically, in cities such as Caracas, vendors have physically appropriated public space in an attempt to secure a living. In this context, public space is a contested site of interaction between a vendor's right to work and the state's attempt to keep public space cleared. Space is a material stage where tension, conflict, appropriation, and negotiation are played out between state and non-state actors.

Most of the 1980s and early 1990s were characterized by uncoordinated policies by different state agencies – clearing, harassment, and relocation was a cyclical process. In 1999, in the wake of a crackdown on street vendors and despite the fact that he did not have clear local authority over public space, President Chávez changed that policy through a series of speeches, from one of harassment to one of apparent safeguarding. The president himself and the constitution now symbolically protect vendors' activities. As a result, street vendors have once again appropriated many of the main streets, boulevards, and plazas in Caracas. Public space no longer represents only a material struggle for vendors' livelihood. It is a space where rights are contested and citizenship exercised. The presidential discourse opened up a public sphere for street vendors to stake claims and exercise their rights. However, rules for appropriating space were also redefined. All this curtailed the enforcement of local regulations, reducing bribes while opening up a private market where the right to work could be acquired through an informal market transaction, often through local "leaders" who claim to protect the vendors' rights.

Both the state and street vendors have recognized that the law is contradictory and difficult to enforce. As a result, they have negotiated informal norms of cooperation to regulate and manage conflict. Different strategies are now implemented to access space, ranging from silently occupying space to approaching the authority and receiving informal support for buying or renting space. Need, demand, and power interact to create economic value for this specifically social situation, where use of space by vendors is nominally prohibited but the confusing and contradictory mandates on the part of different authority structures make such a prohibition ineffective, giving rise to what are in effect de facto systems of market rents.

## Notes

1 This research was made possible with the financial support of the Foundation for Urban and Regional Studies; Center of Latin American Studies, University of Cambridge; Menca de Leoni studentship, Newham College; Cambridge Overseas Trust; Cambridge Political Economy Society Trust and Centre for the Dissemination of Economic Knowledge. Special thanks are due to Wladimir Zanoni, Rocio Guijarro, and Marcos Rodriguez, at CEDICE, who allowed me to collaborate, use survey and exchange ideas with them. I would like to also thank Patrick Boner, the editors, and anonymous readers for their comments and suggestions on this chapter. I am also especially grateful to Noel and Beatriz Garcia for their on-going support. Responsibility for the content is mine.

2 I use street vendors, informal traders, and workers of the informal economy interchangeably and as normally used in the context I am discussing. Locally, these individuals are referred to as *buhoneros* and legislative treatment included non-dependent workers and workers of the informal economy. Metropolitan Caracas has 48,675 people working in the street, 38,458 of which work in the municipality El Libertador. Twenty-six percent of street stands sell garment products (INE 2001; MMO 2002–3) and they are mostly concentrated in "prohibited areas" such as boulevards, plazas, and sidewalks where there is high demand and limited supply of space.

3 Focus group workshop, 30 September 2004. The competitive advantage of location is one of the reasons why policies of relocation do not work and there is little incentive for vendors to relocate.

4 I draw from Bourdieu (1984: 125) to discuss later an initial approximation to street vendors' set of capital, including social, and symbolic. "... the different kinds of capital are one of the fundamental stakes in the struggles between class fractions whose power and privileges are linked to one or the other of these types. In particular, this exchange rate is a stake in the struggle over the dominant principle of domination (economic capital, cultural capital or social capital), which goes on at all times between the different fractions of the dominant class."

5 Vendors were manually counted in these areas block by block; 10 percent of the

total numbers of garment vendors were surveyed (3.55 percent of total vendors in these areas), and 5 percent of those surveyed were then interviewed in depth at a second stage. Garment products represent 32 percent of the products sold on the street, followed by 17 percent pirated CDs and DVDs, among others.

6  Personal interview, 16 March 2005.

7  Ibid.

8  "*ningún mandatario regional podía usar la fuerza publica para atropellar al pueblo.*" Another statement included: "*el soberano tiene derecho a utilizar las vías publicas para trabajar y se llego al extremo de amenazar con cárcel a gobernadores y alcaldes que utilicen a los cuerpos de seguridad para evitar la invasión de la propiedad privada y los bien de domino publico*" (Sotillo Silva 1999).

9  Published *Gaceta Oficial No. 5.152 Extraordinary* of 19 June 1997.

10 The first draft of the article used the term "informal worker," but that was later modified to give a more positive attribution to these workers. It is interesting that entrepreneur, with a more positive but implicitly with a different connotation, was not preferred. The Venezuelan Constitution (1999) recognizes and specifically mentions the right to work of non-dependent or self-employed workers. In the previous Constitution (1961), these individuals were not specially mentioned as a group with legitimate rights to organize and make claims for labor rights. Article 87 of the 1999 Constitution states:

> All persons have the right and duty to work. The state guarantees the adoption of the necessary measures so that every person shall be able to obtain productive work providing him or her with a dignified and decorous living and guaranteeing him or her full exercise of this right. It is an objective of the state to promote employment. Measures tending to guarantee the exercise of the labor rights of self-employed [non-dependent] persons shall be adopted by law. Freedom to work shall be subject only to such restrictions as may be established by law ...

11 The rest did not know or respond.

12 All quotes in the chapter are extracts from open questions included in the 366 surveys gathered.

13 Essentially, this decree establishes that "assemblies of citizens" [*asambleas de ciudadanos*] of the informal economy by geographical sector should be held. It also states that informal traders should work between 8:00 a.m. and 8:00 p.m. and that there should be one day per week when they do not work. Space should be kept clean and their trash disposed of. Cars are not to be used to sell merchandise; metro exits, bus stops, and street corners should remain clear. Fixed structures are prohibited, and for cultural reasons historic locations are to remain free of street vending. A series of studies, commissions, and actions are to be undertaken to seek solutions to the problem of street vending. The municipality commits itself to providing security through the *Policia de Caracas*.

14 Forty-nine percent said they didn't go against the right to work and 4 percent did not know.

15 I use informal and informality as conceptual tools. However, I acknowledge that the formal/informal dichotomy is a continuous field, which feed into each other, representing the same activity but legally treated differently. The formal with a series of rights and benefits, while the informal, lacking security.

16 I draw from an analogy with the traffic-light system in Caracas – used as a reference but not a strict rule to follow. Even when the green light is on, you need to carefully cross a main intersection, as with a red light people can also cross the intersection, especially when there is little traffic. Therefore, even with a green light, that does not mean "go," but rather "yes you legally can go, but with caution as someone else might not follow the same rule."

17 Although not a formal property right, the right to use space or land is recognized by those around the user of the space and by the municipal authority, and over time gives the user a legitimate right over the space and/or ownership by practice. A public policy consequence is that to be relocated or removed s/he must be compensated.

18 Street-vending leader of Sabana Grande and representative of the informal economy on the "Local Council of Public Participation."

19 *Guapear*, the signaling and guarding of one's own, the establishing of "this is mine, not yours," also implies confronting both police violence and organized mafia.

20 Informal conversation.

21 Minimum wage in Venezuela is Bs 350,487 (US$ 163) a month.

22 "*yo te cuadro la gente, pero yo me quedo con algo.*"

23 Personal interview, 28 March 2005; 12 April 2005. Names have been changed.

24 Miriam, a 74-year-old woman working on the Boulevard Sabana Grande, obtained an informal permit directly from the president. She was among a group of senior citizens that wanted to work – according to the ordinance, given her age, she should be allocated a permit – without any police harassment. So one day they decided to seek the president's permission. So, half of the protestors slept on the boulevard and half of the protestors slept at *Miraflores* until they were received by the president, who then called the Municipal Office and ordered that they be allocated a part of the boulevard. "I was there three days until the president himself received us and allowed us to work on the boulevard." Personal interview, 9 April 2005.

25 Other problems identified included: none, 55.52 percent; lack of permit, 2.52 percent; personal insecurity, 4.57 percent; low sales, 1.42 percent; precarious working conditions, 1.26 percent; higher costs, 0.47 percent; other, 1.74 percent.

26 A taxi driver was putting the transaction together. It did not go through because we wanted to sell accessories to complement garment sales in that area and the only product informally permitted is clothing, as it is the area's competitive advantage. People from all of Venezuela go to El Cementerio to buy clothing.

27 "*Ahora no hay dirigentes, sino bandas; y se dan el lujo de vender espacios ... y negociar espacios.*"

28 "*No que la mafia! La mafia está dentro del mismo municipio!*"

29 Rules, expectations, and experience bounded in the practices and minds of actors. For Bourdieu (2000: 19) "I developed the concept of *habitus* to incorporate the objective structures of society and the subjective role of agents within it. The *habitus* is a set of dispositions, reflexes, and forms of behavior people acquire through acting in society. ... Then the question of social agency and political intervention becomes very important."

## Bibliography

Appadurai, A. (1986) *The social life of things: commodities in cultural perspective*, Cambridge: Cambridge University Press.

Bourdieu, P. (1984) *Distinction: a social critique of the judgement of taste*, London: Routledge & Kegan Paul.

—— (1990) *The logic of practice*, Stanford, CA: Stanford University Press.

—— (2005) *The social structures of the economy*, Cambridge: Polity.

Brown, A. and Lloyd-Jones, T. (2002) 'Spatial planning, access and infrastructure,' in C. Rakodi and T. Lloyd-Jones (eds) *Urban livelihoods: a people-centred approach to reducing poverty*, London: Earthscan: xvii, 306.

Buitrago, L. (1985) 'Solo hay 1500 venezolanos entre los 12 mil buhoneros,' *El Nacional*, Caracas: D-14.

Canizales, M. (1999) 'Sabotaje municipal,' *El Universal*, Caracas. Online. Available: http://buscador.eluniversal.com/1999/10/17/apo_art_17117CC.shtml

CEDICE (2004) Research project 'Building consensus to reduce poverty,' financed by Center for Private Initiative (CIPE). Unpublished data base of survey results.

Chichlow, M. (1998) 'Reconfiguring the "informal economy" divide: State, capitalism, and struggle in Trinidad and Tobago,' *Latin American Perspectives*, 25(2): 62–83.

Contreras, A., Hernandez, J. de, and Fonseca, Lady (1992) 'La informalidad como estrategia de sobrevivencia: su dimensión sociológica,' *Serie cuadernos de investigación*, Caracas: Fundación Escuela de Gerencia Social: 117.

Coronil, F. (1997) *The magical state: nature, money, and modernity in Venezuela*, Chicago, IL: University of Chicago Press.

Cross, J. (1998) *Informal politics: street vendors and the state in Mexico City*, Stanford, CA: Stanford University Press.

de Soto, H. (1989) *The other path: the invisible revolution in the Third World*, New York: Harper & Row.

El Nacional (2004) 'Buhoneros vuelven a las calles sin acatar acuerdos y prohibiciones,' *El Nacional*, Caracas: A-1.

El Universal (1985) 'Un Azote de Caracas: la buhonería,' *El Universal*, Caracas, 13 August.

——(1990) 'Reforzada la vigilancia contra la buhonería,' *El Universal*, Caracas: 1–26.

——(2001) 'El Soberano desalojado de Bello Monte,' *El Universal*, Caracas. Online. Available: http://buscador.eluniversal.com/2001/02/06/ccs_art_06401RR.shtml

España, L.P. (2001) 'Superar la pobreza en Venezuela: el camino por recorrer,' *Superar la pobreza: el camino por recorrer UCAB*, Caracas: UCAB/ACPES.

Febres, C., Hernandez, V., and Murzi, G. (1995) 'Aproximación al sector informal urbano en el área metropolitana de Caracas,' *Serie Cuadernos de Investigación*, Caracas: Fundación Escuela de Gerencia Social: 210.

Fernandes, E. and Varley, A. (1998) *Illegal cities: law and urban change in developing countries*, London: Zed Books.

García-Rincón, M.F. (2005) *Matando Tigres: The informal sector of Caracas*, presented at PILAS Annual Conference, University of Cambridge, UK, February.

Habermas, J. (1989) *The structural transformation of the public sphere: an inquiry into a category of bourgeois society*, Cambridge, MA: MIT Press.

Hansen, K.T. (2004) 'Who rules the streets? The politics of vending space in Lusaka,' in K.T. Hansen and M. Vaa (eds) *Reconsidering informality: perspectives from urban Africa*, Uppsala: Nordiska Afrikainstitutet.

Hellinger, D. (2001) 'Tercermundismo and Chavismo,' paper presented at Meeting of the Latin American Studies Association, Washington DC, September.

Herrera, E. (1996) 'Los buhoneros del voto,' *El Naciona*, Caracas, 26 November.

INE (2001) *Censo Nacional*, Caracas: Instituto Nacional de Estadistica.

——(2004) *Encuesta de Hogares por Muestreo: Situación en la fuerza de trabajo en Venezuela*, INE, Caracas: Instituto Nacional de Estadistica: 25.

Lara, G. (1997) *Precarización del Empleo y Sector Informal*, Caracas: Alcaldía de Caracas, ODEU, UNDP: 76.

Lefebvre, H. (1991) *The production of space*, Cambridge, MA: Blackwell.

——, Kofman, E. *et al.* (1996) *Writings on cities*, Cambridge, MA: Blackwell.

Llerena, B. (2005) 'Venezuela: Experiencia en la representación de los trabajadores no dependientes,' in G. Castillo and A. Orsatti (eds) *Trabajo Informal y sindicalismo en American Latina y el Caribe: buenas practicas formativas y organizativas*, Montevideo: CONTERFOR/OIT: 114.

Marquez, P. (undated) *Trabajo Informal y Comercio Informal en Venezuela*, Caracas: Instituto Municipal de Publicaciones.

McCaughan, M. (2004) *The battle of Venezuela*, London: Latin America Bureau.

Mingione, E. (1994) 'Life strategies and social economies in the postfordist age,' *International Journal of Urban and Regional Research*, 18(1): 24–46.

MMO (2002–3) 'Censo Alcaldia Mayor 2002–3,' unpublished presentation with results.

Morales, A. (2001) 'Policy from theory: a critical reconstruction of theory on the "informal economy,"' *Sociological Imagination*, 38(3): 190–203.

Picavet, R. (1989) 'The love-hate relations between government and the informal sector: the case of street-vending in Peru,' in P. Gelder and J. Bijlmer (eds) *About fringes, margins and lucky dips: the informal sector in Third-World countries*, Amsterdam: Free University Press.

Pratt, N. (2002) 'Public space as an asset for sustainable livelihoods: a literature review.' Online. Available: www.cardiff.ac.uk/cplan/mls/pratt_lit-review.pdf (accessed 17 January 2006).

Scott, J.C. (1985) *Weapons of the weak: everyday forms of peasant resistance*, New Haven, CT: Yale University Press.

—— (1998) *Seeing like a state: how certain schemes to improve the human condition have failed*, New Haven, CT: Yale University Press.

Sotillo Silva, Y. (1999) 'Grupos políticos detrás de buhoneros,' *El Globo*, Caracas: 9.

T.N. (1989) 'No habrá mas buhoneros en el centro,' *El Universal*, Caracas: 2–18.

# 4 Legal responses to sidewalk vending

## The case of Los Angeles, California

*Gregg W. Kettles*[1]

## Introduction

In a city park, where sidewalk vending is legal, there are no vendors. Across the street, where sidewalk vending is against the law, vendors ply their trade in broad daylight. This is a scene from the state of sidewalk vending in Los Angeles, California. Aside from two small zones where it is permitted under heavy regulation, sidewalk vending is illegal in Los Angeles. Yet thousands of vendors continue to operate illegally in the area adjacent to one of the legal vending zones and throughout the city. While legal vending has failed, illegal vending has thrived. What went wrong? What should be done now? Should Los Angeles attempt to revive legal vending by aggressively enforcing the prohibition against illegal vending in the rest of the city? Or should Los Angeles lighten the regulatory burden and broadly legalize sidewalk vending? Does broad legalization enjoy any advantages over the current approach of heavily regulating vending where legal, while generally turning a blind eye to vending where it is against the law?

To answer these questions it is necessary to weigh the benefits of unrestricted vending against its perceived costs, which include unfair competition, over-use of public space, facilitation of the commission of crime, and increased risk of injury to consumers. In response to critics of the practice, I argue here that vending enjoys significant benefits. Arguments decrying its social costs are overblown and mask cultural insecurities and perhaps xenophobia, which should not be given weight in the formulation of policy. The solution is neither more criminal enforcement of the prohibition against illegal vending, nor greater promotion of the existing heavy-handed regulatory scheme, nor muddling through with the status quo. Instead, Los Angeles and other communities should broadly legalize sidewalk vending.

## Sidewalk vending in Los Angeles

Los Angeles' experience with sidewalk vending is the latest chapter of an American story about the social and legal tensions posed by informal street commerce and street life generally. New York City (Bluestone 1991) and

Chicago, Illinois (Morales 2000) have been the setting of older (and continuing) struggles over how the law in the United States should respond to vending on the public sidewalk. This chapter's examination of sidewalk vending is symptomatic of a growing interest among legal academics in informal economic activity (Larson 2002).

In Los Angeles, sidewalk vending is a misdemeanor, punishable by up to six months in jail and a $1,000 fine (Los Angeles 2004: 42(b)). This prohibition has been in place since the 1930s, if not earlier (Moffat 1991). In the decades leading up to the 1980s, sidewalk vending appears not to have been a significant public issue. Not much was taking place, or to the extent that it did, it did not attract significant attention (Sanchez 1987). All that changed in the 1980s when three quarters of a million immigrants to the United States identified Los Angeles as their destination (Miles 1992). The Latino population of the city grew by 62 percent (L.A. Times 1991). By the end of the decade, 40 percent of those residing in Los Angeles were foreign born, and 35 percent spoke Spanish (Miles 1992). The number of sidewalk vendors also increased dramatically (Berestein *et al.* 1995). In 1987 the city had 1,000 unlicensed street vendors (Sanchez 1987). A year later, that figure had grown to 2,000 (McMillan 1988). By 1992, the number of vendors in Los Angeles had grown to an estimated 3,000 to 4,000 (L.A. Times 1992; Sahagun 1992). The area surrounding the city's MacArthur Park – a largely Hispanic area about one and one-half miles west of downtown – was one of the most prominent locations for this increased vending activity.

Controversy followed in its wake. MacArthur Park area storefront merchants complained that sidewalk vending was "getting totally out of hand" (Sanchez 1987). To some, vending was not just illegal, it was wrong. Storefront merchants and other critics argued that vendors were unfairly competing with fixed businesses, were not complying with health regulations on food, were attracting crime, and were a source of litter on the streets (McMillan 1988). Others defended vending; they responded to critics by arguing that vendors provided a useful service and were just trying to make a living the only way they knew how (Sahagun 1992; Sanchez 1987). They argued that vending should be broadly legalized throughout the city.

The controversy caught the attention of the Los Angeles city government. After two years of study and debate, in 1992 the city approved, in principle, a compromise (Sahagun 1992). It enacted a reform ordinance that authorized the creation of eight special districts where vending would be legal. The law, however, did not create any districts in reality. Instead it set up a process by which they may be created. In order to establish a sidewalk vending district, a vendor must go through a long and heavily politicized process (May 1995). A vendor must take a petition to the city accompanied by signatures of 20 percent of the business owners and residents of the proposed district (Los Angeles 2004: 42(m)(2)(B)). The Board of Public Works and city council have final authority to approve, modify, or reject the proposed district (Los Angeles 2004: 42(m)(6)).

Once a district is set up, a vendor must go through a complex and expensive four- to six-week process to get a permit (Los Angeles 2004: 42(m)(11), (12)). Among other things, a vendor must obtain public liability and property damage insurance and obtain written permission from the neighbor of the proposed vending location to allow the proposed sidewalk vending activities (Los Angeles 2004: 42(m)(12)(C), (D)). In other words, every storefront merchant has the power to veto vending in front of his or her business. Robert Valdez, the city's sidewalk vending administrator, summed it up best. Establishing a vending district is "a lengthy process. It is very involved. … It has protections for the merchants and the residents" (Rainey 1994).

Once a vendor obtains a permit, she faces detailed and burdensome regulations concerning her vending activities. The reform ordinance requires the use of a pushcart meeting certain specifications (Los Angeles 2004: 42(m)(22)(A)). Placement of advertising on the cart, and of the cart itself in relation to the curb, are also restricted (Los Angeles 2004: 42(m)(22)(B), (I)). The ordinance allows the vendor to use "one small, compact stool or chair," which "shall be placed within four feet of the pushcart" (Los Angeles 2004: 42(m)(22)(D)).

What has been the practical result of the reform legislation? There has been interest in setting up a number of legal vending districts. Initially, at least five areas of the city were targeted (Sahagun 1992). Later, vendor organizations and community groups said they planned to sponsor as many as eight vending districts (Rainey 1994). In the twelve years running from the enactment of the legislation in 1994, however, only two districts have been set up in Los Angeles. One, in the San Pedro area, began with six carts and went downhill from there, closing two years after opening. The other, in MacArthur Park, at its peak had only thirty-three approved vending carts, and closed after operating for five years (Roumani 1999). This is not surprising.

Neighboring fixed businesses are given a number of opportunities in the process to prevent creation of the district, and each neighbor has the power to veto vending in front of their shop (Rainey 1994). A number of people are resistant to the idea of legalizing vending. City leaders dropped proposed districts in the face of opposition from neighboring residents and businesses (Glover 1993; May 1995). Even submitting a petition signed by 20 percent of the merchants and residents in a proposed zone – as required by the ordinance – has not been enough to ensure the opening of a district. When one vendor group collected the requisite number of signatures, the city councilman for that area refused to consider the group's request. The councilman explained that the vendors had failed to generate "sufficient community support" (Chu 1995). The vending ordinance turned out to be, in the words of one vendor advocate, an "inherently bureaucratic piece of legislation" (Rodriguez 1995). Because of these barriers, the more durable vending district whose creation was approved was placed as far from residents and merchants as realistically possible. It is not in front of any private landowner, but is instead in a public park, MacArthur Park. When the MacArthur Park district was established, vendors were not allowed to sell products that competed with those sold by any of the fixed businesses in the neighborhood. The vendors sell food items from their native lands and craft items such as jewelry and artwork (Romney 1999).

In addition to the substantial barriers to setting up a legal vending district, it is not easy to become a legal vendor. Delays in establishing the legal vending district discouraged some vendors from participating (Hallinan 1999). There is a four- to six-week application period for a permit, during which the prospective vendor attends various training workshops (ibid.). These are designed to train vendors in finance, sales promotion, health and safety, and crime prevention (Roumani 1999). The length of this process caused some vendor applicants to withdraw from the program (Hallinan 1999). It is also costly to operate there: Vendors must use carts meeting specific standards instead of cheaper blankets or cardboard boxes (Becker 1995). While the MacArthur Park district operated, securing permits, insurance, and a city-approved cart cost each vendor $700 per year (Hallinan 1999; Roumani 1999).

There were also substantial costs in administering the legal vending program. To manage the district for the first year of its existence, the Institute for Urban Research and Development (IURD) was hired for $235,000 (Romney 1999). The training of vendors was provided by other non-profit entities, such as the University of Southern California (ibid.). The vendors do not pay rent for their carts; that cost is borne by the IURD. Assuming $6,000 per cart for the thirty-three carts in the district means a capital outlay of $198,000. Even during the district's heyday, revenue from fees taken from legal vendors was not enough to cover the costs of the IURD. The IURD continually lost money on the legal vending program (Colletti 2002). When it later lost funding from the City of Los Angeles and State of California, the IURD felt compelled to shut down the district (Plascencia 2006). One cannot help but wonder at how little value the handful of legal vendors, much less the city, derived from these expenditures, which over five years likely totaled more than $1 million.

Likewise, the cost of enforcing the prohibition of sidewalk vending outside the MacArthur Park district was, and continues to be, significant. And since the level of enforcement is making only a small impact on the amount of illegal vending that is taking place, the city is getting little return on its investment.

What has been the practical result of the reform legislation on vending outside the vending district? It has brought no change. Sidewalk vending continues to be a misdemeanor, punishable by up to six months in jail and a $1,000 fine (Los Angeles 2004: 42(b)). Nonetheless, illegal vendors continue to ply their trade in numbers that appear to be no less than before. They sell a variety of goods, including prepared food, videotapes, clothing, jewelry, and books. Some vendors operate from wheeled conveyances, such as carts or suitcases. Others are less mobile: they might sell their wares from a blanket laid out on the sidewalk or from a cardboard box. Sidewalks near the southeast corner of MacArthur Park were home to as many as forty or fifty vendors on a typical weekend afternoon in 1987. Fifteen years and one reform ordinance later, the number was the same. Countywide, street vendors' sales amount to an estimated $250 million per year (Barrett 2002).

The result of all this is that net social welfare has not been improved by the reform legislation. Vendors continue to exist in large numbers and operate in the open. The administrative costs of dealing with vending have increased, and there have been increased costs of complying with the regulations in the legal vending district in MacArthur Park. There continue to be costs associated with attempting to enforce the ban on vending outside the district. Is there a better way?

## Aggressively enforcing the prohibition against sidewalk vending is not the solution

Increased law enforcement is often pointed to as a solution to the problems of sidewalk vending. The police have generally followed a policy of reactive enforcement. They do nothing unless someone complains to them about a particular vendor.

One response might be to make enforcement more aggressive and pro-active. Instead of waiting for a neighbor to complain, government agents could enforce the prohibition on vending on their own initiative. Los Angeles has already experimented with this. The city established a group of city employees known as Pro-Active Code Enforcement (PACE). Rather than wait for neighbors to complain, PACE goes to an area of the city and takes the initiative to enforce the prohibition of sidewalk vending. But short staffing has limited its impact (Portillo 2002).

Clearly the approach PACE has taken has the potential to succeed in substantially reducing illegal sidewalk vending. Why not assign additional city employees to PACE so that it could cover a greater amount of territory more of the time? There are two principal reasons why the cost of doing so is likely to be too high.

First, many vendors ply their trade because they have no choice. They are not vending to get rich. They are vending to survive (Cross 1998: 25; Rainey 1994). Some vendors we talked to explained that they could find no other work. Vendors interviewed for newspaper stories also cite lack of other employment options as a reason to vend (McMillan 1988; Rodriguez 1995). It may not be for lack of trying. Economic recessions and crises in Los Angeles, Mexico City, and Buenos Aires, Argentina all saw increases in informal economic activity, including sidewalk vending (Gurza 1996; La Nacion 2003; Moffat 1991). Given the cyclical nature of economic growth, there will always be periods in which there are large numbers of people who lose their jobs in the formal economy. For many, sidewalk vending is a way to survive an economic downturn.

Another barrier faced by vendors in finding regular work is discrimination.

In Los Angeles most sidewalk vendors are Latinos, and many are immigrants and women (Rainey 1994; Sanchez 1987). Discrimination has historically limited these groups' access to jobs and capital. Although this form of discrimination is illegal, it doubtlessly continues to occur to some extent (Moffat 1991). Many immigrant vendors are also undocumented and therefore prohibited by law from working (McMillan 1988). According to a city official with PACE, as many as 60 percent of sidewalk vendors are undocumented workers (Portillo 2002). Pressures of survival will impel many to vend. "I can't sit with my arms crossed," said one, "or I won't have money to pay my rent or to eat" (McMillan 1988).

A second reason why increased enforcement of the vending ban is likely to be prohibitively expensive is custom. Many of the vendors in Los Angeles are immigrants from Latin American countries, where vending has been practiced for decades (Cross 1998: 163; De Soto 1989: 84–92; Gurza 1996; Kraul 1995; Levine 1992; McMahan 1995; Moffat 1991; Richmond 1975; Sahagun 1992). When asked how they got into vending, three-fourths of the vendors we spoke with said they learned in their native country. The countries named were Guatemala, Mexico, El Salvador, and Trinidad. Of course, sidewalk vending is not legal in the black-letter sense of the word in all of these Latin American countries. Government agents and officials, however, often tolerate sidewalk vending as a matter of fact and practice (Cross 1998: 163; De Soto 1989: 84–92; Gurza 1996; Kraul 1995).

Having come from a culture where sidewalk vending is widely accepted, many vendors (and the customers who keep them in business) have a powerful drive to continue the practice here. Many vendors we spoke with expressed bewilderment as to why sidewalk vending is illegal in Los Angeles. They contrasted their profession with drug dealing and said theirs is an honorable profession and an honest way to make ends meet (Levine 1992). "We are just trying to make a living," reported one vendor. "I don't understand why we are being persecuted" (Rainey 1994).

## Sidewalk vending should be broadly legalized

Instead of assuming that street vending is a "problem" that must be managed or eliminated, in this section I identify a number of benefits that flow from sidewalk vending. I then recount the principal criticisms that have been leveled against the practice. Critics claim that vendors compete unfairly with storefront merchants, and that sidewalk vending leads to over-use and trashing of public space, facilitates the commission of crime, and poses significant risks to consumers. Another criticism, rarely articulated as such but often implied, is that vending signifies the rise of another culture that threatens the status of existing American culture. I will argue that each of these criticisms is overstated. The benefits of sidewalk vending outweigh its social costs. Rather than continue the current practice of periodically suppressing it, Los Angeles should broadly legalize sidewalk vending.

### Sidewalk vending yields substantial benefits

Sidewalk vending offers a number of benefits. As the discussion of "survival" above suggests, vending would appear to have a number of redistributive benefits. It is a way to eke out a living for many individuals who are poor, and to get a grasp on the bottom rung of the ladder of economic success.

Other benefits of sidewalk vending may be described in utilitarian terms. Vending on the sidewalk increases opportunities for trading, yielding gains to vendors and their customers alike. Broadly legalizing sidewalk vending would allow society to enjoy even more of these benefits.

### The social cost of sidewalk vending is minimal and may be controlled by laws of general applicability

A number of criticisms of sidewalk vending are raised periodically. In this section I will describe the principal criticisms and respond to them. The criticisms of vending do not well withstand scrutiny.

#### Vendors' competition with storefront merchants is not unfair

Among the most vocal critics of sidewalk vendors are merchants who retail products inside privately owned buildings. These storefront merchants argue that vendors unfairly compete with fixed businesses. They explain that vendors pay no rent or utilities, and find it easier to avoid paying taxes. This allows them to charge less for their products than fixed businesses do (Berestein *et al.* 1995).

This argument does have some intuitive appeal. One can imagine a merchant leasing storefront space to retail toys to the public, only to have a vendor occupy space on the sidewalk in front of the merchant and sell the same toys. With lower overhead, the vendor charges less and makes a lot of sales. The merchant, who has higher overhead, earns less profit and eventually may be compelled to shut its doors. Such head-to-head competition between a merchant and an adjacent vendor seems unfair.

In fact, though, there is little head-to-head competition between vendors and storefront merchants. Sidewalk vendors avoid selling from places adjacent to merchants selling the same product or products. Instead, vendors set up in locations that are complementary to neighboring fixed business. Vendors try to be "good neighbors" to adjacent merchants. Illegal vendors across the street from MacArthur Park repeatedly denied being hassled by neighboring merchants. According to one vendor we spoke with, she had heard of only one problem between a merchant and a vendor. In that case, a CD vendor set up directly in front of a store selling CDs. The merchant asked the vendor to move on, and the vendor complied. A number of vendors sell products from the sidewalk in front of a casual dining restaurant across the street from MacArthur Park. One vendor there explained that the restaurant does not like vending of food from the sidewalk in front of it. On the days of our observation, the vendors largely appeared to respect the wishes of this restaurateur. While ten vendors had set up in front of the restaurant, none of them sold food. One food vendor did show up, but she was selling from a wheeled cart and lingered for less than five minutes before moving on. There were a number of other vendors of food on the street and they were stationary. But none of them was set up directly in front of the restaurant. And further, none of them, including the woman with the wheeled cart, sold the kind of food sold by the restaurant. The vendors sold a variety of fruit and foods from Latin America. The restaurant sold Japanese food.

The absence of head-to-head competition between merchants and adjacent vendors repeated itself up and down the street. Illegal vendors of fruit never sold in front of restaurants, though several lined the street. Some vendors sold jewelry, but not in front of a jewelry store on the block. Some vendors sold sunglasses, but nowhere on the block was there a store where sunglasses could be purchased. One vendor sold clothing, but not in front of an indoor swap-meet where clothing was sold.

Compared to storefront merchants, sidewalk vendors have a number of handicaps. Sidewalk vendors operate in an open access commons, or at least something that closely approximates it. Having no legal right to exclude others from the sidewalk, theory would predict that individual vendors would be disinclined to make some investments that could make the sidewalk, as a platform for selling goods and services, more productive. While sidewalk vendors often work from the same "spot" on a regular basis, they have no legal right to exclude anyone. And even if an individual vendor may have the power to exclude as a practical matter, this power disappears every night when even the most dedicated vendor must leave the street to rest and restock. This assumes, of course, that the state would bar attempts by vendors to install on the sidewalk permanent improvements. With such a disincentive to invest heavily, sidewalk vending enterprises should, it is predicted, find it difficult to compete with storefront merchants.

Practice supports this theory. One handicap of sidewalk vending relates to the security of vendors' inventory. Because they operate inside and on their own property, storefront merchants find it easier to secure their inventory against theft. Sidewalk vendors are more exposed. There is no secure place on the sidewalk to store inventory. Vendors must take unsold inventory back home or to some other secure location at the end of each day. This limits the variety of products sold. It also results in a higher risk of theft of inventory and business revenue.

Another disadvantage of vending relates to the offering of conveniences to customers. Storefront merchants can offer their customers all manner of amenities, such as shelter from the elements, fitting rooms, chairs, water fountains, bathrooms, and music. By contrast, sidewalk vendors and their customers are completely exposed to the weather. If one is buying a pair of pants from a sidewalk vendor, there is no discreet place there to try them on.

These unique disadvantages of sidewalk vending limit the size of sidewalk vending enterprises. They tend to be low-dollar-volume businesses, run by individuals and families. And perhaps vending represents a better way to market certain kinds of goods and services. In Mexico City, for example, some merchants have contracted with sidewalk vendors to help sell their goods on the streets (Kraul 1995).

### Sidewalk vending does not lead to a tragedy of the commons

Another principal objection raised against sidewalk vending is that it leads to over-use of the public space. Some claim that vending leads to an excessive amount of trash and litter being left on the sidewalk (Berestein *et al.* 1995; Romney 1999). Critics also contend that vendors and their customers block the public sidewalk, impeding the flow of pedestrian traffic (Lueck 2003; Moore 1999).

This argument has some theoretical support. In his influential article, "The Tragedy of the Commons," Garrett Hardin argued that resources owned in common are destined for overuse (Hardin 1968). Each user enjoys all of the benefit from her use of the common resource, but bears only part of the cost of her use, externalizing most of these costs on the other members of the community. Each user's rational pursuit of her own self-interest leads to an over-exploitation of the commonly owned resource, and the entire community suffers. In that lies the tragedy of the commons.

The sidewalk is like a commons. It is publicly owned, and open to all. Because they do not pay to use it, vendors have no reason to economize on their use of the sidewalk. Given the claims by some that vendors contribute greatly to the problem on litter and impede the flow of pedestrian traffic, sidewalk vending presents an opportunity to test the validity of Hardin's argument. Does sidewalk vending lead to more trash on the sidewalk? Do sidewalk vendors and their patrons interfere with the flow of pedestrian traffic? If the answer to either of these questions is yes, is there an acceptable way to regulate vending to address the problem and prevent a tragedy of the commons?

The argument that sidewalk vendors create special problems regarding trash and congestion is somewhat undercut by reality. Notwithstanding the fact that they operate on public property, many sidewalk vendors are con-scientious about not leaving trash where they vend. They are aware of complaints by neighbors about litter. Those with their own, regular spot are especially concerned about keeping the sidewalk clean (Berestein *et al.* 1995; L.A. Times 1999). One vendor we spoke with said that neighboring mer-chants did not complain about her presence because it is understood that as long as she cleans up after herself, she may continue to vend there. Vendor concern for litter extended even to places that did not belong to one vendor, but were instead shared by many vendors whose identities were in a constant state of flux. In order to maintain good relations with the neighboring merchant, one vendor we spoke with periodically hired individuals to clean the sidewalk. Vendors in another area took up a collection to clean up their trash (Rainey 1994).

Street observations of sidewalk vending and traffic flow are likewise encouraging. In my observation, vendors refrain from setting up so as to block movement up and down the sidewalk. Instead, they establish themselves on one side or the other. I never witnessed a vendor set up in front of an entrance to a storefront business. One would expect nothing else. A vendor blocking the sidewalk with her goods would run the risk of having them trampled under foot. Vendors have also demonstrated concern for traffic flow. When selling to patrons in cars at intersections, one illegal vendor refused to make sales when the light was green. "We have to obey the traffic laws, otherwise we can cause accidents" (Berestein *et al.* 1995).

## To ensure that vending continues to be socially beneficial, a continued threat of prosecution is not necessary

One might wonder whether the fact that vendors behave themselves is due to the fact that vending is a crime. One false step and a neighboring storefront merchant will call the police. Legalizing vending would eliminate this source of control, and leave vendors to run amok. Faced with the unfettered and unfair competition of sidewalk vendors, storefront merchants would be driven out of business. Vendors would feel no compunction against blocking pedestrian traffic, either with their goods or the trash they would leave on the sidewalk ankle-deep at the end of each workday. According to this argument, it is better to continue to prohibit vending and muddle through with reactive enforcement.

This is the wrong course to pursue. Broadly legalizing vendors will not give them an unfair advantage over storefront merchants. As a means of retailing goods and services, sidewalk vending suffers from a number of inherent limitations. These limitations put it at a competitive disadvantage with respect to storefront merchants. Because of this disadvantage, it cannot be said as a general matter that vendors' competition with storefront merchants is unfair. Rather, sidewalk vending and storefront merchandising should be viewed as two options among many for the delivery of goods and services, each with its own advantages and disadvantages.

The only impact the prohibition against vending has on competition is anti-competitive in nature. By forcing vendors to avoid head-to-head competition with neighboring merchants, the prohibition is giving storefront merchants an unfair advantage. This is hardly to the benefit of consumers or society as a whole.

Nor would broadly legalizing vending necessarily lead to excessive litter or sidewalk congestion. This is due to vendor self-interest and laws that apply to the public generally. Any residual problems uniquely attributable to sidewalk vending could be addressed by fairly modest measures.

Because vendor products may not be stored on the sidewalk overnight, vendors have incentives to minimize what they bring with them to vend. Many vendors of non-food products do not even provide their patrons with plastic or paper bags in which to carry away their purchases, so vendors create less garbage to dispose of than fixed businesses.

To the extent that there is a trash problem associated with sidewalk vendors of food, it is similar to the problem posed by restaurants that sell food "to go." Both sell food items in disposable containers, and raise a risk of improper disposal. The main difference is that sidewalk vendor patrons are more apt to carry away their purchases on foot, as opposed to in a car, and might be less inclined to hold on to their trash until they found a trash receptacle. The city might solve this problem by putting more public trash cans in public places where there are large numbers of food vendors. In addition, the city might require vendors to pick up trash within a certain distance of their vending spot. Existing common law of nuisance and local ordinances against litter may also encourage good behavior by vendors (Los Angeles 2004; California Supreme Court 1945).

One may protest that citing vendors who trash the sidewalk would be impractical. Their mobility makes it too difficult to identify the vendor responsible for a particular pile of trash. But this assumes that vendors are constantly on the move. Many are not. Vendors often try to sell in the same location on a regular basis (Berestein 1995; Beyette 1990; L.A. Times 1999; Malveaux 1995). They do this in order to build trust and a loyal clientele. Some have been quite successful in this way. By selling from the same street corner day after day, one Los Angeles vendor earned not only regular customers, but also regular suppliers. Merchants provided her with merchandise on credit, even though they did not know where she lived (Levine 1992). Because of this, it is not so difficult to identify who is trashing an area, and whom to cite for littering.

Broadly legalizing sidewalk vending will not necessarily lead to excessive sidewalk congestion, either. The only pedestrian traffic "problem" that sidewalk vendors pose is that in an area already busy with pedestrians, they can contribute to sidewalk congestion by luring additional pedestrians to the area and slowing down those already passing by. Who is harmed? The pedestrian in a hurry has a number of alternate routes, including across the street. The storefront merchant should enjoy having additional pedestrian traffic that vending may bring. If that traffic is slow-moving, all the better. This means more opportunity for a pedestrian to admire the window display, become curious, and wander inside.

Self-interest and law governing public order generally would also help avoid excessive use. If a vendor were foolish enough to block the flow of pedestrian traffic along the sidewalk or the entrance to a storefront merchant, they would suffer the risk having their goods damaged. The vendor could also be cited as a public nuisance.

*Sidewalk vending does not unreasonably facilitate the commission of crime*

Some complain that sidewalk vending facilitates the commission of crime. By operating in the open, so one argument goes, vendors and their patrons make themselves attractive targets for criminals (L.A. Times 1992; Sahagun 1992). But the risk of becoming a victim of street crime is greatest when street life is dead. In her landmark book *The Death and Life of Great American Cities*, Jane Jacobs argued that crime is deterred in places where there are small fixed businesses on the street (Jacobs 1963: 37). These watchful business owners are "eyes upon the street" (ibid.: 35). Allowing sidewalk vendors to operate would put additional eyes on the street, and thereby constitute a further deterrent to crime (Roumani 1999).

Some critics also claim that vendors themselves commit crimes. One type of crime that sidewalk vending allegedly facilitates is trafficking in stolen goods. The sales allegedly involve physical goods that have themselves been stolen, such as cellular phones and stereos (Beyette 1990; Cevallos 1998), and physical goods containing ideas copied in violation of intellectual property laws, such as pirated compact discs (CDs), digital video discs (DVDs), or VHS cassettes containing music or motion pictures (Gurza 1996; Portillo 2002). When I visited the MacArthur Park area, I observed vendors selling cell phones, stereos, CDs, and VHS cassettes. To my untrained eye, it was impossible to say whether any of these products I saw were stolen. Clearly some are not. An official with the City of Los Angeles told me about one vendor who was selling CDs on the sidewalk. When law enforcement approached the vendor, the vendor produced a purchase receipt that demonstrated that the CDs were legitimate. The vendor's only crime was selling on the sidewalk (Portillo 2002). One would imagine that many of the other goods sold by vendors are also legitimate. Enforcing a prohibition on sidewalk vending would prevent a number of otherwise desirable trades.

Critics also complain that vendors do not pay taxes (L.A. Times 1997; SourceMex 1998). According to one study, untaxed sales from corner street vendors in Los Angeles County amount to $250 million annually (Barrett 2002). Unpaid sales tax is not the only type of lost revenue. Unpaid taxes also include excise taxes on cigarettes, and income taxes. Sidewalk vendors tend to be paid in cash. Like any business that deals in cash, there is a temptation to avoid reporting all sales and income earned.

It does not follow, though, that vending should be flatly prohibited. Vending and taxes are not incompatible. The vendors operating in the legal vending district in MacArthur Park pay sales taxes and, presumably, income taxes based on their sales. Broadly legalizing sidewalk vending would be the first, and necessary, step toward increased tax compliance among vendors. Increased compliance might follow from bringing sidewalk vendors in from the cold (Sanchez 1987).

The argument that sidewalk vending should be prohibited because it facilitates the commission of crime is also questionable because it proves too much. When it comes to trafficking in stolen goods, sidewalk vendors hardly have a monopoly. Storefront merchants have also been known to traffic in stolen goods, as a recent spate of newspaper articles reporting sales of pirated music and untaxed cigarettes attests (Conniff 2003; Holloway 2002; Strauss 2002). Businesses in the MacArthur Park area are no different. There I saw one indoor retailer offering video cassettes of well-known feature films whose less than precise packaging and low prices suggested to me that they were pirated.

Similarly, sidewalk vendors are not the only people who are tempted to evade taxes. Other individuals, particularly those who are self-employed service providers, face a similar challenge. Food servers earn a substantial amount of their income in the form of cash tips. The Internal Revenue Service has for years struggled to find a reliable way to ensure this income is reported (Prewitt 2002). This is not all. Consider the tip income earned by taxi drivers, hairdressers, manicurists, and bell hops. Consider also the income earned by individuals and business enterprises that provide services and demand to be paid in cash, or offer a substantial discount for cash. Day laborers, maids, nannies, strippers, and landlords have been known to accept payment in cash and underreport their income at tax time (King 2003). If the government were to outlaw any activity that carried with it a heightened risk of tax evasion, any increase in tax revenue collections would be more than offset by the allocative costs of so many missed opportunities for gains from trade.

Prohibiting sidewalk vending cannot be justified by arguing that it facilitates crime. Too much sidewalk vending is otherwise free of crime, and storefront businesses and others cause too much of the crime complained of.

### Sidewalk vending poses no insurmountable risk to consumers

One other criticism that is periodically raised against sidewalk vending is that it poses risks to consumers. Typically the complaint relates to the vending of food, which critics claim is contaminated and dangerous (Alvarez 1994; Krikorian 1996). While there is some merit to this complaint, it cannot justify a prohibition of sidewalk vending of food, much less a prohibition of sidewalk vending generally.

A common justification for government intervention in markets for consumer goods, be they automobiles, credit, or prescription drugs, is the inability of a typical consumer to judge the safety of the product being purchased. The same can be said about food. Mishandled food is dangerous and can carry disease. Each year preventable food-borne diseases kill thousands of people (Becker 2003). It is also difficult for a consumer to tell if food she is considering buying has been mishandled. Food-borne illnesses may take some time to manifest themselves, making it difficult for the consumer to identify the tainted source. Food sold from the sidewalk carries heightened risks. There is no running water on the street, and thus vendors have no convenient place to wash hands or utensils. Sidewalk vendors lack access to electric refrigeration.

Some of the street food in the MacArthur Park area in particular has been shown to be dangerous. An outbreak of hepatitis was blamed on sidewalk vending: utensils used to prepare food sold by vendors were cleaned with a garden hose that lay on the ground in a backyard where dogs were kept (Portillo 2002). Instead of using ice made from potable water, vendors of shaved ice in Los Angeles have been known to use cheaper industrial ice (ibid.).

The complaint that sidewalk vendors sell dangerous food to their customers invites a number of responses. One is caveat emptor. Anyone who buys food on the street knows they are taking a chance. Further, some of the market imperfections – such as lack of competition and unequal bargaining power – that are used to justify government intervention in other consumer contexts are absent from the retail sale of food. There is plenty of competition for the provision of prepared food, both on and adjacent to the sidewalk. The relative bargaining power between retail food suppliers and consumers is equal, or at least not dramatically unequal.

Just because consumers face special risks in buying food on the street, however, it does not follow that sidewalk vending generally, or even sidewalk vending of food, should be prohibited. The sidewalk is hardly the only place where one can buy dangerous food. It may also be found in homes and restaurants. In her ten-year study of street food in developing countries, Irene Tinker concludes that "food handling practices of vendors generally reflect prevailing local standards and food sold on the street is not significantly more contaminated than that sold in restaurants" (Tinker 1997: 189). In the United States, most people who eat at restaurants on a regular basis have at one time or another suffered from a mild case of food poisoning. In a well-publicized incident, four children from the Seattle, Washington area died after eating contaminated hamburgers sold at a Jack-In-The-Box restaurant (Becker 2003). These incidents are usually greeted not with calls for new legislation, but rather for more enforcement of existing consumer protection laws governing the sale of food.

All California food providers must obtain a permit, issued only after the provider demonstrates that it will comply with the California Uniform Retail Food Facilities Law (the "Retail Food Law") (California 1996: 113920). Providers are subject to inspection. Those found in violation of any provision of the Retail Food Law may have their food seized, and be fined and imprisoned, for violating its requirements (ibid.: 113925). As retail food providers, sidewalk vendors who sell food are covered by the Retail Food Law and bound by its provisions. Vendors are periodically cited for non-compliance (Glover 1993; L.A. Times 1996). If there is a concern with dangerous food being sold on the streets, a better response may be just to increase enforcement of the Retail Food Law.

Street food does not have to be dangerous. One reason many vendors avoid paying taxes and obtaining health permits is because they are still subject to fines and arrest by the police. Vending advocates claim that legalizing sidewalk vending would give food vendors more reason to find ways to comply with the Retail Food Law (Schwada 1993).

There is some evidence that increased compliance can be obtained and street food made safe. The IURD has ensured that food vendors in the legal vending district in MacArthur Park sell safe food. The food is prepared, handled, and stored in compliance with the Retail Food Law. It is clearly possible to sell safe food on the sidewalk. The only question is cost. The IURD spent a substantial sum of money managing the vending district, and it is not clear how much of this was devoted to compliance with the Retail Food Law, and whether compliance could have been obtained with less money.

A complete ban on sidewalk vending of food is not appropriate. And even if it were, problems with food vending could not be used to justify a prohibition of sidewalk vending of non-food items.

## Cultural opposition to sidewalk vending is insufficient to overcome its benefits

All of the foregoing complaints about sidewalk vending relate to traditional concerns of public policy that are familiar and often debated in transparent terms. By contrast, the remaining complaint I wish to discuss revolves around culture. Though rarely expressed directly, many opponents of sidewalk vending reject the practice because it signifies the rise of a foreign culture that threatens the status of their own. Even this concern, though, is overstated.

The people who complain about sidewalk vendors in Los Angeles often speak in terms of money and public health and safety. But another concern, often not clearly expressed, is a loss of status of storefront merchants and their patrons. One might be tempted to view the controversy surrounding sidewalk vending as simple racism. Los Angeles has a long history of white discrimination against Latinos, which some commentators today contend is perpetuated through institutions that appear on the surface to be non-discriminatory (Haney Lopez 2000). But as many of the storefront merchants and patrons are themselves Latinos with deep, multi-generational roots in Los Angeles, the controversy is better characterized as a cultural one that, at its most extreme, assumes the shape of xenophobia. As the *Los Angeles Times* observed, "tackling the issue of street vending means reconciling a confusion of competing values" (Rainey 1994). Neighboring Long Beach, California has had similar experience with street vendors. After police responded to some complaints about vendors, one officer said, "there is that cultural clash" (Cox 1996). Street vending is common in most Latin American countries, but "here we're not used to people vending like that. We're used to going to a store." A Los Angeles resident put it this way: "It's like a Third

World country" (Rainey 1994). Another complained, "But when you look out your window and see someone from who-knows-where coming to sell their wares, I think it is awful" (ibid.). One Los Angeles Police Officer working in the East San Fernando area of Los Angeles reported that he hears "citizens complaining all the time about the vendors making the area like Tijuana" (Schwada 1990).

These encounters between sidewalk vendors and individuals offended by the practice are less frequent than one might suppose. Vendors tend to locate in places where potential customers have a practice of buying from vendors, and selling the products they want. They operate primarily in neighborhoods populated with Latin American immigrants and other Latinos (Levine 1992; Rodriguez 1995; Sanchez 1987). In neighboring Long Beach, California, vendors regularly operated in a neighborhood with a large Latino population. Then redevelopment replaced renters in apartment buildings with middle-class property owners in condominiums. With the change in neighborhood demographics came more complaints about street vendors. When the police responded by cracking down on illegal vendors, the vendors moved to "a more predominantly Latino area" (Cox 1996). "What's interesting," one Long Beach police officer explained, "is that we get very few complaints about vendors in that neighborhood" (ibid.). Similarly, vending is an everyday occurrence in the MacArthur Park area of Los Angeles. The zip code in which the park is situated is home to around 57,000 people, of which nearly 70 percent are Latino or Hispanic (US Census 2000). This part of the city has been called "the heart of the Central American immigrant community" (Beyette 1990). The police receive few complaints because vendors know where they are welcome.

Examining the cultural concerns behind opposition to sidewalk vending also sheds light on the function of the reform legislation that resulted in the creation of the sidewalk vending district in MacArthur Park. Neighbors unaccustomed to vending are not the only ones with a cultural stake in the legality of vending. The vendors and their patrons also hold a stake. For those who vend, becoming legal is a matter of pride. Said one vendor, "the police can still pick us up and move us, just like bits of trash" (Berestein 1995). According to one vending group leader, "it's a question of dignity" (ibid.). The legislation may be seen as a cultural compromise. By continuing the broad prohibition on sidewalk vending and allowing it to take place only in districts approved by local storefront merchants, the city accorded respect or esteem to those who operate storefront businesses and their patrons. On the other hand, by creating a process by which legal vending districts may be established if neighbors approve, the city likewise accorded dignity to the vendors. Through this legislation, the city told the vendors and their patrons that their way of buying and selling is appropriate, at least in the abstract, and may be practiced in certain circumstances. The vending legislation is less about resolving traditional concerns of public policy than it is about placating interest groups whose sense of cultural worth is threatened.

The only significant bar to broadly legalizing sidewalk vending would appear to be an opposition based on culture: That is not how trade is supposed to be conducted in our society. This argument clearly has appeal to a number of people. But given the benefits and low costs of vending, this objection can and should be overcome.

## Conclusion

Sidewalk vending is an issue that is not going to go away. The experience with vending in Los Angeles, California bears a number of lessons for other communities that have become the site of nascent vending activities. Flatly prohibiting all sidewalk vending failed to stop it because the city by and large (and correctly) did not aggressively and pro-actively enforce the law. Instead Los Angeles enacted reform legislation. It created a process for the creation of legal vending zones. The reform legislation failed to move many illegal vendors into newly minted legal vending zones. Instead, by giving neighboring storefront merchants the power to veto the creation of any legal vending districts (where competing businesses might operate), the reform legislation all but assured that few zones would be created. Further, the regulatory burdens imposed by the legislation on vendors are so burdensome that only the most profitable vendors and those with other means of supporting themselves could afford to participate. This was so even though the costs of running the MacArthur Park district were heavily subsidized. During its short operational life, the legislation helped make a single neighborhood more attractive. But even the city and state came to recognize that these benefits were far outweighed by the costs and withdrew funding for continued management. What was seen by savvy observers from the outset has at last become clear to all: the reform legislation is a failure. Illegal vending continues to thrive.

The objection to vending is not based on the merits. It offers society a number of benefits. The alleged costs of sidewalk vending are either exaggerated or can be alleviated by the judicious use of modest legal tools that apply to public conduct generally. The practice of sidewalk vending should be broadly legalized.

Objections to vending are based ultimately on a fear of a foreign culture. For many in Los Angeles, the sight of a vendor is a sign that their culture is devalued and at risk of being replaced by another. Of course, vendors feel a cultural stake in sidewalk vending, too. The fact that it is illegal sends a message to vendors that their culture is not respected here. The changing legal status of vending in Los Angeles can be seen as less a battle over public policy than a process of cultural compromise. The flat prohibition against vending endured for decades as long as the supporters of vending were few in number and politically weak. Decades of immigration from countries where vending is tolerated has changed the power relationship. So much vending took place in defiance of the law that its legitimacy was brought into question. The reform ordinance that legalized vending under certain conditions was perhaps an attempt by the city to accord respect to the culture of which sidewalk vending is a part, without diminishing the respect accorded to those who continue to oppose the practice. The ordinance, however, makes it so difficult to set up legal vending districts, and even harder to maintain them, that even in this sense the ordinance failed to accord much respect to those vendors outside the legal district. The continued existence of the prohibition as reactively enforced black-letter law is less about preventing vending as it is about according esteem to storefront merchants and the culture they represent.

Perhaps sidewalk vending will, over time, reflect the fortunes of salsa. Once it was an exotic condiment rarely consumed by Americans. Today it is a staple familiar and welcome at tables all across the country (Huntington 2004). Who would want to exclude it?

## Note

1   This chapter appears by permission of *Temple Law Review*, which published an earlier version as an article entitled "Regulating Vending in the Sidewalk Commons," at volume 77, copyright 2004 Temple University of the Commonwealth System of Higher Education. I am indebted to a number of entities and individuals who helped me write this book chapter. The Mississippi College School of Law supported the chapter through a summer research grant. A number of individuals generously shared their time and knowledge about sidewalk vending with me. Those individuals include Alexander Bautista, Carolyn Brownwell, Maggie Calderon, Joseph Colletti, Grace Roberts Dyrness, Sandra Plasencia, Samuel Portillo, Dina Serrano, and Angie De La Trinidad. I am also grateful to twenty-one anonymous sidewalk vendors on the east side of Alvarado Street between Sixth and Seventh Streets in Los Angeles, California. Despite their legal vulnerability, they overcame their suspicion and shared their time and their knowledge of vending with me. John Cross, Alfonso Morales, Kathleen Staudt, and one anonymous reader gave me helpful comments on earlier drafts. James and Claudia Spotts graciously let my family and me stay at their Los Angeles area home to enable my wife and me to perform street-level research there. While my wife and I pounded the pavement, Jim and Maxine Cain watched our children. Most of all, I thank my wife, Lorena Manriquez, who helped conceive of, conduct, and interpret interviews with Spanish-speaking vendors. Errors in pulling all of this together in this chapter are mine alone.

## Bibliography

Alvarez, F. (1994) 'City Council Asked to Ban Street Vendors,' *L.A. Times, Ventura West Edition*, 7 March, Metro, at B1.

Barrett, B. (2002) 'Los Angeles County, Calif. Cash Economy Threatens Wages,' *Los Angeles Daily News*, 6 May.

Becker, E. (2003) 'Salmonella Survivor Endorses Push for Food Safety Agency,' *N.Y. Times*, 12 February, at A22.

Becker, M. (1995) 'Street Vendors Appear to be Sold on Budding Designers' Change of Cart; Students Develop Prototypes to Meet New Standards for MacArthur Park Peddlers,' *L.A. Times, Home Edition*, 10 November, at B4.

Berestein, L. (1995) 'For Vendors, the Wheels Turn Slowly,' *L.A. Times, Home Edition*, 15 January, City Times, at 12.

Berestein, L., Munoz, L., Maher, A., and Steinberg, S. (1995) 'Wheeling and Dealing; Street Vendors Risk Citations and the Ire of Other Merchants as They Try to Eke Out a Living,' *L.A. Times, Home Edition*, 2 February, at J12.

Beyette, B. (1990) 'Vendors vs. the Law – Unlicensed Street Merchants: Able Entrepreneurs or Nuisances?' *L.A. Times, Home Edition*, 27 June, at E1.

Bluestone, D.M. (1991) '"The Pushcart Evil:" Peddlers, Merchants, and New York City's Streets, 1890–1940,' *Journal of Urban History*, 18(1): 68–92.

California (1996) Health and Safety Code §§ 113920, 113925.

California Supreme Court (1945) 'Laurenzi v. Vranizan, 25 Cal. 2d 806, 809–10 (1945),' *California Supreme Court Reports 2d*, 25: 806, 809–10.

Cevallos, D. (1998) 'Labor-Mexico: Governor Declares War on Street Vendor Networks,' *Inter Press Service*, 10 June.

Chu, H. (1995) 'Alarcon Rejects Bid for Sidewalk Vending Zone; Pacoima: Councilman Says Request from Vendors for District Along Van Nuys Boulevard Fails to Generate Enough Support,' *L.A. Times, Valley Edition*, 21 April, at B6.

Colletti, J. (2002) Interview by author of Joseph Colletti, Executive Director, The Institute for Urban Research and Development. Los Angeles, California, 16 July.

Conniff, T. (2003) 'Eighteen Retailers Hit With RIAA Suits,' *The Hollywood Rep.* (California), 17 June. Available at *2003 WL 57153544.*

Cox, J. (1996) 'Street Vendors: A Hard Sell in Long Beach,' *L.A. Times, Home Edition*, 3 May, at B2.

Cross, J.C. (1998) *Informal Politics: Street Vendors and the State in Mexico City.* Stanford, CA: Stanford University Press.

De Soto, H. (1989) *The Other Path: The Invisible Revolution in the Third World* (June Abbot trans.), New York: Harper & Row.

Glover, K. (1993) 'L.A. Officials Ponder Creation of Street Vending Zones: Measure Before L.A. City Council Seeks To License Sellers,' *L.A. Business J.*, 19 July, at 25.

Gurza, A. (1996) 'Mexico City Tries To Control Vendors,' *Orange County Reg.* (California), 8 July, at A1. Orange County, California.

Hallinan, K. (1999) 'Sidewalk to Prosperity? Vendors are Taking Their Place in MacArthur Park,' *The San Diego Union-Tribune*, 21 July, Business, at C1.

Haney Lopez, I.F. (2000) 'Institutional Racism: Judicial Conduct and a New Theory of Racial Discrimination,' *Yale Law Journal*, 109: 1717–1884.

Hardin, G. (1968) 'The Tragedy of the Commons,' *Science*, 162: 1243, 1244–45.

Holloway, L. (2002) 'Arrests Illustrate a Growing Concern Over Bootlegged Recordings,' *N.Y. Times*, 2 December, at C10.

Huntington, S.J. (2004) 'A Brief History of Hot Stuff!' *Christian Science Monitor*, 3 February, The Home Forum, at 18.

Jacobs, J. (1963) *The Death and Life of Great American Cities*, New York: Vintage Books.

King, D. (2003) 'Artful Dodgers: From Inner City to Suburbs, Dealing in Cash is King,' *L.A. Business Journal*, 15 December, at 18.

Kraul, C. (1995) 'Mexico's Vending Machine: Nation's Recession Bringing Swarm of Street Hucksters,' *L.A. Times, Home Edition*, 22 December, at 1.

Krikorian, M. (1996) 'Street Sellers Push for Vending District in Boyle Heights,' *L. A. Times, Home Edition*, 23 August, at B5.

La Nacion (2003) 'Crece el Enfrentamiento por la Venta Ilegal en la Calle Florida,' *La Nacion*, 7 January, at 15. Buenos Aires, Argentina.

L.A. Times (1991) 'California's Quiet Revolution: Latinos and Asians Are Increasingly Making Their Presence Felt,' *L.A. Times, Home Edition*, 27 February, Part B, at 6.

——(1992) 'Plan to Legalize Street Vending Comes Under Fire,' *L.A. Times, Home Edition*, 14 January, Metro, Part B, at 2.

——(1996) '34 Van Nuys-Area Street Vendors Cited,' *L.A. Times, Valley Edition*, 31 March, at B3.

——(1997) 'Can Mexico Clean Up War of the Sidewalks?' *L.A. Times, Home Edition*, 22 December , at 1.

——(1999) 'Family Album Deck: Daniel and Reynalda Cruz,' *L.A. Times*, 21 March, at 1.

Larson, J.E. (2002) 'Informality, Illegality, and Inequality,' *Yale Law & Policy Review*, 20: 137–82.

Levine, B. (1992) 'Of Carts and Corners: "Trying to Earn an Honest Living",' *L.A. Times, Home Edition*, 26 January, View, at E1.

Los Angeles (2004) *Municipal Code §§ 42, 64.70.02C.7(a)*, Los Angeles, CA.

Lueck, T.J. (2003) 'Times Sq. Gridlock ... on Sidewalk: Lapse in Law Puts Hawkers in Way and Pedestrians in a Jam,' *N.Y. Times*, 2 December, B, at 1.

Malveaux, J. (1995) 'Street Vendors' Lament,' *The San Francisco Examiner*, 4 June, at B2.

May, T. (1995) "Street Vendors Caught in Catch-22; The City's First Group of Trainees Remains Subject to Fines Until Legal Selling Districts are Established." *L.A. Times, Valley Edition*, 31 March, at B1.

McMahan, C. (1995) 'El Salvador Eager to Blaze Free Market Trail,' *Chicago Tribune, Chicagoland Final Edition*, 4 June, Business, at C4.

McMillan, P. (1988) 'Street Vendors – In Between a Rock and a Hard Place,' *L.A. Times, Home Edition*, 23 December, Metro, 2, at 1.

Miles, J. (1992) 'Blacks vs. Browns: African-Americans and Latinos,' *The Atlantic*, October, at 41.

Moffat, S. (1991) 'Vendors Bring New Way of Life to Los Angeles,' *L.A. Times, Home Edition*, 25 December, Part A, at 1.

Moore, G. (1999) 'Street Vendors Lose Prime Spots,' *Charleston Gazette* (West Virginia), 7 October, at P1A. Charleston, West Virginia.

Morales, A. (2000) 'Peddling Policy: Street Vending in Historical and Contemporary Context,' *International Journal of Sociology and Social Policy*, 20(3): 76–98.

Plascencia, S.R. (2006) Interview by author of Sandra Romero Plascencia, Program Director, Institute for Urban Research and Development. Los Angeles, California, March.

Portillo, S. (2002) Interview by author of Samuel Portillo, Senior Building Mechanical Inspector, Pro-Active Code Enforcement ("PACE"), City of Los Angeles Department of Building and Safety. Los Angeles, California, 24 July.

Prewitt, M. (2002) 'Tip-Income Reporting To IRS On "TRAC," But Audit Fears Fuel Operators' Diligence,' *Nation's Restaurant News*, 16 December, at 34.

Rainey, J. (1994) 'Vendors Cheer as Legalization Wins Final OK,' *L.A. Times, Record Edition*, 5 January, at A1.

Richmond, P. (1975) '*Organizing Strangers: Poor Families in Guatemala City* by Bryan R. Roberts' (book review). *Contemporary Sociology*, 4: 520–21.

Rodriguez, J. (1995) 'Street Vending Law Has Been Rendered Ineffective by Strife, Organizer Says,' *L.A. Times, Home Edition*, 26 February, at 19.

Romney, L. (1999) 'Group of Street Vendors Licensed in Test of Reform,' *L.A. Times, Home Edition*, 7 May, at C1.

Roumani, R. (1999) 'Hernandez Announces Launching of City's First Sidewalk Vending District,' *Metropolitan News Enterprise* (Los Angeles), 4 June, at 11. Los Angeles, California.

Sahagun, L. (1992) 'Council OK's Districts for Street Vendors,' *L.A. Times, Home Edition*, 15 January, at A1.

Sanchez, R.L. (1987) 'Street Vendors Pay High Price for Unlicensed Trade in L.A.,' *L.A. Times, Home Edition*, 26 October, Metro, 2, at 1.

Schwada, J. (1990) 'Compromise to Legalize Street Vending Drafted,' *L.A. Times, Home Edition*, 30 September, at B3.

SourceMex (1998) 'Studies Cite Explosive Growth in Informal Economy in Mexico City,' *SourceMex: Economic News and Analysis on Mexico*, 18 March, Socio-economic Issues. Available at *1998 WL 8779041.*

Strauss, J. (2002) 'Agents Go After Cigarette Sellers Who Won't Cough Up Tax,' *The Indianapolis Star*, 23 October, at 1B.

Tinker, I. (1997) *Street Foods: Urban Food and Employment in Developing Countries.*

United States Census (2000) Data for zip code 90057.

# 5   Street vendors at the border

## From political spectacle to bureaucratic iron cage?

*Kathleen Staudt*

In 1992, media coverage in two large cities on both sides of the El Paso–Ciudad Juárez border dramatized street vendors into sustained front-page news over an extended time period. Normally, vendors are rendered invisible in public affairs communication, at least in El Paso. However, during this period the critics of street vendors on both sides of the border used amazingly similar rhetorical embellishments, whether in the Spanish language or in the English language, to call for the control or abolition of street vendors: congestion, disease, unfair competition, crime, invasion, filth, and overall threat to established, formal businesses.

The Mexico- and US-based street vendors worked within miles, even a few blocks, of one another, but in two very different political systems, with two versions of democracy. Border space was also a site for interactions, as advocates and critics evoked images of *el otro lado* (the other side). In one political system, a democratic process marginalized street vendors and drastically increased their costs of doing business. In the other political system, a veritable standoff occurred, as street vendors used their "weapons of the weak," as James Scott (1985, 1990) would call their tried and tested tactics to pursue income-generating work on public streets. Mexico's street vendors' sheer numbers and connections to organizations and/or political parties call into question their characterization as weak (also see Cross 1998).

This chapter tells the story of street vendor conflicts across two points in time. The first time period is the early 1990s, as conflicts erupted in what was still a relatively open border region, with high-volume international port-of-entry borders under some (yet relaxed) control with border crossing cards. International crossings have a long history of waxing and waning controls (see Romo 2005). The second time period is the current era, after North American trade agreements, the US Border Patrol's Operation Hold the Line, US immigration reforms, and heightened US security concerns, especially after 9/11.

Street vendors have long been visible at the US–Mexico border, especially at the largest metropolitan area along the 2,000-mile border, El Paso and Ciudad Juárez. This trans-border metropolitan area is home to more than two million people, two-thirds of whom live in Cd. Juárez. After the decade of struggle over downtown urban space, the major political stakeholders transformed the political drama of the early 1990s into partially regulated and controlled urban space, especially on the US side of the border. On the Mexico side, street vendors continue to have high-visibility presence.

On both sides of the border, the stakeholders in these struggles are multiple: street vendors; established formal businesses (many of them store owners, herein called "merchants"); local government administrators; and politicians. On the US side of the border, another key stakeholder involved business concessionaire companies with informal contractual links to some of the vendors. Concessionaire companies produce fast food and sell packaged food, from hot, juicy turkey legs and fried cakes (like donuts) to popsicles and ice cream, from musical vans that circulate in neighborhoods. Concessionaires, one could argue, not only provide opportunities to con-tracted day labor (vendors) but also exploit those day laborers economically, with paltry day and sales commission rates. In the process to forge a democratically derived solution to tensions around street vendors, these English-speaking concessionaire owners represented the vendors as their spokespersons.

The chapter is divided into "then" and "now," covering nearly fifteen years of both tension and cooperation among the major stakeholders on both sides of the border. Conceptually, the chapter draws inspiration from some classic theorists whose concise descriptors live on in ways that inspire insights about struggles over urban space. (For theoretical analyses of space, see conceptual sections in Staudt 1998, Chapters 1–2.)

## Theoretical inspirations

The US–Mexico border is a frontline crossroads for globalization. At the border, using a Gramscian approach, the hegemony that celebrates and subsidizes global transnational capital seems to reign supreme. Both Mexican and US federal, state, and local governments facilitate and subsidize capital investment. Historic US tariffs were reduced, in the mid 1960s, to foster growth in the foreign-owned export-processing maquiladora industry in northern Mexico, and then reduced even more with global and North American free-trade agreements in the 1980s and 1990s.

However, counter-hegemonic processes also operate, including informal economic workers and many street vendors within that category. Informal workers resist formal rules and/or use strategies to get around such rules. A study of informal economies at the border looks at these quintessential "free traders" in the NAFTA/North American Free Trade Agreement era (Staudt 1998).

Street vendors use public space for commerce and trade. The costs of doing business are minimal, unless their goods are confiscated and/or fines are high. The credentials for the work are minimal, requiring people skills and math among other talents. Many people can do this sort of income-generating work without degrees and access to large amounts of capital. However, street vendors face much competition, both with other street vendors and with established merchants who own and rent nearby property and face higher business costs, such as utilities and various taxes. Local governments impose regulations to mediate conflict and competition and to extract revenue from licenses and fees.

Street vendors and other informal workers are necessarily free agents. Wages may be paid "off the books" without Social Security benefits paid. Their earnings may be seasonal and less than the minimum wage (see the discussion of agricultural laborers in Staudt and Capps 2004). As this study suggests, some vendors are connected through patron–client relationships to concessionaire companies.

Rather than drawing on globalization theory, this chapter draws inspiration from classic theorists in the social sciences for how they inform struggles among street vendors, merchants, and the state at the globalized border. Street vendor conflicts and their outcomes symbolize a changing economic order, one that privileges regulation and capital. Stakeholders utilize opposing language and graphic images to make their political cases for policies and regulations to benefit themselves. Murray Edelman has contributed much to the analysis of political symbols, rhetoric, and drama; and when he discussed how political decisions perpetuated "problems through policies to ameliorate them" in *Constructing the Political Spectacle* (1988: 25), he could have been talking about street vendor conflicts at the border. Thus, his title inspires mine.

Sociologist Max Weber had much to say about modern bureaucracy. One of his many compelling phrases involves the "iron cage" in which rules and procedures can place stakeholders. Street vendors, especially in El Paso, found themselves in a bureaucratic iron cage, after a US-style democratic process produced regulations to legalize, beautify (through conformity), sanitize, license, tax, and insure their selling operations. While some of these goals may be reasonable, they had serious consequences: a huge increase in the cost of doing business in order to generate enough revenue to cover partial enforcement costs and to reduce competition with established businesses. Many organizational theorists have developed the way in which "goal displacement" occurs in public agencies: public goals are displaced with bureaucratic goals and procedures, all of which consume considerable public resources. Street vendor regulations, discussed later, offer good examples of goal displacement.

Yet street vendors also illuminate what political anthropologist Scott analyzes as the artful craft of domination and subordination (1990). Although many lack formal political clout and resources, street vendors exercise power and control over urban space. Their numbers alone make government regulation costly and inefficient. The speed with which some can relocate as mobile or semi-fixed location vendors adds complexity to enforcement.

Scott's concept of "hidden transcripts" also illustrates the large hegemonic practices wherein capital and state displace and transform street vendors, as shown for the El Paso side of this struggle.

Ironically, more than a decade after the original research, the street-vendor–merchant conflicts in Cd. Juárez are similar, while in El Paso, a new, publicly subsidized $750,000 downtown development plan released in 2006 will propel El Paso's downtown in the twenty-first century with a Mexico-style *mercado* with fixed-locale vendors who rent space on property whose values will, as the public–private partners hope, skyrocket (Negron 2006). In the strategy, the developers will perhaps destroy what once was "real": free public vending sites and the individual street vendors, who will be regulated and finally displaced.

## The border context

El Paso, Texas, and much of the southwest, was once part of northern Mexico. Mexico lost almost half of its land to the United States, and through the Treaty of Guadalupe Hidalgo in 1848, an international boundary line was drawn along the Rio Grande (known as the Río Bravo in Mexico), at least for a thousand miles of the two-thousand mile border between the United States and Mexico.

Today, El Paso, Texas, and Ciudad Juárez, Chihuahua, form a large metro-politan area of more than two million people, divided by an international border (see Figure 5.1). El Paso, with approximately 700,000 people, is the twenty-first largest city in the US, while Juárez, at over 1.5 million people, is Mexico's fifth largest city. In El Paso, Spanish-speaking people of Mexican heritage have long made up the vast majority of the population. The 2000 Census reported that the Hispanic population totaled 78 percent of residents.

Space in downtown El Paso is used for productive purposes and for leisure. The San Jacinto Plaza is a full square block that often bustles with people, sitting on benches, getting on and off buses, or strolling near the alligator fountain (once filled with real animals, now a statue). A site for immigration rallies in March and April 2006, human rights activists have more informally renamed it the Plaza de los Lagartos, reclaiming its name from official Texas history. In this downtown plaza, El Paso's city center reflects many downtowns in Latin American cities, including Cd. Juárez in Mexico.

El Paso's high-rise buildings consist of banks, government buildings, and hotels. The low-rise buildings are occupied with small businesses (on several streets of approximately six blocks from San Antonio Street to the inter-national border). Elsewhere, the low-rise buildings consist of restaurants and law offices. The small businesses near the border cater to pedestrian traffic, largely Mexican consumers. At the downtown bridge, one of several international bridges to cross the border, almost five million pedestrians crossed northward in 1992, according to figures from city planning (vehicle

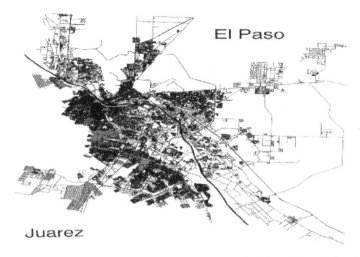

El Paso

Juarez

*Figure 5.1* "The Plan for El Paso" (El Paso: City Plan Commission 1998, in Staudt 1998: 14).

traffic produces larger numbers of crossers, but is spread across multiple international bridges). (For documentation on the 1990s figures, see Staudt 1996 and 1998.) Many pedestrians cross multiple times, for local border passports allow visits for up to 72 hours for shopping and visiting. The language of business is Spanish and Mexican music blares from some businesses.

For established businesses, property tax is high. Texas has no state income tax, so government revenue is generated primarily through property and sales taxes, burdening the "property-poor" geography in the state with respect to educational, social, and public services. Background papers for and presentations at El Paso's Education Summit in 2000 cited its property-poor status: 17th largest US city population size (at the time), but the 157th largest tax base (EPCAE 2000; also see Brenner *et al.* 2003).

Downtown merchants have their own organizations, and many are also affiliated with one of several Chambers of Commerce: the Greater Chamber, the Hispanic Chamber, the Black Chamber, and the Korean Chamber. More recently, the Regional Economic Development Corporation (REDCO) emerged as an offshoot of the Greater Chamber of Commerce, as has the Paso del Norte Group, high-power large investors, businesses, and corporations focusing on a new downtown development plan.

In Mexico, academic and official reports had long documented the extensive size of the informal economy, a common way for people in many "developing" countries to generate income for themselves. Workforce and other surveys query whether people worked in the week prior to the survey, and between a quarter to a third of people report work that Mexico defines as "informal": micro-businesses and income generation without contribution to Mexico's health and pension system, IMSS (Instituto Mexicano de

Seguridad Social). Street vendors occupy spaces in many mobile, semi-fixed, and fixed locations: downtown, the international bridges, busy streets, cemeteries, and public market places, among others. Some vendors became part of municipal government relocation plans, but others remain in what they see as the more profitable downtown streets and near international bridge ports of entry.

The United States prides itself as a "developed," modern economy. The Internal Revenue Service queries potential taxpayers about "self-employment," but relatively small segments of taxpayers report it as their primary occupation. In El Paso, the 1990 figure was just 6 percent. Generally, "informal" economic activity is not part of US official discourse, except for discussions of "tax evasion" and "crime."

A comprehensive study of informal economies at the US–Mexico border (Staudt 1998) found that one in three households that were surveyed generated income on both sides of the border in Cd. Juárez and El Paso. However, in Cd. Juárez, informal worker respondents reported that they earned approximately three times the legal minimum wage (and more than wages in the mostly US-owned export-processing factories, *maquiladoras*). Women informal workers, about two-fifths of the total, earned less than men, however, for there is gender-differentiated value associated with their particular tasks, services, and products. The 1990s research was completed before NAFTA went into effect in 1994; the post-NAFTA border world is far more complex, requiring accountants and lawyers to decipher the rules of "free trade" regimes. That research drew on various samples, from households to interviews with officials and targeted surveys with street vendors. The newspaper clipping file numbered over a hundred articles on street vending.

This chapter reports on the dramatic political spectacle that sharpened and defined the contrasting stakeholders' approaches to street vending in El Paso and Cd. Juárez. In addition, it highlights some of the findings from the street vendor samples, official interviews, participant observation (see Staudt 1996, 1998 for extensive details on multiple methodologies), and update interviews.

## Then: Political spectacles on both sides of the border

In the early 1990s, a proliferation of street vendors occupied space in El Paso's downtown. The year of the political spectacle, 1992, was one year before the Border Patrol's blockade of the international border (renamed Operation Hold the Line) and two years before both NAFTA and the dramatic devaluation of the Mexico peso relative to the US dollar.

### The Cd. Juárez spectacle spills over to El Paso

Juárez had just elected its new Municipal President (Mayor) to his three-year, no re-election position. In Mexico, each new election brings wholesale changes in the cast of characters, from elected to appointed positions in public administration. In the US, civil service systems maintain considerable continuity in the bureaucracy even as politicians change.

The competitive newspaper media in Cd. Juárez provided extensive, high-visibility coverage in articles on the struggles between established merchants and street vendors. Many street vendors are organized, sometimes affiliated with political parties, and their leaders mediate relations between vendors and municipal government (see Cross 1998 on informal politics of street vendor organizations in Mexico City). There is no credible list of street vendors, licensed or unlicensed, and their numbers change with the seasons and days of the week. In an internal review of street vendors, the Cd. Juárez commerce department found that 85 percent of permitted vendors used other vendors' names. This may reflect the time-honored tradition of *prestanombres*, or front people, who obey, but do not fully comply with, the law (*obedezco, pero no cumplo*).

In an earlier study, I estimated a total of 3,000 regular street vendors, but noted that established merchants estimated figures at four to five times that figure (Staudt 1996: 439). Elsewhere, Stone (1997: Ch. 7) analyzed the use of "numeric metaphors" in making persuasive cases in policy analyses. Merchants likely overestimated the size of the street vendor population to create a visual image that hoards of street vendors overran the city.

Technically, licenses are required to vend on the streets, but the process for legalized vending was Byzantine (see two-page flow chart in Staudt 1998: 66–67). Merchants, also organized, complained about street vendors and the costs of doing business amid what they perceived as unfair competition and the congestion on the streets.

Government inspectors periodically check street vendors. Noncompliance can result in several consequences: fines, payments (bribes) to inspectors to avoid fines, other negotiations, or the confiscation of street vendors' goods. Street vendors need "leaders" to mediate this complex reality, and many leaders collect dues from vendors, generating yet other informal income for "leadership." For street vendors, the combination of the above is part of the cost of doing business.

In 1992, Cd. Juárez's new PAN (Partido Acción Nacional) Municipal President sought to control the growth of street vendors and their behavior. PAN is a pro-business (established, formal enterprises) party, riding high not only locally, but also with an historic first governor, Francisco Barrio Terrazas. Even Mexico's dominant political party reflected a neo-liberal (pro-market) agenda, anticipating rapid growth and expansion of modernist formal global and national enterprises. Former President Salinas made a pledge at the dominant PRI (Partido Revolucionario Institucional) national convention, widely covered in all media, "to use all levels of government to eliminate this [street vending] form of unfair competition (*competencia desleal*, literally disloyal competition)" (Staudt 1996: 447).

Bearing down heavily on vendors with burdensome enforcement, some

Mexico-based street vendors moved to other spaces with less surveillance, including vendor relocation sites with fixed and semi-fixed locations that would generate rental revenue and easy value-added tax collection for the Cd. Juárez municipal government, and El Paso's downtown space. Thus, the crackdown in Cd. Juárez provoked an upsurge of vending in El Paso.

### El Paso merchants react, with emergent political drama

El Paso media give far less newspaper space to the economic struggles of working people than Cd. Juárez media. When coverage is visible and sustained, as happened with street vending in 1992, more than the stakeholders notice and the stage gets set for political spectacle. Many more vendors than usual occupied downtown space, numbering in the hundreds (an estimate, as there are no lists), but varying depending on the season and day of the week.

Street vendors, authorized by a 1979 ordinance to operate with licenses if moving (non-stationary, except to make the sale), began to receive citations when stationary. Full compliance with the law was a bureaucratic challenge, since different offices in different locations issued permits: for itinerant vendor license, Texas tax permit, health license for food sales, and fingerprinting with the police. Compliance costs involve time, but the expense was limited to less than $200. Besides their perceptions of unfair competition, merchants complained about garbage, congestion, and the lack of public restrooms.

Police officers enforce laws generally, but they enforce seemingly trivial laws only selectively based on political considerations directed by the Mayor and City Council. The political spectacle offered the context for just such direction. El Paso police officers began to issue citations to vendors. Vendors, ordered to appear in Municipal Court, complied only partially; some did not appear and warrants were issued for their arrest, adding costs to city government. Elected judges reacted sympathetically to some vendors and their struggles for a livelihood, reducing the $62.50 fines to $1. A friendly lawyer took up the case of some vendors, delaying court dates and wasting the time of courts and police officers. Such weapons were employed by the seemingly "weak" in Scott's terms.

I obtained the universe of 89 vendor citations during the most intense period of the conflict (September 1992 through April 1993), along with the legal dispensation of cases. The group was international, as recorded by police officers: "7 Asians, an African (nationality unspecified), two Peruvians, a Puerto Rican, and two Cubans, one of whom alternatively claimed to be a Mexican, Spaniard and Cuban (and called himself 'Batista')" (Staudt 1996: 443). The rest were Mexican or Spanish-surnamed "offenders." Half named an employer, with the remaining half saying, in interviews, that they worked for a boss, *jefe*, or *el patrón*. Family-owned concessionaire companies, discussed above, employed these "contractors."

El Paso's City Council established a Legislative Review Board to mediate stakeholders' interests. A Spanish-speaking, aspiring Anglo councilman chaired the board, and public meetings offered a voice to the stakeholders: officials from different city agencies with a legal or revenue generation stake in licensing, merchants and their organizational leaders, and vendors. The merchants and officials sat at the table, while most vendors ringed the walls at the room's outer periphery. Vendors organized, selecting a member of one of the family-owned concessionaire companies to be their president. He sat at the table as well and did most of his representational work in English.

A compromise was developed to which stakeholders agreed. The city would allot permanent street vending slots through lottery selection. Many could apply (as did 113 in the first lottery), but only 32 spaces would be allotted. Moreover, costs would rise dramatically for street vendors: license fees, insurance, and the cost of carts. While concessionaire companies had the sort of capital to advance for the ten-fold increase in costs, autonomous street vendors were the ones who felt the squeeze. Many reported earnings of just $10–20 per day.

Excitement and tension filled the air of the first lottery selection, with a public drawing at the City Council meeting. As the winners' names were announced, sometimes in triumph for extended concessionaire company family members, with their multiple applications, losers yelled out "*hay fraude!*" (there's fraud!). But the city administered the new procedures, streamlined and perfected them over time, and regulated the allotment of spaces through lottery every three years.

### Now: Early twenty-first century control?

The subheading above contains a question mark, for the answers differ markedly depending on which side of the border is the vantage point. In Cd. Juárez, street vendors are still visible; the municipal elections always put a new cast of official characters in place every three years, and officials by and large continue to negotiate within and among vendors. Perhaps the best descriptor is "standoff." Merchants still struggle with vendors, the latter of whom employ "weapons of the weak."

In contrast, El Paso deepened its regulation and control over urban space, institutionalizing a process of lottery-based selection over a declining number of vending spaces in the downtown area. To use the words of Max Weber, this control might resemble an "iron cage."

As analyzed above, the early 1990s political spectacle resulted in a Legislative Review Committee that produced a compromise solution among downtown merchants, autonomous street vendors, and the concessionaire companies that employ some of the vendors. A lottery drawing occurs every three years to allocate licenses for specific spaces in the downtown area, particularly those that cater to Mexican pedestrian traffic given the close proximity to the international border crossing bridge.

However, from the 32 spaces allocated in the early 1990s, the city now grants only 22 licenses. The process is carefully managed, with public notice in the media and letters sent to all prior applicants. In February 2005, the fourth lottery drawing was held in a special public meeting, not at the City Council. Previous applicants and existing vendors are notified to pre-register for the drawing with special forms. Depending on the location and its prospects for lucrative trade, slots allocated via lottery range from $880 to $1,100 annually. Food vendors must have a food handler's license and a health permit. Applicants also must prove their authorization to work in the US as citizens or resident aliens.

Vendors' costs are considerable, nearly double what they were previously, but the approximately $22,000 revenue generated for the city does not cover the costs of enforcement, management of complaints from merchants and vendors, and processing of applications. Inspectors from the Building, Permit, and Inspection Department issue citations, but usually issue warnings first, hoping for voluntary compliance and for the avoidance of court appearances. Street vending is now nonexistent in El Paso's media.

After merchants complained about the appearance of vending carts and canopies to shade vendors and merchandise from the constant sun, a uniform cart and canopy became required for aesthetic reasons. Both vendors and concessionaire companies organized themselves more fully than during the political spectacle. Still, several concessionaire families employ vendors and supply leadership for these organizations. They negotiate group, rather than individual, insurance rates for the considerable costs of meeting the insurance requirement.

Merchants continue to be well organized, and many of them belong to the Central Business Association. Some old stores are subdivided inside, like a covered market, but with rent paid to landlords. Merchants have come to realize the appeal of street vending, called "sidewalk sales," especially to pedestrian traffic looking for competitive prices. Merchants organized through another Legislative Review Committee to acquire permits to place tables on sidewalks in front of their shops, selling only goods from inside the shop. These permits cost $100 per table, considerably less than those of the food vendors. However, merchants argue that they own or pay rent with sizeable property tax costs. Moreover, they issued a self-tax among themselves for security and clean-up.

Complaints come both from vendors and merchants about the regulated compromise. Merchants watch for unauthorized vending on goods not authorized for sale. Vendors notice that merchants sometimes sell candy and sodas at lower prices, even when the merchants' shops do not offer such products. This behavior runs contrary to the law, and officials mediate conflicts and issue warnings and/or citations. The complaints are all managed in the regulated process that ensued for the more-than-decade-old political spectacle.

## The new era

The context on both sides of the border has changed in many ways, not only for street vendors and downtown merchants, but also for immigrants, crossers, and ordinary citizens and residents. In both cities, formal businesses have become better and more elaborately organized, poised for collaboration with local government in public–private partnerships that capitalize on city "cultures," but without the voices and projected participants of street vendors and their formerly easy entry into income-generating activities. Several new and strong business groups augment El Paso's chambers of commerce, as noted earlier. In Cd. Juárez, the privately funded, high-profile *Plan Estratégico de Juárez* envisions the "city we will become" in 2015 (www. planjuarez.org). Some of this visioning exercise is the result of the tarnished image of the city since 1993, home to more than 400 female homicides (Staudt forthcoming).

In the United States, a 1996 immigration reform now more tightly controls crossing and penalties (Staudt and Capps 2004). Vastly increased numbers of Border Patrol agents monitor the border, occasionally supplemented with private vigilante groups called the Minutemen. A draconian immigration bill (HR 4437) passed the House of Representatives in 2005, but its punitive approaches will likely be negotiated into a compromise solution in 2007.

The PRI's 71-year domination of the presidency in Mexico gave way to PANista President Vicente Fox. He joined another conservative, President George W. Bush, both of them elected in 2000. Their hopes for a bi-national guest-worker program were dashed with the tragedy of 9/11, heightening security concerns, controls, and waits to cross the border for months thereafter. Two children died in the back of their parents' truck as it waited hours to cross, while carbon monoxide crept into the vehicle (Staudt and Coronado 2002: 174).

## Concluding reflections on border street vendors

The analysis of street vendors reveals insights on the relationships of policy regulations to market discipline and cost escalation, both for street vendors and for local government, with inspection fees, fines, and process and mediation labor costs. The analysis also illustrates how established merchants work politically to reduce or eliminate competition and thereby concentrate economic power. At the border, merchants were more successful in El Paso, utilizing "democratic processes" that led to what some might view as a new iron-cage like bureaucratic regime for vendors. Is a bureaucratic iron cage in Cd. Juárez's street vendors' future? Time will tell.

The analysis also challenges conceptions of street vendors as wholly autonomous entrepreneurs. In El Paso, a sizeable portion of vendors are tied through contracting and patron–client relationships with family-owned concessionaire companies. Even without policy regulation and market discipline, many street vendors generated meager earnings as temporary contractors with employers.

The borderlands crossroads may provide portraits of what happens when the globalized economy and its state agents "modernize" the streets. Impoverished street vendors face an economic squeeze, while those with capital have other options. And controls over border crossing have deepened, particularly since 9/11, even as numbers grow. Recent figures for northbound international bridge traffic into El Paso show a total of 8,453,000 pedestrians annually (Fullerton and Tinajero 2005: 14). In April 2005, the US State Department and Homeland Security Agency announced plans that US passports will be required for US crossers. This will add more cost and complexity to movement within the combined metropolitan region.

Is there a place for street vendors in El Paso's future? Architectural plans and downtown development dreams acknowledge consumer preferences for vendors, competitive prices, and a lively public space atmosphere. For El Paso, planners recognize the unique border atmosphere and street vendors' contribution to that atmosphere. Yet if and when spaces open, they would likely open for fixed locations, at considerable fees, and in attractive markets to entice not only an El Paso middle-class consumer clientele to return to the downtown but also wealthy Mexicans from as far away as Mexico City to shop downtown rather than in El Paso's upscale malls.

Many consumers shop already in large malls (as do wealthy shoppers from Cd. Juárez) or the numerous strip malls around the city. In the meantime, semi-fixed vendors, sitting at temporary tables in the shopping malls, rotate from mall to mall to sell their wares. Some are organized, and in one case, their leader pays the whole fee and the individual vendors pay fees to her. Street vendors are alive, but not always well: In El Paso, their costs of doing business are rising in a disciplined regulated manner, whether through the marketplace or the state, in local government guise. Ironically, as the new regulations put their informal competitors out of business, new public–private partnerships may also displace some of the small formal businesses – the merchants – who triumphed in the last dramatic round of conflict with street vendors.

## Bibliography

Brenner, C., Soden, D., and Dalton, E. (2003) "Fiscal Federalism: Financial Flows on the Border," in Brenner, C., Coronado, I., and Soden, D. (Eds.) *Digame! Policy and Politics on the Texas Border*, Dubuque, IA: Kendall/Hunt, 99–126.

Cross, J. C. (1998) *Informal Politics: Street Vendors and the State in Mexico City*, Stanford, CA: Stanford University Press.

Edelman, M. (1988) *Constructing the Political Spectacle*, Chicago, IL: University of Chicago Press.

EPCAE (El Paso Collaborative for Academic Excellence) (2000) *El Paso Education Summit: Building the Best El Paso*, February 18–19.

Fullerton, T. and Tinajero, R. (2005) *Borderplex Economic Outlook: 2005–2007*, El Paso: UTEP Border Region Modeling Project.

Negron, S. (2006) "Downtown El Paso: Make No Little Plans," *Newspaper Tree*, available: www.newspapertree.com, accessed April 3, 2006.

Romo, D. (2005) *Ringside Seat to a Revolution*, El Paso: Cinco Puntos Press.

Scott, J. (1985) *Weapons of the Weak: Everyday Forms of Peasant Resistance*, New Haven, CT: Yale University Press.

—— (1990) *Domination and the Arts of Resistance: Hidden Transcripts*, New Haven, CT: Yale University Press.

Staudt, K. (1996) "Struggles in Urban Space: Street Vendors in El Paso and Ciudad Juarez," *Urban Affairs Review*, 31/4: 435–54.

—— (1998) *Free Trade? Informal Economies at the US-Mexico Border*, Philadelphia, PA: Temple University Press.

—— (forthcoming) *Violence and Activism at the Border: Gender, Fear and Everyday Life*.

Staudt, K. and Coronado, I. (2002) *Fronteras no Mas: Toward Social Justice at the US-Mexico Border*, New York: Palgrave USA.

Staudt, K. and Capps, R. (2004) "Con la ayuda de Dios? El Pasoans Manage the 1996 Welfare and Immigration Law Reforms," in Kretsedemas, P. and Aparicio, A. (Eds.) *Immigrants, Welfare Reform, and the Poverty of Policy*, Westport, CT: Praeger.

Stone, D. A. (1997) *Policy Paradox: The Art of Political Decision Making*, New York: W. W. Norton.

# 6 Street vending in urban India

## The struggle for recognition

*Sharit K. Bhowmik*[1]

Gopal Krishna Kashyap was a union leader of food vendors in Patiala, a town in the state of Punjab. On 24 January 2006, Gopal Krishna walked to the middle of the busy market place carrying a can of kerosene. He started addressing the crowd around him. He told them that his people had been harassed for over two years. They were removed from the place they operated because that space was to be converted to a garden. The authorities had promised him then that the vendors would be settled in an alternative site, but over two years had passed and nothing had happened. His members were starving as they had no work for over two years. The only way, he told his audience, was to sacrifice his life and perhaps then the authorities would take heed. Gopal Krishna then doused himself with kerosene and set himself ablaze before the stunned crowd. He was dead before the ambulance could reach the crowded spot (*Hindustan Times* 2006: 1).

Gopal Krishna's case is not the only one of its kind. A year and a half earlier, on 11 May 2004, Abdul Rafeeq Khan, a leader of a group of street vendors in Lucknow, the capital of the state of Uttar Pradesh, set himself on fire within the precincts of the Municipal Corporation's offices. Abdul Rafeeq and his union had been protesting for long about the Corporation's decision of leasing out pavements (sidewalks) to a local gangster. This person's gang had been threatening street vendors with eviction if they did not pay the fees they had demanded which were five times higher than the tax they used to pay to the municipality. When all negotiations with the municipality seemed to fail, Abdul Rafeeq, in sheer desperation, set himself on fire (*Pioneer* 2005: 3).

These incidents, which are not isolated, show the paradox facing developing countries such as India. On the one hand, the government claims to protect the interests of the urban poor, but on the other hand it not only fails to provide for them, it even prevents them from providing for themselves. This chapter attempts to analyze this paradox. It provides an overview on street vending in India, problems faced by street vendors in conducting their trade, and their efforts to overcome their problems. Specifically, we will discuss how street vendors have organized to improve their legal standing, to the point where national officials have implemented policies to support them. But it also shows that these policies are still largely ignored by state and local officials, indicating that much more work needs to be done.

Street vendors form a very important component of the urban informal sector in India. It is estimated that about 10 million street vendors work in the country (GOI 2004a). They constitute around 2 percent of the total population in the metropolitan cities. A street vendor is a person who offers goods for sale to the public at large without having a permanent built-up structure from which to sell. Street vendors may be stationary in the sense that they occupy space on the pavements or other public/private spaces, or they may be mobile in the sense that they move from place to place by carrying their wares on push carts or in baskets on their heads. The terms "street vendor" and "hawker" have the same meaning and they are often interchanged.

Historically, the urban informal sector, and particularly street vendors, did not attract much interest from academics or trade unionists in India. There are few recent surveys on street vending. This study analyzes the role street vending plays in the urban economy and how merchants are demanding recognition of their positive role. Our focus is empirical rather than theoretical, based partly on my membership in the National Executive of the National Alliance of Street Vendors of India (NASVI) and my long-term association with SEWA, one of the largest street vendor unions in the country. This chapter shows that the experience of India echoes the organized struggles of street merchants around the world. As such it contributes to the debate started by Cross (1998) and continued more recently by Fernandez-Kelly and Shefner (2006) regarding the importance of understanding informality and particularly street vending as a political as well as an economic phenomenon.

## India's informal sector

After India became independent of British colonial rule on 15 August 1947, the new government adopted a supportive view towards factory and plantation labor. Several laws were passed to protect these workers, such as payment of wages, provident fund and gratuity, insurance, and pension. The Industrial Disputes Act of 1947 prevents closure of any factory employing 100 or more workers without the permission of the concerned state government. The working-class movement in general, and the trade union movement in particular, benefited from such laws. However, they included only workers with permanent employers who were expected to administer social security and employment protection laws. Even temporary or casual workers employed in the formal sector were not protected. Unfortunately, the result is that many businesses tried to escape the effect of the law by hiring as few "permanent" employees as possible.

At the same time, there was a growing population of the rural poor who migrated to cities in search of a livelihood. These people worked as construction labor, painters, plumbers, carpenters, etc. on a purely casual basis, moving from one employer to another. Others were compelled to work as rag pickers, waste recyclers, home-based workers, and street vendors. Though they had no direct employers, they were a part of the working class. These workers were out of the ambit of social security, welfare, etc. and remained invisible: both academics and state officials took their very existence as an aberration to the working-class movement.

Although Keith Hart (1973) coined the phrase "informal sector" to describe this kind of work in 1973 and soon after the International Labour Office (ILO) started a series of research and policy formulations for this sector, planners in India ignored the existence of this sector. Despite its growing numbers, the informal sector in India remained marginalized and denied the rights given to formal sector workers. This was probably because India followed industrialized, developed countries in thinking of workers as "industrial man," a factory worker or white collar employee. This notion of worker was exported to developing countries and accepted by their governments even though in these countries the "industrial man" constituted only a small section of the working class. As a result, workers, especially women, who did not fit this mold, remained neglected and their problems were overlooked. In 1969 the report of the first National Labour Commission reflected the prevalent mind-set. The bulk of the report was concerned with industrial labor, "with less than 10 percent of the report, 45 pages out of over 500, explicitly referring to non-industrial workers" (Jhabvala *et al.* 2003: 262).

The dilemma facing India since its independence is the conflict between socialist values and capitalist development. India was the first country outside the Socialist Block to accept planned development wherein the state played a leading role in building up the production process. Though the concept of centralized planning was borrowed from the Soviet Union, India did not have an economy that was totally controlled by the state. It preferred a mix of public and private sectors, with the former playing a lead role in industrialization. The emphasis in the early stages, especially after the Second Five Year Plan (1956–61), was on large-scale production units. These were in heavy industry areas such as steel, coal, and power. The planners believed that these industries would make the country self-sufficient in the basic needs required for building the infrastructure. The emphasis was thus on large-scale industries that would be instrumental in bringing about economic and social transformation. Without entering the debate about the correctness of this path, the fact was that it ignored the informal sector, which the government assumed would be absorbed by the growth of the formal sector. When this failed to happen, it was easier to ignore the failure than to deal with it.

Trade unions followed the same path. Until the mid-1990s, after which the job losses of liberalization were felt, the influence of trade unions was present only in the formal sector. In 1987, informal sector workers constituted just 1 percent of the total trade union membership (Davala 1994: 8–9). Communist unions were often especially harsh on street vendors, referring to them as counter-revolutionary "lumpen proletariat."

The first trade union of informal sector workers was started in Ahmedabad in the 1970s. In 1972, the Textile Labour Union (TLA), a trade union started by Gandhi in 1918, appointed a young woman lawyer called Ela Bhatt to help uplift poor self-employed women in Ahmedabad by teaching them to upgrade their skills. The union viewed this purely as a social service rendered to the poor. However, Bhatt went far beyond her mandate and started unionizing the women, naming the group the Self-Employed Women's Association (SEWA).[2] When Bhatt applied for registration of SEWA as a trade union, the Registrar of Trade Unions refused due to their narrow definition of "workers." It took Bhatt nearly one year to convince the Registrar that SEWA was indeed a trade union. In 1981, SEWA was expelled from the TLA and emerged as an independent trade union. By 1995, SEWA's membership was 250,000, making it the largest trade union in the state of Gujarat. With a membership of over 800,000 in 2005, spread over 10 states, SEWA is now one of the largest trade unions in India. Its members are street vendors, waste recyclers, home-based workers, agricultural and rural non-agricultural workers, and workers in small-scale industries, among others.

From its inception SEWA focused on the problems of the informal sector through national and international forums and it has helped form both national and international unions. These include the National Association of Street Vendors of India (NASVI), Homenet (an international union of home-based workers), Streetnet (an international consortium of street vendors), and Women in Informal Employment: Globalizing and Organizing (WIEGO – an international research and advocacy agency). Ela Bhatt was nominated to the Rajya Sabha, the upper house of the national Parliament, by the President of India. As a Member of Parliament, she framed a comprehensive bill to provide for rights of informal workers, which was introduced in the House but never discussed. Bhatt was later appointed chairperson of the National Commission on Self-Employed Women. The commission's report, *Shram Shakti* (Labor Power), published in 1988, was a landmark as it brought to the forefront the contribution of this section of workers to the national economy and problems relating to their work and wages. The planners started taking note of this sector.

Since 1985, India's economy has been moving gradually away from planned development and towards market governed policies. On 21 July 1991 the Finance Minister, Manmohan Singh (now Prime Minister), signaled the move with an Industrial Policy Statement in tune with the prevalent neo-liberal approach of structural adjustment and globalization of finance and investment. Other developing countries and the former socialist countries (Soviet Union and the East European countries) also changed their policies in a similar manner.

It was only after workers in the formal sector felt the adverse effects of the 1991 economic liberalization policy that the debate actually started.

According to the 1991 Census, conducted a few months before the new policies were introduced, the total labor force in India was 317 million. About 27 million were formal sector employees, about 8.5 percent of the total labor force (Davala 1994: 5). According to a sample survey in 2000, that number had increased slightly to 28 million, but out of a total workforce of 397 million, meaning that the formal sector had actually dropped to 7 percent of the total (GOI 2004b). By 2003, the total number had dropped back to the 27 million level (GOI 2005: 230). In other words, a decade after reforms were introduced, employment in the formal sector has been stagnant, implying that employment growth in the informal sector has been tremendous.

The rapid changes in the composition of the labor force compelled the government to address the problems of the informal sector. This was reflected in the report of the second National Labour Commission, submitted in 2002. Unlike the first report, this report has dealt in detail with the informal sector. It also proposed umbrella legislation for regulation of work and provision of social security to all sections of the working class. The present government, elected in mid-2004, has promised to implement such legislation.

## Street vendors and the urban economy

In most Indian cities, the urban poor survive by working in the informal sector. Poverty and lack of employment in the rural areas and smaller towns drive large numbers of people to the cities for work. These people generally possess low skills and lack the education required for better-paid jobs in the formal sector. In fact, permanent protected jobs in the formal sector are declining, hence even those having the requisite skills are often unable to find proper employment. For these people, work in the informal sector is the only means for survival. Street vending is an important option for these people, as it requires minor financial input and basic skills, though the income is low (see Morales 2000; 2001).

Not just immigrants but those once engaged in the formal sector are also taking to street vending (see Bhowmik 2000; Bhowmik and More 2001; Breman 2001). These people, or their spouses, were once engaged in better-paid jobs in the textile mills in Mumbai and Ahmedabad and engineering firms in Kolkata. Formal sector workers in these three metropolises have had to face large-scale unemployment due to drastic cutbacks of these industries. Many of them have become street vendors in order to eke out a living. A study on street vendors, conducted in these cities, shows that around 30 percent of the street vendors in Ahmedabad and Mumbai and 50 percent in Kolkata were once engaged in the formal sector (Bhowmik 2000). A study conducted by SEWA in Ahmedabad shows that around half of the retrenched textile workers are now street vendors.

Studies on street vendors are few and focus only on select cities. In 2000, NASVI organized the most comprehensive study on hawkers in seven cities which included Mumbai, Kolkata, Bangalore, Bhubaneswar, Patna, Ahmed-abad, and Imphal (Bhowmik 2000). Two other groups also conducted studies on street vendors in Mumbai. In 1998, the Municipal Corporation of Greater Mumbai (MCGM) commissioned Tata Institute of Social Sciences (TISS) and Youth for Unity and Voluntary Action (YUVA) to conduct a census of hawkers on municipal lands (Sharma 1998). In 2001, SNDT Women's University, in collaboration with International Labor Organization, conducted a study on street vendors (SNDT Women's University–ILO 2001).

Over the past few decades, the studies show that there has been a substantial increase in the number of street vendors in the major Indian cities. Mumbai has the largest number of street vendors, numbering around 250,000. Kolkata has more than 150,000 street vendors. Ahmedabad and Patna have around 80,000 each and Indore, Bangalore, and Bhubaneshwar have around 30,000 street vendors (ibid.).

The total employment provided through street vending becomes larger if we consider the fact that they sustain certain industries by providing markets for their products. A lot of the goods sold by street vendors, such as clothes, hosiery, leather, molded plastic goods, and household goods, are manufactured in small-scale or home-based industries. These industries employ a large number of workers and they rely mainly on street vendors to market their products. In this way, street vendors sustain employment in these industries.

An interesting aspect of these studies is that they all find common features among street vendors. Their earnings vary between Rs. 50 to Rs. 80 per day.[3] Women earn between Rs. 40 and Rs. 60 per day. They work under grueling conditions for long hours and are frequently harassed by the municipal authorities and the police. The NASVI study found that around 20 percent of their earnings are taken as bribes by the authorities or intermediaries (discussed further below). The SNDT–ILO study on Mumbai found that around 85 percent of street vendors complained of stress-related diseases – migraine, heartburn, hypertension, and high blood pressure.

In Delhi, the feminist journal *Manushi* (2001) conducted a study on street vendors which showed the stark reality of how these people are exploited and harassed by the authorities. This study provoked the Prime Minister to write to the Lt Governor of the Union Territory of Delhi to change the administration's oppressive policies on street vendors. The Prime Minister's office also issued a concept note on this subject which contained important guidelines, but it is unclear if these pronouncements had any effect.

There are also some interesting studies from town planners. Gitam Tiwari (2000) and Dinesh Mohan, both of Indian Institute of Technology in Delhi, have made significant contributions to research on use of pavement space, pollution control, and use of road space with regard to street vending. They show that street vendors near housing complexes reduce pollution levels; residents do not need to use cars or two-wheelers to buy their daily requirements as these are available on their doorsteps.

The poor are also benefited because of the cheaper cost of the goods sold by street vendors. What was once western history as discussed by Morales (2000) is also common, as shown by Bhowmik (2000) who found that lower-income groups spend a higher proportion of their income on purchases from street vendors mainly because their goods are cheap and thus affordable. Had there been no street vendors in the cities, the plight of the urban poor would be far worse than it is at present. In this way, one section of the urban poor, namely street vendors, helps another section to survive. Though street vendors are viewed as a problem for urban governance, they are in fact the solution to some of the problems of the urban poor. By providing cheaper commodities, street vendors are, in effect, providing subsidies to the urban poor, that the government has refrained from providing.

## Organizing street vendors

Nevertheless, because street vendors are often seen by city officials as problems, they must conduct their businesses amidst a great deal of insecurity. Whenever eviction drives are conducted, their wares are confiscated or destroyed. Even where street vending is permitted by the municipality, the police still have the authority to remove them. Section 34 of the Police Act empowers the police to remove obstructions on the streets. Hence, even if the municipal authorities demarcate areas as street vending zones, the police have the right to evict street vendors in these zones. Even licensed street vendors can be evicted under this law.[4]

In order to overcome these restrictions, street vendors organize themselves into unions or local associations that enable them to continue their activities. These organizations are mainly localized bodies representing street vendors in specific areas of a city. Most of these unions or associations are independent organizations, though some of the unions are affiliates of the larger trade union federations. Since street vending is not officially permitted, the main role of these organizations is to negotiate with the local authorities (the officers in the municipal wards and police stations) for occupying public space. In general, the rate of unionization is low; different studies conducted on street vendors in Mumbai, Delhi, and Ahmedabad show that less than 20 percent are union members. Further research must be conducted regarding gender and unionization but Ahmedabad is an exception, as female vendors constitute a sizeable percentage (40 percent) largely due to the efforts of SEWA. Furthermore, the existence of SEWA has encouraged many women from the urban poor to take to street vending. Thus, Ahmedabad is the only city where male vendors have lower levels of unionization than women.

Trade unions organize protest meetings and demonstrations when street vendors are threatened by the municipalities or the police. If this is not successful, they go to court and obtain stay orders against the action taken by the civic bodies. These are basically stop-gap arrangements; whenever vendors feel threatened, they resort to actions that enable them to continue their business for temporary periods.

One of the reasons that unionization rates are so low is that many street vendors pay bribes (rents) to the authorities to ward off evictions or at least obtain advance warning of attacks, so they forfeit trade union representation for important information. Informal associations negotiate with the local authorities with deals done under the table or through intermediaries to preserve the officials' reputation. In some cases, local musclemen, more often than not with the backing of a political party, collect protection fees through threats. Their links with the local authorities ensure that those who pay will not be disturbed and those who do not pay will face eviction either by the musclemen or the authorities. Indeed, the profitability of this practice may lead many officials to oppose unions because it would cut off their benefits.

These rent-seeking benefits are indeed quite large: The seven-city study of street vendors (Bhowmik 2000) found that street vendors pay between 10 and 20 percent of their earnings as bribes. In Mumbai, the total bribes collected amount to Rs. 4.5 billion ($20 million) annually. In Delhi, Rs. 500 million ($1.2 million) is collected monthly as bribes from vendors and rickshaw drivers (Manushi 2001). These findings were later confirmed by the Central Vigilance Commission, a government watchdog authority.

## Street vendors and public space

Street vendors have existed since time immemorial. In recent times, however, they have come to be regarded as a public nuisance by certain sections of the urban population. Non-governmental organizations (NGOs) representing the elite, especially the residents' associations of the middle and upper-middle classes, are the most vocal proponents of the eviction of street vendors from their neighborhoods. In most of the large cities, such as Mumbai, Delhi, Kolkata, Chennai, and Bangalore, these associations aggressively argue for restoration of pavements as public space only when street vendors "encroach" on them.

One of the more militant NGOs in Mumbai is called Citizens for Protection of Public Space (Citispace). Its affiliates are the middle and upper-middle class residents' associations and the larger shop owners in the city. They collectively represent around 1 percent of the city's population but they wield considerable influence over the policies adopted. The NGO takes great pride in its persistent fight against street vendors. Arguing that "hawking" should be limited only to mobile vendors, they boast that they have filed and won a suit in the State Supreme Court prohibiting stationary vendors from the city streets. If the NGO had its way, all street vendors should be carrying their wares in baskets on their heads! At the same time, these associations encroach on public space by employing private guards regulating persons using public roads that access their residential areas and they cordon off public space by erecting fences and gates.

The media favor the constant tirade by elite NGOs that street vendors deprive pedestrians of their space, inconvenience traffic, and encourage anti-social activities. Municipal authorities act promptly to evict street vendors without consideration to the problems caused to people who find it convenient to purchase from street vendors. That no committee of slum dwellers has ever complained against street vendors is of course irrelevant to the municipal authorities as well as these self-proclaimed defenders of public space.

Though economic elites control the situation one important contravening precedent was set by the Indian Supreme Court. More than a decade ago, the New Delhi Municipal Committee evicted a common street vendor, Sodhan Singh, who sold garments at Janpath in New Delhi. He appealed to the Supreme Court through a Public Interest Litigation claiming that the action violated his fundamental right to carry on business or trade (article 19(1) g of the Constitution of India). Significantly, the Court ruled that,

> If properly regulated according to the exigency of the circumstances, the small traders on the side walks can considerably add to the comfort and convenience of the general public, by making available ordinary articles of everyday use for a comparatively lesser price. An ordinary person, not very affluent, while hurrying towards his home after a day's work can pick up these articles without going out of his way to find a regular market. The right to carry on trade or business mentioned in Article 19(1) g of the Constitution, on street pavements, if properly regulated cannot be denied on the ground that the streets are meant exclusively for passing or re-passing and no other use.
>
> (Sodhan Singh versus NDMC 1989: see GOI 2004a)

The judgment emphasizes several important aspects of street vending and use of public space. First, it notes the positive role of street vendors in providing essential commodities to common people at affordable prices and in convenient places. Second, the judgment notes that street vending cannot be denied a priori under the assumption that the street's only purpose is transit. Third, and most important, is that street vendors are exercising their constitutional right to carry out trade or business, a right that should be regulated in balance with other rights and not abolished.

## Towards a national policy

Reacting to this legal challenge and pressure from groups such as SEWA, a National Taskforce on Street Vendors was formed in August 2001 by the Ministry of Urban Development and Poverty Alleviation. Besides the Minister of State, the members comprised senior officials of the ministry, mayors, municipal commissioners, senior police officials, and representatives of trade unions. After meetings held in Delhi and Ahmedabad a draft policy document was accepted on 30 September 2002 in Mumbai.[5] The policy was approved by the Union Cabinet on 20 January 2004, and was accepted by the subsequent government. The sections below deal briefly with the contents of the policy.

### Policy guidelines

The national policy follows the guidelines of the Supreme Court judgment quoted earlier (all quotes referring to the policy are from GOI 2004a) and restores some dignity to street vendors. Its introduction states: "The role played by the street vendors in the economy as also in the society needs to be given due credit but they are considered as unlawful entities and are subjected to continuous harassment by civic authorities." Furthermore it states, "this policy tries to ensure that this important section of the urban population finds recognition for its contribution to society, and *is conceived of as a major initiative for urban poverty alleviation*." (Emphasis in original.) The main objective of the policy is to "promote a supportive environment for earning livelihoods to the street vendors, as well as ensure absence of congestion and maintenance of hygiene in public spaces and streets." Provisions for hawking need to be made in the urban planning process and existing street vendors need to be settled. The policy tries to tackle these problems through democratic means and collective action. Normally hawking and no-hawking zones are designated by the civic or police authorities in an arbitrary manner and the interests of street vendors and consumers are rarely considered. Under the new policy authorities should demarcate hawking zones in areas that are likely to have consumers.

But, the policy stresses that this process "must be accomplished by a participatory process" that includes representatives of the municipal authority, traffic and local police, associations of shopkeepers, traders, and residents' associations including the association of slum dwellers and representatives of street vendors. The representation of street vendors (40 percent of total number of members of the committee with one-third being women) should be from membership-based organizations. Given that under the prior regime merchants could be evicted for almost any reason one hopes this policy will make vendors' voices heard. For instance, street vendors are often removed from the streets under the guise of beautification of pavements. Potted plants, flower beds, or decorative signs are placed on the pavements to prevent street vendors from plying their trade. The policy therefore states that

> no hawker/street vendor should be arbitrarily evicted in the name of "beautification" of the cityscape. The beautification and clean up programmes undertaken by the states or towns should involve street vendors in a positive way as a part of the beautification programme.

### *Legalizing street vending*

Since, as discussed above, the Police Act empowers the police to remove any obstruction on the streets the policy recommends that states should amend the Police Act of their respective state to add the following rider: "Except in case of street vendors and service providers with certain reasonable regulations."

Licensing merchants allows municipal authorities to keep a check on the number of vendors and earn revenue through license fees and other charges. However, the experience with licensing has been very negative. Licensing intended to remove harassment, extortion, and eviction by authorities makes unlicensed street vendors vulnerable to extortion from various quarters. Additionally, the licensing system may provide new avenues for rent seeking. Numerical limits to licenses have produced new rent-seeking regimes. Legitimate rents are derived from the issue of licenses, but where limited, illegitimate surcharges can be levied since the demand exceeds the (often arbitrary) numerical limits. Moreover, since the demand for merchandise from street vendors exceeds the supply, a number of unlicensed vendors seek to operate, and money is extorted from them during sweeps by law enforcement.

To minimize these predatory practices the policy recommends that instead of licenses there should be a simple registration process and space allocation in accordance with the planning standards and nature of trade/service. Registration is best done by Ward Committees as they are best suited to assess the local situation and issue vendors identity cards. The nominal registration fee will be fixed by the Urban Local Body (ULB). Registration will be renewed every three years. The registration fees and the monthly maintenance charges and fines, if any, will be collected by the Ward Committee on behalf of the ULB. A portion of the revenue collected will be allotted to the Ward Committee for its operations.

Provisions for legal eviction are important. Eviction causes financial hardship and impoverishment, as well as shaming the vendor. The policy decries eviction, but where relocation is necessary, it demands vendors be given a minimum notice of 30 days. The policy suggests that vendors or their representatives should be involved in planning and implementation of relocation and efforts be made to ensure that vendors in the new locality have the opportunity to similar, pre-eviction, warnings. The states are also asked to take comprehensive measures to check and control the practice of forced evictions. While laudable, these policies present their own difficulties, but incremental experimentation with new policies must replace the chaos generated by prior regimes.

## Incorporating vendors into broader policy environments

Street vendors can be assets to the urban system but, being of the marginalized urban poor, they are treated as troublemakers who create chaos on the streets. This attitude prevails against street vendors and other sections of the marginalized poor. The civic authorities and the urban elite regard the majority of the urban population as obstacles to improving the urban environment. Whenever the question of citizens' initiatives for improving cities arises, the reference is invariably to the middle and upper-middle class since it is assumed that these people alone can improve the cities. And which cities are their models? Western cities, who themselves are changing and adapting to new economic realities, often incorporating vendors and markets as part of their development strategy. In other words, the majority is denied the rights of citizenship. Their interests and well being are not considered as legitimate grounds for producing new, locally realistic strategies for social and economic development.

The fact is that no plan for improving the city can be successful without the participation of the urban poor (as Cernea 1991 does for rural development). Merchants should be integrated into the planning process and in campaigns for a better environment. The experience of another marginalized section of the urban workforce, namely rag pickers, has shown this. Rag pickers have been regarded as a nuisance and they are blamed for spreading garbage. They are harassed by the civic authorities and by middle-class residents' associations. In fact they, who form the poorest section of the urban population, are engaged in environmentally important activities as they collect recyclable materials from the city's garbage. Instead of victimizing them, the civic authorities could incorporate them as in Ahmedabad, where SEWA included rag pickers in the "clean city" campaign, and in Mumbai, where the Street Mukti Sangathana and the Forum of Re-Cyclers and Environmentalists (FORCE) mobilized rag pickers and involved them in beautification campaigns. Such moves are beneficial for the urban environment and in restoring citizenship to the marginalized.

Street vendors' involvement in various needs can benefit the urban population if hawking is legalized and regulated. Beautification and other improvement programs should involve street vendors and their organizations. But food vendors present a special difficulty. Food vendors need to operate under hygienic conditions. The new policy replaces health inspectors with self-compliance from food vendors. The policy acknowledges the difficulty of monitoring merchants, "though quality control is essential, the practice of 'health inspector' may not be suitable for the hawkers." This is mainly because such inspections encourage rent-seeking rather than the objective of promoting hygiene. Customers will sanction merchants, but the policy suggests that local government could also be involved by way of the Ward Committee imposing fines or closing businesses.

The new policy attempts to incorporate merchants individually in terms of beautification or hygiene, but it also encourages collective organization among street vendors. One of the objectives is "to promote organizations of street vendors e.g. Unions/Co-operatives/Associations and other forms of organizations to facilitate their empowerment." One important source of empowerment is in terms of credit, social security, and insurance programs recommended in the policy.

### Credit and social security

As street vendors are a part of the urban informal sector they have little or no access to institutional credit. This makes them dependent on private moneylenders who charge high rates of interest, or they depend on their savings as working capital. The policy therefore suggests that banks should encourage street vendors to form self-help groups (SHGs) for income-generating activities. Vendors' associations should be assisted by NGOs and covered in government schemes for poverty alleviation. Federations of SHGs should be formed to create "a financial interface between the vendors and formal sector financial institutions to gain access to larger credit not only for income generation but also for housing, whenever the need arises." Social security generally covers medical care, sickness, maternity benefits, employment injury, inability and survivors' benefits, old age pension, etc., benefits previously unheard of among vendors. The policy recommends that Welfare Boards be created for street vendors on the lines of those existing for construction workers or home-based workers. The policy suggests special insurance schemes should be developed to cover the loss of merchandise due to natural and manmade disturbances. This element of the policy is an important step towards social welfare, securing dignity and safety by way of collective organization.

## Conclusion: Contradictions in urban planning

The new national policy just described makes one think that the government is pro street vendors and that the torments, evictions, and harassments are in the past. Unfortunately, while the policy has been accepted by the Central Government, the implementation is by other authorities. The Urban Local Boards (ULBs) or Municipal Corporations are primarily responsible for implementing policies relating to urban development and thus responsible for implementing the policy. However, changes in municipal codes must be approved by state governments, where the influence of Central Government is limited. The Central Government provides guidelines, which the state governments should follow, but not a single state government has accepted the policy. While the Municipal Corporation of Delhi has agreed to implement the policy by initiating three Ward Committees, an effective implementation requires amending the local legal framework. Only the Government of the Union Territory of Delhi with the cooperation of, again, the Central Government can do this. In this environment the new policy is caught in an interminable web.

In other states the situation is unaltered. On 12 August 2004 the Secretary of the Ministry of Urban Employment and Poverty Alleviation sent letters to all chief secretaries of the state governments asking them about "the status of the action taken by your government in the implementation of the National Policy on Urban Street Vendors" (see GOI 2004a). A year after the letter was sent, not a single Chief Secretary had responded. On 19 October 2006, the Minister of Urban Employment and Poverty Alleviation called a meeting in Delhi of all state and union officials to discover the hurdles to implementing the policy. There was no opposition to the policy, in fact all the officials agreed that it should be implemented. Yet none has made efforts to implement it. This evident disinterest signals indifference at best and corrupt, broken government at worst.

India faces the dilemma of balancing social justice with market-oriented policies demanded by the World Bank and IMF and pressures exerted by multi-national corporations and big business. While the government adopted a national policy for street vendors, which was then largely ignored, on the other hand it subsidizes huge shopping malls and big business. In July 2005, the Prime Minister promised Wal-mart entry to Indian markets. McDonald's and Pizza Hut are already well entrenched. The first step these businesses take is eliminating competition from street vendors by eliminating merchants with the active support of the local authorities under the guise of beautification.

Shopping malls and Wal-marts are welcome additions to the market for choice and prices they provide consumers. However, street vendors deserve a level playing field, but without political clout and influence street vendors are sure to remain marginalized.

Street vendors play a crucial role in Indian cities because they subsidize consumption by the poor. But street vendors face hostile municipal administrations. Though the national policy promises security to them, it is clear that no state will implement this policy without pressure to do so. The pressure could come from below, through the collective action of street vendors. Despite merchants' low level of unionization some umbrella organizations exist promoting unity among vendors. NASVI has had some success, but support from international working-class movements and unions would help in this fight.

StreetNet, a global union of street vendors, is mobilizing international support for local unions. Women in Informal Economy: Globalizing and Organizing (WIEGO) is also carrying the campaign to academics, researchers, and policy makers and acting as a link between mass organizations of street vendors and researchers.[6] These efforts, at the national and international level, in tandem with local initiatives, have the best chance of realizing the promise and potential of India's new policy on street vendors.

## Notes

1 The author acknowledges the insightful comments of the editors and anonymous reviewers, most of which have been incorporated in the chapter.

2  The word *sewa* in most Indian languages means "to serve," emphasizing that the association was formed to serve the interests of the poor working women.
3  All currency terms are given in Indian Rupees (Rs.). The conversion rate with US $ in May 2006 was: $1 = Rs. 45.
4  The Section reads: "No person shall cause obstruction in any street or public place by ... exposing anything for sale in or upon any stall, booth, cask, and basket or in any other way whatsoever."
5  The author was a member of the Task Force as an expert and was also a member of the Drafting Committee.
6  More information on StreetNet and WIEGO can be found on their websites, www. streetnet.org.za and www.wiego.org.

## Bibliography

Bhowmik, S.K. (2000) *Hawkers in the Urban Informal Sector: A Study of Street Vendors in Six Cities*, National Alliance of Street Vendors of India. Online. Available: www.nasvi.org.

Bhowmik, S.K. and More, N. (2001) 'Coping with Urban Poverty: Ex-Textile Mill Workers in Mumbai,' *Economic and Political Weekly*, Mumbai, 36(52): 4822–27.

Breman, J. (2001) 'An Informalised Labour System: End of Labour Market Dualism,' *Economic and Political Weekly*, Mumbai, 36(52): 4804–21.

Cernea, M. (1991) *Putting People First: Sociological Variables in Rural Development*, Oxford: Oxford University Press.

Cross, J. (1998) *Informal Politics: Street Vendors and the State in Mexico City*, Stanford, CA: Stanford University Press.

Davala, S. (ed.) (1994) *Unprotected Labour in India*, Delhi: Friedrich Ebert Stiftung.

Fernandez-Kelly, P. and Shefner, J. (2006) *Out of the Shadows: Political Action and the Informal Economy in Latin America*, University Park, PA: Pennsylvania State Press.

GOI (Government of India) (2004a) *National Policy for Urban Street Vendors/ Hawkers*, Ministry of Urban Employment and Poverty Alleviation. Online. Available: www.meupa/nic.in.

—— (2004b) Ministry of Labour. Online. Available: www.labour/nic.in/ss/ INFORMAL SECTORININDIA.

—— (2005) *Economic Survey for the year 2004–2005*, Ministry of Finance. Online. Available: www.finance/nic.in.

Hart, J.K. (1973) 'Informal Income Opportunities and Urban Employment in Ghana,' *Journal of Modern African Studies*, 11(1): 61–89.

*Hindustan Times* (2006) 'Fiery Protest by Patiala Vendor,' 25 January, Patiala.

Jhabvala, R., Unni, J., and Sudarshan, R. (eds) (2003) *Informal Economy Centrestage*, Delhi: Sage Publications.

Manushi Nagarik Adhikar Manch (tr. Manushi Citizens' Rights Forum) (2001) 'Memorandum Submitted to the Lt. Governor of Delhi on Behalf of Delhi's Street Vendors and Rickshaw Pullers and Owners on 2 October 2001.'

Morales, A. (2000) 'Peddling Policy: Street Vending in Historical and Contemporary Context,' *International Journal of Sociology and Social Policy*, 20(3/4): 76–99.

—— (2001) 'Policy from Theory: A Critical Reconstruction of Theory on the "Informal" Economy,' *Sociological Imagination*, 38(3): 190–203.

*Pioneer* (2005) 'Self-Immolition by Hawker,' 11 May, Lucknow.

Sharma, R.N. (1998) 'Census of Hawkers on Brihanmumbai Municipal Corporation Lands,' prepared by Tata Institute of Social Sciences and Youth for Unity and Voluntary Action, unpublished report.

SNDT Women's University–ILO (2001) 'Street Vendors in Mumbai,' unpublished report.

Tiwari, G. (2000) 'Encroachers or Service Providers?' *Seminar* 491, June. Online. Available: www.seminarindia.org.

# 7 The conflict between street vendors and local authorities

## The case of market traders in Ankara, Turkey

*Recep Varcin*[1]

## Introduction

The purpose of this chapter is to explore the basis and the nature of conflict between informal traders and state and public authorities in Ankara, the capital of Turkey. Since Hart's study (1973), there has been a growing body of literature focusing on different aspects of the informal sector. Although prior research conducted in the informal sector demonstrated that informal occupations are extremely competitive and individualistic, the issue of conflict and competition have received little attention in the informal sector literature.

Some patterns of conflict and cooperation in the informal sector might be analogous to those that are conventionally observed and studied in the formal sector. Bromley and Birkbeck (1984: 186) have, however, pointed out that there are certain ways in which patterns of conflict are different from, and in certain ways more complex than, conventionally studied conflict in the formal sector. Following their approach, I address some aspects of conflict between informal traders and state and public authorities in the case of market traders in Ankara, Turkey.

This chapter consists of five sections. The first section deploys a familiar conceptual framework within which the research question will be examined. The second section introduces the research setting and outlines specific research methods being used in collecting data. The third section describes the heritage of town planning and state intervention in Turkey. The remaining sections address various aspects of conflict between market traders and state and local authorities.

## Conceptual framework

An influential theoretical framework on the state is O'Connor's (1973) theory of the "fiscal crisis of the state." Different classes and groups want the state to spend money for their benefit; however, they are not willing or are unable to pay taxes in order for the state to meet those demands. Government can take actions such as freezing wages and salaries, forcing people to pay higher taxes, or collecting taxes indirectly via inflationary policies. However, the state is not class-blind either in allocating state finances and expenditures or distributing the tax burden among various economic classes.

The theory argues that the capitalist state has two contradictory roles: maintenance of capital accumulation and legitimization (O'Connor 1973; Habermas 1976; Offe 1975). The state tries to create suitable conditions for capital accumulation because it depends on the economy's surplus production capacity and taxes drawn from that surplus. The state legitimizes the social system (O'Connor 1973: 125–68) by using tax revenue to produce services such as social insurance, welfare spending, and education spending. Some of these services and projects, called social consumption, e.g., social insurance, also contribute to lowering the reproduction costs of labor and therefore increasing the rate of profit. But the state loses its legitimacy when its policies too obviously profit one class at the expense of another. Thus, the state is pulled between its obligations to the different social classes in society.

O'Connor draws his argument mainly from the experiences of an advanced capitalist society, particularly the United States, but the concept can also be applied to developing countries, where the contradictions are even more apparent. While the state creates suitable conditions for profitable capital accumulation, it regularly faces legitimization crises, as it does not have the resources to finance consumption that prevents unrest from the lower ranks of society.

A second important feature of the capital accumulation process in developing countries is directly linked to the informal sector and its role in the accumulation process (Portes 1994; Cross 1994, 1998). It has been argued that the economic surplus generated within the informal sector is first transferred to the formal sector of the developing country and then to developed countries. Thus, large-scale capitalist enterprises benefit from the existence of small-scale, informal enterprises. Gerry argues:

> Capital benefited in two ways from the provision of cheap essential goods such as transport, housing, recycled materials, clothing and shoes, entertainment, and petty commerce. It benefited from the downward pressure directly exerted on urban wage levels and also from the indirect effect on the value of urban labor power resulting from these producers' preeminence in the industrial reserve army.
>
> (1987: 112)

While the informal sector contributes to formal sector capital accumulation, its own ability to accumulate capital is lessened since growth brings greater enforcement of costly regulations. Growing disparity between the two produces conflict between the informal enterprises and the state.

The state has political interests (beyond the revenue produced) in incorporating informal enterprises under its control. Informal enterprises resist incorporation, De Soto (1990: 151) argues, because the costs of remaining formal (both in terms of taxes and regulatory costs) outweigh the costs of informality. In a comparative study of Papua New Guinea, West Africa, and Singapore, Eades argues:

> The degree of control over small enterprises is greater when the degree of overlap between the social networks of the small-scale entrepreneurs and the agents of the State is minimal, and where rigid enforcement is monitored by a powerful interest group anxious to avoid any erosion of its dominant position in the economic and political system.
>
> (1985: 215)

Eades argues there are three dimensions to the relationship between the state and small-scale enterprises: first, Eades' argument implies that small-scale enterprises engage in organizing a social network; second, state agents have an interest in controlling small-scale activities; and third, the degree of linkage between social networks of small-scale enterprises and the state agents determines the degree of control over the former by the latter. That is, a powerful interest group applies rigid regulations in order to maintain its dominant position in the economic and political system if the interest of the networks of small-scale enterprises and interest of the agents of the state do not overlap. Bromley (1985: 190) points out that "small enterprises are likely to be tolerated and even mildly supported if they fit in with these interests [of local and foreign elites], but deliberately obstructed or persecuted if they do not."

The local municipality also has an interest in regulating and organizing economic activities in the city. Market traders conflict with municipal authorities because the local municipality creates and maintains the governmentally desired socioeconomic order in the city (Bromley 1985). Local government tries to impose its policy over small-scale enterprises and creates conflict with them. Markets and vendors in public places disproportionately attract the attention of local authorities and city dwellers (Bromley 1982; Morales 2000). Local policy makers are interested in extracting capital from informal entrepreneurs, but congestion is often a more proximate, and costly, political problem. Thus local government frequently persecutes all forms of small enterprise that cause congestion, such as street traders (King 1980; Rogerson and Beavon 1985).

Several foci emerge from the relationship between market traders, the central state, and municipality. First is further study of macro-level state policies on the accumulation process. Second is the study of state policy towards small-scale enterprises. Third are studies of historical and contemporary practices of town planning and municipal government. Finally, further study should be made of traders against the central state and municipal government. Following a discussion of the setting I will examine the relationship between small-scale enterprises and the state and municipality to analyze conflicts and cooperation between market traders, the state, and municipality.

## The research setting and data

In Ankara, market traders provide urban dwellers with fresh vegetables, fruits, and other kinds of food in marketplaces that are located in public fields or on public streets. Marketplaces in Ankara are periodic outlets for fresh vegetables, fruits, and dairy products. Most of the market traders are professional sellers; marketing is their primary business. The market traders in Ankara obtain their supplies either directly from rural producers or from city wholesale commissioners (called *hal*). These marketplaces are neither traditional rural nor town markets. Market traders in Ankara also differ from itinerant sellers who periodically travel from one town market to another supplying industrial goods to local people. Marketplaces in Ankara are considered municipal markets, controlled by local municipalities.

Ankara is a metropolitan city, with a total population of about three million people. It is subdivided into eight suburban municipalities, which bear the responsibility for all marketplaces located within their boundaries. In each suburban area the local municipality provides the market traders with various marketplace facilities. There are 73 marketplaces in the metropolitan city of Ankara which convene once or twice a week depending on the size of neighborhood. The municipality appoints a group of uniformed civil servants (called *zabita*, a kind of municipal law enforcement agency) to each marketplace. There is a *zabita* office in almost every marketplace. The *zabita* usually visit every stall several times a day to check whether the marketing business is going smoothly and to collect fees from the market traders for the various municipal services. In return, the municipality is responsible for the maintenance of the marketplace. The *zabita* are also responsible for making arrangements for the flow of goods and people within the marketplace.

The market traders are represented by a voluntary association, the Chamber of Marketplace Traders (CMT; *Ankara Pazar Yerleri Esnafi Odasi*). It was founded in 1962 by the traders themselves in order to pursue their economic and social interests. The CMT currently has 5730 members. The president and administrative personnel of this organization are elected for a three-year period by the members. The distribution of the stalls and spatial location of the traders in marketplaces was the domain of the CMT in the past, but today this role is often a matter of conflict with the municipal authorities.

For this study I chose six marketplaces meeting on different days of the week. I considered the following criteria in choosing marketplaces: (a) the income level of the neighborhoods (lower-middle income, middle-income, and another in a newly developed suburban area); (b) the physical structure of the marketplace (two are very-well developed with asphalted ground, roofs, and utilities provided, and the other four have none of these); and (c) spatial location of the marketplace (marketplaces, meeting in different suburban municipal zones). The idea was to get a diverse sample of issues faced by different types of market settings. Since social conflict has both hidden and obvious components I combined research methods to collect data. Semi-structured and in-depth interviews with officials and leaders of enterprises, along with participant observation and documentary research, were all employed.

## Heritage of town planning and state intervention

Ankara, the capital of the Turkish Republic since 1923, has a long history, dating back to the Hitite period, about 2000 BC. Throughout its history Ankara has been a good-sized provincial town with a strong history of state intervention in trade activities.

The Ottoman state, through its local administration, closely controlled and taxed trade activities. The local administration intervened in traders' activities, and, in so doing, agglomerated trade activities in bazaars, or traditional shopping malls, called *han* (Faroqhi 1984: 343). This agglomeration made it easy for the tax collector to collect taxes and control trade activities. The Ottoman state's primary interest in collecting trade activities under *han* was to tax them easily but the state also had a political interest in centralizing and controlling trade in the *hans* (Faroqhi 1984: 28).

However, the traders' activities could not all be restricted to *hans*. Some streets and more or less irregular open spaces were used as markets during the Ottoman era and later during the Republican era. These streets and open spaces were named according to the kind of market activities that took place there, such as *at pazari* (horse market), *koyun pazari* (sheep market), *saman pazari* (straw market), *bitpazari* (second-hand market), and *koylupazari* (peasant market). These names still persist. Nonetheless, the state still subjected vendors to various kinds of taxes according to the economic activity such as *bac* (sales tax), *bac-i hamr* (wine tax), *bac-i harir* (tax on silk), and *bac-i meyve* (sales tax on fruit). In these open spaces and street markets, the local administrator appointed market supervisors (*muhtesip*) to control market activity and to collect taxes (Ergenc 1980). They also collected market fees (*bac-i pazar*) from surrounding village people who marketed their foodstuffs in town. These taxes were collected either at the entrances of town or in the marketplace. Faroqhi (1984) describes gate tolls at bridges or roads, but traders tried to evade tax payment by avoiding roads or bridges. When discovered, such traders were severely punished and goods were confiscated.

In this brief historical account, two important issues help shed light on the present: first, the local Ottoman administrators saw trade and commercial activities as an important source of revenue. They applied a variety of taxes to commercial and trade activities in the city. They enforced strict rules and regulations over economic activities, making tax evasion difficult, but also creating conflict between traders, producers-sellers, and city administration.

Second, the local government intervened in the activity of traders by regulating urban space and trade activity. That is, the local administration forced traders to market their produce in covered areas or in designated areas and market supervisors sought to compel traders to obey government laws and regulations.

Thus, state intervention has become a tradition in urban life. The transition from the Ottoman Empire to the Republic of Turkey in 1923 did not break this pattern of intervention but it did lead to a stronger centralized state. As a result, intervention increased dramatically and extended into every area of society, especially the area of collective facilities and urban organization.

### Organization and control of urban space

After Ankara was declared the capital of the Republic in 1923, significant changes occurred and phenomenal growth took place. Initially, urban planning and implementation in Ankara was carried out by the central government. The Ankara Planning Commission under the direction of the Minister of the Interior controlled all forms of public and private development (Danielson and Keles 1985: 60–1). According to these master plans, Ankara's growth would be strictly controlled, with a targeted population of 300,000 in 1980. Ankara, however, reached the targeted population in 1950 and the years through the 1970s brought further massive migration from villages and small towns to the large Turkish metropolitan areas of Istanbul, Ankara, and Izmir. In Ankara accelerated urbanization was not accompanied by corresponding industrialization and newcomers during this period were unlikely to find formal sector jobs or adequate housing. The result was that hundreds of thousands of units of informal housing, *gecekondus* (literally "built overnight"), have been constructed in the outward sprawl of the city.[2] The process of accelerated urbanization in Ankara has been accompanied by a proliferation of income-generating activities at the margin of state regulations that provide essential services to the urban population. New immigrants usually engaged in informal economic activity such as pushing a cart on city streets and selling vegetables and fruits.

Newcomers were usually subjected to a great deal of harassment by authorities who saw them as a threat to the urban plan. The municipality, in association with the state, razed their houses, refused them use of municipal utilities, and did not provide public transportation to their newly founded neighborhoods.[3] The municipal officials who were in charge of checking business offices or stores for permits and controlling all kinds of small trades and transportation harassed street traders and confiscated their goods or foodstuffs and issued monetary fines.

The strong Kemalist[4] state, which was determined to transform society from traditional to modern, Western, and "civilized," intervened in almost every aspect of collective life. According to this elitist plan the increasing numbers of informal economic activities were neither Western, modern, nor "civilized." The centralized state and the municipality, which was no more than an extension of the central state, took several measures to take informal activities under their own control such as building booths on the busiest streets, forcing sellers to obtain municipal permissions, and agglomerating foodstuff sellers in marketplaces. The increasing number of informals produced a transformation in traditional practices, from producer-seller and itinerant merchant markets to markets dominated by professional traders.

## Macro-level state policies

In this section, I will first sketch how the Turkish economy fits with the dual state roles of accumulation and legitimization. Second, I will examine the macro-level state policies towards small-scale enterprises. Finally, in the light of discussion of the above issues, I will examine the relationship between market traders and the state.

The Turkish state facilitates capital accumulation, and sometimes loses legitimacy because it does not hesitate to use its coercive power to do so (Oh and Varcin 2002). The aims of state policies toward small-scale enterprises can be summed up as the following: (a) decreasing unemployment; (b) increasing state revenue; and (c) creating conditions for profitable capital accumulation.

The Turkish state still depends, to a significant degree, on small businesses to draw a variety of taxes and fees. Proliferation of small businesses enables the state to tax them and finance its expenditures. The state applies a direct tax system on small businesses in order to ensure its revenue in advance. In addition to paying income taxes, small businesses pay a variety of taxes and fees to the state and municipality.

Proliferation of small businesses also creates suitable conditions for profitable capital accumulation in the formal sector. Small businesses contribute to capital accumulation in the formal sector via forward and backward linkages. Without making direct investments in distribution, formal enterprises distribute their products via small-scale enterprises. Small-scale enterprises sell products at a minimum profit, transferring profit to formal enterprises. Small-scale enterprises also provide the formal enterprises with low-cost inputs, enabling formal enterprises to accumulate more capital.[5]

Foodstuff distribution occupies a unique place in the informal sector of the economy. Every year, the government sets up prices for agricultural crops, including but not limited to wheat, cotton, tobacco, soybeans, rice, corn, and sugar beet. The state itself is the biggest buyer of these crops, and stores them nation-wide in its storehouses. The state either processes them in its own factories and distributes them to customers via private enterprises or sells these crops on the national or international market. The state also applies dual labor-market policy, one policy for the agriculture sector and the other for the industrial and service sectors. The governmentally set minimum wage for the agricultural sector is lower than the minimum wage for the industrial and service sectors. In addition, the state does not apply the same labor laws for agricultural employees. Widespread practices in agriculture are the use of child labor, forcing employees to work overtime without additional pay and providing no benefits to pregnant women or to new mothers (Seker *et al.* 1987).

It is very important for the state to keep the prices of agricultural produce under control. From this perspective, market traders have long been providing city dwellers with foodstuffs at a lower price, which, in turn, helps keep wages down in both the state and private sectors of the formal economy. For example, foodstuff prices are 10 percent to 90 percent lower in the marketplace than in the formally structured supermarkets. Nevertheless, the state is constantly concerned to keep prices down in order to reduce unrest among the poor who rely on these markets.

One state concern is reducing the power of large-scale market traders that threaten to dominate the market. The Ministry of Finance sporadically places checkpoints in main entrances to the city, as happened during the Ottoman era centuries ago. Trucks carrying foodstuffs to the city have to carry an invoice showing the amount and the kind of foodstuffs, business title, tax number, and shipping address.

The state's second method of intervening in large-scale traders' activity is to tax them. For years, the state has maintained an ambivalent position with respect to taxing small merchants. However, the existence of large-scale market traders in particular, and an increasing number of businesses evading taxes in general, has forced the state to take a more active position.[6] There is increasing discontent among taxpayers, which pushes the state to increase tax compliance. The state loses legitimacy since it is unable to equally distribute the tax burden among various economic classes.

Large-scale traders partially merge into the formal sector in order to overcome the state barrier and to benefit from being formal. Some of the large-scale traders establish a quasi-formal enterprise in the city. For example, an enterprise might have a legal business title but does not comply with all regulations or pay all taxes and fees. The legal business title enables evasion by large-scale traders who ship produce from the production site to the marketplace. This benefit attracts other traders who apply for business licenses with producers or who seek to control the entire commodity chain.

The conflicting state policies of lowering prices and raising taxes places a squeeze on traders. Market traders constantly complain that the state prevents them from providing cheap foodstuffs to the urban population. As one trader argued, "The state does not have as much control over the big business as it does over our business. Those big business people have a tremendous amount of tax evasion; they defer their tax obligation as they wish. The state is not after those big businesses but is after ordinary people like us."[7] Market traders often pointed out that they were viewed by state agencies as potential tax evaders. As one recalled:

A couple of times our trucks were kept at one check-point for no legitimate reason. We were put on TV news as if we were responsible for high prices in the market. They were introducing us like the mafia controlling the foodstuff supply and keeping the prices high in the market. All we do is eliminate the middle person and buy our foodstuffs at the production site and ship them to the market.

In summary, the state directly and indirectly benefits from the existence of the small-scale business, in this case small-scale marketing of foodstuffs to the urban population. The market traders' activity keeps wages down in the state institutions and also in the private sector. Second, the state views small-scale informal enterprises as a solution to unemployment and capriciously imposes taxes and state regulations. Third, the state pays special attention to controlling and keeping foodstuff prices down. Therefore, the existence of small-scale merchants decreases social antagonism by providing employment and low-cost merchandise. However, the state perceives the relative success of some traders as a threat to its interest in accumulating capital and its policy to control food prices. Thus, the state imposes more regulation when the scale of the marketing operation increases.

## Market traders and local municipalities

In Ankara, local municipalities, rather than the central state, impose regulations on the activity of market traders and intervene in various aspects of the marketing business. The Turkish state inherited its strong, centralized, bureaucratized system from the Ottoman Empire. Weiker (1981: 228) calls it "one of the world's most centralized states." The central government assigns responsibility to cities but national officials supervise cities closely, unto the smallest detail. For example, elected mayors are sometimes dismissed from their positions if their policy preferences are in conflict with the central government. Local municipalities are financially dependent on the state. Thus for municipalities to secure revenue from the state they follow the directions and policy preferences of the government. Weiker (1981: 226) points out "most Turkish governments have not hesitated to use their patronage powers and their powers of discretion in authorizing projects to reward their clients and supporters." Thus local municipality regulation of markets should therefore be analyzed within the context of the state and its macro-level policies. The ruling class, political leaders, top bureaucrats, and some business leaders benefit enormously from centralization. This coalition has vested interests in the continuation of the centralized state.

Central state decision makers enable elected officials to punish or to reward local people by implementing projects or by withdrawing urban services. Markets are important urban services. The ruling party in a municipality uses or creates market policies to gain electoral support or extort unearned income. Local authorities in control of marketplaces have several mechanisms to reward or penalize the people in a specific neighborhood.

### Price checking

As mentioned above, local municipalities have historically controlled trade activities in Ankara, and their intervention has expanded. Before the 1980s every marketplace had its own municipality appointed *zabita* officers who had greater responsibilities than market supervisors had during the Ottoman era. In many marketplaces, the *zabita* have an office for their own use. The *zabita* are always on the move, visiting stalls several times a day to check and control various market activities.

Until the late 1980s, the municipality applied strict price control on foodstuff prices. In accordance with the old price policy, the *zabita* checked every stall and required sellers to put a price tag on every item. The price tag was supposed to show no more than 30 percent profit over the cost invoice. These encounters were one of the main sources of conflict between the market traders and the municipality. The *zabita* received the price list from the commissioners of the local wholesale market or *hal*. According to this list, the *zabita* determined the maximum price for every item. If the market traders were unable to show the invoice, the *zabita* issued a price for each item and penalized the trader for not showing the invoice.[8] The poorest vendors would often plead with the *zabita* officers not to issue them a fine because they could not afford it.

In the 1990s, with the liberalization of the economy during the Ozal administration,[9] this strict price control in markets was gradually abandoned. The state began to let prices fluctuate according to the dynamics of supply and demand. However, the *zabita* still check every stall and every item for a price tag, even though they do not ask for invoices or question the cost traders paid for the produce. If traders do not tag items, the *zabita* impose sanctions on the market traders. The *zabita* will remove the trader's scale thus preventing him from doing business. Traders attempt to solve such disputes on an individual basis and are keen to develop good informal relationships with the *zabita* officers. This can be very important when traders break regulations and are supposed to pay fines, which a friendly *zabita* might overlook.

### Controlling the marketplace

The local municipality has also an interest in regulating and organizing economic activities in the city. An important goal of the municipality's intervention in street trading is to raise revenue for its expenditures. The municipality collects fees and fines informally. The local municipality claims the right to operate markets, and it collects mandatory fees from the market traders for using the marketplace. The majority of traders do not object to the municipality's collection of fees per se, but they do object to the amount and timing of the fees. The *zabita* collect the fees right after the traders set up their stalls, which means that traders have to pay before they know whether they will actually earn any money.

This does not greatly affect the larger market traders[10] (semi-formal company owners) since their profit margins are greater than other traders. They ordinarily pay the fee to the *zabita* without much dispute. They also tend to have well-established relationships with *zabita* officers where both parties benefit financially from the relationship. Medium-sized market traders engage in more disputes and arguments because they do not know how much money they will make on a given day. Although traders pay the fees every day they still dispute the payment. Marginal traders are most contentious. These traders object to the payment on all counts. They plead with the *zabita* to exempt them from payment for the simple reason that they do not make a profit, but the argument generally falls on deaf ears.

The municipality's control over the market place leads to other types of confrontation with these marginal traders. One of the official responsibilities of the *zabita* is to make spatial arrangements so as to provide an easy flow of goods and people within the marketplace. Since most of these traders are literally marginal – operating in the walking areas or at the margins of the marketplace – they are usually harassed by the *zabita* for preventing easy flow of traffic. This results in *zabita* yelling at them and giving them dirty looks, or even confiscating their goods. In return, heated arguments emerge between the marginal traders and *zabita*. In one extreme case, a market trader attempted to commit suicide when the *zabita* confiscated his goods.[11] Now I will turn to the relationship between the vendor's organization and the local government.

### Conflict over the distribution of stalls

Traditionally, marketplaces were accessible to any trader or seller as long as they paid fees to the municipality. After the massive immigration into Ankara beginning in the 1950s and the involvement of an increasing number of individuals in market trading, demand for space became higher than supply. For many years the CMT had been responsible for distributing stalls among its members. When a new marketplace is established, the CMT provides large trading companies with at least one stall and then distributes the remaining stalls to its members by lottery. In the last decade, however, some local municipalities have tried to take over the distribution of stalls from the CMT. The most important reason for this shift is that the members of the city council and the mayor want to use stall distribution to expand their access to patronage.

Government has been unable to take complete control of stall distribution. The municipality has two main efforts. First, in one district the government reserved some stalls for each council member and permitted the CMT to distribute the rest of the stalls among its members. The municipality created 591 stalls in the new Mamak marketplace, reserving 120 for itself to be distributed among those members of the city council who were from the same political party as the mayor. According to one local biweekly newspaper,

40 stalls were reserved for each of these members of the city council.[12] These places were purportedly distributed in exchange for money and/or electoral support. The CMT officials and market traders reacted strongly because some of the market traders, who had had stalls in the old marketplace, could not get stalls in the new one. Consequently, the CMT board decided to protest the municipality's decision by not opening stalls for a month until a solution was found (*Mamak Arayis* 1993: 1). As a result of this protest, the municipality made additional stalls available for former market traders.

A different municipality also tried to control the distribution of stalls in a newly established marketplace by making an informal contract with the CMT officials. According to this contract, the municipality provided every CMT official with two stalls for his own use on the promise that the CMT would stay silent and would not engage in any collective protest. According to this deal, the local municipality distributed the reminder of the stalls as it wished. In this way, the city council members made "unearned income" by using their administrative power. The informal agreement between the CMT and this municipality shows that in this case the CMT and the municipality shared similar interests.

As I have shown, the intervention of the municipalities in the marketing business benefits not only the municipality, in terms of raising its revenue, but also those decision-making actors in the municipality who use their posts for personal and political gain. It is precisely because of the political and personal interests of these actors that urban affairs, collective facilities, and economic activities are kept subjected to strict regulation and control.

### Conflict and cooperation over work conditions

The last area of dispute between the municipality and the market traders centers on physical work conditions. One of the characteristics of informal market trading is that work takes place in public places rather than on private premises. The local municipality is responsible for improving work conditions, something that interests both employers and employees alike.

Both employers and employees demand the improvement of work conditions in return for fees paid to the municipality. An ideal workplace, according to the market traders, should be paved, have rest rooms, parking lots for their trucks, roofs, running water for cleaning their produce, drainage systems, adequate lighting, roomy stalls, garbage disposal sites for their perished produce, and regular, thorough cleaning. The lack of some of these services exposes sellers to unhealthy and unsafe working conditions. In the winter, sellers can work in sub-freezing temperatures with no roofing to protect them from snow or rain. A common sickness among sellers is rheumatism, which can be considered an occupation-related illness. Of course there are other work-related health problems such as back pain stemming from lifting heavy boxes or leaning while serving the customers. The municipality considers such work-related health problems as beyond their responsibility.

But there are many work-related problems that the municipality is supposed to solve.

Some influential large-scale market traders and CMT officials are constantly in touch with the local municipalities about improving workplace conditions. They also put out press releases to convey their demands to the municipality through the media. In this way, they attempt to mold public opinion and put pressure on the elected officers. Although the market traders are in close contact with the *zabita*, they rarely take up these issues with them, since the *zabita* do not have the power to mobilize resources to improve the marketplace. Market traders, however, verbalize their demands to the *zabita* to be conveyed to the City Council.

Workplace conditions vary according to the local municipality, largely according to class level. Only one out of the five local municipalities in Ankara has provided market traders with decent work conditions, close to what market traders consider as ideal. The municipality in question is the Cankaya municipality serving the area where upper- and middle-class income neighborhoods are located. Market traders consider this municipality the best among the five local municipalities. But there are some marketplaces in the working class neighborhoods within the boundary of this municipality that are more similar to conditions found in marketplaces in other municipalities.

Improvement of marketplaces in some neighborhoods has had an unintended consequence. Until the late 1980s, none of Ankara's marketplaces had any improvements and unhealthy working conditions were taken for granted by the market traders as the unfortunate characteristic of their business. As some marketplaces were improved and market traders had better work environments, they grew conscious of inequality and desired better work conditions. Once concrete examples were established, traders increased their demands for improved conditions in most market places.

In late 1993, market traders were disputing the deplorable working conditions in a specific marketplace in the region of the Mamak municipality. The CMT officials organized a petition and asked for an appointment with the Mayor in order to discuss the improvement of the working conditions in the Mamak marketplace, which was declined. Afterward, the Board of the CMT decided to take action against the Mayor's indifference. The CMT president issued a press release, declaring, "Our board has decided that if our demand is not going to be met, we will protest the municipality by not opening our stalls for one full month in all of the marketplaces within the Mamak region" (*Mamak Arayis* 1993). Later, an agreement was reached between the municipality and the CMT.

Improvement of work conditions in the marketplaces also becomes an electoral campaign issue. In every local election, new candidates promise to improve the work environment of the market traders in exchange for their electoral support. Many market traders point out that such promises are conveniently forgotten by the elected administrators after the election.

### Solidarity of market traders

As the above example shows, market traders sometimes make collective protests against the local authorities through their associations, and calling for a collective strike is a potent weapon given the important role they play for food provisioning. In another example, the local council of the Yenimahalle district decided to cease marketing activity in the Karsiyaka marketplace and build a shopping mall in the lot where the market was meeting. The CMT officials met the Mayor to ask him to rescind the decision but they were ignored. With this development, the CMT officials decided to protest. They organized a protest and about 1120 market traders joined in. On that particular day, traders went to the marketplace but did not open their stalls. The CMT officials and market traders informed customers about the decision of the municipality and asked for their support in maintaining the marketplace. In the marketplace, the CMT launched a signature campaign supported by the local customers, and collected more than 100,000 signatures. The customers declared their support saying, "We do not want our marketplace condemned. In this marketplace tens of thousands of people shop for foodstuffs. The municipality should stop making decisions against us" (*Zaman* 1992: 13).

Market traders continued their protest by not opening their stalls, while traders and the CMT intensified their propaganda campaigns in that district and across Ankara. This protest and the increasing public support for traders adversely affected the political standing of the Mayor and his political party. The CMT successfully applied to the Seventh Administrative Court to rescind the municipality's decision and keep the marketplace. Market traders demonstrated in front of the municipal building as their president handed in the decision. The CMT press conference was covered by all the national newspapers and the decision reduced the prestige of the municipality and of the Mayor before the public and demonstrated that trader associations could have a large impact on municipal decisions.

As part of the long-term, centralized, authoritarian political system, the elitist politicians holding power generally make decisions without consulting with the traders themselves or their customers.[13] The city council insisted on its decision despite the fact that neither local people nor the market traders approved the decision. As conveyed in the mass media, the city council, by attempting to build a new shopping mall, tried to create new resources for themselves and their supporters. However, their efforts were eventually thwarted by the concerted action of vendors and their customers.

## Conclusion

Turkey's centralized state fits well with capital accumulation theory. Even as the Turkish economy transitions from state control to private sector control, the state still creates conditions for profitable capital accumulation and for keeping wages for its own employees low. Despite superficial changes the centralized state remains intact. Therefore, it is reasonable to argue that state policy towards market trading is designed neither to eliminate it nor to allow it completely to operate under market forces. Rather, state policy in Turkey attempts to keep market trading enterprises healthy enough to make a significant contribution to the downward pressure on wages.

This study reveals that the municipality intervened in various aspects of income-generating activities of informal traders under the direction and close control of the national state. Consistent with the state policy, local municipalities intervene in various aspects of market trading: setting and checking prices; controlling the distributing stalls; and organizing and reorganizing the marketplace. The intervention of the municipality in economic activities of traders sometimes leads to the individual and collective action of market traders. Even so, the conditions are not clear by which traders might secure more autonomy from state control.

## Notes

1 The author would like to express his grateful thanks to Linda Fuller, John Cross, Alfonso Morales, and anonymous reviewers for their helpful and insightful feedback on earlier versions of this chapter.

2 I use the term "informal housing" because settlers either invaded state waste lands or illegally purchased agricultural land. In many cases the residents also participated in the informal street economy.

3 The state and municipality's reactions to the informal housing were mixed: on the one hand the invaded areas disrupted urban growth plans, but on the other the political party in power tried to get electoral support from the inhabitants and therefore did not always enforce laws strictly (see Ozbudun 1976; Nelson 1979: 286).

4 Mustafa Kemal, the first President of the Republic of Turkey, led the overthrow of the Ottoman Empire and established a strong regime designed to "modernize" Turkey along Western lines.

5 Informal carpet manufacturing constitutes a good example for both backward and forward linkages (Ayata 1987).

6 According to various researchers, estimates of unregistered business income ranges from 11.5 percent to 137.8 percent of the Gross National Product (Hurriyet, November 1, 1994: 7). According to the same source, the amount of business tax evasion was about three billion US dollars in 1994 ($1 = TL 36,000).

7 At the time this trader made his comments, two industrialists had escaped abroad to evade a tax loan and debts to their employees.

8 The monetary fine at that time was about half of a worker's daily wage in the market.

9 Unlike other prime ministers and presidents, Turgut Ozal had a background in business and worked for the World Bank. Before he accepted a government post during the military regime, he was the president of an influential union of employers. Turgut Ozal's background led him to follow state policies that were in contrast with the traditional state policies.

10 Large-scale market traders refer to those who have semi-formal businesses, while medium-size market traders are generally lumpen capitalists or regular self-employed. Marginal traders are either retired workers who engage in marketing

for additional income or new city comers. For further information on the scale of operation see Varcin (2000).

11 A 56-year-old market trader opened a stall at the margin of the Karsiyaka marketplace. After the *zabita* confiscated his business, he got on the roof of a six-story building and threatened to commit suicide unless he was given the right to work in the marketplace. The police convinced him not to commit suicide and took him to the police station. At the police station, the trader said in tears, "The *zabita* did not let me open a stall in the marketplace. I have three children and family. I have to feed them. What can I do now?" (*Hurriyet Sehir*, December 22, 1993: 3).

12 According to the same source, each stall was worth the equivalent in Turkish liras to about 1500 to 2000 US dollars.

13 It should be noted that these two Mayors were not reelected in the following local election. Authoritarian, elitist rule was in fact not approved by local people.

# References

Ayata, S. (1987) *Kapitalizm ve Kucuk Ureticilik: Turkiye'de Hali dokumaciligi*, Ankara: Yurt Yayinlari.

Bromley, R. (1982) 'Working in the Streets: Survival Strategy, Necessity, or Unavoidable Evil?' in A. Gilbert, J.E. Hardoy, and R. Ramirez (eds) *Urbanization in Contemporary Latin America*, New York: John Wiley.

—— (ed.) (1985) 'Physical and Legal Constraints: The Heritages of Town Planning, Municipal Government and Policing,' *Planning for Small Enterprises in Third World Cities*, New York: Pergamon Press.

Bromley, R. and Birkbeck, C. (1984) 'Researching Street Occupations of Cali: The Rationale and Methods of What Many Would Call an "Informal Sector Study",' *Regional Development Dialogue*, 5(2): 184–203.

Cross, J. (1994) 'The State and Informal Economic Actors.' Online. Available: www.openair.org/cross/subecon4

—— (1998) *Informal Politics: Street Vendors and the State in Mexico City*, Stanford, CA: Stanford University Press.

Danielson, M.N. and Keles, R. (1985) *The Politics of Rapid Urbanization: Government and Growth in Modern Turkey*, New York: Holmes & Meier.

De Soto, H. (1990) *The Other Path: The Invisible Revolution in the Third World*, New York: Harper and Row.

Eades, J.S. (1985) 'If You Can't Beat 'em, Join 'em: State Regulation of Small Enterprises,' in R. Bromley (ed.) *Planning for Small Enterprises in Third World Cities*, New York: Pergamon Press.

Ergenc, O. (1980) 'XVI Yuzyilin Baslarinda Ankara'nin Yerlesim Durumu Uzerine Bazi Bilgiler,' *Osmanli Arastirmalari* (I): 85–108.

Faroqhi, S. (1984) *Towns and Townsmen of Ottoman Anatolia: Trade, Crafts and Food Production in an Urban Setting, 1520–1650*, Cambridge: Cambridge University Press.

Gerry, C. (1987) 'Developing Economies and the Informal Sector in Historical Perspective,' *The Annals of the American Academy of Political and Social Science*, 493: 100–19.

Habermas, J. (1976) *Legitimation Crisis*, London: Heinemann Press.

Hart, K. (1973) 'Informal Income Opportunities and Urban Employment in Ghana,' *Journal of Modern African Studies*, 11(1): 61–89.

King, A.D. (1980) 'Exporting Planning: The Colonial and Neo-Colonial Experience,' in G.E. Cherry (ed.) *Shaping an Urban World: Planning in the Twentieth Century*, London: Mansell.

*Mamak Arayis* (1993) 'Belediyeyle Pazarci Esnafi Kapisti,' 17 November: 1. Ankara: Mamak Arayis.

Morales, A. (2000) 'Street Vending in Historical and Contemporary Context,' *International Journal of Sociology and Social Policy*, 20(3–4): 76–98.

Nelson, J.M. (1979) *Access to Power: Politics and the Urban Poor in Developing Nations*, Princeton, NJ: Princeton University Press.

O'Connor, J. (1973) *The Fiscal Crisis of the State*, New York: St Martin's Press.

Offe, C. (1975) 'Introduction to Legitimacy Versus Efficiency,' in Lindberg *et al.* (eds) *Stress and Contradiction in Modern Capitalism*, Lexington: Lexington Books.

Oh, I. and Varcin, R. (2002) 'The Mafioso State: State-Led Market Bypassing in South Korea and Turkey,' *Third World Quarterly*, 23(4): 711–23.

Ozbudun, E. (1976) *Social Change and Political Participation in Turkey*, Princeton, NJ: Princeton University Press.

Portes, A. (1994) 'When More Can Be Less: Labor Standards, Development, and the Informal Economy,' in C. Rakowski (ed.) *Contrapunto: The Informal Sector Debate in Latin America*, Albany, NY: State University of New York.

Rogerson, C.M. and Beavon, K.S.O. (1985) 'A Tradition of Repression: The Street Traders of Johannesburg,' in R. Bromley (ed.) *Planning for Small Enterprises in Third World Cities*, New York: Pergamon Press.

Seker, M., Varcin, R., and Turegun, A. (1987) 'Insan Haklari Baglaminda Gezici Tarim iscileri,' *Insan Haklari Yilligi*, Ankara: TODAIE Publication.

Varcin, R. (2000) 'Competition in the Informal Sector of the Economy: The Case of Market Traders in Turkey,' *International Journal of Sociology and Social Policy*, 20(3–4): 5–33.

Weiker, W. (1981) *The Modernization of Turkey*, New York: Holmes and Meier.

*Zaman* (1992) 'Pazarda Bos Tezgah Eylemi,' 30 May: 13. Istanbul: Zaman.

# 8 Pirates on the high streets

## The street as a site of local resistance to globalization

*John C. Cross*

## Introduction

We are sitting around the dinner table eating a savory meatball and rice plate (*albóndigas*) prepared by my host's wife. Eduardo and his wife are hard-working, middle-aged, and stocky; their oldest daughter is going to a private university, their second daughter works with them while she waits for her turn to study tourism. Their youngest child is a teenager in high school who practices soccer in the afternoons or kicks the ball around with the pre-school children in the courtyard of their *vecindad* (housing complex). Small children from neighboring apartments come in and out and one small red-headed girl is invited to stay for dinner, which the boy tenderly feeds to her. The apartment is comfortable and solidly middle-class, the furniture is sensible and sturdy. In sum, this looks like a solid and loving middle-class family, the kind of family that politicians would be proud to claim as the "salt of the earth," with children who happily help their parents at their work and seem to be immune from rebellious drug use that consumes so many young teenagers. However, every few minutes Eduardo gets up and goes to the closet under the stairs to replace 15 hot CDs from his "burners" with 15 blank CDs. Outside the *vecindad* the bustle of the largest illegal market of counterfeit goods in Mexico is just ending for the day, and under my chair are stacks of CD cases we have just prepared. After dinner the cases will be filled with bootleg copies of popular Mexican and American albums, and tomorrow they will take them to their stall on the street and start another day as criminals.

One of the many criticisms of street markets is that it is difficult to control illegalities within them. They may occupy space without a permit, prices may be "fudged" by using inaccurate scales, or hygienic regulations ignored (Bromley 2000: 7–9; Cross 1998: 111). These types of procedural illegalities are what Portes and Castells (1989) refer to as the basis of "informality": providing legal goods or services by violating the normal regulations that apply to such businesses. But street markets may also be places where clearly illegal goods and services are provided, such as prostitution or contraband goods. If these goods are clearly illegal, morally reprehensible in the local population, and fairly easy to spot, such as illegal drugs, they will usually play a relatively minor part of open street market activity, and such markets have not been included within this volume. However, what about illegal goods that are considered morally justifiable by the local community and are thus difficult to take action against?

One example of this is the widespread sale of pirated music and videos by individuals such as Eduardo. In this chapter we will discuss the role of street markets in allowing such "soft-illegalities" to occur, and in particular the local justifications that make it difficult for police to obtain community support against them. In addition, we will consider the following question: while these types of illegalities are often used as an excuse for cracking down on street vending in general (Kettles 2004 and this volume), are they a form of "resistance," as discussed by Scott (1990), to increasingly globalized government and corporate policies that rarely take the needs of the poor (or other minorities) into account?

## Background: The war against piracy

While many people believe that the act of copying and reselling music and movies is a relatively mild offense, the corporations and individuals that produce these products, which I will hereafter refer to as the "cultural industry," do not agree, and there is a quiet global war against Eduardo and his fellow pirates. Copyright rules and protections have been around for a long time, but never have copyrights been such a massive and lucrative business. In the US, copyright and patent licenses account for 5 percent of GNP (Cresanti 2004). Worldwide infringements of copyright protection alone cost US businesses an estimated $25 billion, a figure that does not include internet piracy, which is almost impossible to measure (IIPA 2005). On the other hand, copyright protection, which is supposed to protect individual authors and is ostensibly class neutral, is more and more monopolized by massive corporations which control vast amounts of cultural production – five companies, for example, control 80 percent of worldwide music production (Jones 1996).

Under Mexican law it is a federal crime punishable by up to ten years of prison to make unauthorized copies of intellectual products such as songs, movies, and computer programs "for purposes of profit."[1] In recent years, under pressure from the United States and Europe, and following its treaty obligations under the North American Free Trade Agreement (NAFTA) and the World Intellectual Property Organization (WIPO), Mexico has significantly strengthened the penalties for such activities, popularly called "piracy," and has formed special units within the Federal Attorney General's office, the *Procuraduria General de la República* (PGR), to combat them.

However, it is widely recognized by Mexican authorities, as well as industry associations such as the International Intellectual Property Alliance (IIPA), that cultural piracy has become a massive problem in the country. Mexico is rapidly climbing the list of major world producers of counterfeit CDs and DVDs. According to *El Economista* (2004) the Mexican market loses $1.1 billion a year to piracy sales of 70 million CDs, or 60 percent of all sales, making it the second largest piracy market in Latin America and the fourth largest in the world.[2] The IIPA (2005) estimates that losses to US firms grew from $395.2 million in 1995 to $820 million in 2004.

Unlike the US and Europe where the internet is ubiquitous and most piracy takes the form of downloading songs through file-sharing programs, in developing societies like Mexico, the predominant form of piracy is the sale of counterfeit copies of cassettes, CDs, and DVDs in the street since few people have computers and fewer have broadband access to the internet. This would appear to make enforcement easier, since street sales necessarily take place in plain view of both customers and police, but in fact the sheer scale of such markets and the highly organized nature of street vending have made effective enforcement almost impossible. One of the most important "pirate" markets exists in a working-class neighborhood next to the historical center of Mexico City with a long history of resistance to the legal system. That neighborhood is called Tepito.

The IIPA notes that the main problem with dealing with piracy in Mexico:

> [is] well known pirate marketplaces that remain largely outside the reach of law enforcement – most notably the district of Tepito. Without a government-initiated sustained campaign against well known pirate marketplaces like Tepito, the situation in Mexico is unlikely to change dramatically, regardless of the otherwise fine intentions and work of PGR.
>
> (2005)

In an ongoing research project we have been investigating what it is about Tepito that gives it the ability to "remain largely outside the law," but more specifically why "Tepiteños" feel the need (and the right) to do so. In this chapter we report on some initial research that touches on aspects of this question. Based on ethnographic research, we will illustrate the processes and issues involved in piracy by highlighting the story of three "pirates" who have turned to the sale, and in some cases the production, of illegally copied CDs and DVDs to make ends meet. We will then discuss why piracy has become so easy to do from practical and ecological perspectives. Finally, we will discuss the "justifications" given by pirates for their activity as a way of revealing the "right" that vendors feel they have to carry out an activity that they recognize is legally proscribed. Valid or not, we will argue that these perceptions of rights create a practical and, perhaps in some cases, an ideological form of resistance to the dominant ideology that intellectual property rights form an absolute privilege to control the dissemination of cultural goods.

## Methodology

Our primary objective is to understand why piracy has grown so dramatically in the Tepito area. As a part of that question we need to understand how and why individuals have changed to the sale and/or production of pirated materials as well as the broader impact of changes in the neighborhood as a whole. We also needed to understand how piracy works on a practical level: what makes it a more feasible alternative than other types of products and services that people could offer? A survey was considered far too dangerous politically and personally given the reticence shown by vendors under constant surveillance in a neighborhood subject to violence when merchants fight back against the police raids occurring several times a week.

Thus, we used a qualitative approach utilizing previous contacts in the area. A semi-structured interview schedule was developed to flexibly consider the following five broad questions: (1) What was their family status? (To measure what needs the subject had.) (2) What jobs did the subjects' parents have as a child, and what was their career path? (To measure changes in occupation.) (3) How did they actually operate their pirate business? (Whether selling, burning, or both.) (4) What problems have they had with the police, or other risk factors? (5) What moral qualms did they have about (or justifications for) their activity? The precise wording was not crucial since there was no attempt to get a statistical sample. Instead, in each case the focus was on trying to get as deep an understanding of the issue as possible from the subjects' point of view.

### Access

Over the 15 years that I have been working in Tepito, beginning with my research on street vending in 1991, I have built up a working relationship with a number of street vendors and leaders in the area. During my previous research I would often approach street vendors cold to conduct interviews, but my local contacts recommended against this strategy for vendors selling pirated goods. Even though sales take place in the open, pirates are loath to share information with strangers since they could be investigators or informants for copyright protection associations collecting information for prosecution.[3] In addition, the constant raids in the neighborhood create the constant suspicion that "moles" are supplying information to the police, and if a raid occurred after I had interviewed someone, they or I could be accused of being a stool pigeon.

Instead, I relied upon my previous contacts with leaders who were widely respected in the area. Even then, some leaders were reluctant to risk their reputations. Even those who trusted me were worried that a coincidental raid would make it look as though I had abused their confidence. On one occasion, for example, my best informant advised me not to use a baseball cap with a circular badge that I had worn in the neighborhood. Apparently some vendors thought the badge was an official logo.[4] For the same reason, although I hoped to obtain a snow-ball sample from my initial contacts in order to broaden the sample, this was not possible. Vendors were very reluctant to introduce me to others, not because they distrusted me, but because any mishap could affect their relationship with the friends or neighbors that they had introduced me to. For example, when I asked one of my most cooperative subjects for a referral:

> They ... explained as politely as they could that they would normally never talk about their business, even with others in the neighborhood. It was far too dangerous. Someone might set them up for revenge or for money. They supposed that others would feel the same way and wouldn't feel comfortable recommending me. They suggested I talk to [their street vendor leader] about introducing them to other people, because it was only because he introduced me that they felt safe talking to me and inviting me inside their home to see what they did.
>
> (fieldnotes)

In the end, I was able to interview a total of 12 vendors besides discussions that I had with my long-time informants/associates. Of those, two were fairly brief, but the other ten were each over an hour. In several cases, interviews took all afternoon, and in two cases I continued the interview over several days and met other members of the family. In one case I assisted the family with their work and thus learnt far more about the processes involved than interviews and observations alone would provide. To protect informants I relied exclusively on written notes and names were not asked and never written down. Due to these limitations, the interviews were gathered almost entirely through two organizations (out of almost 40 in the neighborhood) and did not represent as wide a variety of subjects as I had originally hoped. Nevertheless, while this data should be considered to be preliminary it still represents a unique perspective into a complex and secretive form of behavior that has not been studied to date. In the future, I hope to supplement this information with information from other areas.

In the next section we will describe three "case studies" of pirates. Our objective in this section is to show the different variety of approaches to piracy. The names used are fictitious and some of the details have been obscured to prevent any possibility of identification, but the cases are very real. They were selected from the larger sample because they represented different types of vending, although they do not exhaust by any means the variety of possibilities even within that sample.

## "A pirate's life for me"

### *Eduardo: A middle-class pirate (48, married, 3 children, sells CDs)*

Eduardo, who we mentioned above, is proud to call himself a third generation Tepiteño (resident of Tepito). Now in his forties with three grown children that he is putting through college and high school, he sees piracy as the only way to maintain a middle-class lifestyle. He is far from an unskilled laborer. His father used to own a handbag factory with an exclusive contract to supply a high-end retail chain with outlets throughout Mexico. "Unfortunately my father was a very honorable man (*cabal*) and respected his word. But the store didn't." When the store was merged with another in 1981, the contract was cancelled and his father was unable to make another one as retail stores turned to cheaper imported leather goods. The factory was closed and he opened a taco stand for 6 years before retiring, renting the stall out.

Eduardo had a tourist visa for the United States so he made money for a while bringing clothes back from South Texas, but when he got a new passport his visa renewal was denied. So he relied on other importers, selling tennis shoes and later illegally imported electronic goods. He realized that he was getting a bum deal, though, because his supplier wasn't giving him a good price. At this time he won the lottery and tried to become an importer again. Unfortunately, it didn't work out. As his wife said, he insisted on maximizing his earnings by taking all his money up north to buy merchandise, but he was also risking it all. "I tried to do things legally," he said, "but they make it impossible." In the end he lost everything when a shipment was confiscated.

That began the toughest period of their lives together. "We had to put our kids in public schools for the first time, and we went from having two cars to having none." One car was even stolen as they tried to sell it. To make ends meet they worked all day, selling *tortas* (sandwiches) in the mornings in the *vecindad*, tacos outside a local school during lunch time, buying their supplies at the wholesale market (La Merced), and working at different cleaning jobs in the afternoon. Finally, they sold tacos until two in the morning on a neighborhood street. "We worked 29 hours a day – that's how we lifted ourselves back up."

In 1996 a street vendor association built concrete platforms on the sidewalk and his mother paid a down payment for a platform area that he could share with his two brothers. They didn't want to work the stall because it paid so little, so he ended up paying it off himself and got the ownership title from the association. At first they sold baby items that one of his wife's cousins gave them on commission. They didn't sell well so they turned to clothes. Finally, the cousin gave them pirated CDs to sell. But she didn't give them many, so he turned to another man who offered to give him all he could sell.

In 1999 his supplier was raided and five of his associates arrested. The supplier escaped and sold one of his burners to Eduardo who began burning his own CDs. At first he would buy his own originals at Ghandi (a formal bookstore). He wanted to sell something besides the pop artists that everyone else sold, and for a while he was the only vendor selling classical music and jazz. Now others do it too, "but I began it," he says proudly. Business went well, they expanded production and they moved out of the neighborhood, using the house they owned for production and storage only. But in 2003 their house was raided. Six *vecindades* in the area were hit. "They knew exactly where everything was," he said, suggesting the police had informants in the area.

> ... They broke down the door to his house and the door to his "office" and took everything he had – three machines with 10 burners each, about 1,200 original CDs, 5,000 pirated CDs, and about 6,000 blank CDs. Also, they took the cases that went with them – about $30,000 worth of material [author's estimate]. That wiped them out and they had to move back to their house: "They took everything. We didn't even have enough left to pay the rent."
>
> (fieldnotes)

After that they moved back into their house. They got some old burners that didn't work as well and went back into business. Now, they sell about 2,000 CDs a week, but they say earnings are down. The price of pirated CDs has dropped until they make only 1 or 2 pesos profit on each CD (10–20 cents). Sales have also dropped as many vendors who used to buy from them wholesale have learnt to make their own CDs.

### Samuel: The entrepreneurial pirate (42, married to second wife, 4 children, sells DVDs)

From the beginning of our relationship Samuel was very suspicious about my intentions. Before we began our second interview he asked me a series of questions such as: "If you gave your brother $1,000 to hold for you and he had financial difficulties, would you want him to use it?" I told him I hoped he would, but also that he would pay me back if he could. He seemed satisfied but not entirely. He changed his story on several occasions, first claiming that he made CDs, then saying he only sold pirate CDs, then saying his son made the CDs, but they didn't sell them, to finally saying that his son made the CDs and he (Samuel) sold them. And I don't think I have the final story yet.

Samuel is, from what I have seen, a consummate entrepreneur. Every time I have seen him he is always trying to push a new product. A high-level informant told me that Samuel was single-handedly responsible for importing and distributing counterfeit Marlboros in Tepito, going directly to China to get a factory to produce them. The resulting cigarettes used sawdust rather than the normal chemical mix that Marlboro uses to keep the tobacco burning, and the box was a little smaller meaning they only had 18 cigarettes in each, but otherwise they seemed identical – the small differences were explained as a health benefit (fewer chemicals and less cigarettes). Even when I met him, he supplemented the sale of pirated CDs with the sale of smuggled cigarettes from Belize, one of his favored sources. The cigarettes tasted like crap, he said, but they were less than half the price of Mexican cigarettes. All of this was in addition to a liquor store that he owned in the neighborhood that seemed to do a pretty good business.

Other ventures I observed during the month or so over which our interviews continued were a series of hot sauces that he had developed at home and wanted to start bottling (I was a part of his taste-test group), and a liquor that he claimed increased sexual potency. In addition to this, Samuel was constantly involved in importing goods from the US or Belize, whether legally or illegally. Indeed, Samuel complained bitterly about the difficulties of operating legally in Mexico despite the democratic opening and the "Free Trade Agreement," arguing that it was easier before when everything was under the table.

> If you bring something 100 percent illegal you know they will take it so you have to hide it. But if you are 100 percent legal they take it anyway and if you get it back you just get half or sometimes nothing ... Yes, you can import legally, but they ask for authorizations that you can't get. They ask for permits that they won't give you. That is, they reserve them for the people they favor.
>
> (interview)

Samuel argued that everyone worked illegally, including the big companies like Pricemart and Walmart. Free Trade has only made it more complicated, with procedures that only larger businesses could follow.

In fact, when I met him Samuel was in economic straits because he just lost a consignment of lipstick that he was importing. The Secretary of Health asked for a certificate proving that the goods were not counterfeit (one of the new requirements under WIPO rules). "I had a copy faxed, but they wouldn't accept it." To make up for the loss, he was planning to sell a building he owned in the neighborhood. The liquor store, he complained, was a money loser. "This is all 100 percent legal," he said, waving his hands at the bottles of liquor. "We've been open seven years but we're about to close because it isn't convenient. It doesn't earn enough to pay the light, for government costs. A legal business doesn't last." While the street vendors outside his door were protected by large associations and were never inspected, "In here we are inspected six times a year, and they always find something wrong to fine us or get a bribe ... if I do close, I'll dedicate myself full-time to piracy. But if it picks up maybe I'll leave it."

Samuel told me that his son, who lived with his estranged first wife, had become involved with drugs when he was younger and came clean, so he had purchased some burners for him to get his own business and learn responsibility. Before he had worked with a friend but "now he earns more. Up to 400 pesos (US $40) a day." After a few interviews, Samuel showed me the stall where he sells the products, along with smuggled cigarettes and counterfeit cologne. It was a large stall in the middle of a very commercial street, but he didn't do the kind of business people did on the main thoroughfare. At 2 p.m. he showed me his notebook where he kept track of his sales. So far he had only sold 98 DVDs, almost all at the discounted "wholesale" rate, which was just a few pesos over production costs.

### José: A young pirate (22, single, lived with parents and 3 siblings, sells CDs)

Many of the pirates I was introduced to were middle-aged like the two preceding cases. This was largely due to the mode of access: the established leaders who had the respect of vendors knew the oldest vendors the best. But many younger vendors found the sale of pirated CDs and DVDs an easy way to start a business. I met José through his mother, who had noticed me interviewing other vendors and suggested I interview her son. Despite his young age he owned his own stall because he had joined a street invasion seven years before while he was still in high school.[5] "An older man from our neighborhood took me to meet the leader and I had to go to several meetings," he said. In the meantime, he worked at a retail store to save up money for the stall, the closest anyone in his family has come to formal employment. "They didn't treat me good," he says. They kept him late and the pay was poor.

When he got his stall, he sold clothes at first. "The clothes had to be fashionable, so you lost a lot. Fashions change and you need a lot of sizes," so he would get stuck with a lot of merchandise, or it would get ruined in the rain. "You earned, but it was problematical. On one piece you could earn 100 pesos (US $10), but you lost a lot." So after a few years he switched to selling legal CDs. He liked going to record stores and buying CDs on sale. "If something cost 80 pesos I would sell it for 140. And that was a good profit." But, "people wanted more things, and they wanted it cheaper." Pirated CDs at that time were selling for 20 or 30 pesos, "So I decided to start stocking pirated CDs ... I started with a few, as people asked me for them. And now it is more pirated than original." As the price of pirated goods has fallen, it has become more and more difficult to make money selling legitimate CDs, even at cut-rate prices.

But for José, who sees himself as a music connoisseur, the price is not the only factor that gives piracy an edge: "It isn't so much the cheapness but that in the piracy there is all the new stuff when the store only has one artist on a CD and if they have a CD with several it is too expensive ... The sales are for only a few items that don't sell, so the people don't want them." Many of the legitimate CDs that don't sell are new artists or material that just didn't work. Sometimes there might be one or two good songs, but it wouldn't be worth it to buy the whole CD. So, someone would make a pirated CD with a mix of the more popular songs. He pointed to several that looked like copies of legitimate CDs, but he said they were fully produced by pirates by making their own combination of popular songs. These would then get pirated by others.

These three examples of pirates show that piracy is not, at least in the case of Tepito, a matter of "mafias" or criminal masterminds, but largely individuals who have chosen piracy as a means of subsistence. But why is it so easy for these individuals to violate the law? In the following section, we will discuss how technological changes have contributed to this process by allowing individuals and in some cases their families to work together to compete in the "pirate marketplace."

## The mechanics of piracy

Piracy has become far easier to carry out in recent decades due to new computer technology available in the last decade. Paradoxically, when the compact disk was first introduced it was touted as a "pirate free" alternative to the cassette tape, but with the introduction of personal computers with CD burners it became far easier to copy a CD than a cassette. While entertainment companies have developed encryption programs to protect their products, counter-encryption programs can easily defeat these. From there it is a short step to the development of computer towers that can automatically copy five, seven, or more CDs at once. Furthermore, the relaxation of import requirements under NAFTA and GATT means that computer equipment prices, as well as the prices of "raw materials" such as blank disks, have fallen dramatically in countries like Mexico, which used to have strong protectionist tariffs.

Counterfeiting is now as easy to do as making toast. All the relevant elements are readily (and legally) available: all the individual has to do is put them together. Computer towers are sold in Tepito itself, or at a nearby computer market. The blank disks are also sold in bulk in the neighborhood, and often they are brought straight to the stalls or residences of the producers. Prices are so competitive that they actually fluctuate over the day by a few pesos per hundred and are always far lower than in any regular store. The cases are sold by the box load and also delivered to the consumer, although as competition has increased some vendors have switched from plastic cases to plastic bags. An entire street is dedicated to the sale of the "covers"[6] that are copied from original CD cases and printed up in color by the hundreds. All of these practices in themselves are perfectly legal. The only act that violates the law is the physical "burning" of the data from a copyrighted disk onto a blank CD with the intent to sell the product.

Some people, like Eduardo above, handle all aspects of the process themselves. He starts by getting the "covers" of CDs that he wants to make. If necessary, he will also buy a "master," which is a copy of the original CD already de-encrypted. He has the blank CDs and cases delivered to his stall or his house by "runners" who go around the stalls of vendors offering their products. His children then help by folding the covers so that they can be later inserted into their cases. This can be done while watching TV, so it is not considered very onerous. "Encasing" is actually the most laborious part of the process – putting the "covers" into the cases. His children do this around the dining room table in the afternoons after school. One day I asked if I could help:

> They were in the middle of "encasing" and invited me in. The table had stacks of CD cases and the black CD holder that goes inside them. The girls and the boy are all sitting around the table where I join them. They have the printed covers and backs in packets of ten. Girl 1 is sitting next to me and hands me a packet of covers and shows me how to put them together. I have to slip the front cover in the front of the case, and put the back in the back part and then clip the black CD holder part over the back part. The pieces have already been folded, so they should slip right in but generally they are a little big and sometimes we have to cut them with scissors. It takes me a while to get into the rhythm and they go much faster than me. The boy bangs together ten pieces and then takes a short break in the time it takes me to do three or four.
>
> (fieldnotes)

While this is going on, Eduardo is burning CDs, a process that will take much longer. They burn ten at a time in three machines, stacking up the copied CDs with slips of paper in between the different titles so that they know where they will go. He puts the CDs into the cases when he is done, often later at night. When I asked why he didn't start putting the CDs in the cases right away to save time, he politely told me my advice was not needed. "Don't mess up our system. Next thing you know, they will be all mixed up."

The selling is done in the daytime between 9 a.m. and 3 p.m. Usually, the son will load up their dolly with six to seven boxes full of CDs and other assorted supplies and set up the stall. Eduardo does most of the selling, but he is helped by the children if they don't have school. Towards the end of the selling day, if they will need to make more CDs, Eduardo will go shopping for covers again and the cycle will repeat itself as the children pack up the stall.

Other vendors, such as José, do not have their own machines, and sub-contract the copying. "Here it is a chain," said one woman. "Besides the people selling the masters there are the burners, and then the sellers." In some cases, vendors rely on relatives to do the burning. One older couple selling DVDs partnered with a cousin who did the burning. As the sales price has gone down, many vendors have started to do their encasing at the stall (previously a task done by producers) to save time and money.

In sum the act of counterfeiting has become so easy that almost anyone can participate. Like the advent of crack cocaine, which used a cheap and easy technology to turn powder cocaine into a more potent variant, the result has been a rapid increase in competition and a drop in prices. Most vendors reported that 6–7 years ago prices for counterfeit CDs were about 60 pesos (US $5). At the time of research (summer, 2005) CDs were selling in Tepito for as little as 4 pesos (40 cents).

The ease of producing and selling pirated products is only one side of the story, of course. Vitally important to understanding the ability of these vendors to thwart the law is the role of the social ecology of areas such as Tepito and how that ecology makes enforcement in these areas tenuous. Tepito has long been considered a "lawless" area where police presence occurs only in force but, as I have argued elsewhere and will elaborate on in subsequent publications, it is not as much lawless as self-regulating. For example, in Cross (2005) I analyze the role that street vendor organizations in the area play in helping to defend the neighborhood against an all-out assault by police.

In the next section I will focus on another element that makes enforcement difficult – the fact that producers, vendors, and other community members feel that their activity is justified and thus morally worth the risk. This means that despite the sometimes violent enforcement efforts made by authorities, the neighborhood itself helps to protect vendors as they are seen as carrying out a necessary activity. As I will show, even though vendors recognize that they are on the wrong side of the law, they believe in large part that they are in the right, and that the law is wrong. It is not that they deny the rights of the music and producers, however, as much as they believe that those rights have been abused.

## Justifications of piracy

Everyone that I spoke to was clearly aware that piracy was an illegal activity severely sanctioned under Mexican law. In fact, during the research period there was a lively debate in the press about new laws designed to stiffen penalties and apply the conspiracy law (similar to the Racketeer Influenced and Corrupt Organizations (RICO) law in the United States originally applied to organized crime and drug cartels) so that prosecutions could be made more easily. Raids were a regular occurrence in the neighborhood, and usually were carried out in massive operations involving hundreds of police officers led by the elite Federal Agency of Investigation (the Mexican equivalent to the FBI in the United States).

One of the questions that I asked all of my subjects was whether they felt guilty for the negative effect they might have on artists and the companies that produced them. When appropriate I would challenge them by giving arguments made in the press against piracy. As discussed above, their answers were varied, but I categorized them into four basic groups. Furthermore, the reasons given in these free-flowing interviews tend to be mixed together, so in some cases the categories blend together. Rather than formally coding specific responses into distinct categories, therefore, the different categories are described and illustrated with representative quotes from the interviewees. With such a small sample it is impossible to know how representative these views are among vendors, nor whether there might be more, but for now it gives some indication of the tendencies that can be tested with further research.

### Economic need

The most frequent reason given was the most obvious one for anyone who has worked with street markets: economic need. While they worried constantly about being arrested, an older man who said he was trying to look for another type of work because of the high risk and low income asked me "But what else am I going to do?" "We know it isn't legal, but it leaves us two or three pesos and that pays for our salaries," another vendor said. José, who said he had friends in bands and debated the issue with them often, commented, "I don't like it myself but it is my job. Work is work." Many of the vendors blamed the government or economic changes for the lack of viable alternatives. As Samuel said, "There are no jobs here, and if they do provide jobs it is where your expenses are 200 pesos but you only earn 100. Can you live on that?" A leader put it more eloquently, noting that even with their low incomes Tepito raises many families, "Because the government doesn't produce jobs, but it does produce poverty."

One could argue that none of my informants was really in dire need, so their activity was not justified by poverty. But on the one hand their lack of poverty was due to their illicit income. On the other, "need" is defined socially, not in absolutes. The fact is that Tepito is a historically working-class neighborhood that has been hit hard by changes in the Mexican economy as legal jobs have been harder to find. Traditional craft activities that flourished in the area such as shoe making and leatherwork as well as semi-skilled jobs in local industries have been largely displaced by foreign competition with the opening of the Mexican market to "Free Trade" under GATT and NAFTA, and even alternative "soft" illegalities such as the sale of contraband electronic goods have been virtually eliminated as these products are now available legally in formal stores. The increase in both drug sales and abuse in the neighborhood reflects the growing desperation in the area, and vendors of pirated goods may indeed be justified in claiming that they have found a less socially destructive avenue of subsistence.

In fact, many of the vendors compared their activity favorably to the sale of drugs. Samuel asked me, "If you didn't have a job, would you sell drugs, steal, or sell piracy?" After hearing similar arguments from different individuals, I asked one man whether they weren't after all similar in breaking the law. He disagreed strongly: "Don't turn that around [*No le des vuelta con esto*]. Those who sell drugs and steal is one thing, but piracy is due to hunger. If they have something legal to sell, those who sell piracy are content. They do it only because there is no other option." I challenged another vendor, asking if he felt that piracy was an honorable profession. "No, but what honorable job can there be? To switch from piracy to theft?" Continuing as a devil's advocate, I suggested that some people would say they should do neither. "That is the proof of our honesty then – for us to die of hunger! They talk of honesty, but they don't know about our needs."

### Normalization

Closely related to the issue of need was the argument that piracy had become such a staple for the community that it had become normalized. As one informant said, "The truth is that one becomes accustomed to it – being here you see everything and get used to everything." Younger participants especially had literally grown up with it. For example, when I asked one of Eduardo's daughters if she felt guilty she responded simply, "I never thought about it." Another response that is related to this justification is the argument that piracy had become so easy to do (as discussed above) that the fault lay in the technology itself: "The 'gringos' (Americans) are the ones who make the technology to do this," Eduardo's other daughter argued, suggesting that the ease of piracy made it acceptable. A leader agreed that piracy was illegal, and then added, "But customs make the law."

The vast amount of piracy in the neighborhood has a normative effect, but it also has a more competitive effect. Several of the interviewees, like José, had started by selling legal CDs that they obtained on sale from distributors. One woman noted, "It didn't sell a lot, but you earned enough. But [the distributors] started to raise the prices ... Now it is all piracy." Another vendor asked, "If I turn legal, but the guy next to me still sells piracy, what do I do?" Normalization is thus reinforced by or blended with competitive reality.

### Blaming the victim

A popular justification for criminal activity is that the victim deserved it due to some moral lapse. Similarly, in this case, vendors often blamed the artists and producers themselves. The idea that artists who boasted about their wealthy, and sometimes seedy, lifestyle might be affected by their actions did not cause these vendors a lot of grief. The multinational corporations that dominate the music and movie industries met with even less sympathy: if artists could at least be seen as morally suspect but admired individuals (after all, they admired their artistic work enough to copy it), faceless corporations, whether Mexican or foreign, could be seen only as sources of oppression.

Comments critical of the cultural industries were the second most frequent comments after need. When I asked a middle-aged couple whether piracy was a form of robbery, the man agreed, but then added, "Let me explain. Who robs more, them or us? What have the record companies done for the country? What have the movie studios done? What have the presidents done for the country, to make jobs?" His wife added, "They just worry about themselves." The man became so excited that he stood over me to make sure I was writing down every word: "That Free Trade agreement makes the rich richer and the poor more screwed, because to benefit from the trade you have to have a lot of money. Now [Mexican companies] are all trans-nationals, but the poor are worse off."

### *Playing Robin Hood*

Related to this disdain for the cultural industries, some vendors saw them-selves as providing a vital service for the public that those industries failed to deliver: "As someone who sells piracy I screw [*doy en la madre a*] the industry. But who am I helping?" one asked rhetorically, then answered himself: "The people." This viewpoint, shared to a greater or lesser extent by at least half the informants who made similar, if less direct, statements, is also promulgated by a local newsletter put out by an anonymous group that calls itself the "pirates of Tepito." In one issue they responded to the director of a movie called "Don de Tepito" who complained vociferously when his "director's cut" was distributed widely in the market a month before the official release date. "Who is he to complain," the article asked, "when his lousy movie makes everyone in Tepito seem like a criminal or a drug dealer?" In private discussions with members of the group, the argument that multi-national corporations were obtaining intellectual property rights over vital food and medical resources that often originated in the Global South was mixed with the argument that the pirates were making (perhaps less vital but still significant) cultural resources available within the budget of the masses. "With the minimum salary [about 50 pesos (US $5) a day], it isn't possible to buy an original disk for 200 or 300 pesos. They will spend their entire weekly wage. They come here and can find the same quality ... but we can make it cheaper." Another vendor added, "The need of popular culture is to have culture that is accessible for the people. But [the industry] just makes money and more money."

Several times I asked my informants if cultural products such as music and movies are really "necessities" that people need to survive, but I never received a direct response. One could certainly question whether the provision of cheap music and movies, especially the generally low level of quality pumped out by Hollywood, can be compared to Ghandi's challenge of the British salt monopoly in India. However, as I argue above, need is relative. Mexico is a good example of a culture where music is a highly valued social good. Cultural industries have pumped millions of dollars into advertising campaigns to create a "demand" for movies and new brands of music, and then effectively deny that demand through high prices. Furthermore, while historically the Mexican cultural industries supplied most products at a lower price in Mexico compared with First World countries such as the United States (and this is still true, for example, of Mexican cinemas), pricing of CDs and DVDs in formal stores is often higher than comparable prices in the United States. Is it any surprise, then, that people look for an alternative source?

Of course, one could argue that these justifications are simply excuses that any miscreant might make for their activity. The extent to which these justifications are heartfelt or simply defensive will be left to the reader. However, as a research note, I would point out that this was often when subjects became the most animated, actively trying to teach me their point of view. As I tried to keep up with their comments on my notepad, they would often repeat themselves and make sure that I got down every word. With a few exceptions, most of the interviewees appeared to have strong, well thought out beliefs.

Support for the argument that these justifications should be taken seriously was given indirectly by an interview with a top official charged with enforcement of intellectual property rights in Mexico City. When asked about his private opinions about piracy, his comments mirrored the arguments made by pirates. When I asked why they didn't try to arrest more people, he said, "Here it is a problem of social conflict. First, they are unemployed, they don't have opportunities. Also, they are in places where there are many of them and it is difficult to enter because it generates a conflict because they see it as a job that they want to protect, and not a crime." He was particularly loath to arrest vendors because of the possibility of conflict. When I asked him if the penalties were appropriate, he said, "I'm convinced that raising the penalties is not the solution. It is a social and economic problem more than a delinquency problem ... I would prefer to be grabbing drug traffickers than pirates." Like the pirates, he agreed that the cultural industries shared the blame: "It is also a problem of the artists: It isn't possible that a disk that costs 200 pesos just has one good song and all the rest are garbage!" Why, then, do they try to enforce the laws? "It is mostly the internationals – that is, those who squeeze us are the 'gringos' [Americans] for these operations." Interestingly, like the vendors, since I was still writing, he repeated the comment about gringos to make sure I wrote it down.

## Conclusion

Sociologically, whether defensive or heartfelt, the justifications given by individuals involved in the production and sale of "pirated products" pose an ideological challenge to the argument that the issue of piracy is black and white as the cultural industries argue. After all, everyone has justifications, and while the tendency is to privilege the justifications of the rich and power-ful – the need to be able to collect their profits in order to stimulate economic production – we should not dismiss the existence of a counter-claim as simply a matter of criminals excusing their violations of the dominant order.

Rather, our argument is that, in both their practice and their justifications, pirates represent a significant counter-ideology to the hegemony of the cultural industries. It is not a revolutionary ideology by any means, and given that it is carried out within the context of a market economy, it is far from anti-capitalistic. Still, it represents a challenge to the unbridled power that the multinational corporations would like to have to determine unilaterally the prices of their products in the marketplace. To the extent that piracy continues out of control in countries like Mexico this may create a significant problem for companies trying to recoup their costs of production for movies and music, particularly as those costs have soared for "big name" products and increasingly rely on international sales to break even. Paradoxically, however, while much of the counter-ideology of pirates involves expressions of anti-imperialism, the national industries may be affected even more: already many Mexican artists and movies make far more money in the more secure US market than they do in their own country (Iliff 2004).

"Tepiteños" in particular are proud of their resistance to a political and economic system that they consider to be morally bankrupt. Located locally within a context in which they argue they have to be "*chueco*" (crooked) in order to survive, they are little concerned with the broader impacts that their activity may cause. And even if they are concerned, they believe that they can do little about it: after all, as one vendor said, "If I don't sell it, someone else will." Through the stories of three pirates, we have shown that these individuals are far from being stereotypical criminals or radicals: instead, they are young people trying to improve their standard of living, middle-aged couples raising their children, and older people searching for a way to remain economically active. My research suggested there was no "mafia" of pirates, at least in Tepito, despite the huge amount of activity involved and the constant refrains in the press, because the activity was too freewheeling for any one group to control.

What piracy in the streets of Tepito shows, however, is that these individualized "micro-realities" have a powerful effect on the "macro-realities," in this case of both international trade and international diplomacy as the United States puts more and more pressure on countries in the "Global South" to comply with rules that will, arguably, increase the profits of a growing sector of the First World economy.

Thus, while the tendency even within studies of the informal economy is to see street markets as minor nuisances at worst or limited panaceas at best, we have shown that they should also be seen as potential sites of resistance to the dominant ideology of both space and redistributive power. Scholars should focus much more attention on both overt and practical forms of resistance. Scholars should also link the empirical reality of markets and market activities to empirical studies of regulatory regimes and the socio-historical development of those regimes. Street markets not only allow the sale of goods that would normally be controlled by government and corporations, in spaces that would normally be monopolized by the "private sector," they also allow the spread of ideas, and products, that would otherwise be controlled or effectively censored.

In this case, the emerging "counter-ideology" of the street carries a powerful rebuke of the dominant political-economic system: if they had jobs, they would not need to break the law (after all, they are working, not stealing); if prices of movies and music were not so high, they would not have a market advantage (after all, they are merchants, not thieves); if the government were not so corrupt and businesses not so monopolistic, they would not have to break the rules that favor those large businesses (after all, if they are crooked, so much more the ruling elites).

Will any of these issues ever be resolved? That question is far beyond the scope of this modest work. Nevertheless, in the meantime street markets like Tepito constitute a form of "reality" check on the dominant economic and political system. Just like the old King of the Britons who put his throne on the beach to see if the tide would obey his commands, so multinational corporations are finding that they cannot simply abuse their claims of ownership of property rights: in effect, street markets like Tepito will force them to balance their "rights" with those of the societies they wish to serve (or exploit). The ultimate irony of this situation is that Tepito does this through capitalist mechanisms: not because they are altruistic or even particularly well organized but because they are trying to make a living for themselves.

## Notes

1 This is a significant difference from US copyright laws, which prohibit any unauthorized copying whatsoever. For example, making a copy of a CD for a friend would not be illegal in Mexico.
2 In terms of *per capita* production, however, it actually has more piracy than China, India, Russia, and Brazil, the other top-five nations.
3 Under Mexican law, copyright infringement must be denounced by the titular owner of the property or their agent before the police can take action, unlike drug enforcement where the offense is considered to be against society. So copyright associations representing major publishing houses regularly send spies into the neighborhood to get information for complaints such as the name and location of vendors and the specific titles that they are counterfeiting.
4 It was actually a baseball cap from New Orleans that said N.O. Rules. Some vendors may have done an imperfect translation and assumed I was a "Rule" enforcer.
5 Stalls are very hard to obtain in this area, so most of the younger vendors rent them or are employees. The only way of getting a stall without buying it (which costs thousands of dollars) is to join an invasion of an empty street, involving a lot of political work and perhaps the possibility of violence (see Cross 1998).

6 "Covers" refer to the printed sheet of paper that describes the contents of a CD. Typically, pirates buy covers that have been photocopied directly from the original covers of the CD or DVD that they are copying.

## Bibliography

Bromley, R. (2000) "Street Vending and Public Policy: A Global Review," *International Journal of Sociology and Social Policy*, 20/1: 1–28.

Cresanti, R. (2004) "Protecting US Innovations from Intellectual Property Piracy," *Federal Document Clearing House Congressional Testimony*, Capitol Hill Hearing Testimony, September 23.

Cross, J. (1998) *Informal Politics: Street Vendors and the State in Mexico City*, Stanford, CA: Stanford University Press.

—— (2005) "Piratería Callejero, el Estado y la Globalización," paper presented at conference on "Comercio, Cultura e Politicas Publicas en Tempos de Globalizacion," Escola de Servicio Social of the Universidade Federal de Rio de Janeiro, Brazil, May.

*El Economista* (2004) "Mexico Loses $1.1 Bln Annually from Piracy," Mexico, October 13.

IIPA (International Intellectual Property Alliance) (2005) "International Intellectual Property Alliance 2005 Special 301 Report." Online. Available: www.iipa.com (accessed January 3, 2006).

Iliff, L. (2004) "Piracy driving artists to US from Mexico," *The Dallas Morning News*, July 9.

Jones, S. (1996) "Mass Communication, Intellectual Property Rights, International Trade, and the Popular Music Industry," in E. McAnany and K. Wilkinson (eds) *Mass Media and Free Trade: NAFTA and the Cultural Industries*, Austin, TX: University of Texas Press.

Kettles, G. (2004) "Regulating Vending in the Sidewalk Commons," *Temple Law Review*, 77/1: 1–47.

Portes, A. and Castells, M. (1989) "Introduction," in A. Portes, M. Castells, and L. A. Benton (eds) *The Informal Economy: Studies in Advanced and Less Developed Countries*, Baltimore, MA: Johns Hopkins University Press.

Scott, J. (1990) *Domination and the Arts of Resistance: Hidden Transcripts*, New Haven, CT: Yale University Press.

# Part II
# Making the sale
## Strategies, survival, and embeddedness

The chapters in this part focus on specific strategies used by street vendors to survive and succeed, with more of an emphasis on marketing and networking. Obviously, as businesses, such vendors share many concerns with any other business: attracting clients, keeping them, and making a profit (or at least surviving) at the end of the day are chief among them. However, their location in public space makes for some interesting variation in the way they go about their business, as well as creating additional problems, such as security. They are also more directly placed in the public life of the community in a way that few store-front businesses can be: social life literally flows around them, creating a set of problems and opportunities that need to be more closely examined.

Dealing with the reemergent phenomenon of farmers' markets in the United States and Europe, Sage argues that these markets have created a niche for high-quality products and personalized services that were initially overlooked by supermarket chains and discount stores, revisiting the notion raised by a number of authors in this volume and elsewhere that street markets are about more than just monetary exchanges but also social relations. He also makes the point that the reemergence of street markets is far from simply a result of poverty, but also a matter of choices.

This focus on social relationships is continued by Lyon from a different angle in a different context: Ghana. Rather than focusing on street vending simply as a product of necessity, Lyon illustrates the role of social networks and relationships, and especially trader associations, embedded within the context of the history and tribal structure of Ghanian society. His work reveals the diverse organizational forms and inter-organizational relationships developed in the course of street vending. He convincingly argues these relationships cannot be reduced or understood as "informal" but instead are in turn political, economic, and social with important influences that should be understood and accounted for by regulators and development policy makers alike.

This notion of "embeddedness" rooted in the work of Polanyi and Granovetter is continued in the chapter by Stillerman and Sundt, who analyze the street markets of Santiago, Chile, and incorporate a comparison of neighborhood markets (*ferias*) and flea markets to understand the different strategies and relationships created by each. Within the markets themselves, the authors also compare the strategies of different types of vendors in terms of regulatory status – those with permits, and "pirate" vendors who are seen by some as "parasites" and by others as useful accomplices. The analysis does not allow for a black-and-white description of the markets, but rather provides vital insight by showing how relationships create the market by way of a complex interaction of social and regulatory behaviors in this ostensibly simple activity.

The chapters by Pachenkov and Berman (on Russia) and Companion (on Ethiopia) both examine the role of markets as networks in societies under crisis. Pachenkov and Berman argue that the much proclaimed growth of the informal sector in the Russian economy since the collapse of the centralized Soviet economy adapts old systems of survival while also adopting new ones. In this they argue the social role of the marketplace is at least as important as its economic role in transforming the old, soviet-era social and economic relations into the apparent chaos of the post-Soviet period. For them, the market is a matrix of intersecting systems of information and behavior, distinct and complete systems of reason, market and socialist, clashing with resulting crises of legitimacy, legality, and morality. We are fortunate to have a front-seat in this report on the transformation.

While dealing with a much more dramatic example of social collapse, the case of the 1999 famine in Ethiopia, Companion also starts with the idea that the market is an extension of the community, and she finds markets and merchants effective tools for gauging the effect of such famines, and even of predicting famine conditions. She finds current measures of food security benefit from the information available from markets making policy responses more timely and effective. The reader might note the irony of the similarity between Companion's discussion of the importance of local knowledge in Ethiopia's famine situation with Sage's discussion of the importance of local knowledge in the food scares of the wealthy First World.

Finally, De Bruin and Dupuis provide a colorful but theoretically grounded study of a vibrant street market in an impoverished district of a developed economy in New Zealand. They use the metaphor of a mural to encompass both the variety of activities, ethnicities, and purposes in the market as well as, in a broader sense, the relationship between the different market "sectors" – formal, informal, domestic, and so on – which must be seen as constantly interconnected rather than separated. Their close descriptions render clear the interconnectedness of local, regional, and global society terminating in a particular market, reverberating in household dynamics and entrepreneurial choices.

# 9 Trust in markets

## Economies of regard and spaces of contestation in alternative food networks

*Colin Sage*[1]

"Los mercados de alimentación son la sala de espera de la cocina"
("Food markets are the waiting room of cuisine")

Pep Palau (2004: 158)

## Introduction

Around the world, markets[2] are vital places that provide the backbone of the local food economy. Invariably occupying a strategic central location, markets draw together local people in the buying and selling of food. For the traveler, markets are privileged spaces that offer a window into "real life"; an opportunity to observe people engaged in an everyday activity that provides a microscopic lens on the local food culture. In an age when the giant retail chains appear to be sweeping all before them, it is heartening to know that local markets are undergoing something of a renaissance. Whereas supermarkets stock foods largely transformed from their natural states to accommodate the demands of long-distance transportation, central ware-housing, and long shelf life, local markets deal principally in fresh products with shorter life spans and much of it sourced within the region. Consequently, people are gradually returning to markets because they appreciate the human interaction, the character and taste of the food, and the sense of trust that comes from shopping personally.

In recent years, Europe and North America have witnessed a significant growth in new forms of food retailing whereby fresh and high-quality produce is sold directly by the producers themselves. The most visible examples are the development of farmers' markets (FM) in many urban locations, but there has also been a revitalization of street and covered municipal markets as well as the growth of other new retail arrangements such as farm shops, box schemes, community supported agriculture, forms of co-operative bulk purchase, and so on. The common feature of these initiatives is that they serve to reconnect food producers and consumers in a new and direct way, a relationship largely severed in recent years by the dominance of corporate multiple retailers. The term "alternative food networks" is often used as a label to cover this wide variety of innovative forms of production and sales (Renting *et al.* 2003; Goodman 2003).

What lies behind the emergence of these alternative networks and the revitalization of markets as sites of exchange? It is apparent that, particularly in Europe among people with high disposable incomes, there is a generalized disenchantment with the modern food system. This may seem somewhat paradoxical given its apparent success in delivering an unprecedented abundance and diversity of foods while consumers are spending the smallest proportion of their household budget on food. Yet analysis of the wider "external" costs associated with the modern food system reveals numerous environmental problems. These stretch from the fields and feedlots (soil erosion, excessive nutrient loading, loss of biological diversity) to the multiple indirect environmental consequences of global sourcing and centralized distribution[3] (Pretty *et al.* 2005; Church 2005; Paxton 1994; La Trobe and Acott 2000). Moreover, intensification and cost reduction in the livestock sector has probably encouraged the greatest public concern as industry practices produced the BSE crisis, dioxin contamination of poultry feed, foot and mouth disease, salmonella infection in eggs, and so on. Despite these setbacks, the food industry enabled rising meat and dairy product consumption, much to the growing concern of health specialists about the consequences of excessive dietary intakes of saturated fats and refined sugars (Lang and Heasman 2004; Winson 2004).

Above all, the modern food system produced standardization, creating global brands and global consumption patterns (Lind and Barham 2004). The domination of the global food industry by relatively few corporations, such that the top three food companies together had combined sales of almost US$ 100 billion in 2000, is constantly being extended through consolidation and concentration (Lang and Heasman 2004). This process, which we are constantly reassured is in the interests of the consumer in providing convenience, time saving, choice, and low price, has resulted in a fundamental transformation of our food system. Increasing numbers of people are now asking themselves: what are the hidden costs of this "convenience?" Is the time supposedly saved in shopping and in food preparation used for life-enhancing pursuits? And how has the selection, preparation, and consumption of food been reduced to just another chore in the general commodification of life rather than a source of pleasure and enjoyment?

Across Europe and North America, new networks of producers, consumers, and others are beginning to embody an alternative to the more standardized industrial mode of food supply. While they take on a variety of forms, what these networks have in common is an ability to redistribute value throughout the network (other than to find it concentrated in the hands of retailers). The high level of personal interaction that is a hallmark of exchange within these new networks, for example in farmers' markets, offers a novel experience to customers who have become accustomed to the impersonal nature of human contact reduced to the barcode scanning of the contents of their shopping basket. Such experiences have the capacity to recover the collective human experience associated with the preparation and exchange of foods and contribute to the *remoralization* of the food economy (Sage 2003).

This chapter interrogates the meaning of these exchanges, arguing that they go far beyond a simple commercial transaction, and comprise hybrid elements of both moral and money economies. While performing their respective practices and routines, both producers and consumers come to a mutual understanding of the value of the product and of the exchange. Through the grant and pursuit of regard, transacting partners become entangled in a reciprocal relationship whereby the intrinsic benefits of personalized interaction are valued. The central thesis of the chapter is that for too long we have diminished the importance of non-monetary dimensions of exchange and that we need to re-establish the moral economy of food markets.

The chapter makes the case for markets as sites where trust in food can be recovered through the act of buying it directly from the producer. The rise of alternative food networks (AFN), the features of which are discussed in the following section, has enabled some consumers to procure food in this way. One of the most popular and fastest-growing expressions of AFN has been the development of FM, which are outlined in the third section. Farmers' markets potentially embrace all the necessary elements of a moral economy of food, representing the embodiment of the local, more sustainable ways of producing and distributing food, and the recovery of trust between producer and consumer. The issues of trust, embeddedness, and mutual regard are discussed in the fourth section, which highlights the significance of a non-economic (i.e. moral) dimension in market transactions.

Yet, we should not underestimate the power of corporate capital or state bureaucracies to obstruct or refashion the potentially transformative nature of such spaces of exchange. The fifth section provides a case study of recent developments in Ireland that demonstrate how markets also serve as a contested arena between quite different visions of the use of public space and the ways in which we procure our food. Finally, the Conclusion under-lines the importance of public policy in ensuring that markets are enabled to provide people with the opportunity to acquire fresh, local produce at reason-able prices as an alternative to that provided by corporate food retailers. This would help strengthen the recovery of a moral economy around food and re-establish the importance of individual responsibility in food consump-tion practices.

## Features of alternative food networks

In a highly globalized world economic system, it is to be expected that food has become a commodity like any other, to be produced at the lowest price and subject to corporate processes in order to wring out the most profit

(Friedland 2004). Thus, much of the modern food system yields products that have been genetically mutated, irradiated, extruded, and made to appear as natural, nutritious, and "just picked," no matter if they have traveled halfway around the world. It is in relation to these concealed methods of production, the distancing of consumers from their food supply and their growing skepticism and distrust of labeling providing bland reassurances about its "farm-fresh quality," replete with associational images (Watts *et al.* 2005), that has led to a loss of confidence and trust in the conventional food supply system. Cook and Crang refer to a process of fetishization whereby "consumed commodities and their valuations are divorced for and by consumers from the social relations of their production and provision through the construction of ignorances about the biographies and geographies of what we consume" (1996: 135). This may help to explain the fearfulness and disempowerment of consumers at times of food scares. It may also account for the apparent quality "turn" of some consumers away from industrially produced foods and towards products that can demonstrate provenance to a place of origin, and therefore reassurance that it is safe to eat (Goodman 2002).

This "turn to quality" has consequently underpinned the emergence of alternative food networks, or short food supply chains, arising from consumer concerns for human health and food safety as well as other wider ethical considerations (animal welfare, fair trade, sustainability). Such developments have demonstrated that food markets are not the result of some "invisible" hand external to the social world but are produced by various actors in the food chain – consumers, producers, retailers, processors, etc. (Renting *et al.* 2003). This has encouraged the view that alternative food networks might help reverse long-established trends toward corporate concentration in the food sector and improve the share of total value accruing to primary producers. By breaking with the long, complex, and logistically organized supply chains run for the benefit of the major corporations, food networks have the potential to forge new links between producers and consumers. Indeed, by resocializing food, consumers – generally those with higher disposable incomes – are enabled and empowered to exercise a more reflexive and critical judgment about the relative desirability and quality of different food products (Renting *et al.* 2003) and build local food systems for community development (Feenstra 1997).

While claims for the transformational power of short food supply chains may be overstated, there is no question that FM and other new retail forms are bringing together ever-larger numbers of producers and consumers within a fundamentally different type of relationship than that found in conventional supply chains. One reason for this is that the product reaches the consumer embedded with information about the place of production, the methods employed, and the values of the people involved.

Marsden and colleagues (Marsden *et al.* 2000; Renting *et al.* 2003) have developed a three-fold typology of short food supply chains:

1.  *Face to face*: where the consumer purchases a product directly from the grower, farmer, or producer. This category includes farmers' markets, farm shops and roadside stalls, pick-your-own, box schemes, and home deliveries extending to mail order schemes involving telephone or on-line purchases. In all cases, authenticity and trust are mediated through direct personal interaction with the producer.
2.  *Spatial proximity*: although products may travel longer distances they are still predominantly retailed within the region of origin, invariably by people who have knowledge about the producer, the conditions of production, and appreciation of the attributes of the product. While this category includes more complex institutional arrangements for sales, the regional identity of the product is at the forefront. Examples include consumer co-operatives, fairs, gastronomic tourism, arrangements between producer farm shops, regionally themed restaurant menus, and so on.
3.  *Spatially extended*: while distribution into national and even international markets may appear to contradict the notion of *short* supply chains, this category refers to products with reputations and embedded with value-laden information about the place and characteristics of production. Regional specialties such as Parmigiano Reggiano cheese and Champagne wine or fair trade products such as Guatemalan coffee are, in their different ways, products that are strongly differentiated from anonymous commodities, commanding a premium price and often retailed through distinctive supply networks. In order to maintain the "exclusivity" of the product formalized codes, involving independent regulation and certification and established on a juridical basis, have been created to protect it from inferior imitations. Such codes include national and European designation of regional origin (PDO/PGI) or fair trade labeling (Parrott *et al.* 2002; Tregear 2003).

Clearly, as these categories demonstrate, short food supply chains encompass a wide range of different forms of interaction between producers and consumers. However, it is in the reinvigoration of markets in all their various forms where the influence of alternative food networks has become most apparent.

## The growth and significance of farmers' markets

Markets at which food constitutes the principal element (thereby putting to one side "flea" markets, car boot sales, and street markets where cheap clothing is the prevailing item) may still take a number of different forms. There are the municipal markets, mostly of nineteenth-century origin, established by local authorities in the interests of public health and civic planning, which continue to take place in covered, serviced central sites of architectural and civic interest.[4] Next are the periodic street markets that take place one or more days per week in a central square or street. Although such markets remain an important feature of most towns in France and Spain, they have experienced significant decline in Northern Europe in the post-war period under pressure of competition from the convenience of supermarket shopping. However, during the last ten or so years there has been a significant revitalization of street trading including a rapid expansion in the number of farmers' markets. While they are a new expression of a long-established tradition of weekly markets, FM have captured the imagination of consumers, food writers, and many small producers, providing an outlet for the sale of produce.

Farmers' markets appear to be an excellent way by which small growers, farmers, and other food producers can market their produce directly to the public without the high transaction costs or minimum volume requirements associated with conventional food supply chains. Although they are of little relevance for producers of bulk commodities or those involved in contract sales to food manufacturers and retailers, they offer real opportunities for increasing returns to farmers. For example, Pretty (2002) compares the paltry 8–10 percent share of each euro, dollar, or pound spent by consumers on food that finds its way back to the farmer through normal marketing mechanisms with the 80–90 percent when sold by that farmer directly to the consumer.

Starting in the United States, the number of FM there has grown from 1,700 in 1994 to over 3,700 in 2004. According to the US Department of Agriculture in their FM study of 2000, around 19,000 farmers sell their produce only at FM, with aggregate annual turnover exceeding US$ 1 billion. An important feature of the US experience is that 58 percent of FM participate in food poverty schemes, such as accepting food stamps, and in this way help to improve nutrition by facilitating increased consumption of fresh fruit and vegetables (USDA 2005). For the UK, Pretty (2002) reports that in 2001 there were 200 established FM trading, although the National Association of Farmers' Markets (NAFM) has only given its approval to just over half this number of markets that conform to NAFM criteria. In Japan, there are an estimated 2,500 FM, while in Ireland around 90 markets have been established, most of which have developed in the last three or four years. The situation in Ireland is discussed in more detail below. The key question that we have to ask, however, is "what explains this rapid growth and the desire of so many people to want to purchase some of their food from open-air stalls rather than at the supermarket?"

Holloway and Kneafsey, drawing on ideas derived from recent work in geography, approach FM both as a space of consumption and as a terrain where various networks of relationships between actors intersect. Underpinning the emergence of a farmers' market is a shared commitment to the locality and to its social and economic development. However, constructing meanings around the products, their producers, and the act of engaging in a farmers' market can lead to quite contradictory interpretations. On the one hand, Holloway and Kneafsey suggest that FM can be read as a reactionary or nostalgic space attempting to recover some golden age of wholesomeness and rusticity. In their observations of a farmers' market in the English Midlands, they note the presence amongst stallholders of old-fashioned clothing, the prominence of Union Jack flags, and an attempt to evoke a sense of nostalgia for a traditional rural identity. On the other hand, however, a farmers' market constitutes an alternative space that partly subverts the conventional space of food shopping (while celebrating free-market entre-preneurialism). It challenges the dominance of the supermarket retailing-productivist agriculture nexus and provides a means to circumvent the consumption spaces controlled by powerful actors in the food chain. In this way FM

> hold the potential for a challenging of conventional production, retail and consumption patterns by alternatives which embrace discourses of the local, environmental awareness and direct contact between producer and consumer.
>
> (Holloway and Kneafsey 2000: 298)

Indeed, it can be argued that FM present the opportunity to re-embed the exchange process for food into localized social relationships (Kirwan 2004).

## Social embeddedness, trust, and regard

> At a time when the acquisition of products is becoming depersonalized (by supermarkets, hypermarkets, self-service and other modern facili-ties), the public appreciates being able to trust someone who knows the product, someone they can speak to personally, and who can offer information and advice about the origin and the characteristics of the desired purchase.
>
> (Medina 2004: 266)

This desire for face-to-face contact, whether as a reaction to the anonymity and depersonalization of the modern food retailing experience, or in search of human reassurance about the provenance and integrity of a food product, has been a recent feature of modern western consumers. In order to trust the food, one must first trust the producer, and direct personal interaction offers consumers the opportunity to make their own judgment. Such transactions foster new relations of proximity and help to both resocialize food through face-to-face contact and respatialize it on the basis of its local origin. Social relations underpinning economic transactions are what defines the term embeddedness. Originating with the economic historian Karl Polanyi, embeddedness has become a vital concept in the study of alternative food networks, conveying important principles of social connectivity, reciprocity, and trust. These are characteristics which are essential to all economic life in general, but which fundamentally underpin direct agricultural marketing initiatives. In a seminal interpretation of the concept, Mark Granovetter stresses "the role of concrete personal relations and structures (or 'networks') of such relations in generating trust and discouraging malfeasance" (1985: 490).[5]

Within the modern food system, concerns relating to risk, safety, and traceability are placing emphasis on the embeddedness of a product in a particular place or production process, thus establishing its ecologically embedded character ("naturalness") and provenance. This attachment to locality (often made explicit in a place name for the product) conveys a trustworthiness and credibility that can be further verified through short food supply chains. However, according to Murdoch *et al.* (2000), an overly simplistic attachment of embeddedness to spatial proximity can lend itself to a fetishizing of localness while underplaying the qualities embedded *in* the product. Others have taken issue with the tendency to conflate spatial relations (the "local") with social relations of production (Hinrichs 2003), equate "alternativeness" with embeddedness (Winter 2003), or investment in the "local" as a redoubt against globalized mass consumption of "placeless foods" (DuPuis and Goodman 2005).

Yet embeddedness matters and is likely to matter more in the future given rising concerns about food safety and ecological consequences (Murdoch *et al.* 2000). Indeed, there is abundant evidence that corporate retailers are increasingly conscious of it: by the appearance of more "local" and organic foods, in-store promotions providing opportunities for shoppers to meet with specialty food producers, and in a few cases even holding farmers' markets on the supermarket car parks. Social connectivity and trust have consequently become vital elements in transactions around food, although this is not to preclude the relevance of price or instrumental behavior.

In order to further deepen our appreciation for and understanding of the distinctive qualities of social interaction that characterize exchange within farmers' markets, it is helpful to draw upon the notion of regard developed by Avner Offer (1997). Offer's paper addresses the persistence of non-market exchange, where "goods and services continue to be transferred without the benefit of markets or prices, to be exchanged as *gifts*" (450). The preference for reciprocal exchange, he argues,

> ... arises out of the intrinsic benefits of social and personal interaction, from the satisfactions of *regard* ... [and is] ... preferred when trade involves a personal interaction, and when goods and services are unique, expensive, or have many dimensions of quality.
>
> (Offer 1997: 450)

In contrast to neo-classical market exchange, where personal acquaintance is immaterial and the material gains from trade are all that matter, reciprocal exchange embodies a "process benefit, usually in the form of a personal relationship." Offer continues:

Personal interaction ranks very high among the sources of satisfaction. It can take many forms: acknowledgement, attention, acceptance, respect, reputation, status, power, intimacy, love, friendship, kinship, sociability. To wrap it all into one term, interaction is driven by the grant and pursuit of *regard*.

(1997: 451)

Regard provides, according to Offer (1997), a powerful incentive for trust, and trust itself resembles a gift – a unilateral transfer with no certainty of reciprocity. However, trust "economizes on the 'transaction costs' of monitoring, compliance, and enforcement." In this way, regard provides an additional motivation for economic exchange; it offers a transaction benefit.

Roger Lee, in a study of small horticultural nurseries in the south of England, argues that the grant and pursuit of regard may, "through a form of mutually recognized reciprocity between transacting partners, displace narrowly economic relationships (normally imposed by financial evaluations) and enable sub-optimal production and exchange" (Lee 2000: 139). Thus the buyer discounts the uncertainties, idiosyncrasies, and usually higher prices associated with small enterprises heavily reliant upon the labor of their owners. For, in addition to the desired product, the buyer gains insight into the production system, status, and identity associated with the consumption of a good with limited distribution and enhanced expertise, for example ways of preparing or serving the food. The producer, on the other hand, not only realizes the value of the good but also acquires an extension of regard based on their specialized knowledge. This regard, importantly, is not simply acquired at the moment of transaction, but may be extended through a widening of the circle of consumers through the sharing of food and deepened by consumer loyalty.

For small producers selling through local markets, it may be very important to maintain consumer loyalty by establishing the preferences of customers and signaling their efforts to meet them. This personalization of gifts, argues Offer, "serves the function of authenticating the regard signal" (1997: 454). Yet giving gives rise to obligation, argues Offer, creating an emotional bond that some may find excessively intimate and which constrains their "freedom of choice" to shop wherever they like. In a similar vein, Hinrichs (2000) observes in her discussion of community-supported agriculture how members may be unhappy receiving bags of produce with which they are unfamiliar and in quantities they did not request, yet feel obliged to maintain their custom. Even within a nominally "free" market of buyers and sellers of local produce, a sense of entanglement may arise from the hybridity of moral and money economies that impose certain obligations and responsibilities on both transacting parties.

## Contested rights and public space: challenges to the legitimacy of markets in Ireland

Thus far, the chapter has presented an unproblematic view of contemporary markets as spaces where trust, regard, and reciprocity prevail. While the preceding section made the case for a moral economy of market relations, it is necessary to recognize that markets might also be sites of contestation in which competing interests are played out, where conflicts can also take place as much as the grant and pursuit of regard. Clearly, markets offer opportunities for the extraction of rents and the leveraging of differential in the value of goods that are bought and sold. They also occupy a physical space which, in an era of rising land values, might realize more lucrative returns under other forms of commercial development than that generated by a weekly market. The way that markets have evolved and the contemporary pressures they face clearly reflect the particular regional circumstances shaped by history, legal status, and patterns of social and economic development. As an insight into some of the challenges faced by markets today, this section provides examples from Ireland, which has otherwise witnessed a resurgence in street and farmers' markets during recent years. Nevertheless, these two cases illustrate the way in which commercial imperatives and statutory regulation can work to eliminate long-standing market traditions if not challenged by alternative visions that seek to recover a moral economy of food.

The need to dispose of surplus by which to acquire necessities not directly produced by the household gave rise to sites of exchange from earliest times. The gradual formalization of these sites into periodic markets and fairs became an important instrument of political authority and a means to capture economic rent. As in much of the rest of Western Europe, the thirteenth century was a period of economic expansion in Anglo-Norman Ireland and the steady growth in commerce was marked by an increase in the number of fairs and markets. These were generally founded on the basis of a charter by the British crown to local lords and, in return for the right to levy tolls, obliged the founder to provide weights and measures and to preserve law and order (Cronin *et al.* 2001). The granting of rights to hold a fair (effectively an extravagant market held once per year around a feast day for up to 15 days) or market (held in a named place on a specified day of the week) represented a potentially lucrative income from tolls for charter holders. Unsurprisingly these rights were carefully guarded and periodically renewed by royal patent to ensure their legal basis was maintained. This situation prevailed in Ireland until the late nineteenth and early twentieth century when local councils effectively bought out the toll rights of charter holders and set about asserting municipal control. Critically, however, the royal charters also provided the basis for proprietary or customary rights to sell produce on the specified day and in the designated place.

A survey conducted in 1880 revealed that there were 264 towns with market rights in Ireland, where farmers and others were legally entitled to sell their produce in the town on the designated market day (*Irish Farmers Journal* 2003). Yet, under the 1995 Casual Trading Act, market rights may self-extinguish after ten years if they have not been exercised. This has created some confusion and legal incertitude where attempts to "regularize" trading by moving it away from commercial areas and to restrict its development have been challenged by traders seeking to maintain these historic "rights." Two recent cases from West Cork highlight the ways in which market spaces can become sites of competing visions of the "appropriate" use of public space, where private commercial interests seek to prevail over civic values of personal interaction, trust, and regard.

Bantry, a town whose name and reputation far exceeds its size, has long been the site of a weekly market. Indeed, the rights to hold a market were granted by the Crown to the First Earl of Cork in the seventeenth century. On the first Friday of every month the market is known as the "fair day" market, with a larger number of stalls clustering around Wolfe Tone Square and adjacent streets, selling a wide variety of fresh and high-quality craft foods, fish, poultry, clothes, and bric-a-brac. During recent years, however, the shopkeepers of the town had complained that the market was an impediment to business, that market stallholders pay no rates, leave rubbish, are unhygienic, and so on. In response to these complaints Cork County Council decided to establish a dedicated market site close to the foreshore of the bay and well away from the commercial hub of the town using by-laws under the Casual Trading Act of 1995. Market stallholders were unimpressed, arguing that the proposed relocation was unsuitable, remote, and far too small to accommodate the number of traders who traditionally use the Square. Nevertheless, the County Council informed them that from 11 January 2002 they would be required to have a casual trading license to trade in this new area and that to trade elsewhere would constitute a legal infringement.

On the stated day, Toby Simmons, a well-known market trader selling olives and related foods, set up and traded from his stall in the center of town as usual. At 11 a.m. Council officials informed him that he was not trading in the designated area and unless he removed his stall by 12:15 p.m. the *Gardaí* (police) would impound his goods. At 12:45 pm. *Gardaí* closed in on the stall and gave Mr. Simmons a final opportunity to remove his stall. He declined on the grounds of historic market rights to trade. At 1:20 p.m. a council van drew up and *Gardaí* loaded the first barrel of olives into the van, rendering them unfit for resale. His entire stock of olives, and his stall tables, umbrella, and takings for the day were impounded and removed.

By the end of January, Toby Simmons applied for and was granted a temporary injunction preventing Cork County Council from disturbing him while trading, so that on 1 February, fair day, he and others were trading once more. More importantly, however, together with the Irish Organization for Market and Street Traders Ltd, he sought and won an interlocutory injunction at the High Court with Mr. Justice O'Caoimh arguing that powers to regulate casual trading do not extend to defeat the proprietary rights of members of the public (The High Court 2002). Bantry market remains in its long-standing location and continues to attract people from across the region as it has for many years.

Yet despite this ruling, other town councils have sought to intimidate market traders with threats of legal action if they continue to exercise this proprietary right. In Skibbereen, two market traders were arrested by *Gardaí* in 2004, locked up for a day and their stock impounded. The two argued that traditional market rights have existed in the town since the granting of a charter from King Charles II in 1688 and that this made their arrest and subsequent loss wrongful. In 1981, the High Court confirmed the status of market rights in Skibbereen in the Quill v. Skibbereen Urban District Council (UDC) case stating that "the franchise granted by the charter still exists and has not been terminated." Subsequently on 25 July 2005 in Skibbereen, District Court Judge Terence Finn ruled in favor of the two traders and criticized the local authority for their failure to act in the interests of all in dealing with casual trading.

The role of local authorities in facilitating or hindering local market trading is a topic considered in other chapters in this volume. There are numerous examples in the UK and the USA where local town councils and other institutions have played a highly supportive role in facilitating FM by granting licenses, providing publicity, and liaising with other stakeholders. In Ireland this has not been the case so far, and indeed in Skibbereen the UDC has shown little but prevarication and hostility towards efforts to create a local market. It rejected outright proposals from a local group, Growing Awareness (GA), to develop such a market. Subsequently, GA, mostly comprising small organic farmers and growers, established that market rights existed on the "Fair Field," an area in the center of town. Besides the 1688 rights, a second patent was issued to the Townshend family in 1778. In May 1898, a High Court judge conveyed the freehold title of the Fair Field to Skibbereen Town Commissioners subject to market rights and other rights of way. In 1958, the UDC leased the Fair Field to Cork Co-operative Marts Ltd, which then acquired the freehold including the market rights. Subsequently, the company sold the site to property developers. These developers, speculating on the rapidly rising land values in Ireland during the past 15 years, sought and received from the local council permission to build a supermarket for the German discount multiple, Lidl. However, in all of these transactions market rights had not been extinguished.

In May 2001, Growing Awareness began trading on the Fair Field, though as the summer wore on, the developers sought to close access to the site by erecting a steel fence and chaining the access gates. As rights of way exist across the site, GA was able to ensure that the gates remained open, although one of the developers sat in his black Mercedes parked across the entrance restricting access to all but pedestrians on market days. The symbolism of this confrontation possibly captures the struggle to maintain a moral economy of mutual regard between producers and consumers at a time when corporate-controlled production and consumption networks prevail. For on the one side are a group of property developers enjoying the conditions of rampant land speculation and an associated culture of political corruption that rezones land use and provides planning permission for large discount supermarkets that will effectively eliminate much of the retail competition in the town. Opposing them is a more disparate group of growers and artisan food producers, many of whom are non-nationals, but who seek to maintain market rights in the interests of bringing fresh wholesome food to the people of Skibbereen at competitive prices.

The symbolism of this dispute underlines the salience of Holloway and Kneafsey's (2000) observation of the ways in which the spaces of FM hold the potential for challenging conventional retail and consumption patterns by alternatives which embrace discourses of the local, environmental awareness and direct contact between producer and consumer. Moreover, it also attests to the relevance of their call for closer examination of the ways such spaces become increasingly regulated as part of the tendency towards bureaucratic and capitalist appropriation of potentially alternative economic spaces.

## Conclusion

This chapter has presented the case for markets as opportunities for face-to-face transactions between producers and consumers with the potential for recovering a moral economy around food. While recognizing the need to qualify embeddedness, the chapter has argued that the grant and pursuit of regard, involving personal acknowledgement of trust, loyalty, and expertise, is a significant non-monetary reward in its own right. In this respect, markets have a powerful advantage over the highly impersonal conventional food retailing practices.

The power of local markets lies in their providing both a spatial alternative to conventional food supply chains (reducing distances traveled by food, encouraging people to reconnect with their regional "food shed," together with its seasonal possibilities) and a social alternative (encouraging greater community integration, employment opportunities, trust). However, local authorities, statutory agencies (environmental health, planning), and vested economic interests all have the power to facilitate or to thwart efforts to (re-)establish or maintain local markets. There are at least three ways by which the attitudes of such bodies toward local markets might be reflected:

- their ability to recognize the potential of food to become a useful tool of economic policy and the role that markets can play as vital nodes for the retention of value within the region;
- their understanding of how markets may serve as incubators of small businesses, enabling producers to gain first-hand feedback from customers on their tastes and preferences without the high entry costs of other forms of retailing, encouraging competition in the pursuit of quality;

- their vision of town centers as being the historic site of markets where, for hundreds of years, people have mingled and shopped for food, as opposed to car-dominated streets with traffic heading for peripheral urban hypermarkets.

Of course, there are many more criteria that might equally reveal official public attitudes toward the value of local markets. Not least is whether national food policy is effectively a *laissez-faire* matter left to the practices of the global food corporations, or whether there is any connection in public policy between the state of the nation's health and the national diet (Sage 2005). In the absence of political will to raise nutritional standards, for example by encouraging an increase in consumption of fresh fruit and vegetables, then markets might simply be considered an anachronism and supermarket retailers given the green light to build more out of town shopping centers selling processed and packaged foodstuffs. Fortunately there are a growing number of cases where the official attitude towards markets is positive.

Evidence from the United States has demonstrated that markets do have nutritional and health benefits, especially when located in low-income areas, by making fresh affordable food available (FoE 2000). In the UK, the recent rapid expansion in the number of farmers' markets has been welcomed by national government and has involved the active participation of local authorities in supporting local food initiatives (ibid.). In Toronto, of course, markets play a role within a wide range of services that underpins the commitment of that city to food security for all (Toronto Food Policy Council 2005).

While the official view in Ireland remains dominated by a bureaucratic and "hyper-hygienist" approach in which markets are treated with suspicion as a relic from the distant past, growing numbers of people across the country are choosing to buy foods embedded with positive characteristics. Desiring a reassurance of traceability, environmentally sound methods of production, and good taste, consumers enjoy purchasing these products at markets from the producers themselves. For those resourceful individuals seeking new ways of retaining value within the family farm in the face of the remorseless downward pressure on farm-gate prices paid by the corporate food sector, markets offer a valuable outlet for the low-volume, craft-based production of quality foods that they have developed. It is too early, as yet, to speak of this as a national synergy, a new and powerful alliance of consumers and producers coming together in an alternative setting. Yet, although incipient, the growth in the number of farmers' markets across Ireland attests to the desire of people for greater meaning in the quality of their food and the way it is acquired. Whether such markets will challenge conventional retail and consumption patterns through its alternative discourse emphasizing the local, the environment, and a new ethics of production, remains to be seen.

However, it will be ironic if increasing numbers of farmers' markets are established on the grounds of long-standing customary rights originally granted by a foreign medieval monarch.

## Notes

1 I wish to acknowledge the financial support of the Higher Education Authority's Programme for Research in Third Level Institutions, Cycle 3. I would also like to acknowledge the helpful advice of Caroline Robinson, Chairperson of the Irish Food Market Traders Association, Madeline McKeever of Growing Awareness, and an anonymous reviewer of this chapter.
2 The term markets is used here as a generic category to encompass a complex of independent vendors gathered within a defined space, whether open-air or under-cover, unregulated or licensed, under the auspices of a local authority or an individual entrepreneur. The term therefore includes long-standing street trading venues, farmers' markets, as well as municipal covered markets characteristic of many European cities. The central concern of this chapter, however, is with food markets and especially the nature of the relationships formed by market vendors and their customers, the consumers. The generic category of markets is therefore set apart from other forms of food retailing especially that represented by supermarkets.
3 Rising volumes of air-freighted food from around the world and lengthening distances traveled by road are all contributing to rising "food miles." According to Church, "UK imports of food products and animal feed involved transportation by sea, air and road amounting to over 83 billion tonne-kilometres [which] required 1.6 billion litres of fuel ... and ... resulted in 4.1 million tonnes of carbon dioxide emissions" (Church 2005: 4).
4 For example, Cork city possesses a fine municipal covered market. Originally opened in 1788, the English Market was redeveloped during the 1860s by Sir John Benson, whose Italianate design features cast-iron pillars and ornate brackets, brickwork, and a lofty vaulted glass roof. Today the English Market is a cornucopia of delicious ancient and modern foods featuring such Cork specialties as tripe, drisheen, offal, and pigs' feet alongside contemporary European products such as cheese, olives, pasta, champagne, and Belgian chocolates (Sage and Sexton 2005).
5 I am grateful to an anonymous reviewer of this chapter for drawing to my attention the significance of Granovetter's (1985) reworking of embeddedness and its contri-bution to breaking down the traditionalist/modernist binary that has characterized orthodox approaches within the social sciences.

## Bibliography

Chubb, A. (1998) *Farmers' Markets: The UK potential*, Bristol: Eco-logic Books.
Church, N. (2005) *Why our food is so dependent on oil*. Online. Available: www. 321energy.com/editorials/church/church040205.html (accessed 13 April 2005).
Cook, I. and Crang, P. (1996) 'The world on a plate: Culinary culture, displacement and geographical knowledges,' *Journal of Material Culture*, 1(2): 131–53.
Cronin, D., Gilligan, J., and Holton, K. (2001) 'Introduction,' in D. Cronin, J. Gilligan, and K. Holton (eds) *Irish Fairs and Markets: Studies in local history*, Dublin: Four Courts Press.
DuPuis, M. and Goodman, D. (2005) 'Should we go "home" to eat? Towards a reflexive politics of localism,' *Journal of Rural Studies*, 21: 359–71.

Feenstra, G. (1997) 'Local food systems and sustainable communities,' *American Journal of Alternative Agriculture*, 12(1): 28–36.

Friedland, W. (2004) 'Agrifood globalization and commodity systems,' *International Journal of Sociology of Agriculture and Food*, 12: 5–16.

FoE (Friends of the Earth) (2000) *The Economic Benefits of Farmers' Markets*, London: Friends of the Earth Trust.

Goodman, D. (2002) 'Rethinking food production-consumption: Integrative perspectives,' *Sociologia Ruralis*, 42(4): 271–77.

—— (2003) 'Editorial: The quality "turn" and alternative food practices: Reflections and agenda,' *Journal of Rural Studies*, 19: 1–7.

Granovetter, M. (1985) 'Economic action and social structure: The problem of embeddedness,' *American Journal of Sociology*, 91(3): 481–510.

High Court, The (2002) 'Judgement of Mr Justice Aindrias Ó' Caoimh delivered 22 February 2002.' Online. Available: www.austlii.edu.au/~andrew/balilii/IEHC/new/1262p-02_k.rtf (accessed 3 October 2005).

Hinrichs, C. (2000) 'Embeddedness and local food systems: Notes on two types of direct agricultural market,' *Journal of Rural Studies*, 16: 295–303.

—— (2003) 'The practice and politics of food system localization,' *Journal of Rural Studies*, 19: 33–45.

Holloway, L. and Kneafsey, M. (2000) 'Reading the space of the farmers' market: A preliminary investigation from the UK,' *Sociologia Ruralis*, 40(3): 285–99.

*Irish Farmers Journal* (2003) 'Market rights: Use them or lose them.' Online. Available: www.farmersjournal.ie/2003/0823/ruralliving/countrylifestyle/feature.shtml (accessed 3 October 2005).

Kirwan, J. (2004) 'Alternative strategies in the UK agro-food system: Interrogating the alterity of farmers' markets,' *Sociologia Ruralis*, 44(4): 395–415.

Lang, T. and Heasman, M. (2004) *Food Wars: The global battle for mouths, minds and markets*, London: Earthscan.

La Trobe, H. and Acott, T. (2000) 'Localising the global food system,' *International Journal of Sustainable Development and World Economy*, 7: 309–20.

Lee, R. (2000) 'Shelter from the storm? Geographies of regard in the worlds of horticultural consumption and production,' *Geoforum*, 31: 137–57.

Lind, D. and Barham, E. (2004) 'The social life of the tortilla: Food, cultural politics, and contested commodification,' *Agriculture and Human Values*, 21: 47–60.

Marsden, T., Banks, J., and Bristow, G. (2000) 'Food supply chain approaches: Exploring their role in rural development,' *Sociologia Ruralis*, 40(4): 424–38.

Medina, F. X. (2004) 'Los futuros de los mercados: Reflexión y prospective,' in J. Anglí, J. Bacaria *et al.* (eds) *Mercados del Mediterráneo*, Barcelona: Lunwerg Editores.

Murdoch, J., Marsden, T., and Banks, J. (2000) 'Quality, nature, and embeddedness: Some theoretical considerations in the context of the food sector,' *Economic Geography*, 76(2): 107–25.

Offer, A. (1997) 'Between the gift and the market: The economy of regard,' *Economic History Review*, L(3): 450–76.

Palau, P. (2004) 'Colores, aromas y sabores de los mercados mediterráneos (The colors, aromas and tastes of Mediterranean markets),' in J. Anglía, J. Bacaria *et al.* (eds) *Mercados del Mediterráneo*, Barcelona: Lunwerg Editores.

Parrott, N., Wilson, N., and Murdoch, J. (2002) 'Spatializing quality: Regional protection and the alternative geography of food,' *European Urban and Regional Studies*, 9(3): 241–61.

Paxton, A. (1994) *The Food Miles Report*, London: SAFE Alliance.

Pretty, J. (2002) *Agri-culture: Reconnecting people, land and nature*, London: Earthscan.

Pretty, J., Ball, A., Lang, T., and Morrison, J. (2005) 'Farm costs and food miles: An assessment of the full cost of the UK weekly food basket,' *Food Policy*, 30: 1–19.

Renting, H., Marsden, T., and Banks, J. (2003) 'Understanding alternative food networks: Exploring the role of short food supply chain in rural development,' *Environment and Planning A*, 35(3): 393–412.

Sage, C. (2003) 'Social embeddedness and relations of regard: alternative "good food" networks in south-west Ireland,' *Journal of Rural Studies*, 19(1): 47–60.

—— (2005) 'Food for thought,' *Irish Times Health Supplement*, 28 June: 2.

Sage, C. and Sexton, R. (2005) 'The food culture of Cork,' in J. Crowley, R. Devoy, D. Linehan, and P. O'Flanagan (eds) *The Atlas of Cork*, Cork: Cork University Press.

Toronto Food Policy Council (2005) *Annual Report 2004*, Toronto: TFPC.

Tregear, A. (2003) 'From Stilton to Vimto: Using food history to rethink typical products in rural development,' *Sociologia Ruralis*, 43: 91–107.

USDA (United States Department of Agriculture) (2005) Online. Available: www. ams.usda.gov/farmersmarkets (accessed 3 October 2005).

Watts, D., Ilberry, B., and Maye, D. (2005) 'Making reconnections in agro-food geography: Alternative systems of food provision,' *Progress in Human Geography*, 29(1): 22–40.

Winson, A. (2004) 'Bringing political economy into the debate on the obesity epidemic,' *Agriculture and Human Values*, 21: 299–312.

Winter, M. (2003) 'Embeddedness, the new food economy and defensive localism,' *Journal of Rural Studies*, 19: 23–32.

# 10 Institutional perspectives on understanding street retailer behavior and networks

## Cases from Ghana

*Fergus Lyon*[1]

## Introduction

The urban food supply system in Ghana is dominated by street and market traders. Despite considerable hardships, these traders, predominantly women, continue to play a key role in supplying food to urban populations. This chapter examines the roles of these traders in Ghana. It also examines how street vendors and retailers operate, the institutional forms that shape their livelihoods, and how they secure their livelihoods in the context of a highly uncertain and insecure environment.

The chapter also raises important issues for African urban development and food security. It has been estimated that the urban poor in Africa spend 60–80 percent of their income on food (UNCHS 1996). Despite rapid urbanization and increasing levels of urban poverty, urban food systems are rarely considered an issue in urban development in the South (Smith 1998). In addition, the functioning of urban food systems has considerable impacts on the livelihoods of rural producers. However, previous research on agro-food systems has mainly concentrated on the export of produce and the impacts of globalization.

Street trading and marketing is of vital importance to the livelihoods of urban people; it is estimated that 18 percent of Ghana's population is involved in trading (Darkwa and Ackumey 2003, quoting the Ghana Living Standards Survey 1999). Retailing is particularly important for women and one of the most striking aspects of the food marketing system in West Africa is the dominance of women. This is reported in other sectors in Ghana and many African countries (Attah *et al.* 1996; Clark 1994; Handwerker 1981; Harts-Broekhuis and Verkoren 1987; Horn 1994; Onyemelukwe 1970; Porter 1988; Sudarkasa 1973; Trager 1981, 1985). Trager found that the food marketing in all its forms "is historically the domain of women in Yoruba society. Beliefs and institutions recognize women's importance in the market" (Trager 1985: 280). Similarly, Horn (1994: 46) argues that "in Zimbabwe, the link between women [traders] and specific food commodities is rooted in traditional beliefs about the nature of women and their roles as family food provisioners." Babb (1985: 295) stresses the lack of alternatives available to women in urban areas and that trading is preferable to domestic work because of the degree of independence and flexibility it offers. Attah *et al.* (1996: 7) state that in urban Ghana the large numbers of female-headed households result in women being highly economically active although they are often limited to trading.

Much of the literature on the subject therefore draws on early studies on the subject that attributed the large numbers of traders to the lack of choice for employment in urban areas where there is a shortage of capital and the only resource that traders have is their own labor (Bauer 1963: 18; Mintz 1964: 266). In this chapter, I aim to go beyond the common conceptualization of street vendors and retailers as a "residual labor category" without voice or alternative, to demonstrate that, despite the constraints under which traders have to operate, there exists a diversity of activities and behavior, with each trader having an element of agency through which to shape their livelihood. This approach goes beyond agency-centered neoclassical economics approaches that assume that vendors should act as profit maximizing individuals with crude notions of how "rational" actors should respond to "market forces." My approach allows for an understanding of how vendors have an element of agency that is shaped by the social and cultural context in which their actions are embedded.

By taking an institutionalist perspective, this chapter explores how networks and social relationships enable access to opportunities. I will also explore a range of regulatory elements, informal institutional forms, and norms that have evolved in parallel to formal institutions and legal structures of the state. The ways in which these alternative formal and informal institutional forms are developed and exercised are shown to be shaped by the social relations and structural factors in which the actions of the traders are embedded (Granovetter 1985).

Research under the banner of New Institutional Economics (NIE) has attempted to explore the reasons behind collective action of different kinds. NIE has developed as neoclassical economists have attempted to modify their key assumptions to reflect real-world situations more closely. NIE introduces the concept of transaction costs (Williamson 1985) which are omitted from many neoclassical economics analyses because of the assumption about a "frictionless exchange process in which property rights are perfectly and costlessly specified and information is likewise costless to acquire" (North 1990: 11). North (1990) proposes that the key cost of transacting is that of information. The cost comes from measuring the quality of what is being exchanged, as goods may not be homogeneous; protecting rights to the goods being exchanged; and policing and enforcing agreements.

However, in much of the NIE approach there are functionalist views that assume institutions evolve to minimize the transaction costs (Granovetter 1985). While institutions can and do reduce transaction costs in many cases, such a view is based on trying to explain existing institutional forms by assuming institutions appear automatically to reduce transaction costs while not probing why cooperation and other institutions occur in one case and not in another.

## Research methodology

The empirical work took an ethnographic approach and was carried out in four urban markets and surrounding streets in Ghana between 1995 and 1998. The greatest attention was given to Kumasi market, while shorter studies were undertaken in Sunyani, Techiman, and Accra. These markets were selected because of their importance in the marketing systems of agricultural produce, especially tomatoes. This study was part of a wider research project examining the whole marketing chain for tomatoes and is discussed elsewhere (Lyon 2000a; 2000b).

Open-ended questions were used that allowed respondents to describe specific experiences in their own words. The traders were interviewed in the markets and while they were visiting the farmers. Locating the traders when they had time to discuss their work was difficult and a random sample could not be taken. It was necessary to build up relationships with traders over several years. This was achieved by regular visits. Data collection also involved a considerable amount of observation of market transactions and dispute settlements, what Hollier (1986) refers to as "lurking" methodology. The rationale here is that collective action and the social relations of a particular context are best understood through following explanations of important events and disputes by traders themselves.

Small focus groups were used to explore key issues in detail and took place in the market association sheds. These were informally organized and included between three and eight traders who were present at the time. Further focus groups were used to explore the meanings of certain key terms and words in Twi language. These were carried out in the evening with five people of differing backgrounds, although all had good English skills.

## Historical context

The history of how the retail sector evolved in this particular context is useful for understanding how the present institutions operate, and their basis in historical precedent or what North (1990) refers to as "path dependency." Evidence of trade in Ghana goes back at least 1,000 years and its steady growth over time has led to dramatic social changes. Economic activity has involved long-distance trade and the development of trading networks that stretched throughout West and North Africa (McIntosh and McIntosh 1993: 638; Hymer 1970: 39; Lovejoy 1974; Mikell 1989a).

The arrival of Portuguese traders on the southern coast of Ghana in the fifteenth century reduced the dependence on trade routes to the north and diverted many of the traded goods to the south (Szereszewski 1965: 11;

Reynolds 1974: 26). The early European coastal traders did not penetrate far inland and there developed a system of brokers from the Fanti ethnic group who acted as intermediaries between the trading ships and those supplying gold, ivory, and, in later periods, slaves (Hymer 1970: 42; Gould 1960: 11).

These brokers continued to play an important role, and in the seventeenth century this role gave rise to the development of systems of credit (Daaku 1970: 42). These credit systems may have been necessary to secure the goodwill of chiefs and important merchants in the face of the intense rivalry between competing Europeans (Reynolds 1974: 15). The credit system was passed to traders going inland. In 1853, Cruikshank wrote of the trading system that it had:

> become one of simple credit. ... The natural result of this system of trust, was the extensive diffusion of property throughout every class of society, to a degree which can hardly be comprehended by one unacquainted with the peculiar partiality of the natives.
>
> (1853: 35–36)

He goes on to describe debt repayments through the pawning and selling of relatives into slavery. This practice was widely practiced, especially in the Ashanti areas (McCaskie 1995: 40).

Food marketing started when towns emerged and there are reports by Pieter de Marees in 1602 of men selling sugar cane and women selling their produce in the trading ports along the coast, and buying fish:

> By the time these Peasants have sold their Sugar-cane, the Peasant Women are beginning to come to Market with their goods, one bringing a Basket of Oranges or Limes, another Bananas and Bachovens, [sweet] potatoes and Yams, a third Millie, Maize, Rice, Manigette, a forth chickens, Eggs, bread and such necessities as people in the Coastal towns need to buy. ... These women and peasants' wives very often buy fish and carry it to towns in other Countries, in order to make some profit: thus the fish caught in the see is carried well over 100 or 200 miles into the Interior.
>
> (1602: 63)

The letters of Bosman in 1702 quoted in Dickson (1969: 98) describe the marketing of food to the mining towns of southwestern Ghana as well as trade along the coast and fish marketing to the Ashanti areas. Reports in the 1880s indicate the existence of a large market place in Kumasi, although much of the food came from the dependent settlements in the suburbs (McCaskie 1995: 35–36).

Early reports on pre-colonial Ghana show that women played a major role in food supply (de Marees 1602). However, Clark (1994: 6) found that there had been relatively recent shifts in the gender divisions in Kumasi market:

> scholarly accounts of West African market women had often portrayed the markets as supposedly timeless, "traditional" female occupational sector .... [But] Asante men had moved out of market trading in many commodities now considered stereotypical for women around 1910, shortly after colonial conquest, and had moved into cocoa farming, which then brought them higher incomes and better upward mobility prospects.

Women did not have access to the same land and resources and so could not participate in cocoa production to the same extent as men (Clark 1994: 95, 115).

Food marketing incrcascd in the colonial period with rapid urbanization. There had been a long history of food provision for Kumasi and the coastal towns (McCaskie 1995; Clark 1994; Dickson 1969) but new markets appeared with the growth of small mining towns such as Tarkwa and Obuasi. The urban populations in southern Ghana grew at a much faster rate than rural areas due to large-scale emigration by rural dwellers. The patterns of urban migration are shown in Table 10.1. Accra expanded because of its status as a capital city and center of many infrastructural projects, and other smaller towns grew as they became administrative centers.

Kumasi has been an urban center since pre-colonial times with an ethnically varied population because of the large numbers of traders sometimes residing there. It has been the hub of commercial arteries since the nineteenth century when the Ashanti Confederacy forced all trade to pass through the

*Table 10.1* Population of Ghana and urban areas included in this study

| | 1921 | 1948 | 1960 | 1970 | 1984 | 1993 (est.) | 2004 |
|---|---|---|---|---|---|---|---|
| Sunyani | 3,000 | – | 15,810 | 27,500 | 36,100 | 45,000 | 83,900 |
| Wenchi | 5,309 | – | 10,672 | 14,364 | 18,400 | 22,500 | 29,300 |
| Techiman | – | – | 8,755 | 12,463 | 25,200 | – | 41,000 |
| Kumasi | 23,694 | 70,705 | 180,642 | 260,286 | 399,300 | 475,000 | 663,100 |
| Accra | 38,000 | 135,000 | 388,000 | – | 956,000 | 1,264,000 | 1,719,100 |
| Population of Ghana | 2,200,000 | 4,100,000 | 6,730,000 | – | – | 16,000,000 | 20,757,000 |
| Percentage urban | 7.9% | 13.0% | 23.1% | – | 31.0% | 32.0% | 36% |

Sources: IDC (1989), Ghana Statistical Service (1994), Benneh (1990), Population Impact Project (1994), Hilton (1960), Chamlee-Wright (1997), UNDP (2004).

Note: The percentage of urban population refers to those living in settlements of more than 5,000 people.

town. The population of the town itself was estimated to be between 12,000 and 15,000 in 1817, although a figure of 100,000–200,000 was given to include those living in the suburbs and outlying farming villages (Dickson 1969: 247). The British destroyed the city in 1874, although it was able to regain its dominant trading position later (Gould 1960). The population dropped to an estimated 5,500 in 1899 and was reported at 6,250 in 1906. After this the population grew rapidly to 18,853 in 1911 and has expanded rapidly since then. The building of the railway galvanized Kumasi's, and Accra's, central position in the trading system, especially for kola nut and cocoa (Chamlee-Wright 1997: 115; Dickson 1969). The latter crop was a key factor in the rapid growth of Kumasi between 1921 and 1948. The collapse of cocoa and the declining terms of trade for rural producers subsequently led to increasing urbanization since the 1960s (Mikell 1989a; 1989b).

In the post-independence period many of the same policies towards trading continued, although there was increasing political interference as market traders were seen as the cause of agricultural decline. There developed an antagonistic relationship between the state and women traders. On the one hand this came in the form of what Robertson (1983) refers to as "malevolent neglect," although the confrontation could be more explicit. This came to the fore in the early period of Rawlings' regime (1979–83) when traders came under continuing attack from the army and civilian mobs (Clark 1994; Robertson 1983).

## The existing retailing system

The large urban markets are the selling points of the itinerant traders who sell to street vendors and local retailers. The largest market in Ghana is Kumasi Central Market with an estimated 20,000 traders (wholesale and retail) with 7,400 operating in the open areas and tables without fixed stalls (King and Oppong 2003). In 1989 it was estimated that there were 250,000 customers a day (IDC 1989). In the trading systems there are a hierarchy of functions with rural wholesale assemblers and itinerant traders bulking up produce from producers and selling to urban wholesalers who in turn sell to different forms of retailers. These retailers include those that sell from fixed stalls and, of particular interest for this chapter, those that sell in the open and on streets. Wholesalers tend to have access to the physical structures in the large urban markets that are permanent, although there has been large-scale unplanned expansion of wholesale and retail trading making them highly congested. This is especially the case in Kumasi. Street vendors may be working from a fixed location or moving around streets and markets. For those at fixed locations there are no written agreements, although market associations play a role in ensuring there is no conflict. There is a sense of ownership of retailing spots, and women will usually inherit the right to trade on a particular spot from their mothers or aunts.

There is limited storage in all the markets due to lack of space. In addition, traders are keen to sell the produce as quickly as possible to minimize the risk of the produce declining in quality and also so that their capital is not tied up. For those vendors that have been allowed a site, small quantities may be stored for a few days under the stalls. For example, tomato retailers may buy two boxes and not be able to sell them all in the same day. Most markets have security guards, although some traders also like to employ their own guards. Storage by street vendors and hawkers who do not have a stall in the main market is limited to the quantity that they can carry home, unless they are able to make an arrangement to leave produce in a secure place such as a shop.

A large majority of the traders operating in the urban markets are street vendors who tend to start with their mothers and will share the profit while working together. These women make minimal profits, but retailing is popular because of the small amount of capital required to start. They will buy from itinerant traders coming to the market or the wholesale traders who sell on behalf of itinerant traders. They will usually buy one box at a time and take between one and three days to sell the contents. These women have much less working capital than the itinerant traders and many are reliant on receiving the boxes of tomatoes on credit each time and paying the itinerant traders after one or two days. The organization of this system is discussed later.

There are also hawkers who buy from the fixed site street vendors, and carry trays or baskets of produce on their heads around the market, or around other parts of the town. These vendors are predominantly young women and girls and it is seen as a way for teenage girls to learn how to trade. Hawkers may also be working with their retailing mother or relative, while other girls work with their mothers and aunts on their street stalls as another way of learning the necessary skills of trading, such as how to bargain, the conventions of the market, judging the quality and quantity of produce, and how to attract and retain customers. Much of this is tacit knowledge that can only be acquired through these apprentice-type systems. In this way these new traders are also able to inherit the pre-established customer relationships.

## Roles of trader associations

Of particular interest in Ghana is the structure of trader associations, with their formal leadership that draws on traditional chieftaincy structures. In large markets, each commodity has an association and is led by an *ohemma*. In the context of markets, *ohemma* can be translated as market queen, although the term is taken from the traditional title given to the leading woman of a chieftaincy. The *ohemma* is chosen on personal qualities such as age, emotional reliability, familiarity with market affairs, skills in negotiation and dispute settlement, financial independence, and wealth. Wealth is important in order for the *ohemma* to afford the time to carry out her duties (Gore 1978: 292).

She is not paid a wage but receives gifts in kind; the tomato queens receive a number of tomatoes from each crate sold. In Kumasi market she is elected from amongst the elders for life but can be rejected or "de-stooled" (Clark 1994), while in Sunyani the *ohemma* for tomatoes at the time of the research was put in place by the *Sunyanihemma* (the *ohemma* for the chieftaincy of the Sunyani traditional area). Assisting the *ohemma* are a group of elders, *paninfo*, who advise and help her.

Key roles of the associations are the governance of trade and the allocation of space to traders. They are also responsible for lobbying local authorities for improved facilities, although the terrible working conditions (dust, heat, and congestion) and lack of facilities (such as toilets and other buildings) demonstrates that the antagonism between the state and traders limits what influence the associations have. The associations are also responsible for hiring security to guard trader produce.

Associations also play a key role in reducing transaction costs through the settling of disputes and establishing calibration of weights and measures. The leaders of the association are selected for their skills in negotiation and dispute settlement and this allows the traders to work more efficiently, reducing their transaction costs. These costs come in the form of wasted time and the extra costs of ensuring that goods or money are not stolen. This allows traders to operate without bringing in the police or formal court proceedings that are very costly and not trusted by the traders. In settling disputes, both sides openly state their case to the elders and *ohemma* who decide who is to blame and what action should be taken. Clark (1994) describes a range of conflicts in Kumasi Central Market in detail and stresses the importance of group solidarity and respect for the *ohemma* in settling disputes. One of the main punishments or deterrents is the bad publicity and damage to a trader's reputation or creditworthiness. In extreme circumstances traders can be banned by the association for a period of time.

While the traders cannot *fix* prices, they can have an impact on competition, and therefore price, by controlling the supply entering the markets and the number of traders allowed to sell. This has been observed in many West African markets (Bauer 1963: 391; Gore 1978: 300; Ministry of Agriculture 1987: 16; Smith and Luttrell 1994). The control of the market space differs between markets but it occurs, to a certain extent, in all markets in southern Ghana. Linked to the reduction of disputes, the associations act to establish bargaining etiquette and an arena for negotiating prices. The association is made up of retailers and itinerant or sedentary wholesale traders: representatives of each will bargain on behalf of the others. In setting the price, all the traders have to ensure that the produce being sold will be retailed that day or the next, so they will set the price after knowing the supply entering the market that day. The retailers will consider the farm gate price, the marketing costs, and profit margins of the itinerant traders bringing the produce in. The *ohemma* will not play a role unless there is dispute between the two groups that delays the setting of the price for the day. By setting the price at the beginning of the day, the selling of the produce is easier and there is less bargaining on each crate, although prices of unsold produce may drop later in the day. Traders are frequently accused by the media and public figures of fixing prices but a detailed study of the functioning of the associations in Kumasi and Sunyani does not bear this out. There are opportunities for the retailers to bargain if the produce is perceived to be below premium quality or it is later in the day.

When asked about the role of the associations, the consistent reply from traders is that they are there for welfare reasons, and for the support of members at funerals for their relatives. Prestige and status are attributed to the bereaved person and their family members when someone of high status, such as the *ohemma*, comes to the funeral with a large number of her fellow traders. In economic terms, associations assist the bereaved with financial contributions from the other traders. This can be used to defray the cost of the lavish funerals expected among the people of southern Ghana and especially the Akan groups. Those who do not contribute will not have help when they are bereaved and may also suffer from a lack of support in disputes in the market. In his study of Koforidua market, Gore (1978: 292) refers to funeral donations as an insurance scheme to ensure that a trader's working capital is not lost and Dennis and Peprah (1995) refer to it as a "cushion" for unpredictability.

## Institutions for sales to consumers

Retail prices are usually fixed for the day for a given quantity, but retailers try to attract customers by changing the quality of the produce, the size of the piles, and gifts (dash) given after the sale has taken place. There is a wide range of sizes and qualities and some of the consumers pride themselves on being able to select the best buy from what appears to others to be relatively similar qualities and quantities. Consumers will thus examine the piles of vegetables on a range of retailers' tables or mats before selecting.

The size and the quality of the dash given by the retailers depends on the relationship between the retailers and buyer and it is important in retaining custom. It is often as much as 50 percent extra, although it may be of lower quality and is taken from a container under the stall so that other potential customers will not see how much is given, and so will not demand a larger quantity when they buy. This creates serious problems for the collection of retail price data.

There is a convention in markets that traders cannot steal customers or people about to buy from other traders. This reduces the potential for conflict and the relationship between retailers is one of colleagues, rather than competitors. Neighbors will look after each other's stall for long periods of time and sell on behalf of their neighbor even when they have similar products.

Retailers can have piles of produce of different degrees of ripeness, as some consumers like to buy slightly unripe tomatoes that will last a few days. There are also different preferences among consumers belonging to different ethnic groups. Retailers will try to sell the slightly damaged and riper ones first, especially if they are not buying every day. This is an important strategy for the retailers in Sunyani who buy from farmers every Thursday and then sell on Friday, Saturday, and Monday. The definitions of different quality grades can change through the year as produce gets scarce.

Some retailers process or package the vegetables in plastic bags to make them more appealing. Very little is thrown away with the very low-quality tomatoes being sold to those women who prepare cooked food on the street. The low-quality tomatoes, sometimes mixed with chili peppers, are taken to a pulping machine with the pulp collected in plastic bags or pots if the buyer is cooking near by. These machines are run on electricity and managed by men.

## Credit to retailers

Street vendors and itinerant traders/commission agents have customer relationships where the street retailer will obtain the produce on credit and pay when it has been sold, usually at the end of the day.

When giving goods on credit, the trader is repaid at the end of the day or several days later. If the trader does not want to wait they can collect the money the next time they come to the market. In Sunyani weekly market, rural-based itinerant traders will often collect the money from the retailer the following week, rather than wait for them to sell all the produce. There were no reported cases of retailers advancing capital to itinerant traders to buy goods.

The extent of selling on credit is shown in Table 10.2. The percentage of itinerant traders selling on credit is lower in small towns as many of them only sell to consumers. Credit can be given for up to one week and the amount will depend on the quantity the retailer can sell and the trust between the two parties: A young trader in Wenchi stated:

> We start with smaller credit and when the person is truthful and repays each time she buys, we continue to trust her and give more.
> (Eunice Amponsah, Wenchi trader, Interview 13)

The traders need to know the location of the house so that they can follow up any debts:

> I have traded with them for more than five years so I have confidence. ...
> I know the house and the town and I can go to visit them when money delays to see if the person is sick or the business is not going well.
> (Effiah Hemma, Techiman trader, Interview 22)

*Table 10.2* Wholesale traders selling on credit

| | Sunyani small town market | Kumasi central market | Asafo market, Kumasi | Accra: 31st December and Agbogbloshi | Total |
|---|---|---|---|---|---|
| No. interviewed | 16 | 12 | 4 | 5 | 37 |
| Sell on credit | 56.3% | 83.3% | 100% | 100% | 75.7% |
| Don't sell on credit | 37.3% | 8.3% | 0 | 0 | 18.9% |
| Don't know/will not say | 6.3% | 8.3% | 0 | 0 | 5.4% |

Source: Lyon (2000b).

When selling on credit to traders who work in the same market, the risks are reduced as they are members of the same association and know each other, and the close proximity of trading means that they cannot avoid creditors. Proximity is important as even with the rapid increased use of mobile phones by wholesale traders, retailers cannot afford to buy and operate them.

However, most itinerant traders reported that they are owed some money because of retailers and street vendors not being able to pay as they had lost all their money. The itinerant trader can ask the *ohemma* to help settle the dispute but this may not be possible if the retailer has stopped selling. In one case in Accra, there was a dispute over the amount of money owed and the case was taken to the chief:

> One retailer owes me C365,000 from over 6 years ago. The case is before the elders of the Ga chief. She reported that the total amount is not correct.... I won the case and she has deposited C200,000 with the elders about 5 months ago.... I will collect the total amount after full payment.
> (Comfort, Accra trader, Interview 42)

The chief's decision was accepted by the offending trader because if she fails to comply, she could not expect to get support from the chief or other members of the community in future.

In Kumasi Central Market itinerant traders use trusted porters (all originating from the Gao area of Mali) who know street vendors and retailers well to act as guarantors. The itinerant traders would not be able to do this as they do not have the information on the creditworthiness of the retailers, where they sell, or where they live. The Gao will collect the money in the afternoon and if the retailer cannot pay then the Gao is responsible for paying the itinerant trader. In such cases the Gao may use his own money, may borrow from other Gao, or ask the itinerant trader to wait for a few days. It is interesting to note that wholesalers prefer to work with people from different ethnic groups. This was partly attributed to the long-standing relationship with porters from this ethnic community and also the ability of wholesale traders to exclude them from the market in case of any dispute.

# Conclusions

This chapter has examined the range of institutional forms and types of relationships that allow street vendors and retailers to survive and sustain their livelihoods. While recognizing that many may be forced into retailing activities by the lack of alternatives, the research has taken an institutionalist perspective that concentrates on the processes of street vending to show that, despite their disadvantaged position, they are able to shape their working environment to a certain degree, although their actions are inevitably shaped by wider structural factors that limit their opportunities. This approach demonstrates the importance of understanding the institutions that allow those in poverty to access particular markets and also shape how they can participate. The wide range of institutions described here do support exchange but are often ignored by researchers and policy makers as they are not easily identifiable without in-depth research methods, given their less visible nature, and they defy economic formalization (Fafchamps 1997). It should be noted that the institutions such as trader associations and chieftaincy are underpinned by rules and regulations that cannot be termed "informal." Therefore the term informal was not found to be a useful tool for understanding the behavior of the traders.

The types of institutional forms identified include those for learning, cooperating, and regulating trading activity. The institutions of learning are through apprentice-type approaches with family members. This often starts during childhood and raises questions over whether this is a form of education, a household survival strategy, or exploitation of child labor.

The cooperative relations and institutional forms based on trust are vital for the customer relationships with food buyers and for the relationships with wholesalers. Of particular importance are the credit relationships which allow traders to sell produce without the need for capital. However, the fate of those that could not repay debts is not known as they cannot be traced. In the absence of affordable legal representation great reliance is placed on trust rather than legal contracts. In any case, formal written contracts would not be able to cope with the complexity of trade and would undermine the flexibility valued by both parties. Trust is built up through repeated interaction or through having information on the other party acquired through trader associations and other sources (Lyon 2000a).

The case study also demonstrates the important role of non-state-regulatory forms and social norms that operate in parallel to the state. These range from the trader associations excluding people from markets to a reliance on traditional chieftaincy systems for penalizing people. These are explicit forms of exerting power, although cooperation may also be based on less visible forms of power. Such norms of behavior or moral obligations are a form of power that have an impact on behavior and may be internalized as a form of moral economy (Thompson 1971; Scott 1976). In many cases this was found to be routinized compliance in that there is unquestioning acceptance of association elders' authority (Lyon 2003).

A second form of implicit power exertion is through peer pressure, shaming, and the threat of damaging reputations. Shame occurs when someone is seen to have broken a norm and other members of the group can ridicule and undermine the person's prestige and position in the community (Bleek 1981). This pressure can be exerted because they see each other frequently and through knowing where the person lives, so that moral and other pressure can be used. The third form of exerting power over others is more subtle and can be termed surveillance. In this way members of the association observe others and know that they are being observed themselves.

With regard to policy implications, this case demonstrates how urban food supply is shaped by complex institutions that enable food from millions of producers to reach millions of consumers in an environment of minimal legal recourse and very poor infrastructure. Retailing in streets and in open areas of markets is also vital for the livelihoods of hundreds of thousands of poorer women in Ghana. Therefore attempts to reduce poverty should seek to work with street vendors and other retailers, in contrast to the on-going antagonistic approaches adopted by the state, particularly in relation to urban planning schemes.

Policies and interventions therefore need to build on the existing networks and institutional forms and not undermine those forms of regulation parallel to the state that encourage market access for the poor and cannot be used for rent seeking or exploiting other parts of society. This also requires policy makers to disaggregate the types of traders in order to consider the different roles, and identify constraints and opportunities for poverty alleviation. The needs of children involved in trade require particular consideration and also those trading smaller amounts who may not be so well represented by associations.

## Note

1   This chapter is based on research carried out for a PhD and for research funded by Crop Post Harvest Research Project R7149, Department for International Development (DFID) of the United Kingdom. However, the findings, interpretations, and conclusions expressed are entirely those of the author. Thanks to Albert Pappoe who assisted with the study in Kumasi, comments from Gina Porter and Frances Harris, and the comments of editors Alfonso Morales and John Cross as well as anonymous reviewers.

## Bibliography

Attah, M., Apt, N., and Grieco, M. (1996) 'Expected to earn, constrained to trade: Trading a customary role for Ghanaian women,' in M. Grieco, N. Apt, and J. Turner (eds) *At Christmas and on Rainy Days: Transport, Travel and the Female Traders of Accra*, Aldershot: Avebury: 3–18.

Babb, F. (1985) 'Middlemen and "marginal" women: Marketeers and dependency in Peru's informal sector,' in S. Plattner (ed.) *Markets and Marketing*, Boston, MA: University Press of America: 287–332.

Bauer, P.T. (1963) *West African Trade: A Study of Competition, Oligopoly and Monopoly in a Changing Economy*, 2nd edn, London: Routledge and Kegan Paul.

Benneh, G. (1990) *Population Growth and Development in Ghana*, Legon: Population Impact Project, University of Ghana.

Bleek, W. (1981) 'Avoiding shame: The ethical context of abortion in Ghana,' *Anthropological Quarterly*, 54(4): 203–09.

Chamlee-Wright, E. (1997) *The Cultural Foundations of Economic Development: Urban Female Entrepreneurship in Ghana*, London: Routledge.

Clark, G. (1994) *Onions Are My Husband: Survival and Accumulation by West African Market Women*, Chicago, IL: University of Chicago Press.

Cruikshank, B. (1853) *Eighteen Years on the Gold Coast of Africa Volume 2*, London: Hurst and Blacket.

Daaku, K.Y. (1970) *Trade and Politics on the Gold Coast 1600–1720: A Study of the African Reaction to European Trade*, London: Oxford University Press.

Darkwa, A. and Ackumey, M. (2003) 'Confronting global forces at the local level: Trade policies and the Ghanaian Trader,' *Centre for Social Policy Studies Policy Brief*, 10: 1.

de Marees, P. (1602) *Chronical of the Gold Coast of Guinea*. Translated in 1985 by A.V. Danzig and A. Smith. Oxford: Oxford University Press.

Dennis, C. and Peprah, E. (1995) 'Coping with transition: Techiman market, Ghana,' *Gender and Development*, 3(3): 43–48.

Dickson, K.B. (1969) *A Historical Geography of Ghana*, Cambridge: Cambridge University Press.

Fafchamps, M. (1997) 'Markets in sub-Saharan Africa,' *World Development*, 25(5): 733–54.

Ghana Statistical Service (1994) 'Ghana Demographic and Health Survey,' Accra: Ghana Statistical Service.

Gore, C. (1978) 'Food Marketing and Rural Development: A Study of an Urban Supply System in Ghana,' unpublished Ph.D. Dissertation, Pennsylvania State University.

Gould, P.R. (1960) *The Development of the Transportation Pattern in Ghana*, Studies in Geography No. 5, Evanston, IL: Northwestern University.

Granovetter, M. (1985) 'Economic action and social structure: The problem of embeddedness,' *American Journal of Sociology*, 91(3): 481–510.

Handwerker, W.P. (1981) 'African marketing institutions and rural development policy,' *African Urban Studies*, 10: 5–20.

Harts-Broekhuis, E.J.A. and Verkoren, O. (1987) 'Gender differentiation among market-traders in Central Mali,' *Tijdschrift voor Econ. en Soc. Geografie*, 78(3): 214–21.

Hilton, T.E. (1960) *Ghana Population Atlas: The Distribution and Density of Population in the Gold Coast and Togo Land Under UK Trusteeship*, London: University College of Ghana/Thomas Nelson and Sons.

Hollier, G.P. (1986) 'The marketing of gari in North-West Province, Cameroon,' *Geographiska Annaler*, 68B(1): 59–68.

Horn, N.E. (1994) *Cultivating Customers: Market Women in Harare, Zimbabwe*, London: Lynne Rienner.

Hymer, S.H. (1970) 'Economic forms in pre-colonial Ghana,' *Journal of Economic History*, 30(1): 33–50.

IDC (1989) 'Kumasi Central Market Study,' Integrated Development Consultants, Unpublished Report.

King, J. and Oppong, A. (2003) 'Influencing policy: Urban market women and Kumasi Central Market,' in *Demanding Dignity*. Online. Available: www.nsi-ins. ca/english/pdf/gera/14e_ghana.pdf

Lovejoy, P.E. (1974) 'Interregional monetary flows in the precolonial trade of Nigeria,' *Journal of African History*, 15(4): 563–85.

Lyon, F. (2000a) 'Trust, networks and norms: The creation of social capital in agricultural economies in Ghana,' *World Development*, 28(4): 663–882.

—— (2000b) 'Trust and power in farmer-trader relations: A study of small-scale vegetable production and marketing systems in Ghana,' unpublished PhD Dissertation, University of Durham, UK.

—— (2003) 'Trader associations and urban food systems in Ghana: Institutionalist approaches to understanding urban collective action,' *International Journal of Urban and Regional Research*, 27(1): 11–23.

McCaskie, T. (1995) *State and Society in Pre-Colonial Asante*, Cambridge: Cambridge University Press.

McIntosh, S.K. and McIntosh, R.J. (1993) 'Cities without citadels: Towards an understanding,' in T. Shaw, P. Sinclair, B. Andah, and A. Okpoko (eds) *The Archaeology of Africa: Food, Metals and Towns*, London: Routledge: 622–41.

Mikell, G. (1989a) *Cocoa and Chaos in Ghana*, New York: Paragon House.

—— (1989b) 'Peasant politicisation and economic recuperation in Ghana: Local and national dilemmas,' *Journal of Modern African Studies*, 27(3): 455–78.

Ministry of Agriculture (1987) 'National Agricultural Marketing Development Plan, Ghana,' Ministry of Agriculture, Ghana: Accra.

Mintz, S.W. (1964) 'The employment of capital by market women in Haiti,' in R. Firth and B.S. Yamey (eds) *Capital, Savings and Credit in Peasant Societies*, London: George Allen and Unwin: 256–86.

North, D.C. (1990) *Institutions, Institutional Change and Economic Performance*, Cambridge: Cambridge University Press.

Onyemelukwe, J.O.C. (1970) 'Aspects of staple foods trade in Onitsha Market,' *Nigerian Geographical Journal*, 12(2): 121–39.

Population Impact Project (1994) *Population and Development in Ghana*, Legon: PIP/Ghana, University of Ghana.

Porter, G. (1988) 'Perspectives on trade, mobility and gender in a rural market system: Borno, North-east Nigeria,' *Tijdschrift voor Econ. en Soc. Geografie*, 79(2): 82–92.

Reynolds, E. (1974) *Trade and Economic Change on the Gold Coast, 1807–1874*, Harlow, Essex: Longman Group.

Robertson, C.C. (1983) 'The death of Makola and other tragedies,' *Canadian Journal of African Studies*, 17(3): 469–95.

Scott, J.C. (1976) *The Moral Economy of the Peasant*, New Haven, CT: Yale University Press.

Smith, D.W. (1998) 'Urban food systems and the poor in developing countries,' *Transactions of the Institute of British Geographers*, 23(2): 207–19.

Smith, H.M. and Luttrell, M.E. (1994) 'Cartels in an "Nth-Best" world: The wholesale foodstuff trade in Ibadan, Nigeria,' *World Development*, 22(3): 323–35.

Sudarkasa, N. (1973) 'Where Women Work: A Study of Yoruba Women in the

Market Place and in the Home,' Anthropological Papers, No. 53. University of Michigan, Ann Arbor.

Szereszewski, R. (1965) *Structural Changes in the Economy of the Gold Coast, 1891–1911*, London: Weidenfeld and Nicolson.

Thompson, E.P. (1971) 'The moral economy of the English crowd in the eighteenth century,' *Past and Present,* 50: 76–136.

Trager, L. (1981) 'Customers and creditors: Variations in economic personalism in a Nigerian marketing system,' *Ethnology,* 20(2): 133–46.

—— (1985) 'From yams to beer in a Nigerian city: Expansion and change in informal sector trade activity', in S. Plattner (ed.) *Markets and Marketing,* Boston, MA: University Press of America.

UNCHS (1996) *An Urbanizing World: Global Report on Human Settlements, 1996,* Oxford: Oxford University Press.

Williamson, O.E. (1985) *The Economic Institutions of Capitalism: Firms, Markets and Relational Contracting,* London: Macmillan.

# 11 Embeddedness and business strategies among Santiago, Chile's street and flea market vendors

*Joel Stillerman and Catherine Sundt*[1]

## Introduction

The informal economy has been a principal focus within studies of Latin America since the 1960s. Growing out of a discussion of urban marginality and building on analyses of street trading in Africa, students of the informal sector have been particularly interested in its relationship with the formal sector, its potential (or lack thereof) to spur economic development, and its role in poor people's employment and survival strategies. Within this discussion, street vending has been an important focus because of its visibility in Latin American cities and because it challenges state regulation on two fronts: illegal commerce calls into question the state's ability to collect taxes, raise revenue, and provide services; and street commerce (legal or illegal) potentially blocks street access to vehicles, pedestrians, or residents.

Notwithstanding the substantial body of work dedicated to the informal sector and specifically to street commerce, authors have directed less attention to vendors' entrepreneurial strategies. These strategies are important to understand because they may provide insight into the sector's economic potential as well as its relationship to urban redevelopment and employment policies. With this gap in mind, we explore the strategies developed by licensed and illegal vendors in several Santiago, Chile street markets (*ferias*) and flea markets. While many studies contrast the formal and the informal sectors, following Cross (1998), we utilize the intermediate category of semi-formality to classify these vendors because they pay for licenses and are partially monitored by the state, though they evade some regulations: they are distinct from both formal and informal firms.

We found key concepts from economic sociology useful in understanding vendor strategies as well as key differences between street vendors' (*feriantes*) and flea market vendors' business strategies. While economic sociologists have focused on leading-edge firms in the technology, auto, and garment sectors, we found similar dynamics in the economically and legally precarious setting of street vending. Much like their partners in more established industries, vendors' strategies rely on their embeddedness in networks of personal relations (Granovetter 1985) and rely on enforceable trust and bounded solidarity with network partners in order to identify crucial information, reduce risks, and effectively compete in a challenging legal and economic context (Portes 1994; Light 2004).

We found that in both settings vendors utilize long-term personal ties to hire workers, identify supplies, obtain and reciprocate support from peers, and prevent theft. Nonetheless, *feriantes* maintain a regular clientele, while flea market vendors have competitive, short-term ties with shoppers, reflecting their different customer bases as well as each setting's distinct retail culture. Additionally, *feriantes* have hostile and competitive relations with unlicensed vendors (*coleros*), while some flea market vendors collude with their unlicensed counterparts. These differences reflect the fact that flea market vendors may perceive short-term gains from unlicensed vendors' sales, while *feriantes* see *coleros* as their key competition. Additionally, flea market vendors' short-term time horizons for relationships with customers make them less concerned about maintaining an honorable relationship with an established clientele; *feriantes* rely on this reputation to maintain a regular clientele and customers regularly monitor their behavior. Each setting's distinct network ties, business orientations, and cultures explain these differences and demonstrate the semi-formal retail sector's heterogeneity. In both settings, vendors' reliance on embedded ties with suppliers, peers, and customers (for *feriantes*) may restrict their opportunities for expanding profits because it narrows their circuit of contacts and may reflect a risk averse orientation toward new markets and potential business partnerships.

Our argument proceeds as follows. We first review the literature on the informal economy and key concepts in economic sociology, and continue with context on vending in Chile as well as a discussion of our research design and methods. We proceed to examine the study's findings and conclude with an analysis of the differences between street and flea markets and relate this discussion to broader issues in economic sociology.

## Business strategies within informal retail settings

Much of the discussion of the informal economy focuses on delineating the boundary between formal and informal economic activity, legal rules that regulate or economically inhibit informal actors, and the role of informal activity in micro- and macro-level economic performance. We build on one stream of research (De Soto 1989; Cross 1998) that distinguishes between formal, semi-formal, and informal activities to highlight competition between licensed and informal vendors. We extend the discussion of informality via economic sociologists' analyses of networks, enforceable trust, and bounded solidarity. While economic sociologists have argued that informal network relations within and between formal firms help foster leading economic sectors' and firms' success, we found similar dynamics in businesses often considered anachronistic, backward, and unprofitable.

These observations strengthen the argument that most economic behavior is rooted in interpersonal relations (Granovetter 1985) because it encompasses both leading firms and informal actors with a precarious legal status, little capital, and scarce formal education.

For our purposes, the informal economy "comprises economic actions that bypass the costs and are excluded from the protection of laws and administrative rules covering 'property relationships, commercial licensing, labor contracts, torts, financial credit, and social security systems'" (Feige quoted in Portes 1994: 428). The informal sector is characterized by avoidance, noncompliance, or partial compliance with legal regulations (Portes and Schauffler 1993; Portes 1994; Staudt 1996), and is an undocumented way of doing legitimate business (Light 2004).

Without dwelling on the intricacies of a complex debate, we wish to briefly situate this chapter in relation to the three main perspectives on informality. De Soto (1989) developed the legalist approach, arguing that governments' denial of property rights to informal economic actors has hamstrung an energetic and potentially profitable sector. State repression and haphazard regulation of informal activities along with the high costs of operating formal firms have prevented this sector from becoming the prime engine of economic development.

Tokman (2001) and his colleagues at the International Labor Organization (ILO) have developed the dualist approach, arguing that the formal and informal sectors are separate and the latter is a safety net that absorbs the surplus labor created as a consequence of stunted economic development or economic crisis. The sector consists of low-productivity enterprises developed by individuals who cannot gain access to limited available formal employment. He advocates a single, consistent, regulatory framework for the informal sector to boost workers' and entrepreneurs' human capital and help these enterprises become more productive and profitable (Tokman 2001).

Finally, the structuralist perspective, identified with Portes and others, states that the informal sector is interrelated with the formal sector, and the two will often expand and contract together in developing nations. Although informal actors are independent, they belong to a dense network of relationships. Informal enterprises may exploit opportunities left by legal relations; larger formal firms may subcontract via informal companies. This perspective emphasizes the interdependence of formal and informal enterprises, and the benefits formal enterprises receive from subcontracting relationships. Because we highlight the web of relations between suppliers and vendors, we find this perspective most appropriate to the case of Santiago, Chile (Portes 1989, 1994; Portes and Schauffler 1993).

While identifying with the structuralist approach, one of our principal foci is on competition between semi-formal and informal businesses. As Cross argues,

> informal firms may begin to formalize in some respects while remaining informal in others. For example, a business owner may obtain a permit

for her business, but remain outside the tax system, fail to follow labor regulations, and otherwise operate informally ... But, as De Soto notes, semiformality can also mean that the government actively negotiates the implementation of regulatory norms without, however, changing actual regulations.

(1998: 35; see also De Soto 1989: chapter 3)

These two elements characterize the situation of the street and flea markets we studied in Santiago. As we outline below (see also Salazar 2003; Contreras and Weihert 1988 on Chile), local and national governments have partially regulated these markets, thus creating a distinction between formal, semi-formal, and informal markets. However, the formalization of these markets is incomplete in that vendors use family labor and verbal contracts, and often do not pay sales or social security taxes. They are legally and economically located in between formal and informal actors.

While this scholarship has taken us a long way toward understanding informal firms' position within national economic and legal contexts, with few exceptions (see Portes 1994; Polakoff 1985; Aliaga 2002; Morales 1993) students of the informal economy have not examined entrepreneurs' business strategies. Here, we can learn a great deal from economic sociologists, who have argued that interpersonal networks undergird much (if not all) economic activity, serving as means to enforce agreements, reduce uncertainty and risk, and spur innovation.

Granovetter (1985) provides a starting point for this discussion. He criticizes Williamson's assumption that all transactions occur between atomized economic actors and the argument that the large multi-divisional firm emerged to reduce "transaction costs" that market actors bear because they have difficulty avoiding others' malfeasance in market interactions. In contrast to Williamson, Granovetter emphasizes "the role of concrete personal relations and structures (or 'networks') of such relations in generating trust and discouraging malfeasance" (1985: 490). He goes on to show that personal relations that generate trust and permit the enforcement of agreements facilitate inter-firm relationships via interlocking corporate boards and shared information on employees, smooth the flow of information and completion of tasks within firms, increase the flow of information in decentralized sectors like construction, and permit fraud and graft via the collusion of trust-based groups. Thus, interpersonal relations that many economists believed characterized pre-industrial economies are central to modern economic life.

Others argue that network-based relationships between firms in diverse sectors and activities (manufacturing, information- and bio-technology, publishing, construction, joint ventures) facilitate learning and innovation and hence profitability (Sabel 1994; Powell 1990; Powell and Smith-Doerr 1994). This is so because decentralized firms do not restrict individual initiative and creativity as bureaucratic firms often do, long-term network ties facilitate trust and information exchange, and small firm networks can quickly adapt to changing markets and build skills. Additionally, repeated interactions between individuals and the expectation of future exchanges facilitate the growth of trust and cooperation (Uzzi 2001: 214–16; Powell and Smith-Doerr 1994: 370, 388; Polakoff 1985: 176–77; Sabel 1994: 155–57). In a complementary vein, Clarke (1999) shows how direct sales organizations are highly effective because of their integration of sociability, personal networks, and trust in the service of profit (see also Zelizer 2005).

These phenomena present in cutting-edge firms are more pronounced with informal economic activities:

> The dynamics of economic action that Granovetter (1985) labeled "the problem of embeddedness" are nowhere clearer than in transactions where the only recourse against malfeasance is mutual trust by virtue of common membership in a group. Trust in informal exchanges is generated both by shared identities and feelings and by the expectation that fraudulent actions will be penalized by the exclusion of the violator from key social networks.
>
> (Portes 1994: 430)

The absence of state supervision or other formal means to guarantee agreements between informal economic actors necessitates the embedded social relations that are so central to formal firms and can only be carried out via "enforceable trust" that relies on the bounded solidarity shared by community members (Portes 1994: 431).

Consequently, street vendors, as a subset of informal economic actors, rely on social networks in order to guarantee agreements and take advantage of economic opportunities. Morales (1993) shows that Chicago street vendors enter the trade with knowledge from childhood observations or parental socialization, and rely on family and friends as workers, sources of licit and illicit merchandise, customers, and to secure a stable space within the market. Similarly, Polakoff (1985) notes that butchers in Bolivia rely on long-term ties with customers, competitors, and vendor associations to manage risk and engage in profitable, but illicit business practices. While we can find similar mechanisms at work in informal and high performance firms, Aliaga's (2002) study in Lima, Perú cautions that ambulant vendors utilize "bonding" social capital with family and friends as business resources rather than "bridging" social capital with persons only known indirectly. These localized and closed networks facilitate vendors' survival strategies but preclude great capital accumulation because they express vendors' generalized *distrust* of actors outside their small circle with whom they might make profitable connections and reflect a defensive and risk-averse business orientation (compare Uzzi 2001).

Our data on Santiago street and flea market vendors builds on discussions of both semi-formality and embeddedness. Additionally, the presence or absence of enforceable trust and bounded solidarity in vending relationships helps explain the differences between these two retail forms. Street vendors develop long-term ties with customers and suppliers because of their ability to elicit shoppers' trust and to monitor debtors in their own community. Moreover, because local governments are reluctant to repress illegal vendors, semi-formal merchants must rely on their own political organizing to compete with both large formal firms and informal actors. Finally, street vendors' location in neighborhoods and customers' ability to monitor their behavior leads vendors to perceive a long time horizon in their relations with specific clients: it would be self-defeating to cheat regular customers.

Flea market vendors also rely on enforceable trust with colleagues and suppliers, but cannot depend on this mechanism with customers. This is so because, rather than relying on a regular clientele they can easily monitor, vendors have intermittent contacts with customers from the metro area and throughout the country. They cannot offer them credit or develop long-term ties with them. In contrast to street vendors, they have perceived a short time horizon for customer relations, and are thus more likely to view them instrumentally. This is one reason why some flea market vendors collude with unlicensed vendors: they can profit from illicit sales with one-time customers. Unlicensed vendors also benefit from logistical restrictions on guards and police that shield them from prosecution. We outline these findings below.

## Chilean context

Like many Latin American countries, Chile experienced substantial industrialization and public sector growth from the 1940s to 1970s, but the demand for employment outpaced its supply. In the absence of adequate unemployment insurance, many poor people worked in the informal sector (Portes 1989: 8). Portes and Hoffman (2003: 53) found that still in 1998, between one-third and half of the urban economically active population in Latin America worked in informal employment, representing the largest segment of the workforce.

The Santiago metro area, whose population in 2003 was 5,040,001 (INE 2004), consists of 32 semi-autonomous municipal governments.[2] In 1985, Santiago represented 33.8 percent of the country's total population and 40.6 percent of its urban population, though its rate of growth declined from 1952 to 1982 (Portes 1989: 14–15). While Chile's government has traditionally been highly centralized, the Pinochet dictatorship (1973–90) subdivided the municipalities to double their number from 16 to 32, increasing local municipalities' political importance as service providers (Portes 1989: 21–23; Greaves 2005: 199; Salcedo 2004: 173).

The liberalization of land markets and external trade under the dictatorship facilitated the rise in consumer goods imports and the growth of big-box supermarkets and malls. In 1999, large supermarkets sold 53 percent of food and personal items (D'Andrea *et al.* 2004: 5). In 1997, the ten most important malls in Chile had two billion dollars in sales, and in 2002, there were eleven regional malls in the Santiago metropolitan region (Salcedo 2003: 1093–94).

Nevertheless, in 2002, small supermarkets (four checkouts or less), corner stores, open-air markets, and outdoor kiosks sold 47 percent of food and personal items (D'Andrea *et al.* 2004: 4–5). Santiago's neighborhood street markets have more than $2 billion in annual sales (*El Mostrador* 2005) and the metropolitan region hosts 401 neighborhood street markets (*Punto Final* 2005). Vendors purchase licenses from city governments (though may not pay taxes, pension, or health benefits), but many unlicensed vendors squat at market entrances.

The markets, while legally recognized, can thus be considered part of Chile's informal sector, which Portes and Hoffman (2003: 56) calculate at 30.8 percent of the urban economically active population (including micro-entrepreneurs – employers of four workers or less, own account workers, and nannies). Furthermore, according to a 1997 survey, micro-enterprises (defined in the survey as firms with nine employees or less) constituted 80 percent of Chilean firms and 40 percent of the employed (Valenzuela and Venegas 2001: 19, 22–23). With the exception of government efforts to ban street commerce downtown (Contreras and Weihert 1988), government authorities are reluctant to repress unlicensed street vendors because they generate so much employment at little or no government expense, and shutting down markets could produce a political backlash (see Seligmann 1997 on this issue in Cuzco, Perú). Street vendors thus face significant competition from other legal vendors, illegal vendors, and the growing supermarket sector. They have built on their social networks to strengthen their economic and legal position in relation to competitors.

## Research design

Research for this chapter was conducted during June and July 2001, July 2003, and December 2005 to January 2006. The data comes from 120 hours of participant and non-participant observation by Stillerman (along with two research assistants) in several street markets and in meetings of the national street market vendors' association (ASOF). The street markets observed on the first visit are located in low- and mixed-income areas. Research on the second visit focused on two street markets in the Cerro Navia municipality in western Santiago and the Bío Bío flea market on the southern edge of the Santiago municipality. Stillerman and his assistants jotted down schematic notes immediately following field visits, wrote longhand notes as soon as possible afterward, and typed completed notes onto a portable computer.

Additionally, Stillerman conducted 24 formal interviews with street market merchants; scholars with expertise in the area; government researchers; and marketing professionals in banks, department stores, supermarkets, and shopping malls. He took longhand notes during interviews and computerized the notes afterward. In addition to ethnographic and interview-based research, he collected relevant published documents, including newspaper articles, marketing studies, government data and studies, and NGO reports.

## Market vendors as embedded actors

In the street and flea markets we observed, vendors face many challenges toward their goal of maintaining and expanding profitable businesses. These include identifying and maintaining a regular clientele, securing labor and supplies, maintaining cooperative relations with other vendors, guaranteeing their own and their customers' safety, and gaining adequate government services. Vendors' strategies rely heavily on practices of reciprocity via kin and non-kin networks, while they address government via collective political action to improve markets' legal and economic status. These strategies point to vendors' flexibility in identifying business opportunities, gaining needed information and obtaining resources, as well as their embeddedness in trust-based long-term relationships. Street and flea market vendors are differentiated by their long and short time horizons for sales that affect their relations with customers and unlicensed vendors. Before reviewing our findings, we provide background on the two types of markets.

### Street markets

Santiago's street markets (*ferias*) have existed since before the colonial era. While the city's plaza was the site of seasonal markets and festivals during the colonial era, city and church officials forced these activities into the urban periphery in the nineteenth century and later prohibited neighborhood carnivals and fiestas they considered immoral. Periodically, unlicensed food vendors attempted to sell goods near downtown public markets, but city government pushed them back into urban neighborhoods. From the late 1930s until the mid-1950s, the national government legalized these neighborhood markets to reduce food prices by allowing producers' direct sales. In reality, vendors who purchased from farmers at wholesale markets came to dominate street markets (Salazar 2003; compare De Soto 1989 on Lima and Cross 1998 on Mexico City). In 1976, the dictatorship revoked the 1939 law regulating street markets, leaving vendors at the mercy of local government officials.[3]

Today, virtually every Santiago neighborhood has a *feria* that rotates between different streets on different days. Municipal governments grant a market access to a given street on a particular day of the week and close off the street. Though markets originally only sold fresh produce, they now include other foods, household goods, clothing, and entertainment items. Legal vendors (*feriantes*), organized as small family businesses of two to four members (often multi-generational), purchase permits (costing on average $120 every six months) from the relevant municipality and pay smaller fees for waste disposal and portable toilet rental. Vendors park their cars or pickup trucks that hold their merchandise, and set up tables in front with a tarp or awning over their table. Vendors of canned foods and household goods have more elaborate, store-like carts, as do fish and meat salespeople.

Unlicensed vendors (*coleros*) spread their goods on blankets on the ground, tend to work alone, squat at the entrance of the market or along perpendicular streets (where they risk ejection by police), and specialize in new and used clothing sales with a minority selling pirated CDs and DVDs and small electronic items. Thus, *coleros* could potentially attract shoppers' attention and thus draw them toward the *ferias*, or they could compete with *feriantes* either by selling the same goods for lower prices or by capturing a large portion of shoppers' disposable income. They are divided among the unemployed who cannot afford license fees; those who purchase cheaper provisional licenses ($10 or $20 US) and sell new goods; and more prosperous entrepreneurs (their car ownership and large stock indicate they could afford license fees) who flout the law (Salazar 2003: 87–89; Leemira Consultores 2004: 6–7, 126–27, 132; Stillerman 2006a).

*Feriantes* purchase goods in wholesale markets. Most *ferias* are located in the low- and moderate-income sectors of northern, southern, and western Santiago, and satisfy a market niche among residents with modest incomes and often-sporadic employment. These residents may lack transit access to supermarkets and formal credit, have limited incomes that require them to buy products in small sizes, and prefer the quality fresh produce and personal relationships they maintain with local vendors. (Some middle- and upper-class citizens also attend markets to buy fresh foods.) (Salazar 2003: 87–93; Leemira Consultores 2004: 6–7, 126–27; Stillerman 2006a; ASOF 2005.)

### Flea markets

While flea markets originated as antique stores near downtown Santiago (they are today known as *ferias persas* or *mercados persas* – literally "Persian markets" evoking images of the Middle Eastern bazaar), these markets now offer more diverse products. Today, Santiago hosts several indoor flea markets that attract large crowds, especially on weekends. The Bío Bío market is the best known and is located in an older neighborhood near downtown Santiago. The market hosts individual vendors crowded in several defunct factory buildings and covers approximately one square mile. Originally a street market, city authorities forced vendors indoors during the 1970s and again in 1995 (Salcedo 2004: 95), though a smaller number of street vendors today still work on the sidewalks, especially on weekends.

Products sold include clothing, furniture, computer goods, antiques, tools, and bric-a-brac. Individual vendors or families rent stalls, and specific types of products are grouped in specific sections of a building or in different buildings. For example, used goods and hardware share space with antiques, while there are separate buildings for computers, furniture, and bicycles.

The market sits alongside the city's defunct stockyards, which the government moved to an outlying district during the 1960s, though many small restaurants, butchers, and fresh fish stores still operate there. Much of the clothing and software is clearly pirated merchandise, and citizens widely believe that many of the used goods sold there are stolen. In addition to its reputation among some as a thieves' market, the neighborhood is known for high assault rates, though crime does not seem to deter the large crowds the market attracts.

## Identifying and maintaining clientele

*Feriantes* make use of the markets' neighborhood context to develop variegated networks with their peers, suppliers, and customers. Since many markets have remained on the same neighborhood for decades, customers can find, within a few blocks of their homes, the same merchants operating once or twice per week on a regular basis. Because of the *ferias'* permanence in residential areas, vendors are able to rely on long-term relationships with their regular customers, or *caseros*. Vendors may set aside quality merchandise, place special orders, or provide trust-based credit to their *caseros*.

Many customers who do not have access to formal credit shop at street markets, and utilize the *abono* or *fiado* system in which customers pay off items by installments. This system offers regular customers flexible payment options based on trust developed over the long term, while it permits vendors to expand their sales base in low-income areas. Vendors also use several techniques to reduce the risk of customer default, including extending credit to family members of current customers, surveying potential debtors' homes to assess their income and responsibility, and visiting customers' homes on a weekly basis to collect payment. Laura, a clothing and furniture vendor, explains: "I've changed the way I provide credit. I'm more careful now. I go out and evaluate their homes before I offer credit. They can be poor, but I want to make sure their homes are clean. That tells me they're more responsible."[4] The neighborhood location of *ferias* and regular accessibility of clients allows vendors to obtain effective information regarding clients' reputations, monitor their behavior, and build the trust and loyalty that keeps customers returning and up-to-date with their bills. Vendors' direct monitoring of debtors' homes and use of family members as entry points for expanding their customer base exemplify the phenomenon of enforceable trust.

*Feriantes* use a variety of tactics to attract customers. Produce vendors repeat sales pitches, while others play music or banter and joke with customers. Once customers are interested, vendors talk to their customers about their products' health benefits. Laura gives her *caseros* Christmas presents, a strategy she learned from her father, a lifelong merchant. Other vendors make a point of listening intently to customers' personal problems, taking on a quasi-therapeutic role.[5]

Flea market vendors are less able to rely on enforceable trust with customers. Because of their metropolitan-wide clientele, vendors do not develop the close ties with regular customers evident in the street markets.[6] Vendors do not extend credit to shoppers, as their short-term interactions create higher default risks: "Almost no one accepts credit cards here ... We accept some checks, but it's problematic because we don't have the verification service that mall stores do."[7] In contrast to *feriantes*, flea market vendors maintain a short time horizon for sales – they are less likely to have regular customers.

A less tangible factor affecting arm's-length ties between vendors and customers is the market's retail culture. The Bío Bío market is widely known as a source of great deals, but vendors may cheat customers or sell them defective, pirated, or stolen goods. Thus, buyers and sellers are modestly distrustful of one another and seek to outsmart their counterparts.

For example, furniture vendors start prices high because they know customers will try to haggle, and some salespersons change the asking price depending on how much they guess a person can afford. They use scripted lines such as saying an article is the last item they have in stock, and repeating the quality, options, prices, and guarantees that come with each product. According to Leon, a vendor, each salesperson may lower the price enough to keep a customer. While vendors are less likely to have a regular clientele (except restaurateurs who buy large lots of furniture on a regular basis), they mimic *feria* vendors' personalized style in the effort to attract customers who frequent the *ferias*. In an atypical example, a salesman hoped regular customers of Asian heritage might refer compatriots because of his low prices. He also mentioned he had received a $5,000 loan based on a handshake from a Taiwanese immigrant friend.[8]

The gamesmanship noted above is evident in the following staged performance reminiscent of Erving Goffman's observations of confidence artists' "front stage" routines:

> Maria [business owner] and Leon [employee] collaborate on a sale:
>
> Maria – "It costs $15. Leon, how much is it?"
> Leon – "For the lady, $12."
>
> I asked about the practice.
>
> M – We reverse the roles as well. Leon will ask me how much it costs even though he already knows the price range he can use.
>
> Another customer comes.
>
> L – "Maria, how much do the presidential chairs cost?"
> Leon takes out calculator: "It's $175."[9]

In another humorous example of trickery, itinerant vendors sold what appeared to be substantially discounted copies of the Walt Disney film

*Pocohontas*, but in fact the tapes were blank.[10] Thus, unlike street market vendors who are embedded in long-term ties with shoppers, flea market salespeople cannot rely on enforceable trust in relation to customers and both vendors and customers in this latter setting may compete to outsmart one another.

## Labor and supplies

While *feriantes* and flea market vendors differ in the nature and duration of their network ties with customers, they mobilize labor and secure supplies in similar ways. In both settings, vendors operate multigenerational family businesses using unpaid family labor or verbal contracts without paying health or pension benefits. One can find several family members working at different stalls in the same or separate businesses in both settings. After dismissing an employee who was not a family member for theft, a Bío Bío furniture retailer emphasized that only family members are trustworthy employees.[11]

Kin and non-kin network ties become important sources of supplies. While produce vendors maintain arm's-length ties with wholesale vendors, furniture and clothing vendors in both settings rely on long-term ties with suppliers. Laura, quoted above, uses a wide range of suppliers for clothing, including her sister and Korean vendors (with whom she haggles and at times buys without a receipt in an act of collusion so the wholesaler can avoid tax payment). She also follows up on "cold call" suppliers who arrive at her stall, seeking new sources if she learns the goods offered are not stolen. Finally, she purchases clothing from a local seamstress, thereby maintaining particularistic ties with neighborhood producers: "I buy from her all the time. She supports herself with clothing sales, so I have to buy from her"[12] (compare Uzzi 2001). A shoe vendor in the same market also prefers purchasing high-quality leather shoes from small workshops (most of which failed in the face of low-cost foreign competitors).[13]

Bío Bío vendors also rely on personal networks for regular purchases as well as in emergencies. The furniture business we studied relies on a regular set of small furniture workshops located in Southern Santiago. They extend credit to these suppliers until they arrive with shipments. On one occasion, the male co-owner's brother had requested a "loan" of 24 chairs, generating tension with his wife who argued the brother was too cheap to purchase chairs himself. In contrast, she might buy more expensive chairs from a personal contact when in need, arguing that it was necessary to invest in relationships.[14] In both these settings, vendors rely on long-term, trust-based relationships in hiring personnel and acquiring supplies.

Used-goods salespeople also rely on friendship networks for information regarding supplies, and here, the vendor's ability to identify under priced items that could receive a substantial resale markup is essential to an effective business. One vendor with family ties in both *ferias* and flea markets comments, "I have a lot of friends who are *coleros* working in the *feria*, and sometimes they say, 'hey *negrito*, I have something to sell you, are you interested?' and I say, 'Let's take a look.' If it's worth it, I buy it to resell."[15] In this case, personal contacts are critical sources of information on undervalued merchandise that can be resold at a hefty profit in a different venue.

### Cooperation with other vendors

In both settings, personal networks and acts of reciprocity are significant in relationships among vendors and between vendors and customers. In the *feria*, long-term relationships foster bounded solidarity among vendors or between vendors and customers. In Cerro Navia, a vendor procured a wheelchair from shoppers to take a fellow vendor suffering from terminal cancer on trips outside Santiago.[16] A northern Santiago vendor who was mugged at the wholesale market and lost money destined for goods purchases received spare clothing from wholesale vendors and loans from other *feriantes*.[17] Finally, a southern Santiago patron of a local market with long-term relations with vendors received food donations from vendors when her granddaughter suffered severe burns in a fire.[18]

Bío Bío vendors lend supplies to peers as needed, agree not to sell the same products as vendors in neighboring stalls, jointly care for dogs located in the market, take collections for medical treatment and funerals of fellow vendors, and also collaborate in sales of complementary items when a customer seeks an item an individual vendor does not stock.[19] In both settings, bounded solidarity among vendors facilitates resource sharing for mundane tasks and extraordinary events like the death of a workmate.

### Security

Since *ferias* and flea markets do not have the resources to install surveillance cameras or hire a full security staff, they must rely on other means to create a safe environment for themselves and their customers. In some *ferias*, vendors are aggressive in their own protection, given the lack of security guards and the portability of their merchandise. In some poor areas, *feriantes* will mete out vigilante justice against thieves. However, vendors are more likely to collectively monitor the streets to identify thieves as well as collaborate with community-based police.[20]

In Bío Bío, private security guards survey the premises in an effort to prevent theft, control unlicensed merchants, maintain security, and keep order. Vendors attempt to apprehend thieves immediately because security is short staffed. Police are most visible on the weekends, when customer volume is highest, but are less reliable during the week.[21] In each of these settings, vendors often rely on their own informal networks to maintain a secure environment.

### Relations with unlicensed vendors

The *feria* and flea market vendors studied are licensed merchants, though municipal governments, police, and building administrators (in the flea market case) do not exclude unlicensed vendors from operating nearby. As a consequence, *feriantes* have organized collectively at the local, city-wide, and national level to improve their legal and economic status, while some flea market vendors have pressured their building administrator to expel unlicensed vendors.

As noted above, *coleros* who do not pay the approximately $240 per year in license fees plus smaller fees for garbage disposal and toilet facilities set up their blankets on the streets next to *ferias* (where shoppers enter) or on streets perpendicular to the *ferias*. While there is no easy way to measure *coleros'* economic impact on *feriantes*, vendors and a recent survey indicate three ways *coleros'* sales might directly compete with *feriantes* while operating at a lower cost. First, for those *feriantes* who sell comparable items to *coleros*, the latter can charge lower prices for these products because they do not pay license fees. Second, vendors complain that customers see the *coleros* first as they enter the *feria*, spend money on the cheap items, and thus have less money to spend in the *feria*. Third, in many neighborhoods, particularly on weekends, there are two to three times as many *coleros* as *feriantes*. For example, Puente Alto, a fast-growing Santiago suburb, has 3,500 licensed vendors and 10,000 *coleros*. Thus, *feriantes* fear that none of the vendors will profit because sales are spread too thinly. While the presence of a small group of *coleros* might attract customers to the *feria* and thus benefit all vendors, the massive number of *coleros* undercuts these possible benefits to *feriantes*.[22]

Neighborhood-level *feriantes'* organizations have pressured city government to remove *coleros* or *feriantes* operating with falsified licenses, but authorities either ignore these demands, only compel *coleros* to move down the block, or offer unlicensed vendors inexpensive provisional or used goods licenses. A city official commented that the mayor was reluctant to crack down on *coleros* because of high unemployment rates.[23]

As we argue elsewhere (Stillerman 2006b), vendors' inability to gain local government enforcement of vending laws results from political and economic changes under Chile's 1973–90 dictatorship. In brief, the military government suspended the *feria* law in 1976, placing vendors under the rule of general retail laws that did not take into account the specific circumstances of street vending and left vendors at the mercy of mayors appointed by the generals. Moreover, the dictatorship refused to recognize or negotiate with existing vendors' organizations, and a subdivision of municipalities left some *ferias* straddling municipal boundaries. Free-market economic and social policies made jobs less stable and economic downturns in 1982–83 and 2001–03 created massive unemployment, filling the ranks of taxi drivers and salespeople. *Ferias* were thus subject to an ineffectual regulatory system, mayors' arbitrary rule, and competition from unlicensed vendors.

In the 1990s, vendors in the La Florida suburb built a citywide organization, thanks in part to their political ties to a sympathetic congressman, an agronomist in Santiago's largest wholesale market that supplies the *ferias*, and advocates in the non-profit sector. Through these connections and their own experiences as political activists prior to the military coup, vendors created the National Association of Feria Organizations (ASOF). This organization has had modest success gaining government grants to train vendors in accounting and retail service, bank loans for vendors, and other services. They helped draft a pending bill that would stabilize vendors' positions in existing markets, and are currently conducting a pilot program with the United Nations Food and Agricultural Organization to use the *ferias* as conduits for public health and food security campaigns that would link them with small farmers. These modest successes reflect vendors' political experiences, network ties with powerful figures, and the fact that some *feriantes'* demands resonate with government anti-poverty initiatives. These projects have not effectively addressed the fundamental un- and under-employment problem that produces thousands of *coleros*.

In the Bío Bío market, some individuals work completely outside regulations and without registration or fees. Unlicensed vendors (*piratas*) make money by approaching customers, assisting them in finding an item, charging more than its sales price, and pocketing the difference. Many vendors dislike the pirates and refer to them as parasites, but cannot do much to stop them. Pedro, a *pirata*, is the son of a furniture manufacturer and worked as a licensed vendor for two years before becoming an unlicensed vendor. As a consequence, he understands the business as well as sales practices in the market and claims to have had much success in his business, earning enough to pay a car loan and a mortgage.[24]

Understanding the *piratas'* ability to ply their trade requires an examination of administrators' and guards' limited ability to prove their guilt, licensed vendors' own illegal behaviors, police indifference, and *piratas'* own forms of self-governance and cooperation. The building's administrator and security guards express frustration at their inability to remove the *piratas*:

> The administrator stopped by Maria and Isaac's stall. "I've got 125 delinquents inside here and I'm not talking about someone that steals a little thing from you. They defraud people. The licensed vendors sell at $60 and the pirate sells it elsewhere at $200."

> Guard – "And as a guard, if I call it to the person's attention, I'm the bad guy."

> A – "The police can't do anything about it if they don't see it – it's the vendor's word vs. the pirate's. If the cop sees it, he brings the complaint to a judge and the judge decides. They came here once to interview us without letting us know ahead of time and they shut this place down for a whole day. We work every day of the year except Christmas and New

Year so it hurt the vendors a lot. Seventy percent of the people here work illegally without papers. So they closed this place down. SERCOTEC [government agency promoting small business development] did the study. The police and detectives don't come inside here. Some people carry knives here. There are only seven of us [administrators] here, and it's dangerous here, but the owners support us. This place is like a closed world where no one [from outside] gets involved."[25]

On a separate occasion, the administrator commented, "I have to deal with twelve lawsuits against the market, the majority of which result from vendors' non-payment of social security and health benefits to employees."[26] Here, the administrator points to several difficulties in apprehending the pirates. It is difficult for short-staffed guards to catch pirates "in the act." Since police are in the building infrequently, are unlikely to see crimes as they occur, and they file crime reports, a court judgment is unlikely to favor licensed vendors and/or the market's administration. The manager also insinuates that she does not wish to draw government attention to the markets because vendors do not pay their employees legally required benefits. Additionally, by describing the markets as a "closed world," she suggests that, with few exceptions, government authorities may fear entering an apparently dangerous setting or may have an agreement with the owners not to interfere with market activities.

In addition, two guards and one pirate note the collusion between some vendors and pirates. A guard comments, "The pirates get along well with the licensed vendors because if they have the choice between selling nothing and selling something, they prefer to sell. The problem is that often the pirates lie and try to defraud customers. They keep their surcharge without giving customers the merchandise they purchased."[27] Pedro continues, "For businesses, it's cheaper to use a pirate than to pay salary and commission to an employee."[28] Thus, while some vendors resent the pirates because they think their unscrupulous practices (charging large surcharges or refusing to deliver purchased merchandise) scare away customers, others cooperate with them to gain short-term profits at shoppers' expense, and may shield *piratas* from apprehension.

The *piratas* limit their own behaviors in order to prevent major conflicts with licensed vendors:

> The most important thing of all (so as not to fight with the owners) is not to take a client away from a store. That is to say, if a client was interested in something before a *pirata* arrived, he must respect the rights of the store, and he can't take him away. The other rule is that the *piratas* must not interfere when another *pirata* is helping a customer.[29]

Thus, unlike the relationship between *feriantes* and *coleros*, which are largely antagonistic, some flea market businesses tacitly collaborate with *piratas*.

Additionally, apathetic policing in the markets, licensed vendors' own routine violations of labor law, and the difficulty of proving *piratas*' fraudulent acts provide these unlicensed vendors ample room for maneuver. The collusion between vendors and *piratas* reinforces the point that embedded relations may promote illegal actions because effective criminals act in concert (Granovetter 1985; Polakoff 1985). Additionally, vendors' short-term ties with customers may help them justify participating in unscrupulous sales practices.

## Conclusion

While much scholarship on the informal sector has attempted to determine its role in a nation's economy and its relationship with the formal sector, we have focused on semiformal street and flea market vendors' business strategies. This analysis has demonstrated the complex ways vendors utilize kin- and non-kin network ties with peers, suppliers, customers, and political authorities to prosper, manage risks, and effectively compete. Their emphasis on flexible networks, enforceable trust, and bounded solidarity, we argue, serves them well in a legally precarious and inhospitable context.

In both cases, vendors use embedded networks with peers and suppliers in order to intensify sales and manage risks. Additionally, vendors' instrumental use of these ties also spills over into acts of reciprocity in which no immediate return is expected. In both settings, vendors exchange favors and engage in solidary acts with their peers. In this regard, networks are multifaceted: business relations blur into friendships and the two are mutually reinforcing (compare Uzzi 2001: 214; Padgett and Ansell 1993).

The different forms of network ties *feriantes* and flea market vendors maintain with customers and unlicensed vendors explain, in part, their distinct relationships with these two groups. Because they operate over the long-term in residential neighborhoods, *feriantes* are able to develop embedded ties with customers that benefit both parties and shape the character of doing business. In contrast, because flea market customers make one-time purchases and come to the market irregularly, vendors have arm's-length network ties with them and operate based on short time horizons.

The differences in vendor–customer ties between these two settings also result from their distinct retail cultures. *Ferias* are understood as safe, family spaces where one participates in their community by neighboring and visiting with regular vendors (see Salazar 2003; Stillerman 2006a). In contrast, Bío Bío market vendors and customers adopt a competitive stance toward one another and understand that the likelihood of malfeasance and deviance are ever present. These cultural differences underscore the point that economic behavior should not be understood simply as instrumental action constrained by network ties. Rather, cultural beliefs and practices are inextricably linked to and shape economic behavior (Zelizer 1989, 2005; Clarke 1999).

Variations in relations between licensed and unlicensed vendors in *ferias* and flea markets also reflect their distinct network ties and relations with government officials. Because they are physically separated and see their activities in direct competition, *feriantes* remain aloof from *coleros*. Indeed, they see *coleros* as the main source of their economic problems, and as free riders in a setting where they comply with the law. As a consequence, they attempt (mostly unsuccessfully) to persuade local officials to remove them.

Some flea market vendors, in contrast, collude with *piratas* because they gain an immediate economic benefit from increased sales (even though *piratas* may scare off customers over the long run). Moreover, vendors who collude with guards can shield them from apprehension by guards, and market administrators fear excessive government oversight of licensed vendors' often-illegal activities.

These findings point to the usefulness of concepts from economic sociology for understanding informal vendors' entrepreneurial strategies as well as variations across different types of markets. The fact that ideas used to understand the auto, garment, high-technology, and other industries would also apply to undercapitalized sectors with a precarious legal status speaks to the general relevance of the concepts of embeddedness, enforceable trust, and bounded solidarity for understanding economic behavior. Nonetheless, it is important to underscore the differences between these vendors and leading-edge businesses. While the businesses we studied are more economically stable than ambulant vendors in Lima, Perú (Aliaga 2002), these vendors have very different opportunities for profit growth than, for example, high-technology entrepreneurs in Silicon Valley or Japanese auto company subcontractors. Much like the Lima vendors, *feriantes* and flea market vendors have limited formal education and utilize their network ties as a means of survival and in the hopes of funding their children's education, but cannot be described as "innovators" who will transform Chile's retail sector. Their preference for "bonding" rather than "bridging" social capital means that they operate within a small social circle and may harbor a risk-averse business orientation, thereby inhibiting potential profit opportunities. However, the usefulness of these concepts suggests that the study of street vending can move on from developing overarching definitions of the informal sector as a whole to exploring the complex and diverse strategies street vendors use to survive and thrive.

## Notes

1 The authors gratefully acknowledge funding support for portions of this research from the International Studies Program, Office of Research and Development, and Student Summer Scholars (S3) program, Grand Valley State University. We also very much appreciate the valuable comments we received on an earlier version of the chapter by two anonymous reviewers and volume editors John Cross and Alfonso Morales.

2 The metropolitan region, which includes a number of rural counties, has a population of six million. However, Santiago county (*provincia*) is normally

understood as the metropolitan area. It includes 32 municipalities, though Puente Alto and San Bernardo, located in separate counties, are now considered part of the metro area.

3 *Punto Final* (2005).

4 Field notes, Feria El Montijo, Cerro Navia, western Santiago, 13 July 2003. Interviews conducted by Stillerman and Tomás Ariztía in Santiago, Chile and translated by Stillerman. Observations conducted by Stillerman, Ariztía, and Patricio García. Individuals who wished to be identified by a pseudonym appear as first name only; all others appear with first and last names.

5 Field notes, Feria El Montijo, Cerro Navia, western Santiago, 13 July 2003.

6 Close ties with customers may exist in the food sales area, though we did not gain entrée with these vendors.

7 Field notes, Las Gangas building, Bío Bío market, 13 July 2001. This vendor's wife, a partner in the business, commented that they had received a check with insufficient funds from an upper-class patron: field notes, Las Gangas building, Bío Bío market, 1 July 2001.

8 Field notes, Las Gangas building, Bío Bío market, 11 July 2003; field notes, Mercado Placer, Bío Bío market, 26 July 2003.

9 Field notes, Las Gangas building, Bío Bío market, 26 July 2003.

10 Interview with Arturo, 24 July 2003.

11 Field notes, Las Gangas building, Bío Bío market, 24 December 2005.

12 Field notes, Feria El Montijo, Cerro Navia, western Santiago, 13 July 2003; Feria Las Viñitas, 22 July 2003; El Montijo Christmas market, 22 December 2006.

13 Field notes, Feria El Montijo, Cerro Navia, western Santiago, 13 July 2003.

14 Field notes, Las Gangas building, Bío Bío market, 26 July 2003.

15 Interview with Arturo, 24 July 2003.

16 Field notes, Feria Las Viñitas, 22 July 2003.

17 Field notes, Chilean Street Market Vendors' Association (ASOF) meeting, 22 July 2003.

18 Field notes, San Ramon feria, 5 August 2001.

19 Field notes, Las Gangas building, Bío Bío market, 8, 11, 18, 26 July, 2003.

20 Interview with Arturo, 24 July 2003; interview with Raúl, La Granja municipality, 29 July 2003.

21 Field notes, Las Gangas building, Bío Bío market, 11 July 2003; interview with Manuel, Bío Bío market, 26 July 2003.

22 See Leemira Consultores (2004: 132–35); *Punto Final* (2005); field notes, ASOF meeting, 15 July 2003.

23 Field notes, ASOF meeting, 15 July 2003, 31 July 2001; interview with Carlos, Peñalolen market, 22 July 2001; interview with Raúl, La Granja municipality, 29 July 2003.

24 Interview with Pedro, 7 August 2003.

25 Field notes, Las Gangas building, Bío Bío market, 26 July 2003.

26 Field notes, Las Gangas building, Bío Bío market, 7 August 2003.

27 Field notes, Las Gangas building, Bío Bío market, 7 August 2003.

28 Interview with Pedro, 7 August 2003.

29 Interview with Pedro, 7 August 2003.

## Bibliography

Aliaga Linares, L. (2002) *Sumas y restas: El capital social como recurso en la informalidad*, Lima, Perú: Alternativa.

ASOF (Asociación Chilena de Organizaciones de Ferias Libres) (2005) *Sistema primario de información feria libre, S.I.F.L.*, Power Point presentation given at

Universidad ARCIS, 18 April, Santiago, Chile, 62 pp.

Clarke, A. (1999) *Tupperware: The Promise of Plastic in 1950s America*, Washington, DC: Smithsonian Institution Press.

Contreras, V. and Weihert, U. (1988) *Sobrevivir en la calle: el comercio ambulante en Santiago*, Santiago: Programa Regional de Empleo para América Latina (PREALC).

Cross, J. C. (1998) *Informal Politics: Street Vendors and the State in Mexico City*, Stanford, CA: Stanford University Press.

D'Andrea, G., Stengel, A., and Goebel-Krstelj, A. (2004) 'Six Truths about Emerging Market Consumers,' *Strategy + Business*, 34: 2–12.

De Soto, H. (1989) *The Other Path: The Invisible Revolution in the Third World*, New York: HarperCollins.

*El Mostrador* (2005) 'Santiago: Mas de $173.000 milliones anuales venden ferias libres,' *El Mostrador*, 13 January 2005. Online. Available: www.elmostrador.cl/modulos/noticias/constructor/noticia.asp?id_noticia=151813 (accessed 5 July 2005).

Granovetter, M. (1985) 'Economic Structure and Social Action: The Problem of Embeddedness,' *American Journal of Sociology*, 91(3): 481–510.

Greaves, E. (2005) 'Panoptic Municipalities, the Spatial Dimensions of the Political, and Passive Revolution in Post-dictatorship Chile,' *City & Community*, 4(2): 189–215.

INE (Instituto Nacional de Estadisticas) (1999) *V Encuesta de Presupuestos Familiares, 1996–1997, Versión Resumida*, Santiago, Chile.

—— (2004) 'Estimaciones de Población por Regiones, Provincias, y Comunas, según sexo.' Online. Available: www.ine.cl/12-pobla/Ambossantia.htm (accessed 22 July 2005).

Leemira Consultores Asociados Limitados (2004) *Estudio y catastro de las ferias libres del Gran Santiago*, Santiago: Leemira Consultores Asociados Limitados.

Light, D. W. (2004) 'From Migrant Enclaves to Mainstream: Reconceptualizing Informal Economic Behavior,' *Theory and Society*, 33(6): 705–37.

Morales, A. (1993) *Making Money at the Market: The Social and Economic Logic of Informal Markets*, PhD dissertation, Evanston, IL: Northwestern University.

Padgett, J. F. and Ansell, C. K. (1993) 'Robust Action and the Rise of the Medici, 1400–1434,' *American Journal of Sociology*, 98(6): 1259–1319.

Polakoff, E. G. (1985) *Butchers, Bribes and Bandits: Market Relations in Cochabamba, Bolivia*, PhD dissertation, Ithaca, NY: Cornell University.

Portes, A. (1989) 'Latin American Urbanization during the Years of the Crisis,' *Latin American Research Review*, 24(3): 7–44.

—— (1994) 'The Informal Economy and its Paradoxes,' in N. Smelser and R. Swedberg (eds) *The Handbook of Economic Sociology*, Princeton, NJ: Princeton University Press, and New York: Russell Sage Foundation: 426–52.

Portes, A. and Schauffler, R. (1993) 'Competing Perspectives on the Latin American Informal Sector,' *Population and Development Review*, 19(1): 33–60.

Portes, A. and Hoffman, K. (2003) 'Latin American Class Structures: Their Composition and Change during the Neoliberal Era,' *Latin American Research Review*, 38(1): 41–82.

Powell, W. (1990) 'Neither Market nor Hierarchy: Network Forms of Organization,' *Research in Organizational Behavior*, 12: 295–336.

Powell, W. and Smith-Doerr, L. (1994) 'Networks and Economic Life,' in N. Smelser and R. Swedberg (eds) *The Handbook of Economic Sociology*, Princeton, NJ: Princeton University Press, and New York: Russell Sage Foundation: 368–402.

*Punto Final* (2005) 'Ferias libres contra Goliat,' *Punto Final*, 27 May 2005. Online. Available: www.puntofinal.cl (accessed 7 July 2005).

Sabel, C. (1994) 'Learning by Monitoring: The Institutions of Economic Development,' in N. Smelser and R. Swedberg (eds) *The Handbook of Economic Sociology*, Princeton, NJ: Princeton University Press, and New York: Russell Sage Foundation: 137–65.

Salazar, G. (2003) *Ferias libres: Espacio residual de soberanía ciudadana*, Santiago, Chile: Ediciones SUR.

Salcedo, R. (2003) 'When the Global Meets the Local at the Mall,' *American Behavioral Scientist*, 46(8): 1084–1103.

—— (2004) *Towards a reconceptualization of post-public spaces*, PhD dissertation, Chicago, IL: University of Illinois at Chicago.

Seligmann, L. (1997) 'Market Women in Peru in the Age of Neoliberalism,' in L. Phillips (ed.) *The Third Wave of Modernization in Latin America*, Wilmington, DE: SR Books: 65–82.

Staudt, K. (1996) 'Struggles in Urban Space: Street Vendors in El Paso and Ciudad Juárez,' *Urban Affairs Review*, 31(4): 435–41.

Stillerman, J. (2006a) 'Private, Parochial and Public Realms in Santiago, Chile's Retail Sector,' *City & Community*, 5(3), September: 293–317.

—— (forthcoming 2006b) 'The Politics of Space and Culture in Santiago, Chile's Street Markets,' *Qualitative Sociology,* 29(4): 507–930.

Tokman, V. (2001) 'Integrating the Informal Sector into the Modernization Process,' *SAIS Review*, 21(1): 45–60.

Uzzi, B. (2001) 'Social Structure and Competition in Interfirm Networks: The Paradox of Embeddedness,' in M. Granovetter and R. Swedberg (eds) *The Sociology of Economic Life*, 2nd edn, Boulder, CO: Westview Press: 207–40.

Valenzuela, M.E. and Venegas, S. (2001) *Mitos y realidades de la microempresa en Chile: Un análisis de género*, Santiago, Chile: Centro de Estudios de la Mujer.

Zelizer, V. (1989) 'The Social Meaning of Money: "Special Monies",' *American Journal of Sociology*, 95(2): 342–77.

—— (2005) 'Culture and Consumption,' in N. Smelser and R. Swedberg (eds) *Handbook of Economic Sociology*, 2nd edn, Princeton, NJ: Princeton University Press, and New York: Russell Sage Foundation.

# 12 Spaces of conflict and camaraderie

## The contradictory logics of a postsocialist flea market

*Oleg Pachenkov and Danielle Berman*[1]

### Introduction

On a sunny weekend day during St Petersburg's fleeting summer months the bustling market place at Udelnaya fills with vendors, as many as 3,000 of them, haphazardly overflowing its off-season boundaries. Bordered by a park at one end and a highway crossing at the other, the market stretches narrowly along a mile of railway track, spanning only 80–100 feet. On weekends and holidays, it operates from nine in the morning until late in the afternoon, except in summer when the market, like the northern sun, extends its hours. On a typical day, there are between 1,500 and 2,000 vendors, and two to three times as many shoppers. The vendors arrange themselves in about eight rows, resembling streets winding through the park. Signs that once marked the rows have long since disappeared, but people continue to reproduce the original structure, with only slight variations. There are no stalls, so they stand in their place to sell their wares; everything lies right on the ground in front of them. The shoppers who frequent Udelnaya are similar to those observed at flea markets anywhere; they come to bargain-hunt, search for something special, or just to spend the day "loafing around" (Damsar 1998).

It was at Udelnaya, the largest market in St Petersburg, that five scholars from the Centre for Independent Social Research (CISR) worked as vendors from July 2003 to June 2004, participating in, and observing, the phenomenon of street vending in postsocialist Russia. Based on these observations and interviews with vendors, we analyze how the flea market, as a social and economic institution embedded in the particularities of the postsocialist context, provides a space for Russians to negotiate emergent contradictions between their longstanding practices of everyday economy and the instrumental rationality introduced with the market economy. As the varied experiences of individual vendors illustrate, how one responds to the new economic order is fraught with interpersonal and internal conflict, and entails real consequences for their place in the new socio-economic hierarchy.

In this chapter, we argue that street vending in postsocialist Russia is not simply an economic phenomenon; it is a complex, and often contradictory, social phenomenon reflecting broad societal transformations. Street vending at Udelnaya, as elsewhere in Russia and around the world, reflects the social embeddedness of economic action (Granovetter 1985; Polanyi 1957). The particular character of social and economic integration in contemporary Russia, however, cannot be understood without reference to the social and historical context of post-Soviet societies. While this implies a degree of path dependency, we, like Agnes Czako and Endre Sik (1999: 715), view this as "not simply a fashionable and sophisticated revival of historical determinism. In its original form this approach assumes an institutional framework in which actors make 'embedded' but not fully determined decisions." Thus, while flea market vending practices have their roots in the informal (or "second") economy activities common throughout Russia in the late-Soviet period, the explosion of small-scale trading in the early 1990s reflects a dynamic response to the transformation of Russia's social, political, and economic institutions.

In response to the structural transformation of Russian society, the vendors at Udelnaya both adapt old practices and adopt new strategies in their everyday lives. Jurgen Habermas's (1984) interpretive framework helps to provide a vocabulary for describing how the communicative rationality of everyday "lifeworlds" is challenged by the expanding influence of the instrumental rationality characteristic of the capitalist "system." Thus, the transition from state socialism to market capitalism can be understood as the shift from one *system* to another, in which the political-bureaucratic logic of state socialism loses its force and the economic rationality of capitalism begins to take hold. The realm of social life in which individuals must meet the challenges brought on by this shift is what we refer to as the "everyday economy"; that part of everyday life that confronts, through resistance or adaptation, the colonizing force of the system.

The flea market, as an institution that constitutes the everyday economy, provides a site to study the reproduction of post-Soviet culture, allowing people to reproduce or adapt familiar patterns of consumption and everyday life. At the same time, participation in flea market vending signifies a departure from Soviet life and the adoption of new economic survival strategies. In order to permit generalization beyond the flea market we situate market activity in the vendors' everyday lives as well as the context of broader social changes. These changes – brought on by the shift from a state-administered bureaucratic system to one organized around market economics – entail an increased dependence on market activity for economic security and survival, a rising dominance of market rationality used to determine prices, and thereby values, and the transformation of the social, economic, and moral bases undergirding interpersonal relationships.

In this chapter we use concrete examples to (1) show the ways in which the everyday economy of vendors is rooted in the particular social-historical context of postsocialist society, and (2) examine what happens when this conflicts with the capitalist logic. Furthermore, we suggest that variation in one's ability and willingness to conform to economic principles entails real consequences for individuals in terms of their location in a new social-economic hierarchy. Thus, by situating market-centered activities among social phenomena more generally, and by addressing how basic features of social life accompany street vending, our explanation aims to deepen and broaden existing approaches to understanding the place of the flea market in postsocialist life.

The empirical data presented below was collected by five researchers from the Centre for Independent Social Research (CISR) in St Petersburg from July 2003 to June 2004. Their period of observation began in April 2003 when they participated in the marketplace as shoppers before establishing themselves as vendors in July. Through these different roles, the research team carried out hundreds of hours of participant observation, which included numerous informal conversations with sellers, buyers, and the market leadership. The researchers also conducted both biographical and problem-oriented interviews with approximately 30 vendors.[2] In addition, more than 150 pages of field diaries were collected as well as notes on the personal life stories of approximately 25 vendors learned through ordinary conversation.

## Udelnaya's history in postsocialist context

We begin by situating the development of Udelnaya in the historical changes of the late Soviet and postsocialist periods. There are many ways to interpret the shift from a state socialist to a capitalist market economy and the associated changes in the mode, character, and legitimacy of private economic activity. Stark (1986), Szelenyi (1978), and later Bodnar (1998) each make use of Polanyi's (1957) three basic forms of socio-economic relations – reciprocity, redistribution, and market exchange – to characterize differences between capitalist economies where market exchange is primary and Soviet economies which were dominated by state redistribution. In both cases, the primary economic forms proved insufficient to meet the needs of the population, compelling capitalist states to employ redistributive measures to compensate for market failings, and the Soviet state to permit (or at least acquiesce to) market exchange to meet needs left unfulfilled by state planning. Importantly, reciprocity, based on social networks and inter-personal relationships, provided the basis for market activity in Soviet society. Thus, as Bodnar (1998) argues in her analysis of Hungary, the role and practices of the market that constituted this supplemental "second economy" in Soviet times differed sharply from the meaning of the market as organizing principle of the economy.

To some degree, postsocialist informal economic activities have their roots in the Soviet second economy, where market exchange operated through social networks. Throughout the USSR, particularly in the 1980s with Gorbachev's *glasnost* reforms, open-air markets (bazaars) including book markets, flea markets, pet markets, *fartzofschiki*[3] trade, as well as *virtual* real-estate markets camouflaged as "accommodation exchange," accounted for a well-developed, if generally illegal, second economy (Ladanyi 2003; Romanov and Suvorova 2003). Private commercial activity was criminal throughout the Soviet period, by virtue of the fact that only the state owned property. The pervasive cultural and ideological characterization of entrepreneurship as "wrong," "suspicious," or "anti-Soviet" helped maintain the criminal character of this activity. Even now, despite the formalization and legalization of commercial activity, many of these attitudes persist, as does tight and often arbitrary state regulation of private commercial activity. Thus, the contemporary character of Udelnaya cannot be understood without reference to how its history is intertwined with the rapid transformation of the Soviet Union and Russia. Udelnaya, like many such markets, both prefigures and echoes the transformation of the Soviet and now postsocialist Russian economy and society.

The combined forces of "large-scale marketization" (Bodnar 1998: 512) and a generalized breakdown of economic, political, and social structures (Shanin 1999: 11–13) that characterized the early postsocialist years in Russia spurred expansion of small-scale, marginal economic activity. Numerous studies document factory closures and widespread unemployment, salary arrears among those with jobs, sharp declines in industrial and manufacturing productivity, and a general withdrawal of state provided social services (Åslund 1995; Burawoy 2001; Shanin 1999; Gerber and Hout 1998; Gerber 2002). As a result of this economic dislocation, people sought alternative employment or sources of income. The legalization of private cooperative and individual entrepreneurship in the early 1990s, and the mass privatization that followed, facilitated the growth of small-scale trading which soon expanded to become a primary employment activity in the country.[4]

In the early nineties traders quickly filled the streets of major cities like St Petersburg. Everyone was selling something; along the streets people sold food and goods, and newspapers were full of advertisements for services. One could easily find a member of the Academy of Sciences selling vegetables at a bazaar, a philologist selling bed linens at an improvised market stall, or an engineer selling hand-made wool socks in the street. Students resold cheap beer from stores for a small profit near metro stations; factory workers who were paid with products rather than paychecks (a common practice due to a general shortage of cash) sold tea kettles, plates, spoons, or if they were lucky enough to work at these factories, shoes and clothing. Shuttle trading between former Soviet states or distant regions grew, as relatives transported and sold goods their kin received at their places of work. More recently, international shuttle trading emerged to bring goods in from Poland, Turkey, and China.

With time, small kiosks began to crowd the sidewalks along major streets. There was no systematic organization or official documentation for trading and the majority of vendors paid no heed to taxes. Open air markets and street vending places formed spontaneously throughout the city, most commonly near metro stations. Like Udelnaya, few markets had stalls or fences, and only a couple of people, if any, represented anything approximating a market administration. Bandit gangs often served as a *kreisha* (roof), providing protection from other gangs or occasional pilferers. The situation was completely new and uncertain; the rules of the "market economy" game were unknown. A flurry of new laws and decrees, intended to regulate private business activity, further contributed to the sense of ambiguity toward market activity that pervaded government and society. People devised rules, the government empowered and formalized controlling institutions, improved the tax system, and issued licenses that transformed criminal gangs into security agencies. By the mid-1990s, street vending and market trading became more structured, controlled, and institutionalized. Despite this process of institutionalization, however, street and flea market vending continues to have a non- or semi-formal status.

Long-term residents of the district where Udelnaya is located recall that prior to 1995, when the large market that exists today took shape, it was a place where a small group of ten or twenty people, mostly pensioners and alcoholics, gathered to try to earn extra money by selling hand-made crafts or odds and ends from home. The pensioners typically sold fruits, vegetables, or flowers they cultivated at their dachas,[5] alcoholics sold old trash they found around their homes, while homeless people sold junk collected from dumpsters. As was typical across the Soviet Union, the market originally formed by the railway station because of the steady stream of people traveling to and from their dachas on the outskirts of the city in the summertime, and because it was convenient for those arriving on the train with food to sell from their dachas. By the mid-1990s, Udelnaya provided a space for hundreds of people to sell their wares, despite its illegality.

At the time of the field work, the market still lacked formal infrastructure such as fences, permanent stalls, electric lighting, even toilets. Privileged actors in the market, including the administration representatives, could use the toilet at the nearby "ordinary" marketplace, which had electricity, a roof overhead, and stalls. The director explained why Udelnaya continues to lack such basic amenities:

> ... we cannot do it, because we are open two times a week and someone has to watch them the rest of the week, otherwise they will be taken immediately! The same with the fences – we cannot place them around here, they will be completely disassembled immediately. Instead, we follow the foreign model, we come, we trade, and we clean everything after we leave.

At one time there was even an initiative to use the stalls of the neighboring market, but "people totally disliked it, it is too dark there, and uncomfortable to stay [at the stall], whereas here there's a lot of space and one can see everything."

Thus, the particular social-historical context of postsocialist society conditions the patterns and possibilities for change, imparting a degree of path dependency. While Udelnaya's vendors cannot be understood in isolation of the particular postsocialist context and the historical experience this entails, their activities nonetheless reflect a dynamism and responsiveness that cannot be accounted for by history alone. The close integration of social and economic relations that shaped informal exchange in the "second economy" imparted a personalized character to market activity. As the dominance of state redistribution gives way to market allocation, the character of the market, and its very meaning, must be reconstructed. The flea market, therefore, provides a space in which people reproduce familiar patterns of market exchange even as they adapt their practices and understandings to a market-based "first economy." This process can be seen by attending to (1) the development of Udelnaya's administrative structure and its relationship to law enforcement, (2) the population that comprises Udelnaya's vendors, and (3) how vendors describe their own motivations for participation in the marketplace.

### Emerging administrative structure

In the mid-1990s, when the market's present form initially emerged, people had repeated confrontations with the police, who would come, take items and money from vendors, arrest them, fine them, and sometimes destroy the items they tried to sell. Luba, a middle-aged woman who is the current director of the flea market and was a vendor at that time, describes the situation this way:

> ... the police came, ... they just came up and arrested people .... Elderly people, pensioners, disabled, and the police who came started a fire – they had brought firewood with them – the policemen threw into the fire and burned everything that they took from the people, everything: children's shoes, picture frames ... just burned them.

Troubled by the situation, especially since the social and economic collapse of the early 1990s exacerbated reliance on the market for income, 72 vendors organized in defense of the marketplace. With Luba as the informal leader, the group started visiting local authorities, politicians, and deputies of the city parliament to "push the deal." After a lengthy process of meetings and negotiations, they agreed that future legal and practical problems would be solved between the police and local authorities and the market director. The market was granted legal status as a club for pensioners; members gained the right to gather and socialize, but not to trade. In addition, by failing to issue financial documents or pay taxes, many vendors' participation in trading involves the violation of several laws. This semi-legal position is maintained by corruption; the administration collects money from vendors in order to pay bribes to the local police. The administration also provides several "invisible guards," intentionally shadowy figures, who, according to Luba, are intelligence officers who patrol the market, and who almost nobody knows by face. This service is provided thanks to Luba's personal agreement with a friend, a former KGB officer. The guards provide internal security and watch for trade in illegal goods so that the market administration can avoid potential problems with police.

While the vendors, who no longer have to communicate personally with police officers, are pleased with the arrangement, Luba must continually reassert her legitimacy both in her role as negotiator for the market with local authorities and as collector of a form of rent from the vendors. The administration (Luba, her husband, and several colleagues and friends) collects a small fee from the majority of vendors, about 5–10 rubles (less than a dollar), and from 50 to 250 rubles ($1.50 to $8) from those vendors selling "new" items from the trunks of their cars. Vendors continuously complain about paying even this nominal amount in rent for their trading place. They justify their obstinacy by pointing to the fact that they are poor, or that Udelnaya is not a proper marketplace, that it lacks infrastructure, even toilets, and that they are selling their own second-hand clothes, all of which makes rent payments unfair. It is deemed immoral, in principle, that people who worked for the state, "for the better part of their lives," now receive pensions so small that they don't cover the cost of living and are forced to sell at the flea market to earn money. Luba, on the other hand, justifies the practice:

> People here terrorize me by asking "why do we take money from them?" but we collect kopecks in fact! Not more than three thousand rubles per day. And it means we have to pay to the cleaner, we pay the most for cleaning – the area is huge and should be cleaned ... the other part we pay as a bribe.

The development of administrative structures at Udelnaya illustrates how conflicts in the marketplace reflect the abundant contradictions of Russia's social and economic transition. Even as individuals respond to the economic dislocation of market reforms through expanding their own participation in the marketplace, formal laws governing trade protect authorities' claims to a financial share of market activity. Their claims are successful, in part, because of the moral ambivalence vendors feel about the activities in which they participate. Despite the imperatives of the market system, vendors resist adopting an economic logic even as their livelihoods increasingly depend on it. The market administration operates at the nexus of this conflict between the emerging institutional manifestations of capitalism and the persisting ideological ambiguity of market relations. Thus, they hire an internal police force to enforce "legal" market activities while paying outside authorities in continued recognition of the illegal aspects of market activity in postsocialist life. Over time, it seems that the payment of bribes is gradually transformed from a practice that reinforces and legitimizes the arbitrary enforcement of laws into a form of rent or service fee that solidifies property rights and supports the development of market infrastructure.

### *The changing faces of Udelnaya*

The postsocialist transition has also brought a widening gap between the wealthy "new Russians" and the "new poor." The combined effects of unemployment, wage arrears, and inflation devastated much of the former Soviet middle class, leaving them without assets or a stable income. This population, according to Vadim Radaev (2000), constitutes about 60 percent of the contemporary Russian population. They rely primarily on state subsidized social benefits, social networks, and an informal barter economy for survival. Tikhonova and Shkaratan (2001) describe these economic activities of the new poor as an "economy of survival."

The majority of vendors at Udelnaya can be considered part of this new poor. Although some vendors are homeless people or alcoholics, they are in the minority, and are treated as marginal by the flea market community.[6] Flea market vendors tend, instead, to be from the middle or working class, including pensioners and poor people with small salaries. There are more women than men, and middle-aged or elderly people predominate. They mainly sell their own second-hand clothes and domestic items. Sometimes these goods are mixed with foods produced at their dacha, such as cans of conserved vegetables and jam. Women may also bring handicrafts, such as knit socks or lace handkerchiefs. The prevalence of women at the market arises from a convergence of the effects of economic dislocation in the early 1990s and the role of women in Soviet society. High unemployment rates, the reduction in (or loss of) many social welfare benefits, and rapid inflation affected women, especially widowed pensioners, with particular severity (Gerber 2002). Despite these conditions of hardship, women continue to bear primary responsibility for caring and providing for their families, and children in particular (Haney 1999). Street vending provides one of many strategies to obtain cash needed to provide for the family. For most female vendors, the items they sell are brought from home; old items that they no longer need or hand-made items they produce both to minimize their own expenses and to sell for additional income (Bridger *et al.* 1996). Thus, even within the subsidiary activity of small-scale trading, women tend to be marginalized and are less likely to engage in the buying and selling of new items.[7]

Another population of vendors, who gather together along the railroad tracks, comprises men selling technical devices and spare parts. They bring plumbing supplies, hand-made axes, or spare electronic parts, sometimes purchased at lower prices from known suppliers, but usually garnered (or stolen) from their primary jobs as technicians or electricians. Still another group of specialized vendors can be described as "collectors" who sell postage stamps, coins, medals, and other antiques such as silver spoons or candlesticks. Some specialize in World War II (the Great Patriotic War) paraphernalia including weapons, military equipment, or uniforms. Others offer nostalgic items from the Soviet era such as old books with photos of Lenin on the first page, or books and posters printed under Stalin. These specialized traders are, nevertheless, exceptions, occupying their own small niche in the marketplace dominated by ordinary people selling everyday items.

In recent years, increasing numbers of professional traders selling new, cheap, primarily Chinese-made imported goods or imported second-hand clothes from Finland have begun to dominate the area at the entrance to the flea market, pushing the poor flea market vendors deep into the park. Another group of professional "shuttle traders" gathers at the edge of the market, where they can park their cars in a line and sell their wares directly from the trunk. They commonly offer second-hand technical devices brought from Finnish flea markets: old-model VCRs, TV sets, stereos, microwaves, and other household appliances. They may also specialize in sports equipment, household cleaning products, or inexpensive brand-name items bought at the duty-free shops on the border. The expanding presence of these professional vendors at the market is due, in part, to the contradictory semi-legal status of the flea market and the need it creates for the administration to collect money from vendors for the bribe and maintenance costs. Even as the administration actively supports the market for its social functions as much as its economic activity, the willingness of professional traders to contribute significantly to the administration's collection, in contrast to the poor vendors, makes them increasingly important for the market's overall survival. In 2003, Luba recognized the need to maintain a balance between the typical flea market traders and professionals who, if allowed to dominate the market, would transform Udelnaya into an ordinary open air market.

Thus, in addition to the numerous poor vendors, there are smaller groups that constitute distinct subpopulations of vendors in terms of their demographics, goods, and roles in the market. The organization of the marketplace itself arises out of the clustering of these different populations of vendors. As one vendor told us:

> ... Most already have a regular place, they are like cats, they get used to their place, they would never switch to another spot, each one has their favorite place ... the situation is friendly enough ... , they are always encouraging each other, we shopkeepers have a good, healthy co-operation in selling. ... In general, the situation is very sane. Even if they are alcoholics, or drug addicts ... they're dirty but what's there to do? They have their own group. People are all very different.
>
> (Vendor, 40, mother of two)

## Shifting motivations: communication, survival, and everyday life

### *Market as communicative space*

Despite the growth of other groups of vendors, the field work and interviews that inform this analysis focused on the vendors who constitute the "new poor." Similar to observations from flea markets throughout the world, these vendors at Udelnaya identify communication as a basic feature of the flea market as a social institution, one that differentiates these markets from other locales of market exchange. Many scholars investigating flea markets stress that people visit them for conversation, leisure, socializing, and to share or pick up news (Damsar 1998; Maisel 1974; Sherry 1990a, 1990b). The importance of communication at flea markets provided the basis for Robert Maisel's study of the flea market as "an action scene" (Maisel 1974). Damsar's study highlights the importance of flea markets as social settings, particularly for elders in societies who lack alternative informal spaces for spontaneous communication (Damsar 1998).

Contemporary Russia provides an interesting context for understanding the social interactions of consumers and vendors alike. From the beginning, Udelnaya's market administration recognized that the social opportunities the market provided were as important as the economic ones.

> ... people come here, all these elderly, disabled, sick, they come here not just to sell, but to rest. Just to relax. We wanted to put benches here especially [for this purpose]. They say, "I pay for my [trading] place, but I relax," or, "I come here to rest, I don't need anything, I just come here to chat a bit – at home I have no one to talk with." So this is like a club, for people to meet, to rest. People sometimes organize picnics here, set up tables, they take it easy, celebrate. We support all of this and help them.
>
> (Luba, market director)

The elderly, in particular, reported coming to the flea market to meet and chat with their friends. Elderly women complained that younger family members did not understand them, and that they looked forward to the weekend when they could come to the flea market and meet others with whom they could share their thoughts, feelings, knowledge, and interests. Many elderly women said their children disapprove of selling at the flea market, because they view it as a sign of poverty. If the family is not poor, they cannot understand why their parents so stubbornly go to the flea market. But as the following quote illustrates, these elderly vendors are not primarily motivated by economic need; they seek a venue where they are able to socialize with their peers:

... let's imagine for example a pensioner, sitting at home for five days with his family. And then he comes to the market, he socializes, he breathes fresh air, but you wouldn't just go out and spend all day walking around the park for no reason. [The market offers] a way for many to socialize. Like her, ... Lydia Ivanovna, who's over there; she says: "I wait for Saturday all week long. I wait as though here ... Well, like it is some kind of event." She's a pensioner, she lives alone now, and she has some money, but now that's not the most important thing for her. For her – socializing is more important.

(Female vendor, 50 years old)

Social circles at the flea market are not only defined by age; gender also circumscribes market behavior. It is common for both men and women to come to the flea market to meet friends and to take a break from their spouses and family obligations; men visit the flea market when their wives are doing housework, while women seek the marketplace when their husbands are spending the weekend "lying under their lovely cars." These social processes reflect both continuity in gendered social relations and emerging communicative gaps along gender and generational dimensions in contemporary Russian society.

Thus, the flea market serves an important social function as a place for the communication that is central to developing and preserving social relationships. Vendors organize gatherings, old women sit and chat, a man ostensibly selling guitars may play them instead, while men gather around him to sing, talk, and drink. Many are old friends who welcome the opportunity provided by the market to share news and catch up on experiences of the week. These practices reflect the integration of social and economic relationships that characterized Soviet society and that continues to be critical for coping strategies in the postsocialist context (Caldwell 2004). Particularly for the elderly pensioners, the flea market is an important venue that, in addition to providing entertainment and relaxation, provides a setting for establishing and maintaining the network of social relationships vital to their emotional, personal, and economic security.

### Market as survival strategy

Many vendors attribute their activities at the market to their reluctance to throw away their belongings, especially when they are "almost new," "almost never used," or "could be used again." In the shortage economy of Soviet times people bought as much as they could of whatever they could find in the shops. If the items were never, or rarely, used, they were kept for the next generation, without concern for changing fashions. Baby and children's clothes were given as gifts to grandchildren or children of younger friends or relatives, thereby redistributing these items through social networks.

As a culture of consumption gradually replaces this culture of scarcity, the younger generation adopts new social and economic relations, and internalizes patterns of Western consumer culture that eschews inheriting old and out-of-fashion clothes. Since the older generation, accustomed to the culture of scarcity, still cannot bear to throw away "almost new" things, but now lacks a generation of willing recipients, they adopt new patterns of capitalist relations, intermixing them with the familiar patterns. Thus, vendors bring old, long-stored items to the market, both to avoid throwing them away and to earn an "extra kopeck." This practical rationality of post-Soviet people is widely reflected at the flea market:

> Well how did we live? ... there was a shortage you know. Then we got used to always having to stock up on things. ... And here are these stored up things, they were absolutely new, still with price tags ... We were standing here like this, holding this stuff in our hands, selling after work, on the weekends. And gradually we made up our mind, that even though it wasn't much income, at least you received cash ... Right. So we received it in cash, and didn't wait for the salaries the enterprise would give us ...
>
> (Female vendor, 50 years old)

Another manifestation of the culture of scarcity is the tendency to repair, rather than replace, broken items. Although this predilection stems from a context of absolute shortage where no replacement items were available, now the practice is encouraged by the shortage of money needed to buy costly replacements. The flea market provides a source of spare parts and small components needed to fix old stereo systems or appliances at people's homes or dachas.

> I remember that when our pipes broke we bought some kind of connecter right there because there weren't any in the stores ... Firstly, I know that's how father bought all the plumbing, it's true. Secondly, one fellow, who's still at the market, had this kind of wire, that is, to clean waste pipes, it's pushed in there and turned through [to snake the drain]. That is, there were none in the stores. And there we, for five rubles, if that, bought it. Aren't we clever!
>
> (Female shopper, 45 years old)

This quotation also reflects a certain pride in "making do," the sense of accomplishment that accompanied a successful shopping excursion, the satisfaction of overcoming the obstacles to meeting one's basic needs (Caldwell 2004). Strategies of making do are also seen among the men at Udelnaya who offer repair services, for items such as watches, stereo systems, or garden tools. By offering these services for a fee, post-Soviet people adapt practices developed to compensate for a shortage of goods, to meet the needs of the current situation in which money is short.

## *Market as everyday life*

For most vendors, flea market sales are just one of many small-scale economic activities in their complex strategy of economic survival. They are often employed at several low-paying jobs, with women often working as cleaners and men as night security guards. Many of the women work for 24 hours, followed by two or three days off when they stay home to take care of children or grandchildren. Pensions and social welfare benefits further supplement the income earned from these activities, and this population continues to rely on dense social networks for a range of goods and services. As a result of their constant struggle to make ends meet, the flea market is both a place of leisure and enjoyment and a setting where those dissatisfied with their lives gather.

Vendors also take advantage of every available opportunity to sell products, including several flea markets in St Petersburg, free classified ads, pawn shops, or commission shops. Some buy cheap imported goods from acquaintances who work as professional retail traders, and resell them to friends, or to kindergartens for children. In the summer they sell fruits and vegetables grown at their dachas. Thus, the goods they sell reflect how interwoven vending is with their daily life. For both men and women the goods they bring to the market are often "leftover" from their everyday life; women bring handmade clothes or prepared foods that their own family does not need, and men bring surplus supplies from their "formal" place of employment.

Through analyzing our informants' way of life and the activities that filled the rest of their week, we realized that although market activities appear to be governed by an economic logic, their everyday concerns that value family and social relationships continue to take precedence over profit making. For example, one female vendor cares for her two sons and her husband, who works for the state and earns a small, but stable, salary in a socially protected position, as well as her elderly, infirm mother-in-law. To earn money, she buys children's clothes from a relative to sell to kindergartens and children's clinics, works as a security guard for 24 hours every three days, and sells paper, notebooks, and old clothes every weekend at Udelnaya. Despite her need for income, she shared this account of her choice of employment:

> When I used to work at *Prodprom*, I was sent to the pioneer camp *Ogonek*, and I was offered any position that I wanted. Understand, I had higher education. … They offered me the position of director of the camp or manager, but I was there because of my children. That's why I said, "Either you let me work as the building cleaner and run the English lessons or I won't come here at all!" Of course, [the director] wanted me to at least be a tutor. But to be a tutor meant that your child is abandoned, that he is alone all day long, and with the river nearby anything could

happen to the child, and as it is [working as a cleaner] you clean and you are free all day. The river, blackberries – all this was ours. ...

(Vendor, 40, mother of two)

Here we see this vendor clearly prioritize her life project over economic gain. Her choice of work is not based solely on increasing income; instead the main criterion is that it not interfere with her social and moral obligations. This decision highlights the contradictory moralities at work in the logic of the market economy and the logic of life worlds. While the life of Russia's new poor is, in part, characterized by the demands of an economy of survival, their everyday practices continue to subordinate economic logic to the logic of everyday life. With their everyday practices they resist, or defend against, the moral and social imperatives of the market system. Such a challenge to the system is, however, not without cost. The varying degrees to which those at Udelnaya, whether administration, vendors, or shoppers, understand the flea market on the basis of the logic of everyday life and value it for extra-economic reasons gives rise to conflicts that emerge between and among these actors. Interactions among vendors and between customers and vendors, often having little to do with trading, occasionally lead to heated arguments and physical struggles. In addition to these visible confrontations, many vendors experience internal conflicts about their activities at the marketplace. We suggest that this discord is rooted in broader conflicts between the economic and moral realms of social life.

## Conflicts at Udelnaya

### *Conflicts of legitimacy and legality*

The conflicts over rent payments, described earlier, illustrate contradictory understandings about the marketplace and its dominant morality. These perspectives can differ so sharply that arguments between representatives of the market administration and vendors over rent payments for their trading place sometimes lead to physical fights. Poor vendors continue to view this payment as robbery and extortion. Vendors do not consider themselves to be *real* merchants selling commodities, nor do they consider the flea market an ordinary marketplace. They come to Udelnaya in part to socialize and relax, and, in part, to sell fragments of their everyday life – not *commodities*. Even if they sell to earn money, their motive is survival, not personal enrichment. Moreover, many feel forced to take part in the shameful practice of selling their everyday lives. From their point of view, taking money from them for rent is both unjustifiable and unjust. Although rent payments make sense within the market economy logic, it does not fit the logic of everyday life based on moral evaluations and a non-instrumental rationality.

Nonetheless, these vendors recognize an expansion of an economic logic in the changes they witness in the spirit of Udelnaya flea market. They are disappointed by, and struggle with, the growing influence of economic rationality, divorced from the social and moral imperatives that they are accustomed to including in their economic calculus.

> All the same, it's been bastardized. Earlier, gardeners sat there, they exchanged seeds, seeds could be bought there, and of such quality! And they would tell you how to sow them, during what season, and what they will grow for you. But the last time I bought seeds there, instead of flowers I had some kind of noxious weed come up. So, basically everything, was bastardized. ... it's purely mercantile interest. ... If only it wasn't necessary for pensioners to earn their own bread. Well of course, there's a certain group of people for whom their conscience comes first, but unfortunately not too many of them remain ...
>
> (Female vendor, 45 years old)

To use the language of Habermas, this process can be understood as the *colonization* of the flea market space and its embeddedness in the interpersonal relations of everyday life by the logic of the *system*. Other vendors continue to view the flea market as a singular phenomenon, a world with its own rules, way of life, and practices. These vendors want to save this world; protect it from colonization by a rationality that fails to value human concerns and relationships:

> That's why ... in general ... the market is generally an interesting little world ... with its own rituals, customs, idiosyncrasies, problems, and all kinds of other stuff. And, of course, it's a shame that the city ... does not pay attention to it ... or at least not prevent selling in these markets. Nobody's saying that they need to help, they formed themselves, and organized themselves. It's just the police chase, you could say, the police chase their own people. ... the most poor and the most defenseless. To chase them ... it's not right.
>
> (Female vendor, 50 years old)

### Conflicting rationalities

Conflicts between vendors and consumers also arise from the contradictory nature of this space, and by a misunderstanding emerging between those who consider Udelnaya as a marketplace and those who see it as a space of everyday economy. The former expect to encounter market relations that conform to economic logic and rationality, while the latter seek camaraderie and interpersonal relationships as they do what they must to survive. Disputes often arise between vendors and customers when customers express doubts about the quality of goods sold, or when they try to get steep discounts, wanting to pay next to nothing. On the other hand, vendors may chat leisurely with shoppers and never attempt to make a sale.

For many vendors, the goods they bring to the flea market are not commodities, but pieces of their everyday life experiences. This complicates the assignment of price, since it does not map neatly onto understandings of value. What should the price be for a doll, bought for their child thirty years ago, that has been almost a member of their family? The price is the expression of positive, warm feelings, the expression of sympathy, sharing your own everyday experience and personal memory with the vendor – this is a good price that a consumer might offer, and some vendors accept it with pleasure. This is the social and emotional reciprocity observed in situations when consumers and vendors talk with each other at length, sharing life stories as they relate to certain goods sold by the vendor. If, at the end, the consumer leaves without buying anything, both consumer and vendor are nonetheless satisfied. Similarly, items are given for free because "to give something as a gift is more enjoyable than to sell it for kopecks," as one vendor explained when she gave a scarf to a gypsy girl for free.

This same dynamic gives rise to confrontation and conflict when consumers fail to recognize and participate in the social basis of the market. When consumers treat a vendor's goods simply as commodities, and communicate this through bargaining strategies that seek the lowest possible price, they risk offending the vendor. Sometimes vendors do not know the price of the items they sell, or even their function. Vendors claim it is immoral when, after suggesting what they consider a fair price for an item, greedy consumers want to buy it for nothing. Likewise, they take offense when shoppers insist on bargaining over an item of personal significance or sentimental value. A vendor may respond with outright refusal to sell the item, reasserting the logic of everyday life that shapes their terms of exchange.

### Conflicting moralities

Moral categories are an integral part of interactions at the flea market, and often contradict purely economic, capitalist, or market rationality and its moral implications. Everyday life is always organized around morality and moral judgments (Silverman 1985: 135–36), so the frequency of moral judgments in flea market discourse signifies the invisible presence of people's life worlds at this market space. The significance of non-economic moral categories in the context of economic transactions extends the boundaries of the flea market beyond the marketplace. Moreover, it is precisely those activities that reflect an economic logic and rationality that postsocialist people identify most often as immoral. Many internalized the Soviet ideological opposition toward market-based, *wild* capitalism, and condemn this sort of everyday activity. At the same time, Soviet people, dissatisfied with the inefficient and inadequate system of state redistribution, grew accustomed to cheating the state and devising alternative strategies based on social networks, or *blat*, and the second economy. Thus, people are accustomed to living in a world characterized by two economies and know how to manipulate this structural situation in order to minimize risks (Bodnar 1998: 512). Moreover, this situation of a "double life" was not only institutionalized but also morally justified (Ledeneva 1998; Voronkov and Chikadze 1997).

The practices of contemporary St Petersburg street vendors continue to reflect these ambivalent, even contradictory, attitudes toward the market and their participation in market relations. Their disdain for the very practice they participate in reflects this contradiction that exists at structural, interactional, and intrapsychical levels in postsocialist Russia. The Soviet ideology that vilified and even criminalized involvement in trading persists in the minds of vendors who see the activity as immoral and shameful. One vendor, a 50-year-old woman, expressed this sentiment in harsh terms:

> So here I was just let go [at the factory]. I had to go to the market, it is not terrible if you're not educated … it's nothing; where unfortunate people stand, … but in this way we, in general, also seem like prostitutes …[8]

Her characterization reflects a common feeling among vendors that the market is a place for the downtrodden who feel that they do not measure up to social standards and for those thrown into poverty by an economic upheaval they did not bring about. She also described how her family views her market activities:

> … My own family does not really understand. No, my husband works, he has never traded, never … It is a position of principle. He would never come, but trading here is a way to … to raise money, or socialize. He doesn't understand, not his relatives either. They will sit without money: "We have no money!" and I give them money, but he won't go to trade, "It's not for me! I am above it," he says, and I say, "And, I am not? Plainly not!"

The disdain felt toward entrepreneurial market activity is extended to those who take part in it. Those who traded in goods were held in low esteem, as they profited off speculation rather than labor.

> I am always telling grandpa to go. I say: "Come on, papa, go already! You don't have to do anything anyways, go, try it." … No, the stubborn fool, he doesn't go! … he says that he's from a well-bred family, he never had to, that is, his parents were never traders, and he certainly won't do it!
> (Female shopper, 45 years old)

Nonetheless, as under the Soviet system, people do what is necessary to plug the gaps in the dominant system of provision, vendors overcome the shame they feel, and do what they must to get by. A 75-year-old pensioner put it this way:

> I began to walk around, to look, but of course I felt embarrassed, to be carrying all of this and everyone thinks that you are going to sell ... It is terribly awkward when you go, dragging all these bags and you put them all on display, then when everything is laid out, and people come up and ask about them, then you have to forget everything else and concentrate on selling.

To some degree, this characterization reflects the stark reality of the growing social and economic differentiation in Russian society and the centrality of the market in determining and reinforcing this inequality. With state salaries and pensions too meager for families to survive on, many well-educated professionals are compelled to take part in petty trade to get by. While similar practices served this population well throughout Soviet times, including small-scale barter and market exchange rooted in social networks and the reciprocity they entailed, they no longer suffice to offset the sharp decline in their economic wellbeing in the postsocialist context. Moreover, the more they must rely on these activities, the further they fall in economic status in their own eyes. As economic status increasingly determines social status, the deeply held values of reciprocity and social interdependence are challenged by the logic of the capitalist system giving rise to interpersonal and internal conflicts. While individual vendors may characterize their economic activities as either resistance or adaptation to the imperatives of the market system depending on their own understanding of these practices and the priority they give to them, the material implications of economic and social dislocation are unambiguous.

## Conclusion

Following Habermas, we claim that at the micro level the core issue of the transformation of postsocialist society is the conflict between the everyday life worlds of the Russian people and the extension of the new economic system. The particular historical and cultural context of postsocialist societies leads to sharper conflicts and more brutal consequences for people. In Soviet times, people's life worlds were also under attack, although by a different system, one governed by a bureaucratic logic, and people devised "tactics of resistance" (to borrow the terminology of Michael de Certeau (1984)) to confront colonization. Despite their resistance, people appropriate elements of the system, making them a part of their everyday life worlds, and, in the process, adapt to structural transformations in society. With the fall of the Iron Curtain, the everyday life worlds of former Soviet peoples faced new challenges from the economic order imposed by the capitalist economic system. Practices developed to resist the Soviet system were inappropriate to protect life worlds from this new system that emphasizes economic relations and market exchange. Vendors' market activities, and the conflicts they produce, provide a window onto the current process of resistance and appropriation. As the Udelnaya market case seems to show, the transformation of postsocialist societies cannot be reduced to, or explained by, purely economic processes.

The macro transformation of society entails the destruction of structures and practices of everyday life due to pressure from the system, which strives to colonize the life worlds of post-Soviet people. Understood in this way, the destruction of everyday life worlds may cause the feelings of uncertainty and defenselessness characteristic of post-Soviet people (Hann 2002; Humphrey 2002; Humphrey and Mandel 2002; Humphrey and Sneath 1995; Sampson 1994; Burawoy and Verdery 1999). Some adjust their life projects according to the demands of macro social structures, while others try to maintain their habitual life worlds. The new system establishes a new social hierarchy rooted in economic logic. Correspondingly, social phenomena, and individuals, that do not conform to economic principles and logic are accorded low status. Those who refuse to (or cannot) change their life worlds and habitual logic are relegated to the bottom of the hierarchy, forming the new poor. Out of this resistance, a repertoire of new micro practices emerges. These sets of micro practices form institutions of the everyday economy, many of which structure flea market behavior. By functioning both as an institution of the economy of survival and of everyday economy it serves as a venue where postsocialist people can adapt to new system challenges, develop new forms of resistance, and repair their broken, but habitual, life worlds.

## Notes

1 This research project was supported by the Independent Institute for Social Policy, with financial support from the Ford Foundation. The authors wish to acknowledge the contributions of Olga Brednikova, Lilia Voronkova, Zoyza Solovieva, and Maria Kudriavtseva from the Centre for Independent Social Research in St Petersburg, whose skillful ethnographic field work produced the data for this chapter. We are grateful for the helpful comments by Alfonso Morales and two anonymous reviewers. The comments and suggestions from Aya Hirata, Abby Kinchy, Kaelyn Stiles, and Andrea Voyer on an early draft of this chapter are also greatly appreciated. The authors are solely responsible for any errors of interpretation or analysis that remain.

2 Seven of these interviews were recorded and transcribed in full for analysis, while records of other interviews consist of notes taken during and after the interviews.

3 People who had access to foreign goods (through relatives from diplomatic corps, or sportsmen, etc.) and sold these goods in Russia to friends, relatives, etc. or to retailers. These retailers were called *fartzofschiki*. This activity took place because, "In planned economies of shortage, the set price of goods, which varied from country to country, along with their usually poor quality and extremely limited range, meant that those who could cross the border – and had some money as well – could buy cheaper, finer and better goods or could access things that they could not buy at home" (Czako and Sik 1999: 719).

4 This process of legalization should not be overstated – it entailed onerous tax obligations and complicated licensing procedures. So although the activity itself was technically legal, to practice it legally required a level of compliance that few even attempted to achieve.

5 In this context, *dacha* refers to small, rustic cottages outside of the city that the majority of Russians rely on as both an escape from urban conditions in the summer and a place to grow food that will supplement their diet throughout the year. Although suburban vacation homes for the elite are also referred to as dachas, they are certainly not the norm. For ethnographies of dacha life see Zavisca (2003) or Caldwell (2004).
6 The initial expectation of the field researchers was that underclass people, e.g. homeless and alcoholics, would dominate the marketplace. This turned out not to be the case.
7 This explanation only hints at the complexities of the position of women in postsocialist Russia. For further discussion see, for example, Gal and Kligman (2000), Moghadam (1993), Posadskaya (1994), and Wejnert and Spencer (1996).
8 The word used in the original Russian was *panel*, which is used as slang to play on the formal meaning of a place to sell something on the street, and is used here to imply selling oneself. *Panel* is used in Russian slang to mean streetwalker, or to start turning tricks.

## Bibliography

Åslund, A. (1995) *How Russia Became a Market Economy*, Washington, DC: The Brookings Institution.
Bodnar, J. (1998) 'Assembling the Square: Social Transformation in Public Space and the Broken Mirage of the Second Economy in Postsocialist Budapest,' *Slavic Review*, 57(3): 489–515.
Bridger, S., Kay, R., and Pinnick, K. (1996) *No More Heroines? Russia, Women and the Market*, New York: Routledge.
Burawoy, M. (2001) 'Transition without Transformation: Russia's Involutionary Road to Capitalism,' *East European Politics and Societies*, 15(2): 269–90.
—— and Verdery, K. (eds) (1999) *Uncertain Transition: Ethnographies of Change in the Postsocialist World*, Lanham, MD: Rowman and Littlefield.
Caldwell, M. (2004) *Not by Bread Alone: Social Support in the New Russia*, Berkeley, CA: University of California Press.
Certeau, M. de (1984) *The Practice of Everyday Life*, Berkeley, CA: University of California Press.
Czako, A. and Sik, E. (1999) 'Characteristics and Origin of the Comecon Open-air Market in Hungary,' *Journal of Urban and Regional Research*, 23(4): 715–37.
Damsar (1998) 'Socialisation at the German Flea Market,' unpublished paper, Bielefeld University.
Gal, S. and Kligman, G. (eds) (2000) *Reproducing Gender: Politics, Publics, and Everyday Life After Socialism*, Princeton, NJ: Princeton University Press.
Gerber, T.P. (2002) 'Structural Change and Post-Socialist Stratification: Labor Market Transitions in Contemporary Russia,' *American Sociological Review*, 67(5): 629–59.
Gerber, T.P. and Hout, M. (1998) 'More Shock Than Therapy: Market Transition, Employment, and Income in Russia, 1991–95,' *American Journal of Sociology*, 104(1): 1–50.
Granovetter, M. (1985) 'Economic Action and Social Structure: The Problem of Embeddedness,' *American Journal of Sociology*, 91(3): 481–510.
Habermas, J. (1984) *Theory of Communicative Action*, Boston, MA: Beacon Press.
Haney, L. (1999) '"But We Are Still Mothers": Gender, the State, and the

Construction of Need in Postsocialist Hungary,' in M. Burawoy and K. Verdery (eds) *Uncertain Transition: Ethnographies of Change in the Postsocialist World*, Lanham, MD: Rowman and Littlefield: 151–88.

Hann, C. (ed.) (2002) *Postsocialism: Ideals, Ideologies, and Practices in Eurasia*, London: Routledge.

Humphrey, C. (2002) *Unmaking of Soviet Life: Everyday Economies After Socialism*, Ithaca, NY: Cornell University Press.

—— and Sneath, D. (eds) (1995) 'Culture and Environment in Inner Asia,' *Final report of the Cambridge University MacArthur Project for Environmental and Cultural Conservation in Inner Asia*, vols 1–3.

—— and Mandel, R. (eds) (2002) *Markets and Moralities: Ethnographies of Postsocialism*, Oxford: Berg.

Ladanyi, J. (2003) 'Neformalnie socialnie seti I ih vliyanie na rost stroitel'stva chastnogo jilya v vengrii,' in Irina Olimpieva and Oleg Pachenkov (eds) *Neformalnaya ekonomika kak socialnaya I issledovatel'skaya problema*, St Petersburg: CISR.

Ledeneva, A. (1998) *Russia's Economy of Favours: Blat, Networking and Informal Exchange*, Cambridge: Cambridge University Press.

Maisel, R. (1974) 'The Flea Market as an Action Scene,' *Urban Life and Culture*, 2(4): 488–505.

Moghadam, V. (ed.) (1993) *Democratic Reform and the Position of Women in Transitional Economies*, Oxford: Clarendon Press.

Polanyi, K. (1957) 'The Economy as Instituted Process,' in K. Polanyi, C.M. Arensberg, and H.W. Pearson (eds) *The Trade and Market in the Early Empires*, Glencoe: Free Press.

Posadskaya, A. (ed.) (1994) *Women in Russia: A New Era in Russian Feminism*, London: Verso.

Radaev, V. (2000) 'Corruption and Violence in Russian Business in the Late 90s,' in A. Ledeneva and M. Kurkchiyan (eds) *Economic Crime in Russia*, London: Kluwer Law International.

Romanov, P. and Suvorova, M. (2003) '"Chistaya fartza": socizlniy opyt vzaimodeistviya gosudarstva I spekul'antov,' in I. Olimpieva and O. Pachenkov (eds) *Neformalnaya ekonomika kak socialnaya I issledovatel'skaya problema*, St Petersburg: CISR.

Sampson, S.L. (1994) 'Money Without Culture, Culture Without Money. Eastern Europe's Nouveaux Riches,' *Anthropological Journal on European Cultures*, 3(1): 7–29.

Shanin, T. (1999) 'Expolary Structures and Informal Economy in Contemporary Russia,' in T. Shanin (ed.) *Informal Economy: Russia and World*, Moscow: Logos: 11–32.

Sherry, J.F. (1990a) *Market Journal of Consumer Research*, 17(1): 13–31.

—— (1990b) 'Dealers and Dealing in a Periodic Market: Informal Retailing in Ethnographic Perspective,' *Journal of Retailing*, 66(2): 174–201.

Silverman, D. (1985) *Qualitative Methodology and Sociology*. Aldershot: Gower.

Stark, D. (1986) 'Rethinking Internal Labor Markets – New Insights From a Comparative Perspective,' *American Sociology Review*, 51: 492–504.

Szelenyi, I. (1978) 'Social Inequalities in State Socialist Redistributive Economies,' *International Journal of Comparative Sociology*, 19(1–2): 63–87.

Tikhonova, N. and Shkaratan, O. (2001) 'Russian Social Politics: A Choice Without Alternatives?' *Social'nie issledovaniya*, 3: 21–31.

Voronkov, V. and Chikadze, E. (1997) 'Leningrad Jews: Ethnicity and Context,' in V. Voronkov and E. Zdravomyslova (eds) *Biographical Perspectives on Post-socialist Societies*, CISR Working Papers, vol. 5, St Petersburg: CISR.

Wejnert, B. and Spencer, M. (eds) (1996) *Women in Post-Communism*, Greenwich, CT: JAI Press.

Zavisca, J. (2003) 'Contesting Capitalism at the Post-Soviet Dacha: The Meaning of Food Cultivation for Urban Russians,' *Slavic Review*, 62(4): 786–810.

# 13 Adaptability and survival

## A case study of street vendor responses to famine conditions in Ethiopia, 1999

*Michèle Companion*[1]

## Introduction

Local street markets play a central role in livelihood security. They represent physical places where resources vital to household economies are traded. As Seaman (2000) notes, "most economic shocks don't lead to starvation, rather, to impoverishment from the sale of assets" (134). As the epicenter of local commerce, street markets play a critical role in interpreting and analyzing the nature of crisis conditions. They are also hubs of information exchange and socializing. Thus, their dynamics are crucial to understanding both food availability and access (Lautze 1999). Vendor knowledge is also vital. As observers of and participants in their communities, they are keenly aware of changes in demand for and availability of goods and services. Because they are embedded in localized contexts, information that they provide can enhance interpretations of price fluctuations.

Despite this importance, data gleaned from markets is usually limited to economic factors such as animal to grain/cereal price ratios,[2] infra-structural availability, distance to markets, and access to roads. Vendor struggles have generally been overlooked in discussions of food crisis. Markets and vendors are treated as givens – part of the overall structure of food availability and access systems. Sociological variables that capture the nature of livelihood systems of vendors and their ability to adjust to local stressors are not emphasized in community assessments.

This case study seeks to remedy this gap. Vendors in Ethiopian markets at different levels of urbanization were interviewed during the height of the food crisis in 1999. This provides a glimpse into vendor responses to famine conditions and highlights their potential as an underutilized/understudied source of information about local conditions, making a significant contribution to the existing literature. The study begins by demonstrating the centrality of local street markets to food security. Gaps in development and humanitarian response literature are then identified and elaborated upon. Finally, summaries of the survey and its findings are presented.

First, however, a brief note is necessary to clarify the position of vendors in the larger context of livelihood security. The studies discussed below deal with markets in more rural settings. The development community acknowledges that urban and rural markets are differently impacted by exogenous factors, such as the influx of food aid (see Tshirley *et al.* 1996), or other sociopolitical dynamics (see Clark 1991; Hammond and Maxwell 2002). Urban markets are subject to more rigid and formal regulations, as well as more direct government oversight. Similarly, vulnerable populations in urban settings may have more direct access to power structures and more elaborate and dense communication networks than those in rural areas, allowing them to create pressure for aid. There are also more established organizational channels and infrastructure in place to distribute resources to urban populations. These factors influence adaptation to changing socioeconomic conditions, regardless of cause.

Urban food security situations have largely been understudied, because rural populations have generally been identified as the most vulnerable. Thus, rural areas have received more attention and been the subject of more study. This is a significant gap in development and humanitarian response literature. While it is beyond the scope of this study to investigate or discuss the broader conditions of urban marketplaces, it is important to note that a much clearer picture of street markets and vendor responses to food stress and crisis climates would be provided by additional research in this area.

## Food security and local street markets

To understand the importance of local street markets and the contribution that vendors can make to interpreting crisis events, it is necessary to situate them in a larger food/livelihood security context. Food security is a complex concept that involves a wide range of interrelated biological, socioeconomic, political, cultural, and environmental factors. To be food secure, individuals and households must be able to obtain enough food to meet the requirements of a nutritious diet and be healthy enough to allow for maximum biological utilization of the micronutrients throughout the year. Availability does not mean that food is accessible to the most vulnerable populations (Seaman 2000; Maxwell and Frankenberger 1992; Sen 1992; FANTA 1999). Individual or household ability to acquire sufficient food diminishes as the value of production and work activities decline relative to the cost of staple foods. Unfavorable terms of trade can limit the effectiveness of traditional coping strategies. It can also increase the speed at which coping strategies are rendered useless.

Coping strategies involve changes in behavior patterns combined with the disposal of assets. The sequence in which strategies are employed and the types used fluctuate depending on the frequency of food shortage cycles and the ability to rebuild assets during "good years" between episodes. Greater frequencies and duration of droughts in Ethiopia make it less likely that households will be able to sufficiently rebuild their asset base, leaving them increasingly vulnerable to new cycles of destitution (Webb and Harinarayan 1999; Buchanan-Smith and Davies 1995). Consequently, as more assets are liquidated, it becomes difficult for the food insecure to return to their "normal" food access levels.

As the crisis deepens and alternative resource bases are depleted, behaviors gradually shift from reversible to irreversible strategies (Walker 1999; Bryson and Hansch 1993; Buchanan-Smith and Davies 1995; De Waal 1989, 1997). Reversible strategies can be more easily recovered from once conditions begin to change. Irreversible strategies are those from which economic and social recovery are not very feasible or impossible. During the early phases of food insecurity, households and individuals will alter short-term consumption patterns or reduce food intake in order to preserve long-term productive assets. Eating unripe crops and gathering wild foods, borrowing food or money from family or neighbors, calling in loans, selling off less important assets, working as day laborers, increasing petty trading activities, temporary migration of adult family members in search of work, and the sale of animals that are surplus to requirements are all reversible strategies.

In what Walker (1999) identifies as the second stage of destitution, strategies that undermine livelihood systems are implemented. These are irreversible strategies.[3] Walker notes that this marks the shift from normal seasonal stressors and cycles of food shortage to true famine. Reproductive females and other animals required for subsistence, agricultural tools, seeds, and land are lost through death, banditry, or sales. Money or food is borrowed from merchants. Children are taken out of school. As the last resort, children may be taken into bondage and out-migration to cities, towns, or refugee camps in search of food or work occurs.

The overall effectiveness of these strategies depends on the duration of the crisis, the breadth of geographic impact, and the interstitial between events. Natural resources such as wild foods, medicinal plants, and fuel wood can be exhausted through overuse. As both Maxwell and Frankenberger (1992) and Buchanan-Smith and Davies (1995) point out, market forces also mediate the effectiveness of these strategies because they reflect changes in real income. Terms of trade between livestock and grains/cereals plummet as more people engage in divestment or asset stripping and flood the market simultaneously.[4] The same holds true for jewelry, cultural items, art and crafts, radios, tools, and other household goods. As Walker (1999) notes, the value of household assets shifts from being derived from social and cultural practices to being entirely dependent on market forces that determine salability, to the disadvantage of the most vulnerable. The large-scale sale of assets generally occurs simultaneously with a reduction in demand. As fewer people have the means to purchase non-food items, their value is reduced as demand for food is causing those prices to rise. This impacts the value of cash and food crops, livestock, and non-farm items, thereby altering purchasing power. Thus, local street markets become a critical arena for peasant survival.

During a crisis, the effects of rapid inflation, falling real wages, and loss of productive capacity in households are all evident in local street markets, as they reflect current conditions across multiple sources of risk for household food security and overall livelihood security. Changes in the cost of maintenance are reflected in the cost or value of productive capital, including land, agricultural inputs such as fertilizers, insecticides, and seeds, tools, and machinery. As noted, non-productive capital, such as jewelry, appear in greater quantity during times of stress, causing a drop in salable value (Cuny 1999; Lautze *et al.* 2003).

Sale of services, or the value of human capital, is also subject to variation based on local and national conditions. Because markets tend to be more centralized and attract people from a wider area, they also serve as vast information networks for those seeking work or laborers. Changes in the ethnicity, age, sex, and number of people seeking work in street markets indicate stress.

It is logical that shocks to any of these sources appear very quickly in local street markets, impacting household ability to purchase grain or staple foods in the crisis period. As Maxwell and Frankenberger (1992) note, poor households, especially female-headed ones, are disadvantaged by market shifts. They tend to run out of food earlier and have fewer cash and asset reserves. Local shocks also foster simultaneous responses by vendors. This study demonstrates how vendors alter their marketing strategies in response-changing conditions.

### Limitations of data gathered from local street markets

Development studies[5] and non-governmental organizations (NGOs)[6] have long acknowledged the need for incorporating more sociological variables to help contextualize findings from rapid food security appraisals (RFSA) and other techniques dealing with disaster response and mitigation. Markets are intertwined with primary food security indicators such as income, total household expenditures, food expenditures, caloric consumption, nutritional status, and variation of diet. However, they overlook the importance of expanding variables specifically relating to local street markets or vendors.

Maxwell and Frankenberger (1992) support expanding research into the role of local street markets by noting that shifts in the numbers and types of vendors may prove to be better indicators of food crisis. They suggest, "a rise in petty trading may be a more reliable indicator of stress than price fluctuations" (88). This is supported by my findings, below.

Freudenberger (1999) believes that expanding the role of markets in famine analysis will help overcome limitations of other data. Market data can be used to get at larger social and economic contexts, food acquisition strategies, food consumption patterns, price variations, and availability.

Market/price data are also good for establishing food security time lines, so that price fluctuations can be charted along with rains, harvest, or government interventions.

Literature on food and livelihood security artificially separates "vulnerable households" that rely on markets to gain access to food from those who are reliant on local street markets as supplemental or primary income generators. As this study demonstrates, the majority of people engaged in selling activities in the street markets are themselves vulnerable to changes in purchasing power and food shortages. The critiques above suggest expanding research on local street markets along three primary dimensions to help incorporate coping mechanisms and livelihood protection strategies of vendors into discussions of food crisis. The first examines shifting food acquisition strategies and food consumption patterns among purchasers. The second dimension captures the impact of changes in income-generating strategies on vendor income. Finally, vendor responses to these conditions, such as shifts in the types of products offered and marketing patterns, are included.

## Data and study sites

Data for the survey were gathered in Ethiopia in October 1999. Parts of Ethiopia, particularly the southern regions, had suffered a catastrophic failure of both the *belg* and *meher* crop seasons due to lack of rainfall.[7] The food security crisis from these two events compounded problems created by progressive drought conditions, unpredictable rains, and crop failures over the previous four years.

Markets in Nazaret were chosen due to the centrality of the location (99 km south of Addis), the size of its population,[8] and its large livestock and grain markets. Data from these markets are used for United States Agency for International Development's (USAID) livestock/grain price ratio calculations.[9] The other surveys were implemented in Liben District, Borena Zone, near the Somali border. This area was selected because it was the heart of the drought impact zone.[10] Three primary markets in Negelle, the central town in this area, and in a village within the Pastoral Association of Balambel are included.

Modifying De Waal's (1989) classifications, the markets in Nazaret would be classified as "upper tier." They are the major markets for the region. They are open air, meet daily, offer commercial products, and are patronized by a substantial residential population. A formal committee controls Amede Market, the larger of the two.[11] They collect rents from those occupying the "brick and mortar" stalls encircling the open area and from vendors wishing to erect informal ones. Informal stalls are designed to provide shelter from the sun and are constructed out of sticks and the remainders of burlap sacks or humanitarian aid distribution tarps, like those pictured in Figure 13.1. Jakala Market has a less formal market committee. There are no rents

*Figure 13.1* Permanent vendors at Amede Market (photo by the author).

collected, because the market is located on public property. However, location of the stalls is controlled by historical occupation and collective enforcement. Neither market sold livestock or small animals.

Negelle is the major "urban" area for Liben District.[12] The town is much smaller and less developed than Nazaret. The markets in Negelle would be considered "second tier." These are rural markets that are dominated by agricultural products. There is no formal committee that collects fees and no permanent structures or shelters have been erected. While there are vendors who work these jobs full time daily, the bulk of trading is conducted on major market days twice a week. Of these, Central Market is the largest and longest established. It is located near the center of the town and has been a designated market area for "as long as anyone can remember." It occupies a large open-air area and maintains a fairly fluid set of traders.

Border Market and Somali Market are both small, informal markets located on opposite ends of town. Each serves a specific sub-population. Somali Market is located to the south in an area containing mostly Somali refugees who have fled ethnic and political violence. Due to ethnic conflict with Negelle's majority group, most Somalis only shop here and this market predominantly serves them. This area has been growing for three or four years. Border Market is on the northern edge of town and is also a recent growth area. It has been established for about a year. The majority of the traders have been in Negelle for less than one year and have come as part of the larger out-migration from rural villages to cities in search of work and food.

The last market is in the village of Balambel (estimated population is 150). Balambel was chosen because it is one of the few traditional communities in the area to have its own centrally located market. Other communities report walking five hours on average to reach markets. This would be considered a "lower-tier" market. Most of the products available are seasonal and depend entirely on local production. These markets are periodic and only occur one day a week.

Sellers are classified based on frequency of marketing activity. Permanent vendors consider this as their full-time occupation and they are in the market every day. Semi-regular traders are in the market for all traditional market days (once or twice a week), but also engage in additional livelihood practices. Itinerant sellers are only in the market as necessary or when they are able to find things to sell.

A combination of observation and survey techniques were used to gather data. The survey instrument was drafted in English and translated into Amharic. The majority of the questions were posed in a closed format. However, room was left on the questionnaires for open-ended responses. Informal interviews were conducted to gather supplemental information. Whenever possible, buyers were asked informal questions to help contextualize their situations. Enumerator training took place between 11 and 12 October 1999 as part of a larger RFSA workshop sponsored by SCF-USA/ DHR and SCF-USA/EFO. During the training period, interviewers familiarized themselves with the questionnaire, recording formats, and interview techniques. Responses were recorded in English or Amharic and then translated. Each survey took approximately 10–15 minutes to administer.

The first section of the survey instrument is designed to capture information about vendors and their wares. Many questions allow for data collection through observation, in the event that vendors decline to be interviewed.[13] These include the number of vendors in a given location and the types of items they are selling. A blanket survey technique was used with the goal of interviewing all vendors in the market areas.

In addition to personal information (Table 13.1), vendors were asked questions addressing larger trade issues (Table 13.2). These elicit data about changes in food acquisition strategies and food consumption patterns in and around the market area. This captures shifting numbers of sellers, changes in the ethnic composition of buyers and sellers, and the types of products being offered. The impact of these changes on their own economic conditions and adaptive strategies is shown in Table 13.3. Vendors' perceptions of the current situation were collected through informal interviews (Table 13.6). The data were entered and analyzed using STATA 6.0.

*Table 13.1* General characteristics of vendors/traders

| Vendor characteristics | Market area | | | | | |
|---|---|---|---|---|---|---|
| | Nazaret | | Negelle | | | Balambel |
| | Jakala | Amede[a] | Somali | Central | Border | |
| No. of men | 10 | 17 | 2 | 7 | 0 | 0 |
| No. of women | 17 | 47 | 9 | 25 | 22 | 3 |
| Permanent | 11 | 23/64 19/40 | 11[b] | 9 | 3 | 1 |
| Semi-regular | 10 | 13/40 | — | 17 | 7 | 2 |
| Itinerant | 6 | 8/40 | — | 4 | 12 | 0 |
| Average time in area | | | | | | |
| Permanent | 7.8y | 6.4y | 1.9y | 5.2y | 1.4y | 10y |
| Semi-regular | 1.5y | 2.1y | — | 2.7y | 10m | 7y |
| Itinerant | 8m | 6.7m | — | 4.9m | 3.6m | – |
| Average items sold (perm. only) | 5 | 7 | 4 | 6 | 3 | 2 |
| % selling grains | 48 | 17 (64) | 0 | 9 | 0 | 0 |
| No. selling corn only | 4 | 7 (64) | 0 | 0 | 0 | 0 |
| No. selling raw coffee only | 3 | 4 (64) | 0 | 0 | 0 | 0 |
| % selling one item | 44 | 38 (64) | 18 | 22 | 55 | 67 |
| % selling cooked foods | 5 | 1 (64) | 0 | 6 | 18 | 33 |
| N | 27 | 40 | 11 | 32 | 22 | 3 |

Notes
a  A visual survey of the number of sellers, number of physical structures, and the types of food sold was conducted for this entire section of the market. However, only 40 interviews were granted.
b  We were at this market on a non-market day. As a result, we were only able to get general estimates on the number of semi-regulars and itinerant sellers.

## Findings

### *Vendor characteristics*

Permanent vendors represent a smaller proportion of the sample in each market surveyed (Table 13.1). They are consistently more likely to have been in the area for longer periods of time.[14] This allows for the establishment of wider trade networks to procure things to sell in the market. It is not surprising that they had a greater array of items available than did either the semi-regular or itinerant traders.

Itinerant traders generally sell one item, usually a cooked "snack food" like bean cakes, roasted chickpeas, or small ears of feed corn. However, many said they would sell anything they could. The majority of itinerant traders in all markets reported needing cash to purchase grain or medicine. Almost all reported having liquidated their own personal assets, such as

*Table 13.2* Changes in food acquisition strategies and consumption patterns identified by vendors/traders

| Food acquisition strategies (Based on last 6 mo. of trade) | Market area | | | | | Balambel |
|---|---|---|---|---|---|---|
| | Nazaret | | Negelle | | | |
| | Jakala | Amede | Somali | Central | Border | |
| % Increase in bartering | 82 | 91 | 100 | 88 | 45[a] | 100 |
| Increase in personal items | 93 | 21 | 100 | 88 | 100 | 100 |
| Change in number of petty traders | 100 | 100 | 100 | 100 | 100 | N/A |
| Increased competition | 100 | 93 | 100 | 88 | 100 | 0 |
| More traders than last year?[b] | | | | | | N/A |
| Yes | 17/21 | 27/32 | 9/9 | 19/26 | 1/1 | |
| No | 0/21 | 2/32 | 0/9 | 0/26 | 0/1 | |
| Not Sure | 4/21 | 3/32 | 0/9 | 7/26 | 0/1 | |
| Are increases seasonal?[b] | | | | | | N/A |
| Yes | 0/21 | 0/32 | 0/9 | 2/26 | 0/1 | |
| No | 15/21 | 27/32 | 9/9 | 17/26 | 1/1 | |
| Not Sure | 6/21 | 5/32 | 0/9 | 7/26 | 0/1 | |
| Staying in the area longer?[b] | | | | | | N/A |
| Yes | 14/21 | 22/32 | 9/9 | 16/26 | 1/1 | |
| No | 5/21 | 2/32 | 0/9 | 2/26 | 0/1 | |
| Not Sure | 2/21 | 8/32 | 0/9 | 8/26 | 0/1 | |
| Vendors' distance greater than usual in seasonal cycles?[b] | | | | | | N/A |
| Yes | 17/21 | 25/32 | 9/9 | 18/26 | 1/1 | |
| No | 0/21 | 0/32 | 0/9 | 2/26 | 0/1 | |
| Not Sure | 4/21 | 7/32 | 0/9 | 6/26 | 0/1 | |
| *Food consumption patterns (Based on last 6 mo. of trade)* | | | | | | |
| Reduction in no. of daily sales | 62[a] | 74[a] | 82 | 79 | 45[a] | 100 |
| Reduction in quantity per sale | 74 | 82 | 82 | 79 | 45[a] | 100 |
| *Client base* | | | | | | |
| Change in client base | 70 | 65 | 32 | 88 | 45 | 0 |
| Ethnicity of migrants | 62 | 71 | 100 | 88 | 60 | N/A |
| N | 27 | 40 | 11 | 32 | 22 | 3 |

Notes
a Itinerants were unsure.
b Question posed only to people who had been in the area one year or longer.

household goods or jewelry.[15] Fatima, who was selling bean cakes at the edge of Amede Market, lamented that she had been forced to sell off her dowry necklaces for a very meager return.[16] "The hunger has robbed me of my beauty. My own daughters have none. There is no one to give them [beads]. If we survive this [hungry time], how will they marry?"

While a number of the semi-regular traders also sell single items, they are more likely to be selling goods with higher cash returns such as raw coffee or maize, as shown in Figure 13.2. Correlating with the data presented in Table 13.3, semi-regular traders all report that they used to offer more than one

*Figure 13.2* Maize and coffee petty trading (photo by the author).

*Table 13.3* Impacts of local changes on vendor/trader livelihood

| Economic impact (Based on last 6 mo. of trade) | Market area | | | | | |
|---|---|---|---|---|---|---|
| | Nazaret | | Negelle | | | Balambel |
| | Jakala | Amede | Somali | Central | Border | |
| % reporting loss of profit | 78[a] | 76[a] | 82 | 88[a] | 45[a] | 100 |
| Average length of time of decline in profit | 4 mo. | 7 mo. | – | 9 mo. | – | 1.2 yr |
| % Higher cost of doing business | 100 | 100 | 100 | 100 | 45[a] | 100 |
| *Vendor adaptations* | | | | | | |
| % Selling normal no. of items | | | | | | |
| More | 0 | 0 | 0 | 0 | 0 | 0 |
| Less | 82 | 91 | 82 | 88 | 77 | 100 |
| Same | 18 | 9 | 18 | 12 | 23 | 0 |
| Average times no. of items reduced in last month | 3 | 1 | 5 | 4 | 6 | 2 |
| Changes are due to normal seasonal factors | | | | | | |
| Yes | 0 | 0 | 0 | 0 | 0 | 0 |
| No | 100 | 100 | 100 | 100 | 100 | 100 |
| N | 27 | 40 | 11 | 32 | 22 | 3 |

Note
a Itinerants were unsure.

item, some as many as nine or ten. This included fragile or perishable items such as tomatoes, chilies, cabbage, lettuce, and carrots. All of the semi-regular traders noted that it was increasingly difficult to procure most vegetables and not profitable for them to sell. Reduction in the number of items and changes in the types of items being sold is an adaptive livelihood strategy.

### Impacts of local changes on vendor livelihood

All vendors and traders were asked questions designed to capture market sensitivity to larger social and environmental changes (Tables 13.2 and 13.3). The questions were derived from traditional coping strategies implemented in times of food stress. They focus on changes in overall profit from market activities,[17] including increased competition from itinerant petty traders, higher personal cost of doing business from climbing food prices, a reduction in the number of daily transactions, and reductions in the quantity of goods purchased per sale.

## Direct economic effects

The majority of vendors and traders reported a steady decline in profit over the last six months. Respondents were asked if these changes were related to seasonal cycles of shortage associated with the agricultural calendar. "No" was the unanimous response. All respondents report that their current situation is much more extreme, intense, and longer lasting than the traditional seasonal shortages. Of those able to identify the time frame of profit decline,[18] the reported average is much longer in Balambel than other markets. This is the heart of the drought impact area. Similarly, Central Market has a longer time frame than the urban markets. Not surprisingly, this indicates that food stressors are felt more immediately in the regions that are hardest hit. As the duration of the crisis expands, the impact is felt at greater distances.

Most vendors cite increased competition in the markets and along the streets as a primary reason for declining profits.[19] At Amede Market, there were complaints that too many people were selling small produce items like shallots or potatoes. One noted,

> I feel bad for the people in the country. Things must be very bad for us to see so many old women reduced to sitting in the dust on the side of the road pleading for people to buy from them. Where are their husbands? But it is starting to hurt us badly too. People who can buy are being spread very thin and getting thinner across those who need to sell. I fear the buyers will soon be as thin as air while the sellers are as thick as dung. What will become of us then?

Other long-term vendors noted that the current situation was different than seasonal fluctuations in the past. The sheer volume of competition was much greater than normal, reminding several of the famine in 1984 and 1985 (Table 13.6).

Competition is also a common reason cited for reducing the number of items being offered for sale. According to those interviewed, too many traders were selling the same range of items (maize, raw coffee, sorghum). This number was increasing while the number of buyers was decreasing, despite a stronger flow of migrants into the cities. One trader waved her arm in a sweeping motion across the market and said, "I must feed my children on what little I can earn [in the market]. I am losing customers to [the new traders]. If the drought continues, there will be no one left to buy!"

Uniformly, sellers report an increase in their personal cost of doing business. As grains and perishable foods increase in scarcity due to agricultural production shortfalls, they pay higher costs to wholesalers or farmers. These costs must then be passed on to their clientele. Table 13.4 shows the trend in average grain prices. They are presented for the month of October 1996, considered the last "good year," and for 1999. As can be seen, all grain prices are significantly higher.

*Table 13.4* Food grain prices in October months

| Food grains | | Price per quintal in Birr during October | |
|---|---|---|---|
| | | *1996* | *1999* |
| Sorghum: | White | 85.05 | 106.95 |
| | Red | 73.75 | 94.67 |
| Wheat | | 122.41 | 205.77 |
| Teff: | White | 163.91 | 273.90 |
| | Red | 135.73 | 250.85 |
| | Mixed | 136.25 | 261.85 |
| Maize | | 58.20 | 102.24 |
| Barley | | 111.98 | 181.60 |

Source: SCF/US – Negelle, Gennale, Haraqallo, Jidolo, and Wadera Markets.

While other studies have reported hoarding by traders during agricultural shortfalls in order to drive up market prices (see Lautze 1999 and Lautze *et al*. 2003), there was no indication of this behavior among any of the vendors surveyed. Rather, all were eager to unload their products to generate cash for themselves so that they could purchase needed goods. While expressing sympathy for those who could not afford the food, they all noted that the survival of their families was at stake as well. Said one vendor at Jakala Market, "It is costing me more money to get sorghum and maize. Even though I know people will have to buy less with the money they have, what can I do? I have to eat and so do my children!"

Permanent vendors and semi-regular traders in all markets reported a reduction in both the number of daily sales and quantities purchased per sale. One woman noted that, rather than buying one potato per person in a household, purchasers were now getting one or two to be shared. Observation of sales in all of the markets supports this.

Somali Market represents an exception, with two male vendors reporting opposite trends. They were seeing profit increases and higher numbers of daily sales. Both men were selling *chat*, large leaves from a perennial bush that are chewed and the juices swallowed.[20] *Chat* is a narcotic. Despite being illegal in this region and looked down upon by some local cultures, they reported that their business had increased. *Chat* is cheaper than most food items and, due to its stimulant effect, reduces feelings of hunger and suppresses appetite while maintaining energy levels. For them, the heightening famine was creating a greater niche for their product. Said one man, "Misery is not good. Hunger is not good. But, if I am not selling [this], someone else will. I have many mouths and now there are more coming.[21] What is wrong with me being able to fill them?"

The hunger and food shortages were expanding their market beyond their cultural group and into others that had previously looked down on them. Stated the other vendor,

I was making charcoal bricks and sweeping sidewalks. It is hot dirty work. Too many others are doing the same thing. The money is small. *Chat* is easy! It does not require much tending. The money is bigger. Now I have boys who work for me! This [gives] me standing. They can bring something to their families. It is easier for me to feed mine.

Vendors and traders also identified changes in buyer purchasing styles. Increases in the amount and intensity of bartering, including asking for credit, and in the number of people trying to exchange personal items such as jewelry, small craft pieces, or labor for food were reported. Amede Market is the exception. Given its size and the active trade in commercial and manufactured goods, respondents reported that other vendors would purchase such items. Therefore, most people had cash on hand.

Both sellers and buyers reported that access to cash was a major factor limiting quantities of purchases. By this point, many expendable household assets had been liquidated. As a result, greater numbers of people were taking animals to market, to get cash for grain and food purchases. Because of the flood of animals onto the market and deteriorated physical conditions due to water shortages and poor grazing areas, the price of livestock was falling (Table 13.5). This had a negative impact on terms of trade in the markets.[22] States one vendor,

Things are very bad. I have not seen [the market] this bad. People come to me with only [pennies] in hand. They buy only little bits and haggle very hard for them. They complain bitterly about the price of my wares. They tell me they have sold all that they have. Too many have told me that they have no animals left.

*Table 13.5* Livestock prices in October months

| Livestock | | Price per head in Birr during October | |
|---|---|---|---|
| | | *1996* | *1999* |
| Oxen: | Large | 885.44 | 663.30 |
| | Medium | – | 404.60 |
| | Small | 468.82 | 279.07 |
| Cow | | 470.29 | 381.72 |
| Heifer | | 563.51 | 415.46 |
| Sheep: | Male | 101.13 | 85.55 |
| | Female | 100.72 | 72.87 |
| Goats: | Male | 87.06 | 78.88 |
| | Female | 65.16 | 64.75 |
| Camels: | Male | 575.55 | 714.38 |
| | Female | 744.37 | 708.80 |

Source: SCF/US – Negelle Market.

Another notes, "Many beg for discounts for maize. Too many say their animals are sickly and do not fetch good prices. They wonder if they will ever be able to get them back. I am [hurting] for them, but I have to live also."

### Changing dynamics in the markets

Though fewer people are making purchases, all vendors reported very crowded conditions in and around the markets. They commented on inter- action dynamics and crowd behaviors. They saw market areas being used as a source of information about day labor, potential water sources for cattle, livestock prices at markets farther away, or the availability of food aid. This echoes De Waal's (1989) findings from Sudan. Traders repeatedly com- plained that browsers and those who were looking for information were distracting them and driving away business. Says one man in Jakala Market, "It is not good to have so many people milling around. They make people who might come to buy think the market is too crowded and they will go elsewhere." Others were worried about theft. "They ask all sorts of questions. While you try to answer, their friends will take potatoes!"

An increase in the number of people, usually women, on the streets selling pre-cooked food at the edge of the markets was also reported.[23] Several sellers commented that the price of fuel wood had been climbing as pressure from population increases and petty trading in wood-intensive activities grew. As a result, those who weren't able to collect wood themselves often couldn't buy it either. They were relying on pre-cooked items to take home or were purchasing just enough to stave off hunger and consuming it on the spot. Their observations show that stress migration is creating new niches for itinerant sellers while altering the trading patterns for permanent vendors and semi-regular traders.

Respondents noted changes in the composition of crowds in the markets, particularly a marked rise in the number of beggars. Begging is considered very lowly and shameful. It is something only those in the most dire straits would do. In a sentiment expressed by many others, one vendor at Amede Market noted, "Begging is demeaning. To beg for your babies is to admit that your family has failed. It is a source of much shame. To see so many doing this bad thing means that things have become very bad indeed."

Vendors also pointed to a change in the ethnic composition of both their clientele and their competition. The majority of permanent vendors and semi-regular traders were able to identify different ethnicities of migrants and the general areas they were from based on style of dress, ornamentation, hair styles, accents, tattooing, and scarification patterns. Length of time in a given location was strongly related to this ability. This allowed many respon- dents to state with certainty that the migrant pool was different from normal seasonal cycles of food shortage. People were coming from greater distances and staying longer or not returning to their villages at all. One vendor at Amede Market pointed to a group of men who were milling around, noting that they had come a significant distance in search of day labor:

Afar [region] men are noted for their herds [of camels]. If they are in the city, their camels are either sold or dead. This is a sign of very bad things. Either way, they have [lost face] among their people. Maybe they will never go home.

At Border Market, a higher percentage of itinerant sellers were able to evaluate distance traveled because they recognized friends and neighbors who had abandoned villages to move into the area. However, the sheer volume was surprising to many of them. One man said he was very surprised to see his neighbor looking for wage labor in the market. This man had access to decent grazing areas and had been able to support a large herd. "If he is here, he is not with his cattle. If he is not with his cattle, he has lost everything! If *he* has lost everything, the suffering of others must be great indeed."

Somali Market was similar. Despite serving a restricted clientele, which corresponds to the low figures for changes in client base, vendors are able to distinguish among sub-groups of refugees by style of dress and color of cloth. In Balambel, the change in the ethnicity of the client base is zero. However, when they took this to mean a loss of clients, the figure was 100 percent. States one woman,

We have lost so many people. It is difficult to say when they will return. If the hunger continues, they may never return. What will become of the ancestors they leave behind? Their spirits will grow lean and angry. They may drive away the rest of us who stayed.

### Adaptive strategies

Vendors and traders were asked about their adaptive strategies to these changes. The majority report reducing the number of items offered for sale. As noted above, increased competition is a primary reason for this. A secondary reason involves minimizing losses from spoilage or damage. As discussed, many vendors have shifted to durable items such as raw coffee or maize, which are easy to move and store without damage and are resistant to spoilage.

Semi-regular traders also changed item types. They noted that it was much harder to get vegetables. They had to travel farther away to find people selling them, increasing their own cost of doing business. This takes time away from other income-generating activities. Thus, they had to pass on the cost to their clientele.

This was becoming a zero-sum game for many. Costs associated with procuring resources had outstripped local ability to buy, especially in Balambel. Many said they were spending more time on market-related activities only to be generating less income. Several in each of the market areas admitted to having taken their children out of school to save on fees. They were also trying to diversify their income-generating activities by having their children scrounge through dumps and trash piles for salvageable goods that could be sold as raw material or used to create crafts objects.

In addition, many semi-regular traders noted that the foods they could buy were of poor quality. They went bad quickly and had to be sold at a cheaper price, representing a loss. "Farmers beg me to buy their vegetables," notes a trader in Central Market. "They are desperate. I want to help them, but no one will buy from me. The tomatoes are stunted and mealy and bruised." As seen in Figures 13.1 and 13.2, sturdier products such as potatoes and other root vegetables, lentils, chickpeas, shallots, maize, and raw coffee dominated most markets.

Itinerant sellers described a constant struggle to find items to sell. They use the lowest cost, and sometimes quality, ingredients to sell singly, such as cups of roasted chickpeas. In all of the market areas, women set up small charcoal braziers. They were selling segments of ears of feed corn, a low-quality corn that has been engineered for animal consumption only.

Ingredients are also combined into snack foods such as bean cakes or sauces. Itinerant sellers reported reclaiming damaged or spoiled foods from the trash and from other vendors. They were quick to note that these items, which others might not buy, still have edible parts and could be blended with other ingredients to minimize the unsightliness. This type of commerce fills an important niche during food crisis situations. They provide calories for people who cannot afford higher quality foods, the separate ingredients needed to cook a meal, or, as noted earlier, fuel wood. While itinerant sellers cater to the desperation market or those in need of quick sustenance, they provide an important function for semi-regular and permanent vendors as well. They are willing to purchase less desirable items that might be thrown away at a complete loss, helping other traders to mitigate some of their damages.

### *Comparability to previous events*

Through informal interviews, vendors provided supplemental information about their perceptions of the food crisis. They compared current conditions to previous years (Table 13.6). Uniformly, rainfall was below average, making overall conditions worse than the previous year. They believed food prices to be much higher than average, having gone up considerably from the same time period last year.

A number of those interviewed remembered the famine in 1984 and 1985. While most agreed that their current situation is better than it was then, many noted similarities. The large movement of people from the country to the city areas was particularly striking. One seller remarked, "I am reminded of that bad time and I have much fear. Things still are much better but if the [rains] continue to fail, it will be that way again." Another noted, "We seem to be walking down that same path. [Food resources] are growing scarce and the cost of things is rising quickly. Competition is great. Soon neighbors will turn away from each other because they can only look after their own."

*Table 13.6* Seller perceptions of famine and current conditions

| Perceptions | Market area | | | | | |
| --- | --- | --- | --- | --- | --- | --- |
| | *Nazaret* | | *Negelle* | | | *Balambel* |
| | *Jakala* | *Amede* | *Somali* | *Central* | *Border* | |
| No. of men | 4 | 3 | 2 | 3 | 0 | 0 |
| No. of women | 3 | 9 | 3 | 6 | 10 | 3 |
| Vendor type | | | | | | |
| Permanent | 4 | 3 | 5 | 2 | 3 | 1 |
| Semi-regular | 1 | 5 | – | 7 | 4 | 2 |
| Itinerant | 2 | 4 | – | 0 | 3 | 0 |
| This year's rain | | | | | | |
| Below average | 3 | 4 | 0 | 1 | 0 | 0 |
| Poor | 4 | 8 | 5 | 8 | 10 | 3 |
| Compared to last year's rain | | | | | | |
| Worse | 2 | 2 | 0 | 0 | 0 | 0 |
| Much worse | 5 | 10 | 5 | 9 | 10 | 3 |
| This year's food prices | | | | | | |
| Very much higher | 1 | 0 | 3 | 5 | 8 | 3 |
| Higher than average | 6 | 10 | 2 | 4 | 2 | 0 |
| Compared to last year's food prices | | | | | | |
| Above average | 7 | 10 | 5 | 9 | 10 | 3 |
| Remember 1984/85 | 6 | 10 | 1 | 6 | 9 | 2 |
| Now compared to 1984/85 | | | | | | |
| Better | 5 | 8 | 0 | 2 | 1 | 0 |
| Same/similar | 1 | 2 | 1 | 4 | 8 | 3 |
| Reason for coming here[a] | | | | | | N/A |
| To look for work | 3 | 4 | 2 | 1 | 5 | |
| Need money | 3 | 4 | 2 | 1 | 5 | |
| Conditions at home | 3 | 4 | 2 | 1 | 5 | |
| Family here | 1 | 2 | 2 | 1 | 4 | |
| Arrived here first | 2 | 2 | 0 | 0 | 1 | N/A |
| Remitting money | 2 | 2 | 0 | 0 | 1 | N/A |
| Return to village? | | | | | | N/A |
| Yes | 1 | 1 | 0 | 1 | 2 | |
| No | 1 | 1 | 2 | – | 0 | |
| Unsure/conditional | 1 | 2 | 0 | | 3 | |
| *N* | 7 | 12 | 5 | 9 | 10 | 3 |

Note
a  This question was asked to those who had been in the area six months or less.

# Conclusion

Due to the embeddedness of vendors and local street markets within larger community structures, they are subject to the same social, cultural, political, and environmental stressors. The consequences of these stressors manifest themselves in the markets in the form of shifting food acquisition strategies and consumption patterns among both clientele and vendors. These result from reductions in the availability of or ability to purchase food and other necessary goods.

Vendors and traders must continually adapt to these changing local conditions to ensure their own livelihood survival. However, vendor responses to crisis have been overlooked in livelihood security discussions. This case study makes a significant contribution to the existing literature by identifying vendor responses to famine conditions in Ethiopia. While more research needs to be done to accurately map coping strategies across complex emergencies, this study provides a solid starting point.

This study also highlights another potential contribution of vendor knowledge. Food security indicators, used to monitor and track famine conditions, do not utilize the wealth of information available at local markets. By incorporating vendors and dynamics in local markets into these indicators, a more sensitive picture of local conditions could be created. Information provided by the vendors in this study contextualizes the severity of local conditions. Not only were vendors able to address changes in costs of goods over time, they were also able to identify atypical migration patterns. While a more detailed investigation needs to be conducted to determine the cost effectiveness and utility of indicator expansion, the results presented here provide preliminary support for their greater inclusion.

# Notes

1 The author wishes to thank Save the Children Federation's Ethiopia Field Office for the opportunity to pursue this study and for access to Liben District. Much thanks goes to members of the Negelle Field Office for their volunteered time, efforts, and translation assistance. The author also wishes to thank the three anonymous reviewers and Alfonso Morales for comments and suggestions made on earlier drafts.

2 This involves comparing the market value of different types of animals to their equivalent value in grain purchases.

3 See also Bryson and Hansch (1993).

4 As drought conditions worsen, so does the physical condition of livestock. Because of their centrality to household economies, cattle are unloaded onto the market at the last possible moment to prevent their loss from death or disease. This reduces their value at the same time grain prices rise due to shortage. See Lautze *et al.* (2003), Khan (1994), Bryson and Hansch (1993), and De Waal (1989) for good discussions of livestock/grain terms of trade.

5 See for example Harris *et al.* (2001).

6 See for example: CARE, East Africa Region (2000), Maxwell (2001), and USAID/BHR (1999).

7 *Belg* rains fall in the first half of the year. They are important for minor crops such as potatoes. However, they are critical for ground preparation for the longer crop cycles (*meher*) associated with sorghum, maize, and other grains, usually planted in June and July.

8 The 1984 census estimates the population at 77,256. By 1999, the population was estimated to have swelled to over 139,000 due to the 1984/85 famine and mass migration occurring in this drought cycle.

9 Data for price ratios are collected through observation. Five to ten transactions per product (maize, female goat, etc.) are observed at different sections of the markets for a standard unit of measure. In Ethiopia this is the quintal. Prices are averaged and the figures are reported in Birr, the Ethiopian unit of currency.

10 Access to these areas was provided by Save the Children Federation (SCF)/ USA's Division of Humanitarian Response (DHR) and the SCF-Ethiopia Field Office (EFO).

11 Amede Market has many commercial goods such as shoes, small household items, and cloth, with tailors available as well. To ensure comparability with the other markets, interviews were only conducted in the produce and grain area. The fuel wood and durable goods markets were excluded. Due to its size, each of the seven enumerators in this market and Jakala Market were randomly assigned grids and a site map, drawn by a team supervisor the previous week. The vendor surveys in Amede and Jakala Markets were administered by members of Ethiopian government ministries and CARE and SCF/EFO personnel.

12 Surveys in Negelle and Balambel were administered and translated with the help of three SCF/EFO personnel.

13 This was an issue in Amede Market, where only 60 percent of vendors agreed to be interviewed. Response was 100 percent in the other five markets.

14 Somali and Border Markets have much shorter averages for time spent in the area. This is due to their relatively recent demand-based emergence. They predominantly serve refugees or internally displaced populations. All full-time vendors in both markets are female heads of household who came early in the stress migration phase.

15 As noted above, utilization of this coping strategy indicates more severe conditions.

16 In her home region, young girls are given strands of beads as gifts by possible suitors. The number of strands worn is an indicator of beauty and desirability and thus status.

17 Itinerant sellers were generally unable to answer the question about tracking loss of profit over time. Most stated that they did not have the resources to be in the market consistently enough. This was particularly true in Border Market, which had a large proportion of recent arrivals, as identified in Table 13.1.

18 None of the respondents from Somali Market was able to pinpoint this exactly. All reported that they were feeling marketing shifts "recently." Similarly, those interviewed at Border Market reported declines "since I've been here."

19 A notable exception is Balambel Market. A significant decrease was reported due to people vacating the village. Stress migration is an act of extreme desperation, indicating the level of the crisis had become severe. Many who used to trade in that market no longer do so because they don't have goods available nor are there enough people with the ability to buy.

20 *Chat* (*Catha edulis*) is also seen as a better production risk because it is less vulnerable to drought.

21 He was referring to extended family members migrating into the city from outlying areas.

22 For an excellent discussion of livestock/grain terms of trade in markets, see Khan (1994), Ateng (1987), and De Waal (1989).
23 This finding was not applicable in Balambel, as this area had seen rapid and severe out-migration of local traders.

## Bibliography

Ateng, B. (1987) 'Food Marketing Activities of Low-Income Households,' in J. Price, J.L. Gittinger, and C. Hoisington (eds) *Food Policy: Integrating Supply, Distribution, and Consumption*, Baltimore, MD: The Johns Hopkins University Press: 304–08.

Bryson, J.C. and Hansch, S. (1993) *Food/cash for Work Interventions in Famine Mitigation*. Washington, DC: Office of US Foreign Disaster Assistance, Prevention, Mitigation and Preparedness Division, OFDA/USDA Famine Mitigation Activity PASA, PASA # AFR-1526-P-AG-1129-00.

Buchanan-Smith, M. and Davies, S. (1995) *Famine Early Warning and Response – The Missing Link*, London: Intermediate Technologies Publications.

CARE, East Africa Region (2000) 'Preparing for a Rapid Livelihood Security Asessment (RLSA): Guidelines and Checklist,' Addis Ababa, Ethiopia: CARE International.

Clark, G. (1991) 'Food Traders and Food Security in Ghana,' in R.E. Downs, D.O. Kerner, and S.P. Reyna (eds) *Food and Nutrition in History and Anthropology*, vol. 9, Philadelphia, PA: Gordon and Breach Science Publishers: 227–56.

Cuny, F.C. (1999) *Famine, Conflict, and Response: A Basic Guide*, West Harford, CT: Kumarian Press.

De Waal, A. (1989) *Famine that Kills: Darfur, Sudan, 1984–1985*, New York: Oxford University Press.

—— (1997) *Famine Crimes: Politics and the Disaster Relief Industry in Africa*, Bloomington, IN: Indiana University Press.

FANTA (1999) *Food Security Indicators and Framework for Use in the Monitoring and Evaluation of Food Aim Program*, Washington, DC: Food & Nutrition Technical Assistance.

Freudenberger, K.S. (1996) *Rapid Rural Appraisal and Participatory Rural Appraisal: A Manual for CRS Field Workers and Partners*, Baltimore, MD: Catholic Relief Services.

Hammond, L. and Maxwell, D. (2002) 'The Ethiopian Crisis of 1999–2000: Lessons Learned, Questions Unanswered,' *Disasters*, 26(3): 262–79.

Harris, J.M., Wise, T.A., Gallagher, K.P., and Goodwin, N.R. (2001) *A Survey of Sustainable Development: Social and Economic Dimensions*, Washington, DC: Island Press.

Khan, M.M. (1994) 'Market-based Early Warning Indicators of Famine for the Pastoral Households of the Sahel,' *World Development*, 22(2): 189–99.

Lautze, S. (1999) 'Saving Lives and Livelihoods: The Fundamentals of Livelihoods Strategy,' Feinstein International Famine Center.

Lautze, S., Aklilu, Y., Raven-Roberts, A., Young, H., Kebeded, G., and Leaning, J. (June 2003) 'Risk and Vulnerability in Ethiopia: Learning from the Past, Responding to the Present, Preparing for the Future,' a report for the US Agency for International Development.

Maxwell, D. (2001) 'Understanding Nutritional Data and Nutritional Indicators,' Atlanta, GA: CARE International.

Maxwell, S. and Frankenberger, T.R. (1992) *Household Food Security: Concepts, Indicators, Measurements*, Washington, DC: United Nations Children's Fund and International Fund for Agricultural Development.

Seaman, J. (2000) 'Making Exchange Entitlements Operational: The Food Economy Approach to Famine Prediction and the Risk Map Computer Program,' *Disasters*, 24(2): 133–52.

Sen, A. (1992) *Poverty and Famines: An Essay on Entitlement and Deprivation*, New York: Oxford University Press.

Tshirley, D., Donovan, C., and Weber, M.T. (1996) 'Food Aid and Food Markets: Lessons from Mozambique,' *Food Policy*, 21(2): 189–209.

USAID/BHR (1999) 'Menu of Sector-Specific Humanitarian Assistance Perform- ance Indicators: Definition, Unit of Measure and Possible Data Sources,' Washington, DC: United States Agency for International Development.

Walker, P.J.C. (1999) 'Indigenous Knowledge and Famine Relief in the Horn of Africa,' in D.M. Warren, L.J. Slikkerveer, and D. Brokensha (eds) *The Cultural Dimension of Development: Indigenous Knowledge Systems*, London: Inter- mediate Technology Publications, 147–57.

Webb, P. and Harinarayan, A. (1999) 'A Measure of Uncertainty: The Nature of Vulnerability and Its Relationship to Malnutrition,' *Disasters*, 23(4): 292–305.

# 14 Indelible intersections

## Insights from New Zealand's largest street market

*Anne de Bruin and Ann Dupuis*[1]

## Introduction

Traditionally, the informal economy is viewed as a feature of developing economies and invaluable in providing employment and income for those who otherwise would be marginalized in the formal economy (Maldonado 1995). Thus it is recognized as a means of poverty alleviation and a pathway to development (Bromley 1990). This chapter, however, is on "street vending" in a developed economy, and explores the dynamics of the largest and best example of New Zealand's street commerce: the Otara Flea Market. As such, it differs somewhat from those studies that describe and analyze the operation of vendors in the context of developing countries, where the distinction between the formal and informal sectors of economies is more clear-cut.

In this chapter we highlight the intersections that characterize the formal–informal domains of economic activity, as well as those that exemplify the impact of global factors on localized economic activity. It shows that the very nature and organization of some of the small-scale enterprises in this market are frequently based on the operation of the intricate networks of global connections. Hence, this chapter argues that the dual intersections of informal–formal and local–global are an indelible, or ingrained, part of urban street market activity. This is not to say, however, that such interconnections are not fluid. Indeed, we use the metaphor of a mural to portray a sense of non-fragility while simultaneously illustrating factors of both change and continuity. The artistic qualities of a painted mural are in synergy with the creativity of micro-enterprise operators in their responses to the forces of change and their ability to tap into the opportunity this affords them to engage in business.

While street markets are often seen as one of the most visible manifestations of the informal economy (Thomas 1992: 14), our intention is to move away from the focus on differentiating between sectors and adopt instead an approach to the economic analysis of street markets which emphasizes intersections. As such, the issues discussed here are informed by a broad position akin to that of Harding and Jenkins (1989) which looks critically at the dualistic notion of the existence of a discrete informal economy, separated from a formal economy. We argue that, particularly in developed economies like New Zealand, it is less than meaningful to divide the economy into separate spheres. We disagree, therefore, with writers such as Davis (1972) who attempted to analyze economic activity in the United Kingdom in terms of four distinct sub-economies, the market economy, the redistributive economy, the domestic economy, and the gift economy, each of which are governed by different types of regulations or rules, and Gershuny (1983) who recognizes three forms of informal productive activity (household, communal, and underground) that exist outside the formal economy. Instead, we believe that these activities are best understood as integrated strategies. Our position has similarities to that of Morales (2001) who argues strongly against positivistic tendencies to reify economic activities, thus abstracting them from their social contexts, and recommends instead a focus on a range of decision-making processes.

A key point reinforced throughout is the importance of taking context firmly into consideration. Hence, we argue that to understand the microlevel dynamics of the Otara Flea Market it is necessary to locate the analysis in a wider framework that takes account of macro-transformations in a globalized era. While our analysis focuses on the unique connections made at the global, national, and local community levels, the general argument made regarding the value of a contextual analysis could be applied elsewhere. We draw on interview data from selected stallholders at the Otara Flea Market to provide empirical support for our position.

Our research into the Otara Flea Market has also provided us with a lens through which to view a range of wider social and economic issues currently being played out in the New Zealand context. A selection of these issues is presented later under the heading of "Close-ups of the mural." In the penultimate section, we further reinforce the need for contextual analysis – in this instance within a discussion of the entrepreneurial underpinnings of the activity of street vendors. Here our discussion hinges mainly on a transaction cost approach to provide new insights into street commerce.

## The Otara Flea Market

The Otara Flea Market is located in the labor-market-disadvantaged, multicultural community of Otara, an area in the south of Auckland, New Zealand's largest center of population. The market, which operates every Saturday morning, exudes the atmosphere of an open-air Polynesian market. Like street markets around the world, the Otara Flea Market is colorful, vibrant, and noisy. In one corner, a young Pacific Island man fervently preaches to bystanders of the changes that have taken place in his life since he found Jesus Christ. In another corner, the sounds of urban Pacific music pulsate through the air as a Pacific Island band performs, almost appearing to bring to life the wall mural which forms their backdrop. An elderly woman buys her supply of freshly baked *rewana*, or Maori bread; a child pesters his mother for a cheap, battery driven, musical toy; a German tourist purchases a New Zealand souvenir T-shirt with sheep on it; and a visitor to the market carefully selects a carved bone pendant. These images form only a small part of the kaleidoscope of sight, sound, and smell that makes up the Otara Flea Market.

The market itself is held in a large open-air car park, normally used by Otara shoppers and staff and students of Manukau Institute of Technology, a large polytechnic in central Otara. Around one-fifth of the stalls are located in a local recreation center that adjoins the car park. The stalls on the nearly 400 sites which constitute the market sell the usual range of products: fruit, vegetables, and other fresh produce, fast foods, new and second-hand clothing, household goods and bric-a-brac, toys, jewelry, and other small consumer goods. In recent times, the Otara Market has been promoted as an attraction where tourists can experience the Polynesian flavor of Auckland, the city with the world's largest Polynesian population. Nevertheless, the specific demand-driven nature of many of the products on sale makes it clear that the market caters to both the low-income community in which it is located and the ethnic preferences of a large Polynesian clientele. Thus, fresh produce on sale ranges from such vegetables as potatoes, beans, and carrots to the Pacific Island staple of taro, and the Maori delicacies of watercress and *puha* (or sow thistle). The Maori and Pacific Island cultural products on sale, while of possible interest to overseas tourists, are largely bought by local consumers. For example, brightly colored leis, graveside wreaths made from cheap, gauzy fabric to simulate flowers, and imitation tapa cloth Bible covers, are intended to cater mostly to a low-income Pacific Island market. The revival of Maori ethnic identity (Spoonley 1993, 1995) is represented by an interest in such products as finely woven flax *kete* (bags), carved Maori flutes, jewelry, and other items of personal adornment, weaponry, and toys. It also provides solutions for labor-market-disadvan-taged new Asian migrants who are selling the type of low-quality merchandise indistinguishable from that sold in many street markets across the world: Balinese hair combs, cheap watches, and battery operated toy cars made in China.

Unlike many street markets in the developed world which have a long history of operation, some for more than a century, the Otara Flea Market has only been running since 1977. Though a relative newcomer, it was very soon successfully established as New Zealand's premier street market. To the casual observer it might appear that its beginnings, steady expansion in size over the years, and embeddedness in the life of the community has occurred spontaneously. Though seemingly a natural, organic occurrence, the origins and growth of the Flea Market have been, in fact, a contrived and staged affair. There was a threefold impetus for the commencement of a Flea Market in Otara. First, the Flea Market was conceived of as a viable means of raising funds for the local branch of the New Zealand Labour Party which, at least for the past 75 years, has been one of New Zealand's two major political parties. Second, it was believed that the Flea Market would serve as a good source of cheap clothing, foodstuffs, and other household goods and necessities for a community already beginning to feel the impact of the wider economic decline. Third, it was thought that the Flea Market would assist in the provision of revenue for the recently established Te Puke O Tara Community Centre. The Centre was the realization of a dream of a group of local high-school students to promote positive activities for the young people of the area in a harmonious, multicultural environment (Reid 1974).

Initially, the Flea Market ran within a loose regulatory framework and was circumscribed only by health matters and vehicle parking requirements. By the 1980s, however, tensions between the various parties involved became apparent. The three chief players here were a group of dissenting local business people who, with the widespread introduction of Saturday retail shopping in New Zealand, saw the Flea Market as a threat to their businesses; conservative elements within the local government bureaucracy who disapproved of a portion of the monetary benefits from the Flea Market being channeled to Labour Party coffers; and activists belonging to the Te Puke O Tara Incorporated Society, who felt that a greater share of the proceeds from the rentals should devolve to the Society to assist in the operation of the Centre and thus benefit the Otara community more directly.

The tensions between local stakeholders were resolved through a written agreement dated 20 February 1981, which specified that both groups would form a combined subcommittee designated as "The United Fleamarket of Otara Committee," to jointly maintain the Otara Flea Market. The remuneration clause of this agreement laid down that both groups would share equally the net weekly profit from the Flea Market, with an additional proviso that the local Labour Electorate Committee would ensure that 5 percent of their share of the profits would form a special community fund which would be utilized to support Otara people. With the clarification of organizational aspects under this agreement, the local business community accepted that the Flea Market was there to stay. Local government reorganization in 1989 also necessitated the formalization of the process of market operations in the Council-owned car park. This resulted in considerable negotiation and discussion with the various stakeholders in the community and culminated, in 1992, with the issuing of an occupation license with attendant conditions laid down (Manukau City Council 1992). These form the current regulatory framework for the market, ensure that the market operates in an orderly manner, restrict the number of stalls that can sell food, prohibit the sale of fish, lay down the maximum number of sites available for stalls selling fruit and/or vegetables, provide the conditions relating to garbage removal, specify the hours of operation on Saturdays from 5 a.m. to 12 noon, and draw attention to environmental health operating conditions. A key facet of the agreement was also the setting of an occupation fee to be paid on a weekly basis to the City Council for each car park space.

**The wider context**

New Zealand is a country in the southern Pacific Ocean, approximately 1,600 kilometers east of Australia. With a total land area of 266,171 square kilometers, it is sparsely populated with a population of just over 4 million people. More than three quarters of the population are of European descent (76.8 percent), while the New Zealand Maori ethnic group constitutes 14.1 percent of the population, Pacific peoples make up 6.2 percent, with 6.4 percent of the population identified as Asian (Statistics New Zealand 2005).

The Auckland region, within which Otara is located, is New Zealand's largest center of population with approximately 1.2 million residents. The local authority ward of Otara, where the Flea Market is sited, differs markedly in its demographic characteristics from both the Auckland region and New Zealand more generally. Otara is a multicultural community of approximately 35,000 people, belonging to the City of Manukau, in the south of Auckland. It is a clearly identifiable ethnic minority community having the largest concentration of Pacific peoples in New Zealand, with 63 percent of its population belonging to that group. Those identifying as European constitute 20 percent of the ward's population, with Maori making up 21 percent and Asian people a further 9 percent.[2] Furthermore, Otara stands out as a youthful community with around 49 percent of its people under the age of 25.

New Zealand's economy has undergone significant change since the commencement of economic liberalization in 1984. While the altered welfare state principles and policy directions of the "New Zealand reform model" is well documented (see Galt 2000 for a good summary), the impact of such reform on small communities, such as Otara, and on individuals who must operate within changed circumstances, is less well known.

Otara itself was a deliberate creation of the welfare state. Its development in the 1950s was vitally linked to the central government's state-provided housing policy which aimed at eliminating Auckland's inner-city slum areas. Additionally, Otara was intended to house a low-income labor force in close proximity to a growing manufacturing region in South Auckland. Otara as an urban community, therefore, was a product of the welfare state's housing and industrial policies. While always a low socioeconomic area, the economic restructuring of the 1980s has had a severely detrimental effect on Otara, caught as it was between economic restructuring on the one hand and welfare state benefit cutbacks on the other. Economic restructuring resulting in the closure or downsizing of industries such as meat works, car assembly plants, and other manufacturing industries in the region meant job losses and few job opportunities for the largely unskilled or low-skilled population of Otara. Poverty levels of the majority of people in the Otara community were further aggravated after 1991 by drastic reductions in welfare benefits coupled with the introduction of market rentals for state housing. By the mid-1990s Otara was an example of a community severely affected by the structural changes of the economy, caught as it was between global transformation and the new international division of labor on the one hand and the national response to these changes leading to radical welfare state restructuring on the other.

While New Zealand's economy is generally much more buoyant now than it was a decade ago, statistics indicate that Otara still suffers from economic disadvantage. Data on sources of income show that 40 percent of census respondents were on some form of state income support (with only approximately 5 percent on an age-related superannuation benefit). Home ownership rates also point to economic disadvantage. In 2001, some 68 percent of the nation's households were privately owned. However, only 42 percent of Otara's households fell into this category. Employment data also indicate a tendency for the employed in Otara to be clustered in low-skilled occupations (Statistics New Zealand 2002). Otara is one of the most economically deprived communities in New Zealand, yet it still stands out as a special community. It is the multicultural hub of New Zealand. This rich and diverse cultural make-up and young and vibrant population gives Otara a unique quality which is visibly manifested in the atmosphere of the Flea Market itself.

## Research approach

The research on which this chapter is based was part of a larger project intended to close the information gap that exists in understanding the way that less formalized economic activity operates as part of the coping strategies of people in communities caught by the domestic response to changes in the global economy. Our broad concern was to assess the extent to which such activity can provide sustainable income. The methods used in the Otara Flea Market component of our research included participant observation at the market which allowed us to categorize the nature of the retail sales, classify the size of operations, develop a profile of the vendors themselves, and document analysis of legal papers relating to the regulatory framework of the market and newspaper reports of the market's history and operations. These research activities were augmented by a range of interviews with people involved in the market, including key players in the early years of the operation of the market, those currently involved in its administration and management, and local retailers from established businesses in the Otara Town Centre. Most important, however, were in-depth interviews with a stratified sample of 24 Flea Market vendors. While these were conducted in 1998, they were followed up with various on-going, informal research activities at the market over the following five years.

Informed by a qualitative methodology, the interviews aimed at capturing the understandings and experiences of the research participants and interpreting the meaningful explanations participants gave to their own and others' actions. Our intention was not, therefore, for the interviews to be read as part of a "scientific," generalizable survey. Instead, the interviews were intended to be exploratory in nature, in order to better inform an understanding of the mechanisms of advanced economy street commerce. Our chief purpose was to capture the nuances of street commerce in a specific, urban New Zealand context, albeit one with a strikingly Polynesian market influence.

## Demonstrating the interconnections: spatial and sectoral

In this section we draw on interview data to illustrate our contention that conceptualizing a dual economy comprising formal and informal sectors tends to disguise the interconnections between the two. While these links may not be very obvious they are, nevertheless, integral to the operation of the activities of many stallholders at the market. Similarly, spatial intersections are illustrated with particular reference to social and economic networks that extend well beyond the confines of the local region, inter-regionally and internationally.

An example of the overlap between the organized formal sector and informal sector as well as global intersections of economic activity is provided by Mrs Manu, who had been a permanent stallholder at the Otara Flea Market for a number of years.[3] Mrs Manu took pleasure in making her stall attractive; in decorating her stall with brightly colored umbrellas and drapery to create a feel of the Pacific Islands which reflected her Samoan heritage. The major part of her stall was devoted to her own label of women's clothing, designed primarily with Pacific themes which drew on her knowledge of Pacific Island cultures. For example, one of her creations was a bright red dress embossed with a gold design of a traditional kava bowl,[4] intended for a young Pacific Island woman celebrating a formal occasion such as a wedding or twenty-first birthday party.

Characteristics of both the formal and informal sectors were manifest in Mrs Manu's business activity. Product branding, which characterizes much formal sector activity, was sought through the distinctive labeling of her high-quality Pacific-style fashion garments. She displayed the formal-sector business characteristic of product differentiation through attention to design detail, the use of distinctively Polynesian fabrics, and made-to-measure garments. She also attempted to gain formal recognition in the fashion industry by participation in the annual national Pacific fashion awards, where her work had been well received. Typical of the informal sector, however, she chose to limit the size of her activities by confining the display and sale of her garments to the Flea Market. Quite deliberately, she opted to retain the small scale of her business, although she recognized that with her previous experience in fashion, she could have employed staff and developed a larger workroom-type operation. She also visibly contained the level of the overhead costs of her economic activity by using her Flea Market stall as business premises to take orders for made-to-measure fashion garments. The circumvention of governmental taxation and other regulatory charges were additional informal sector characteristics Mrs Manu exhibited.

Mrs Manu's activities symbolized the manner in which social networks cut across national boundaries to facilitate small-scale economic activity. She drew on social capital in the form of family connections to source goods for her stall. The T-shirts she sold were sent to her from her sister in Hawaii. Although she had lived for 30 years in New Zealand, Mrs Manu still maintained her strong Samoan connections. Hence, it was easy for her to obtain the select range of Pacific-style coconut shell earrings and hair accessories and shell choker necklaces made by Apia craftspeople. Thus Mrs Manu's Flea Market activity presented a microcosm of the synergistic tendencies of the global economy.[5]

Another example, that of Mr Watson, further highlights the inter-connectedness between the formal and informal sectors, with his Flea Market operation forming an extension of formal sector economic activity. Mr Watson owned a large-scale flower growing operation quite some distance away from Otara, but used the Flea Market as a profitable outlet to dispose of flowers that were rejected by the export market or other formal sector outlets. Frequently he supplemented his own stock by buying produce other than flowers from the wholesale market or other suppliers.

Furthermore, Mr Watson also exemplified the interconnected nature of economic and social factors in motivating human behavior. He had been a Flea Market stallholder for well over a decade. Economic considerations were only one motivating factor to work at the Flea Market – social connections were also important. Not only did a life-long friend work the adjoining stall, but close friendships had also developed with a number of other nearby stallholders, and warm relationships had been built up over time with his regular Flea Market clientele. His activities clearly demonstrate that the pursuit of economic goals is normally accompanied by the pursuit of non-economic goals such as sociability (Granovetter 1992).

Our interviews yielded two further, particularly strong, examples where street market activity played an important role in maintaining the viability of the formal sector operations of the stallholders. Mr Fraser ran his own carpet retailing business in another area of Auckland. Together with a relative, he had worked the Flea Market on a permanent basis for nearly 15 years. He used the Flea Market as a low-overhead outlet to dispose of short ends and carpet seconds and also sell a range of small mats and rugs for cars, entries, and bathrooms. Almost all the goods he sold at the Flea Market were aimed at the low-income, local community. A significant proportion of Mr Fraser's customers were Pacific Island people who purchased a particular range of brightly colored, patterned carpet that suited their taste. Mr Fraser stressed that the stall gave him a good "cash flow" that was a useful addition to his earnings in the formal sector.

Mrs Patel, along with her husband, was the co-owner of a well-established, inner city shop that sold primarily T-shirts and catered to the international tourism market. Her Flea Market stall catered to both local and tourist markets, although 80 percent of sales were tourism related, with the T-shirts being bought by tourists themselves or purchased by locals to take as gifts when they traveled overseas. Interestingly, Mrs Patel also had another casual stall across the walkway where a family member sold seconds at a cheaper price. The high turnover of the Flea Market enabled her to sustain the viability of the city shop even though she sold the identical T-shirts at a lower price at the Flea Market. The high foot traffic and low overheads of the Flea Market gave both Mr Fraser and Mrs Patel a low-risk adjunct to their formal sector activities.

Another stallholder, who had as his main source of income the carving of large size, traditional Maori sculptural forms on a commission basis, but sold New Zealand greenstone (nephrite) jewelry at the Flea Market, further illustrates the crossover between the informal and formal sectors. He stated that not only was the market a culturally appropriate and lucrative outlet for the sale of his wares, but also provided him with the opportunity to talk to possible buyers for his commissioned works. Additionally, the market helped in ensuring the viability of his main business in that he was able to use the stone that had been left as off-cuts from his larger commissioned works to create items of jewelry.

The foregoing examples serve to highlight definitional inadequacies of sub-sectoral analyses that do not recognize the interwoven nature of the formal and informal sectors. While we might not go as far as Harding and Jenkins (1989), who argue that there are no separate economies as such, the above examples are intended to stress the idea that the notion of separate economies is problematic. We do, however, acknowledge the attempts by Harding and Jenkins (1989) to take into account the intricacies and connections between the economic and the social, which they claim can best be characterized as a "well-darned and seamed web that is the complexity (and confusion) of a social-democratic market economy." (Harding and Jenkins 1989: 179.)

This web imagery, while attractive, implies elements of fragility, non-resilience, and possible transience, elements that were not apparent to us in our research into the Otara Flea Market. Instead, our research led us to suggest that the image of a contemporary mural would be more appropriate to convey the characteristics and feel, at least of the Otara Flea Market. This mural imagery presents not the delicate and fragile image of a web but rather that of a changing, vivid, living painting, constantly being added to by the brushstrokes of representations of local, multicultural identities. In doing so, it shifts the focus from Harding and Jenkins' (1989) social-democratic market economy to one that better captures the feel of the niche market operations of a local economy increasingly shaped around postmodern ethnic identities. Yet, unlike a web, the mural as we see it has a robustness that ensures it cannot be whisked away by an "invisible hand." We recognize, however, that the "visible hand" of the state, particularly local government regulatory bodies, could whisk away street vending activities with the click of a mouse. In addition, the mix and merging of colors of the mural symbolizes the crossovers and interconnectedness of different sectors of the economy, as well as the variety of motivations that drives market activity.

## Close-ups of the mural

This section focuses on cases which illustrate three issues that arose during our study of the Otara Flea Market: job creation through harnessing ethnic cultural capital; immigration and employment issues in New Zealand; and local charitable support through altruistic behavior. These issues, while not necessarily connected to one another, nevertheless highlight particular features of the local and/or national context.

In earlier work, we argued that in order to mitigate ethnic unemployment differentials in New Zealand, special efforts were necessary to create employment at the community level. Given the low formal educational qualifications of ethnic minorities, these efforts should concentrate on the harnessing of ethnic riches and the cultural capital of the community (de Bruin and Dupuis 1995; de Bruin 1997). At that time, as a consequence of extensive economic reform in New Zealand, ethnic unemployment rates were very high. For example, for the June quarter of 1995, while the unemployment rate of the New Zealand European ethnic group was 4.4 percent, the unemployment rates for Maori and Pacific peoples were 16.1 percent and 17 percent respectively (Statistics New Zealand 1995). A decade later, unemployment levels in New Zealand are very low. At 3.7 percent, the overall unemployment rate, however, still masks ethnic differentials. For the June quarter of 2005, the unemployment rate for New Zealand Europeans was 2.5 percent, whereas for Maori it was 8.6 percent and 6 percent for Pacific people (*The Jobs Letter* 2005). Tapping into cultural capital in order to create employment is still, therefore, a valuable strategy. Exemplifying the idea of how cultural capital can be harnessed for job creation at the local level in Otara, we draw attention to the Flea Market operations of a local Maori trust. Through fostering traditional carving skills but modifying traditional products and patterns to cater to changing consumer tastes and preferences, the trust was able to transform cultural capital into sustainable employment for a group of local men who were then able to sell their products at a lucrative outlet in the Otara Flea Market.

New Zealand exhibits similar demographic trends as other Western nations, such as low birth rates, an aging population, the encouragement of immigration as a means of ensuring population growth, and increasing the flow of skilled immigrants in order to meet contemporary labor market requirements. However, the issue of immigration is one that is hotly debated in New Zealand, particularly as it relates to immigrants from East Asia. Since the 1980s, the country's immigration policy has been aimed at attracting and building up a skilled work force. After the removal of the traditional source-countries preference in 1986, a points system for skilled immigrants was introduced in 1991, revised in 1996, again in 1998, and from time to time thereafter. A criticism made of the various immigration policy changes, however, has been that immigrants to New Zealand have shown relatively high rates of unemployment and underemployment, thus at the personal level not being able to utilize their skills, and at a broader level not benefiting New Zealand with respect to human capital recruitment (Trlin *et al.* 2004: 205–06).

A longitudinal New Zealand study entitled the New Settlers Programme interviewed both Chinese and Indian immigrants and provided significant insights into a range of issues facing new migrants. This study offered a number of explanations for the unemployment and underemployment of immigrants which include: a lack of New Zealand experience and qualifications; low English language proficiency; possible discrimination by employers; the fact that some occupations appeared to be more difficult to enter than others; and problems with both personnel recruitment agencies and the state agencies in helping immigrants secure employment. Research associated with the study conducted between 1998 and 2002 has shown a range of coping strategies used by Chinese and Indian immigrants when faced with such problems as these, including: taking whatever employment is available; becoming a self-employed worker; studying to improve English language competency; studying to gain New Zealand qualifications; and engaging in onward or return migration (Trlin *et al.* 2004: 210–13).

A stereotypical image portrayed in media reports, particularly of Chinese migrants, is that they are rich, exhibit little commitment to their new host society, keep to their own group, and have come to New Zealand only to pursue their own economic self-interest (Friesen 1993). Our interview with Mr Tan, an Otara Flea Market stallholder, showed, however, that this identified stereotype did not fit his case and that he was caught in a similar situation as the immigrants reported on in the New Settlers Programme. Mr Tan was a relatively recent mainland Chinese immigrant to New Zealand. In China he had been a business manager, but after 15 months in New Zealand was still unemployed. As a casual stallholder at the market, he sold cheap toys and watches which he had purchased from a Chinese wholesale agency. Clearly a qualified and experienced professional with an overwhelming drive to work in the formal sector, he was extremely unhappy about his present employment situation. His skills alone were not sufficient for him to obtain any employment in the formal sector. When we questioned him as to his motivation for working at the market, he pointed out that he, like other Chinese, wanted nothing more than to work. The idea of staying at home and being on a benefit was repugnant to him. He saw an opportunity for work at the market during the pre-Christmas season when the toys and other wares he sold were in greater demand, hence his choice of merchandise.

Altruistic behavior was shown by several of the stallholders. For example, Mrs Chambers, an elderly European woman and committed Christian, had run a stall at the Flea Market for 14 years. She sold home-made jams and pickles and second-hand items donated to her by others in order to earn money for a range of charitable works but chiefly to support two overseas children she sponsored through an international aid agency.

### The underpinnings of entrepreneurial activity

Whether they had been "pulled" into Flea Market activity by the lure of the possibilities of supplementing their income and the "buzz" of the market, or "pushed" into street market vending, all the vendors demonstrated entrepreneurial spirit. This section, therefore, is an attempt to understand further this feature. It first draws attention to a transaction cost economization rationale to provide enhanced theoretical understanding of street commerce operations. It then emphasizes the need for a contextual as well as an individual-based approach to exploring entrepreneurial activity.

For street markets such as the Otara Flea Market the economization of transaction costs is an important facet of their economic activity (de Bruin and Dupuis 1999).[6] For instance, social networks can be viewed as part and parcel of the transaction costs economization process. In an earlier section, we pointed out the social connections of Mrs Manu to illustrate how social networks can cut across national boundaries and span the local–global divide. Utilization of social networks, such as family members, in order to source goods for sale provides not only a basis for their trading for several of the Flea Market vendors, but also lowers transaction costs. The enhanced trust mechanisms of these relationships avoid the need for legally binding and costly written contracts, and the associated higher transaction costs thereof, which are a feature of formal sector enterprise. Additionally, the simple nature of the contractual agreement between vendors and the Flea Market organizers, which involves essentially nothing more than the collection of a minimal and set site rental charge, ensures low fixed costs for their enterprise and also low transaction costs relative to the more complex requirements of operating, for example, in a shopping mall. This does not mean to say that the Flea Market itself does not operate under a regulatory framework. In fact, the regulations regarding the range of goods sold by individual stallholders and the overall number of stalls with a particular category of products are very clear cut, as is the contract that covers the way the site rental fees are apportioned and utilized by the market's regulatory body. However, there is simplicity of contractual arrangement between each of the individual market vendors and the market organizers, which lies outside the more complex regulatory framework of the operation of the market itself. As Cross and Peña (2006) argue, the social organization of the market allows transaction costs to be minimized without the expense of complex regulations.

The transaction cost economics assumption of bounded rationality[7] is applicable here since it recognizes that the women vendors are working within a framework of constraints, the most important of which we identify as their intrinsic information bounds. These chiefly involve the limitations faced in terms of selling labor in the formal sector. The primary research question we pursued was how do the women in our study, "... given limited competence, ... organize so as to utilize their limited competence to best advantage?" (Williamson 1985: 46). While Williamson refers to competence here in terms of "cognitive competence," the competence of the women we interviewed is limited by their information and knowledge constraints. These arise chiefly from their current low levels of education and training and few formal sector business contacts and networks which could give them entry into more lucrative income producing market opportunities. We found that the lack of information constrained the capability of the women vendors to operate successfully in a range of economic locales. They do not have the requisite qualifications for formal sector work, other than those that would secure them less-skilled or service-type jobs in the secondary labor market. The skills they do possess and use in their endeavors in the Flea Market have not resulted from formal education but rather are skills acquired through previous employment in the sunset manufacturing industries in New Zealand, or domestic skills developed through life experience.

Informal economic activity from a transaction costs economization perspective can also involve evasion and avoidance aspects. In the first instance, formal institutional rules and regulations in terms of tax and central and local governmental imposts such as Accident Compensation premiums and import duties and tariffs are evaded. Here, however, we need to ask the question of whether or not this evasion can be interpreted in terms of Williamson's other behavioral assumption of "self interest seeking with guile" (Williamson 1985: 47). The answer to this question must, however, consider the information constraints that several street vendors face. Perhaps it is the case that, given their educational and existing competence levels, rather than acting with guile, they simply might not be able to comply with the accounting standards demanded by the formal tax regime (see also Morales 1998). Secondly, the costliness of gathering information in order to operate successfully in the tax-regulated sector of the economy is avoided. This kind of information includes learning about formal sector jobs, knowing how to apply and interview for these jobs, striking a legal contract with suppliers of goods for sale, or negotiating a competitive wage. For Uzzell (1994: 257) this involves "a very complex and fluid array of kinds of information in addition to the education or technical knowledge required actually to perform the work." This kind of information is not the sort of information many vendors in our study, namely those whose dominant sphere of activity was the informal sector of street commerce, could easily draw on.

Mrs Manu illustrates the situation of vendors whom we believe are constrained to a sphere of operation by their information bounds. While it was obvious that she has considerable design and sewing skills, and might well have worked in the formal sector had she been better able to market herself, she chose street vending. It should be noted, however, that her capability to enter this domain is constrained by her lack of information. For example, she has less facility to negotiate favorable contract terms with fashion buyers, or the knowledge to be able to hire herself out as a fashion designer. To do the latter she would need to know, for example, what her charge-out rate would be and she would need to have suitable industry contacts. Such information would not be readily accessible to her, and to acquire it would require considerable effort and cost on her part. Hence, by operating in the informal sector she demonstrates bounded rationality, and within her existing knowledge bounds her Flea Market business is an optimal choice. If she were to attempt to market her garments profitably in the formal sector, she would also need to follow standard business practices, incurring increased costs. She evades both formal sector rules and regulations and avoids the costliness of information-gathering that would enable her to sell her labor as a fashion designer, or fulfill written contractual agreements of supplying goods herself; she is, therefore, a transaction costs economizer.

We also wish to point out that a narrow focus on theoretical slants – in this case the transaction costs economization aspect – tends to underplay both entrepreneurial qualities at an individual level as well as the conduct of entrepreneurial activity at a broader contextual level. Thus, consideration of Flea Market enterprise within a broader contextual approach might involve an examination of such factors as the impact of economic restructuring, the inability of new immigrants to obtain employment in line with their skills and educational levels, and hidden employer discrimination of some groups of people such as older workers and migrants with a non-English-speaking background. Attention to the individual level highlights constraints that some stallholders face and their entrepreneurialism in seeking to overcome these constraints.

## Conclusion

Our examination of the intricate social and economic dynamics of the Otara market has provided us with a vantage point from which we can enter into the debate regarding the utility of the dichotomous separation of formal and informal economic activity. Taking up this argument, we also provide new imagery to capture the special qualities of street vending that we have observed in our research on the Otara Flea Market.

We have argued that in order to understand the complex social and economic dynamics of the Otara market, it is necessary to set out the overarching global and national context of change that impacts individuals at the micro level. While our analysis has focused on the particularities of one street market, the general approach we have taken could well be applied to an analysis of street markets in a variety of contexts. We presented an extension to the critique of approaches that attempt to separate out and specify the peculiar characteristics of distinct segments of economic activity. To better inform this critique we developed a more apt image – that of the contemporary mural – to capture the vibrancy, flexibility yet resilience, and capacity for modification that typically characterizes street markets. The mural image also conveys the importance of local ethnic identities in a postmodern world.

By way of a corollary discussion, this chapter examined the application of a transaction costs perspective to street market activity and also highlighted the need to view the entrepreneurial activity of vendors in terms of the constraints they face. Street vending can thus be framed within an analysis of overcoming these constraints which might be at an institutional and structural level, e.g. the role and perception of women in society and immigration policy deficiencies, or at a more individual level, e.g. the human capital and cognitive limitations of the vendors themselves.

## Notes

1 We wish to thank Alfonso Morales, John Cross, and an anonymous referee for helpful comments and suggestions for this chapter. This feedback helped extend our thinking on the topic of street vending generally. Any limitations remain the responsibility of the authors.
2 The New Zealand census question on ethnicity allows individuals to identify with more than one ethnic group.
3 Fictitious names have been given to stallholders, and in some cases other distinguishing details have been modified in order to ensure that research participants cannot be identified.
4 Kava is a Polynesian drink, made from the roots of a local plant.
5 Interestingly, our research showed the reverse process to that described by Besnier (2004) in the second-hand marketplace in the Tongan capital of Nuku'alofa, where Tongans sold objects their relatives overseas had sent them instead of remittances.
6 Transaction cost analysis, a core aspect of the New Institutional Economics, achieved prominence chiefly through the work of Williamson (1975, 1985). It offers an alternative view of economic behavior to that of the mainstream neo-classical approach. For its suitability in terms of application to a small-scale micro-analysis like the one undertaken in this chapter, we follow the definition of transaction costs offered by Swedberg (1990: 115) as "costs other than price incurred in trading goods and services."
7 A succinct definition of bounded rationality is: "*intendedly* rational but only *limitedly* so" (Simon 1961: xxiv).

## Bibilography

Besnier, N. (2004) "Consumption and Cosmopolitanism: Practicing Modernity at the Second-Hand Marketplace in Nuku'alofa, Tonga," *Anthropological Quarterly*, 77(1): 7–45.
Bromley, R. (1990) "A New Path to Development? The Significance and Impact of Hernando de Soto's Ideas on Underdevelopment, Production and Reproduction," *Economic Geography*, 66: 328–48.
Cross, J. and Peña, S. (2006) "Risk and Regulation in Informal and Illegal Markets," in P. Fernandez-Kelly and J. Shefner (eds) *Out of the Shadows: Political Action and the Informal Economy in Latin America*. University Park, PA: Pennsylvania State University Press.

Davis, J. (1972) "Gifts and the UK Economy," *Man*, 7(3): 408–29.

de Bruin, A. (1997) "Transformation of the Welfare State in New Zealand With Special Reference to Employment," unpublished PhD thesis, New Zealand: Massey University.

de Bruin, A. and Dupuis, A. (1995) "A Closer Look at New Zealand's Superior Economic Performance: Ethnic Employment Issues," *British Review of New Zealand Studies*, 8: 85–97.

—— (1999) "Towards a Synthesis of Transaction Cost Economics and a Feminist Oriented Network Analysis: An Application of Women's Street Commerce," *American Journal of Economics and Sociology*, 58: 807–27.

Friesen, W. (1993) "New Asian Migrants in Auckland: Issues of Employment and Status," in P. Morrison (ed.) *Labour Employment and Work in New Zealand: Proceedings of the Fifth Conference 1992*, Wellington: Victoria University of Wellington.

Galt, D. (2000) "New Zealand's Economic Growth," *Treasury Working Paper*, 00/09. Online. Available: www.treasury.govt.nz/workingpapers (accessed 31 August 2004).

Gershuny, J. (1983) *Social Innovation and the Division of Labour*, Oxford: Oxford University Press.

Granovetter, M. (1992) "Economic Institutions as Social Constructions: A Framework for Analysis," *Acta Sociologica*, 35: 3–11.

Harding, P. and Jenkins, R. (1989) *The Myth of the Hidden Economy*, Milton Keynes: Open University Press.

Maldonado, C. (1995) "The Informal Sector: Legalization or Laissez-Faire?" *International Labour Review*, 134(6): 705–29.

Manukau City Council (1992) *Planning and Resource Management Planning Hearing, Commissioner Report*, 29 September, File PRM 6058/IR.

Morales, A. (1998) "Income Tax Compliance and Alternative Views of Ethics and Human Nature," *Journal of Accounting, Ethics and Public Policy*, 1(3): 380–400.

—— (2001) "Policy from Theory: A Critical Reconstruction of Theory on the 'Informal' Economy," 38(3): 190–203.

Reid, T. (1974) "Otara: We Want Everything in One Place," *New Zealand Listener*, 4 May.

Simon, H. (1961) *Administrative Behavior*, 2nd edn, New York: Macmillan.

Spoonley, P. (1993) *Racism and Ethnicity*, 2nd edn, Auckland: Oxford University Press.

—— (1995) "Constructing Ourselves: The Post-colonial Politics of Pakeha," in M. Wilson and A. Yeatman (eds) *Justice and Identity: Antipodean Practices*, Wellington: Bridget Williams Books.

Statistics New Zealand (various years) *Household Labour Force Survey*, Wellington: GP Press.

—— (2003) *New Zealand Census 2001.*

Swedberg, R. (1990) *Economics and Sociology: Redefining their Boundaries*, Princeton, NJ: Princeton University Press.

*The Jobs Letter* (2005) No. 237, 17 August 2005. Online. Available: www.jobsletter. org.nz/pdf/jbl237.pdf (accessed 20 October 2005).

Thomas, J. (1992) *Informal Economic Activity*, Hemel Hempstead: Harvester Wheatsheaf.

Trlin, A., Henderson, A., and North, N. (2004) "Skilled Chinese and Indian

Immigrant Workers," in P. Spoonley, A. Dupuis, and A. de Bruin (eds) *Work and Working in Twenty-first Century New Zealand*, Palmerston North: Dunmore Press: 205–19.

Uzzell, J.D. (1994) "Transaction Costs, Formal Plans, and Formal Informality: Alternatives to the Informal Sector," in C. Rakowski (ed.) *Contrapunta: The Informal Sector Debate in Latin America*, Albany, NY: State University of New York Press.

Williamson, O. (1975) *Markets and Hierarchies: Analysis and Antitrust Implications*, New York: Free Press.

—— (1985) *The Economic Institutions of Capitalism: Firms, Markets, Relational Contracting*, New York: Free Press.

# 15 Conclusion

## Law, deviance, and defining vendors and vending

*Alfonso Morales*[1]

We began this book with something of a conundrum: how is it that vendors and vending have survived, even thrived, through epochal changes in economy and society? In this conclusion, I argue that the answer is deceptively simple: merchants and markets are deeply embedded in all facets of the economic, political, and social. Thus, they shape and are shaped by the choice and chance variation found in each institution, in society, and in relationship to our broader environment (Companion, this volume). The deception lies in the vast variety of organizational forms produced by small changes in institutional contexts. Numerous variables critically impact vendors and vending. For instance, changing political variables create a more welcoming or hostile environment for merchants (essays in Part I). Or, if social variables such as household structure change, fewer or more people are present to help with business (essays in Part II). Finally, shifts in economic variables like the merchandise demanded, the local labor market, or the sources of merchandise influence whether businesses grow or fail (essays throughout the book). Changes in institutional (or ecological) variables motivate individual changes that produce organizational changes, in turn stimulating institutional responses.

Whatever the variables we analyze, vendors innovate. They are continuously recreating the canvas we seek to interpret. Merchants demand our attention for humanistic reasons as well as those relating to the social sciences. Markets and merchants have roused great poetry and novels measuring the human spirit. Measurement plagues the social scientist. Difficulties pervade most economic estimates of vending. But historical, ethnographic, and experimental techniques reveal merchants' human characteristics and social processes. Vendors share with us who they are. They tell us how they came to this occupation and life, about their concerns and goals, the demands they must meet, and the excitement and esteem they feel from conducting business effectively. They also share with us the personal and economic benefits that come from sociability in public places.

In this conclusion, I will describe the larger political/economic context enveloping merchants around the world. I argue that when policy makers find markets "unattractive," the problem is not wholly in the phenomenon occurring in their streets. Rather, it is in preconceived notions of the "appropriate" or legitimate (read western or modernist) ways of retailing merchandise or using public space (Cross and Karides, this volume). Street vending's renascent legitimacy derives from government locating microentrepreneurship on policy agendas. I argue for pragmatic (Tamanaha 1997; Morales 2001) investigations encompassing *facilitative* as well as restrictive (non)governmental policy and policy-making activities.

The essays in this volume make clear the relevance of new investigations of street vendors from mostly every disciplinary perspective. Early analysts of trade and markets found exchange relationships cementing non-economic realities (they continue to do so today). Contemporary street markets embed even more political, social, and economic information. Each merchant processes that information in creating and transforming familial, political, and economic realities. Markets exist and thrive in varied historical, household, and political-economic contexts.

Over the last century in the United States, successive waves of social legislation and local policy intersected with rural to urban and international immigration, creating the context for merchants and markets. In a centripetal fashion, various Progressive Era government policies (e.g. standardizing weights and measures, regulating food safety, and reducing unemployment) were focused through street markets and street vendors. During this time markets thrived, "street vendor" was a recognized occupational category in the US census, and existing citizens and new immigrants benefited from both entrepreneurial opportunities and inexpensive consumer goods. Exceptional merchants and market denizens attributed their success in various professions to the experience and lessons learned from markets (Eastwood 2002; Eshel and Schatz 2004; Morales 2006).

By 1940, markets and vendors passed from policy interest and mass consumption came to dominate the economic environment. Merchants and markets never completely disappeared, but instead faded into myth, were predicted to disappear (Wirth 1928 on Chicago's Maxwell Street followed by Modernization theory of the 1960s), and became characters of novels (Motley 1947, 1958) and poetry (Sandberg's *The Fish Cryer*) and the focus of social reformers (Berkow 1977; Adelman 1980; Morales 2000). However, this brief interregnum was soon followed by varied interests producing a resurgence of markets and merchants. Organic and sustainable agriculture found a consumer niche, thus expanding farmers' markets. Urban consumers stretched their decreasing dollars purchasing new and used merchandise at all kinds of street markets. Disaffected employees became entrepreneurs in those markets. New immigrants recreated their lives shopping and selling in markets. Local government realized economic development, tourism, and sustainability goals by way of markets. Markets became a catch-all response or a multipurpose tool for various concerns and interests.

Outside industrialized countries, merchants and markets were rarely, if ever, found on policy agendas or used as tools of public policy. Instead, vendors were exploited by corrupt governments and reacted to repressive political and economic conditions. In much of the Third World, street markets provide much of the locally available consumer goods. Likewise markets employ vast numbers of people. The bulk of this economic activity (sales and employment) goes uncounted by government. Government responses to markets are contingent on the local circumstances; in this they are no different than the United States or Europe. Government neglect or repression of markets and merchants and extortion from them is much greater in weak, developing nations than older, developed countries. Yet, the essays in this volume demonstrate variation in government policy toward markets. More importantly, they show how governments and merchants regularly renegotiate their relationships: markets and vendors are repressed in one moment, cultivated in the next, ignored thereafter, and quite often only shown symbolic support.

Likewise, essays in Part II show similar markets found in very different countries, due to some homogenization of consumption and intersection of interests. Street merchants in farmers' markets combined Progressive Era concerns of food quality with new post-Fordist awareness of environmental degradation, satisfying consumers with both interests. Merchants cater to a broad class of consumers. Vendors occupy niches created by demand for antiques, fair trade, organic, sustainably produced, and unique merchandise from around the world. Middle-class consumers the world over stretch their shrinking pay checks by shopping in markets, working-class people demonstrate entrepreneurial skills earning income in markets, and many merchants and businesses developed from markets into store-front enterprises. Other markets and vendors offer a myriad of merchandise from cut-rate fashion to building materials and much more. In essays throughout the book we learn how basic economic needs are satisfied but essays also incorporate the postmodern interest in identity by showing how vendors develop, express, and reconcile new selves in the course of doing business.

When we step back to consider this larger picture, the broader encompassing theme is law. Law makes available legitimacy by defining when vendors are "employed" or not (Cross), what acceptable business places (Part I), practices, and products are (Part II), and shapes the various relationships that govern participation in economic activity (essays throughout). Street vendors adapt to niches created by law and by the absence of law or legal enforcement. They also self-define themselves as legitimate against socio-legal marginalization. Even accepting capitalism's rules of action, vendors rarely benefit from law and regulations to the same degree as larger businesses, especially corporations.[2] Instead, law has shadowed markets, persecuting merchants or making them the targets of corrupt administrators. Laws and regulations are central to legitimate definitions of vendors and markets and more research should focus on the normative justifications of law as well as the creation and administration of law, policy, and regulations around markets and merchants.

Readers are reminded not to neglect the broader research agenda that includes mapping the variety of vendors and markets around the world, their political-regulatory contexts, household interactions, and other individual level variables (Pachenkov and Berman provide a particularly illustrative elaboration on relationships in markets). Some topics of interest include investigations of merchants' supply chain management (an example is de Bruin and Dupuis), state tax policy, vendor licensing, labor, and other matters. However, the heretofore present but incompletely examined research topic is facilitative government and non-governmental organizations, their practices, policy, and research agendas, funding plans, and advocacy on behalf of markets and vendors. Government defines the legitimate, and non-governmental organizations convey legitimacy to their beneficiaries. As with law and regulation, government has two distinct faces. Government in its regulatory guise is distinct from government in its facilitative guise. Until now, most research has focused on the former monitoring the legitimate over the latter affirming the legitimate (exceptions include Cross 1998; Morales 2000) but Varcin, Kettles, Companion, Cross and Morales, and other authors in this volume take up government in its facilitative or legitimizing role.

For decades, research on markets and merchants has focused on government regulation and vendor evasion or self-regulation (García-Rincón; Lyon; Cross and Karides). The root finding is one of contingency and from it has developed the notion of legal pluralism that spawned research into various other empirical situations. Research uncovered a variety of legitimate normative orders developed by different combinations of state/merchant activity, varying historically by political and economic context. Legitimacy is at the core of this relationship between merchants and the state. Vendors see the state as (il)legitimate and the state sees vendors as (il)legitimate by how markets are created and regulated or business organized and practiced. Of course there are many other reasons for the parties to judge each other's legitimacy, but their first source of information about each other is in the order established in the market. Dozens of case studies describe how merchants self-create order. Occasionally the state provides stable and flexible marketplaces. If the government fails to provide these, vendors create order themselves or establish coping mechanisms to deal with corrupt state officials. In one way or another, however, marketplaces are established and persist.

However, government and non-governmental organizations play an increasingly important facilitative role with respect to markets and merchants. Governments allocate resources, legitimacy, attention, and matters for policy (Companion, Sage, this volume) by census and other statistical practices. In the United States, after a 70-year hiatus, the United States Department of Agriculture is again enumerating farmers' markets. This is currently being done by way of periodic census of markets and merchants. Government reports estimate the monetary impact of farmers' markets, assessing their importance to food chains and to the small and medium sized producer. Local governments around the United States invigorate economic development strategies by organizing new markets and regulating and promoting existing markets. Important non-governmental organizations, like the Urban Land Institute and the Program for Public Space, assess existing markets and attempt to measure their various impacts (Spitzer and Baum 1995). Likewise, around the world organizations are playing an increasingly important role in redefining markets and merchants. For instance, in Indonesia, the Urban Poor Consortium vigorously advocates for vendors. In India, national legislation has been passed on their behalf. Additionally, one of the largest and most important organizations is Women in Informal Employment: Globalizing and Organizing (WIEGO), which has among its five missions the study of women in markets as well as policy advocacy on their behalf.

Individual merchants struggle with illegitimate aspects of their business. Merchants contingently comply with regulations and law, hence the labels "underground" or "informal." However, no business is always in complete compliance with law and regulation, and slowly we are discovering how vendors reconcile their "illegal" activity with their needs (Cross, this volume; Morales 1998). Such research is increasingly important, especially as micro-entrepreneurship becomes more legitimate. Since the success of the Grameen Bank (Counts 1996), microentrepreneurship is playing a larger role in development schemes around the world. The Ford Foundation and the Kauffman Foundation have invested important funds in supporting demonstration projects inclusive of street vendors as microentrepreneurs. The international year of micro credit was 2005 and micro credit/microentrepreneurship is expected to play a significant role in millennial development goals. Public policy is notoriously subject to political winds, but in the United States conscientious efforts have been made to build inter-agency programs to support communities in creating "vibrant local economies and markets in which microentrepreneurs can fully participate" (US Government Documents 2000: 1). I am more optimistic about the prospects for farmers' markets than about street markets in the United States but it seems to me that vendors of every type can thrive in markets contributing to our overall economy. We need more research into the household-level dynamics of (il)legitimate activities, how identities are shaped by these activities, and the implications for family life, but we also need more research into the political and organizational framing processes used by governmental and nongovernmental organizations.

Research is needed to describe the activities of these (non)governmental organizations, map their diversity, understand their goals and relationships, and evaluate their practices. Each of these organizations mediates the merchants/markets and state/society relationship. Each organization supports definitions of these relationships, creates policy or policy recommendations, and serves as a conduit of resources to merchants as well as being a voice of merchants. What lobbying practices and resources do these organizations use? What alliances do they pursue and with what contradictions for business and government? We can easily imagine organizations defining and dividing themselves between "legitimate" entrepreneurs and others, but will they and with what implications for how markets and merchants are perceived and incorporated into economic policy?

Finally I would call for research which incorporates household, organizational, and institutional dynamics. Such research examines household responses to various legal and economic (dis)incentives, but incorporates research questions about street markets as "cases" or "business models," in order to investigate how street markets operate and how they fit with existing business models of economic activity. Many street markets, Pikes Place in Seattle for instance, were proven economically viable prior to public or private investment. This implies, I believe, that street markets are no less businesses than any other business and so the existing infrastructure of business support services, advertising, accounting, and the like, must be educated about the street merchant as a niche consumer of their services and must learn to adapt to the street market setting.

Likewise, more research will reveal the various responses corporations have to vendors and vending. There is no straight-line determinism in play here. Many essays in this volume illustrated the variety of such interactions. Staudt, and Cross and Karides, allude to businesses integrating street merchants into their operational plans. On the other hand, Bhowmik describes how business captures government, obviating the need for opposition to vendors, while Varcin describes historical changes illustrating trajectories. Finally, Stillerman and Sundt make clear how merchants are not immune to internecine conflict. Clearly we can see how complex political-economic environments or neoliberal policies favoring "formal" business might blind policy makers to the effectiveness of vending as a policy tool, but we have much to learn about government in its facilitative initiatives and relationships to business and nongovernmental organizations.

Markets and merchants fascinate artists and scientists alike for the complexity hidden in ostensibly simple activities. The visible thrill and visceral excitement entice everyone's participation. The manifold perspectives and purposes intersecting in markets invite many analyses and subsequent disagreement over the interpretations. When policy makers incorporate merchants and markets into economic policy we can expect an increase in government revenues and more important benefits to the local population (Morales *et al.* 1995). But where ignored or persecuted we will continue to see people use markets for themselves against business and the state. Either way, markets and merchants are here to stay.

## Notes

1 Thanks to Michèle Companion, Howie Erlanger, Kathy Staudt, John Cross, and Danielle Berman for their comments on this conclusion. Incomplete citations refer to chapters in this book.
2 In Weber's description, a:

> cosmos into which the individual is born, and which presents itself to him, at least as an individual, as an unalterable order of things in which he must live. It forces the individual, in so far as he is involved in the system of market relationships, to conform to capitalist rules of action. The manufacturer who, in the long run, acts counter to these norms, will just as inevitably be eliminated from the economic scene as the worker who cannot or will not adapt himself to them will be thrown into the streets without a job.

(1930: 54–55)

Street merchants swiftly adopted "capitalist rules of action," providing for consumers' demand by way of manufacturers' overproduction, niche production, or recycling used goods.

## Bibliography

Adelman, William J. 1980. "Robber Barons and Social Reformers." *Inland Architect*, 24(3): 12–15.

Berkow, Ira. 1977. *Maxwell Street: Survival in a Bazaar*. Garden City, NY: Doubleday.

Bowles, Samuel, Durlauf, Steven N., and Hoff, Karla, editors. 2006. *Poverty Traps*. Princeton, NJ: Princeton University Press.

Counts, Alex. 1996. *Give Us Credit*. New York: Times Books.

Cross, John. 1998. *Informal Politics: Street Vendors and the State in Mexico City*. Palo Alto, CA: Stanford University Press.

Eastwood, Carolyn. 2002. *Near West Side Stories*. Chicago, IL: Lake Claremont Press.

Eshel, Shuli and Schatz, Roger. 2004. *Jewish Maxwell Street Stories*. Chicago, IL: Arcadia Publishing.

Flanagan, Maureen A. 1990. "Gender and Urban Political Reform: The City Club and the Woman's City Club of Chicago in the Progressive Era." *American Historical Review*, 95: 1032–50.

Morales, Alfonso. 1998. "Income Tax Compliance and Alternative Views of Ethics and Human Nature." *Journal of Accounting, Ethics and Public Policy*, 1(3): 380–400.

—— 2000. "Peddling Policy: Street Vending in Historical and Contemporary Context." *International Journal of Sociology and Social Policy*, 20(3/4): 76–99.

—— 2001. "Policy from Theory: A Critical Reconstruction of Theory on the 'Informal' Economy." *Sociological Imagination*, 38(3): 190–203.

—— 2006. "Chicago's Maxwell Street Market: Promise and Prospects." Prepared for the Maxwell Street Foundation.

Morales, Alfonso, Balkin, Steve, and Persky, Joe. 1995. "The Value of Benefits of a Public Street Market: The Case of Maxwell Street." *Economic Development Quarterly*, 9(4): 304–20.

Motley, Willard. 1947. *Knock On Any Door*. New York: Signet Books.

—— 1958. *Let No Man Write My Epitaph*. New York: Random House.

Sandberg, Carl. *The Fish Cryer*, archived at www.openair.org, last accessed August 1, 2006.

Spitzer, Theodore Morrow and Baum, Hilary. 1995. *Public Markets and Community Revitalization*. Washington, DC: ULI – the Urban Land Institute and Project for Public Spaces.

Tamanaha, Brian Z. 1997. *Realistic Socio-Legal Theory: Pragmatism and a Social Theory of Law*. Oxford: Clarendon Press.

US Government Documents, 2000. Small Business Administration, www.sba.gov/microenter/policypaperaugust2000.pdf. Last accessed August 13, 2006.

Weber, Max. 1930. *The Protestant Ethic and the Spirit of Capitalism*. London: Allen and Unwin.

Wirth, Louis. 1928. *The Ghetto*. Chicago, IL: University of Chicago Press.

# Index